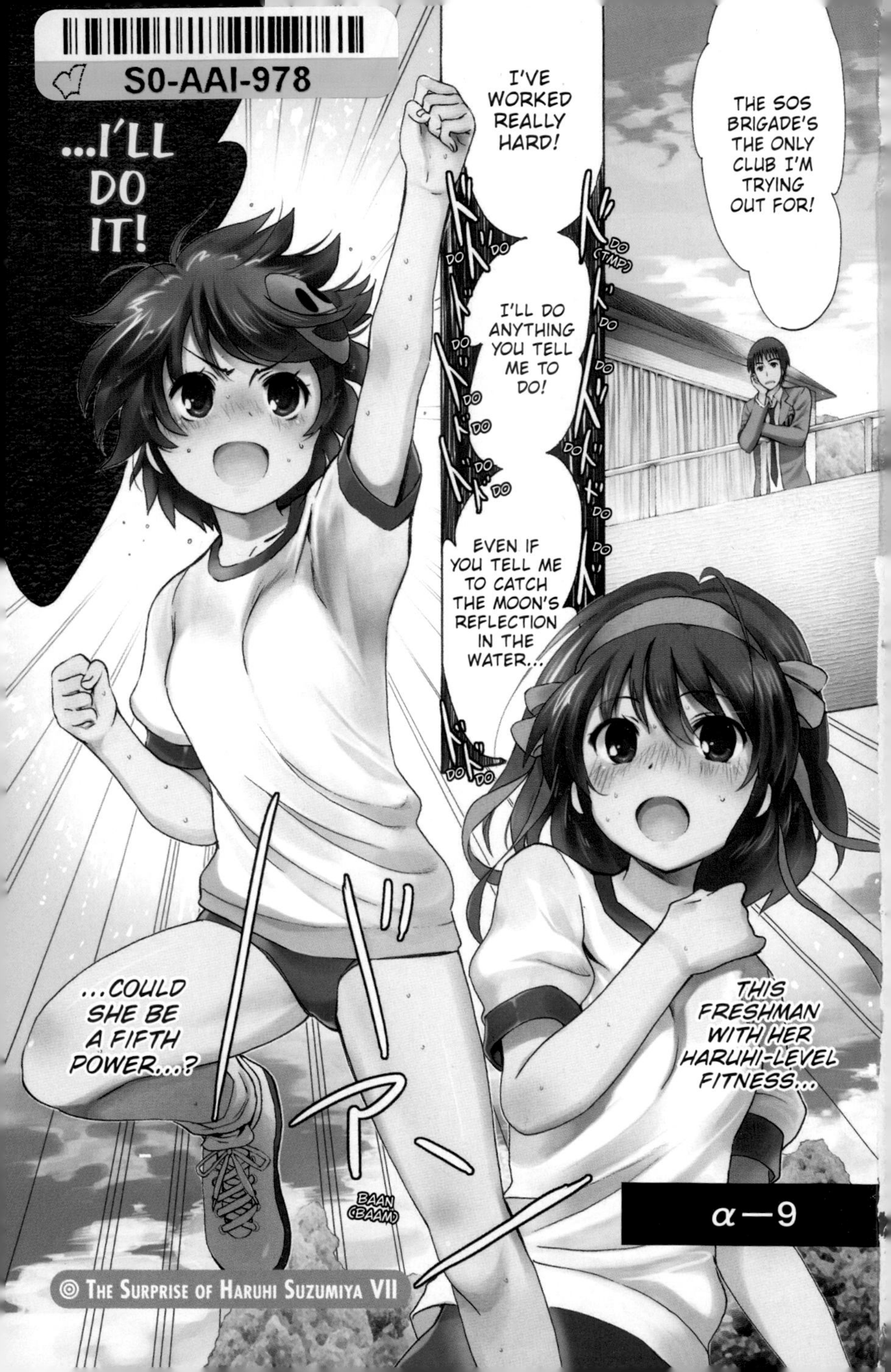
THE SOS BRIGADE'S THE ONLY CLUB I'M TRYING OUT FOR!
I'VE WORKED REALLY HARD!
DO (TMP)
DO DO
I'LL DO ANYTHING YOU TELL ME TO DO!
EVEN IF YOU TELL ME TO CATCH THE MOON'S REFLECTION IN THE WATER...
DO DO
...I'LL DO IT!
THIS FRESHMAN WITH HER HARUHI-LEVEL FITNESS...
...COULD SHE BE A FIFTH POWER...?
BAAN (BAAM)
α—9
© THE SURPRISE OF HARUHI SUZUMIYA VII

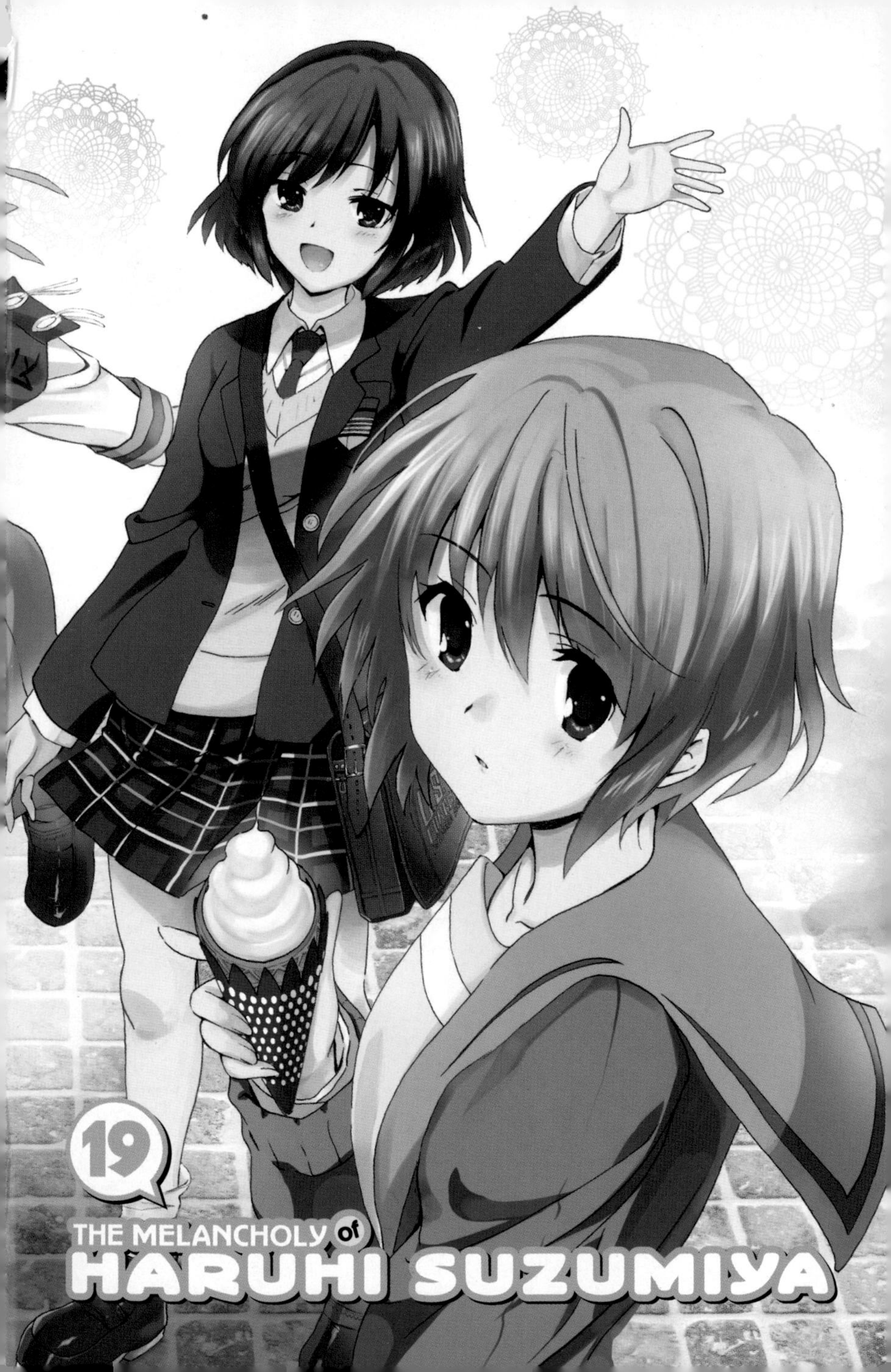
19
THE MELANCHOLY of
HARUHI SUZUMIYA

ORIGINAL STORY **NAGARU TANIGAWA**

MANGA **GAKU TSUGANO**

CHARACTER DESIGN:
**NOIZI ITO**

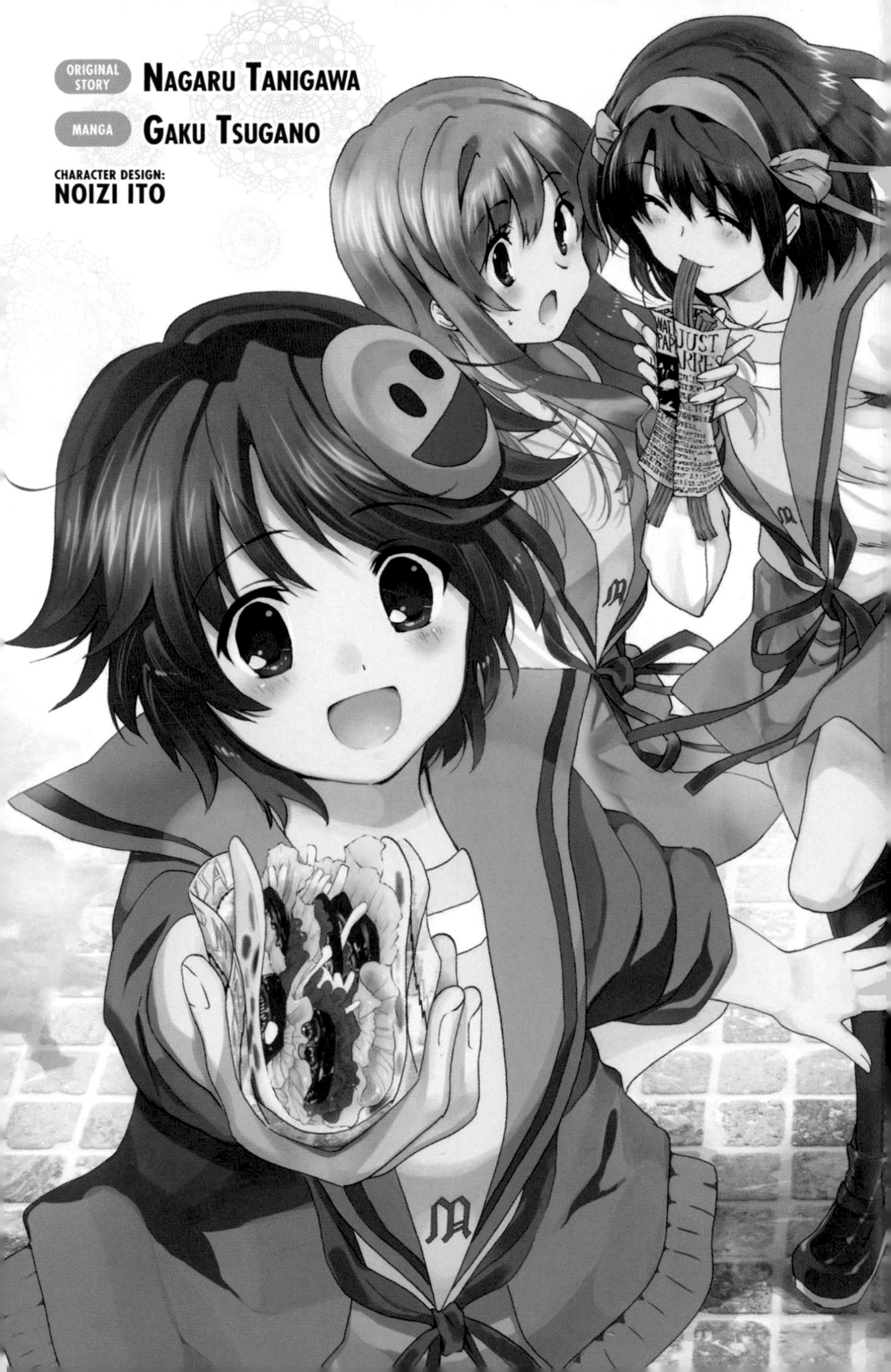

# CONTENTS

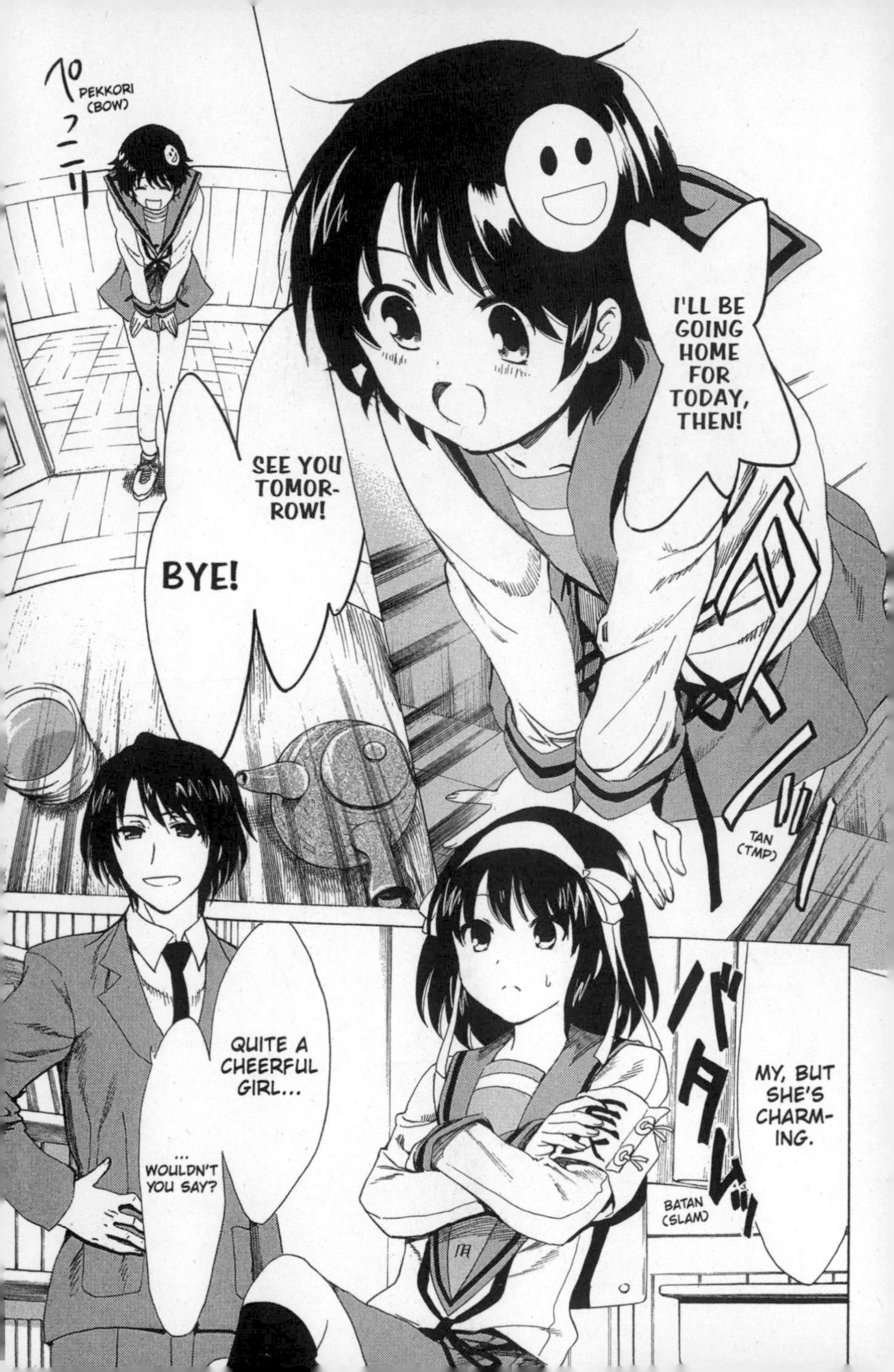
I'LL BE GOING HOME FOR TODAY, THEN!
TAN (TMP)
PEKKORI (BOW)
SEE YOU TOMORROW!
BYE!
BATAN (SLAM)
MY, BUT SHE'S CHARMING.
QUITE A CHEERFUL GIRL...
...WOULDN'T YOU SAY?

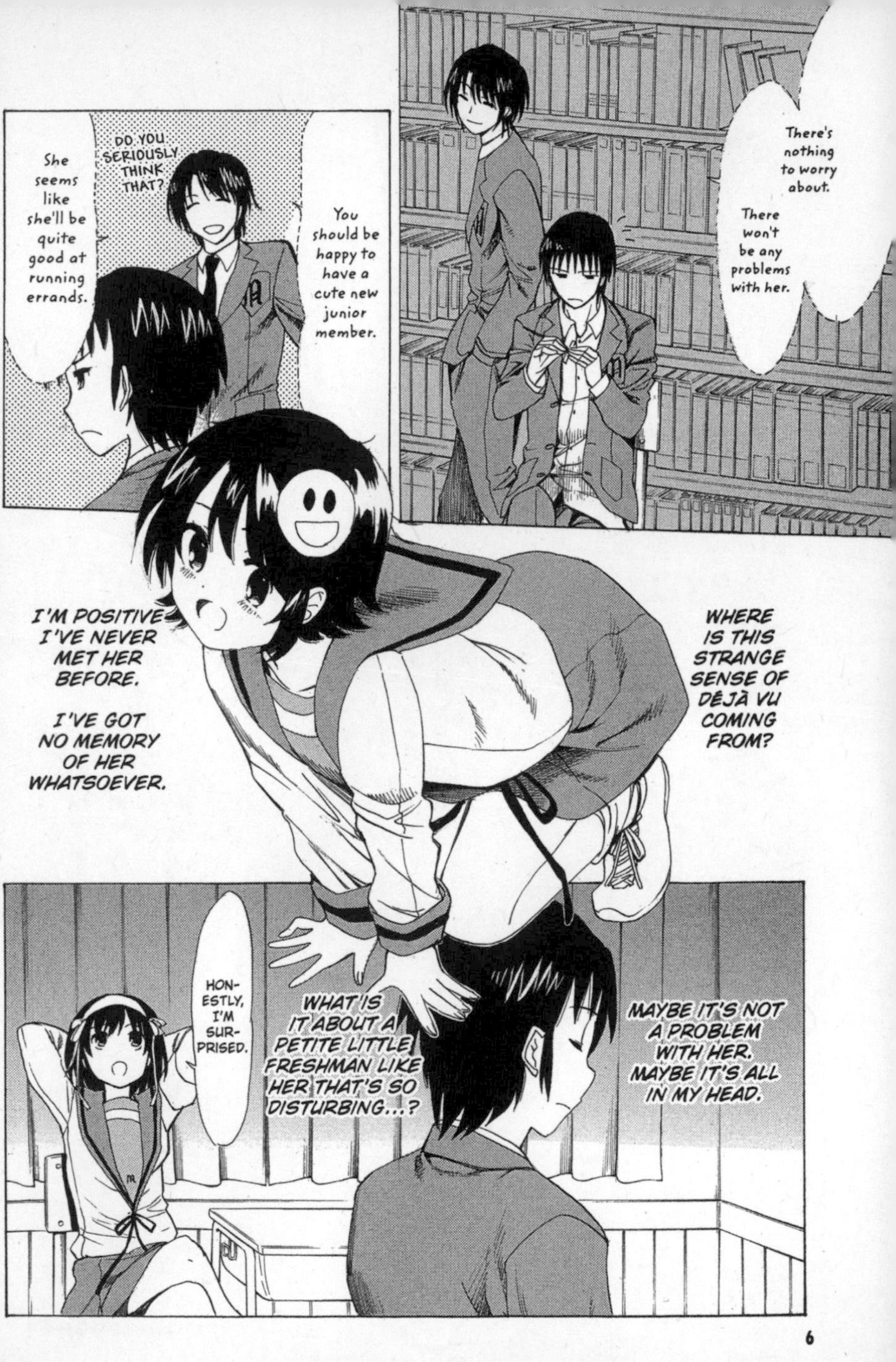
There's nothing to worry about.
There won't be any problems with her.
You should be happy to have a cute new junior member.
DO YOU SERIOUSLY THINK THAT?
She seems like she'll be quite good at running errands.
WHERE IS THIS STRANGE SENSE OF DÉJÀ VU COMING FROM?
I'M POSITIVE I'VE NEVER MET HER BEFORE.
I'VE GOT NO MEMORY OF HER WHATSOEVER.
MAYBE IT'S NOT A PROBLEM WITH HER. MAYBE IT'S ALL IN MY HEAD.
WHAT IS IT ABOUT A PETITE LITTLE FRESHMAN LIKE HER THAT'S SO DISTURBING...?
HON-ESTLY, I'M SUR-PRISED.

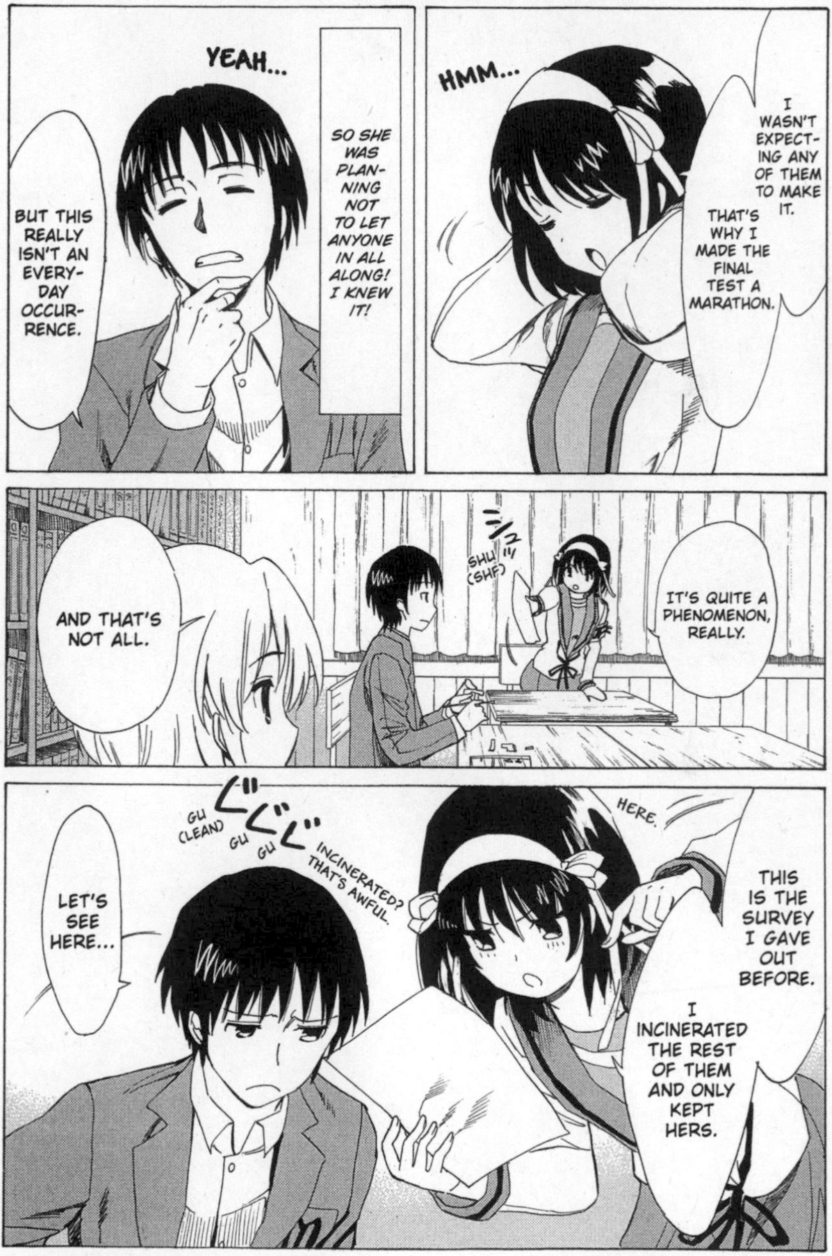
HMM...
I WASN'T EXPECTING ANY OF THEM TO MAKE IT.
THAT'S WHY I MADE THE FINAL TEST A MARATHON.
YEAH...
SO SHE WAS PLANNING NOT TO LET ANYONE IN ALL ALONG! I KNEW IT!
BUT THIS REALLY ISN'T AN EVERYDAY OCCURRENCE.
IT'S QUITE A PHENOMENON, REALLY.
SHU (SHF)
AND THAT'S NOT ALL.
HERE.
THIS IS THE SURVEY I GAVE OUT BEFORE.
I INCINERATED THE REST OF THEM AND ONLY KEPT HERS.
INCINERATED? THAT'S AWFUL.
GU (CLEAN) GU GU
LET'S SEE HERE...

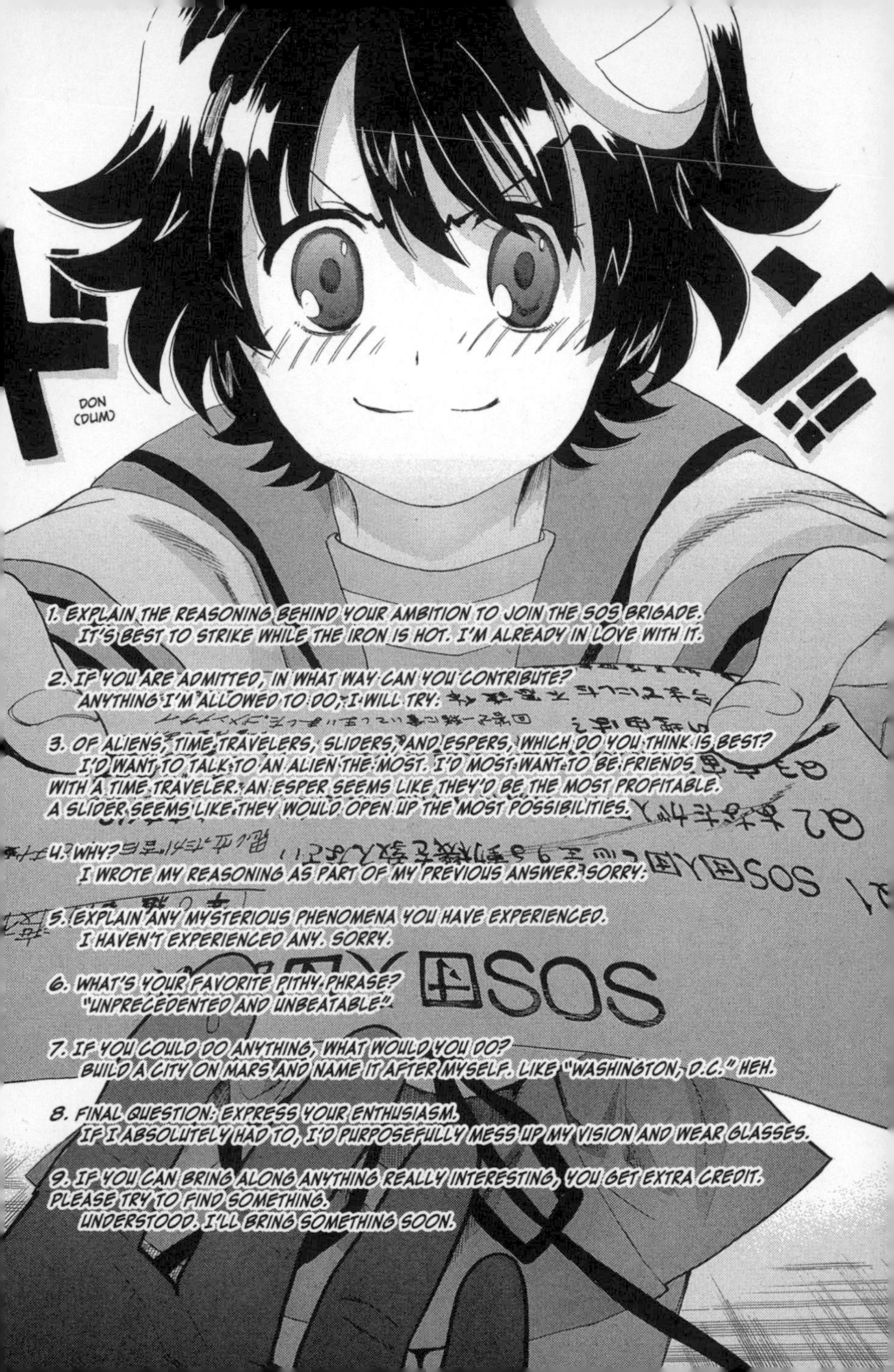
DON (DUM)
1. EXPLAIN THE REASONING BEHIND YOUR AMBITION TO JOIN THE SOS BRIGADE.
IT'S BEST TO STRIKE WHILE THE IRON IS HOT. I'M ALREADY IN LOVE WITH IT.
2. IF YOU ARE ADMITTED, IN WHAT WAY CAN YOU CONTRIBUTE?
ANYTHING I'M ALLOWED TO DO, I WILL TRY.
3. OF ALIENS, TIME TRAVELERS, SLIDERS, AND ESPERS, WHICH DO YOU THINK IS BEST?
I'D WANT TO TALK TO AN ALIEN THE MOST. I'D MOST WANT TO BE FRIENDS WITH A TIME TRAVELER. AN ESPER SEEMS LIKE THEY'D BE THE MOST PROFITABLE. A SLIDER SEEMS LIKE THEY WOULD OPEN UP THE MOST POSSIBILITIES.
4. WHY?
I WROTE MY REASONING AS PART OF MY PREVIOUS ANSWER. SORRY.
5. EXPLAIN ANY MYSTERIOUS PHENOMENA YOU HAVE EXPERIENCED.
I HAVEN'T EXPERIENCED ANY. SORRY.
6. WHAT'S YOUR FAVORITE PITHY PHRASE?
"UNPRECEDENTED AND UNBEATABLE."
7. IF YOU COULD DO ANYTHING, WHAT WOULD YOU DO?
BUILD A CITY ON MARS AND NAME IT AFTER MYSELF. LIKE "WASHINGTON, D.C." HEH.
8. FINAL QUESTION: EXPRESS YOUR ENTHUSIASM.
IF I ABSOLUTELY HAD TO, I'D PURPOSEFULLY MESS UP MY VISION AND WEAR GLASSES.
9. IF YOU CAN BRING ALONG ANYTHING REALLY INTERESTING, YOU GET EXTRA CREDIT. PLEASE TRY TO FIND SOMETHING.
UNDERSTOOD. I'LL BRING SOMETHING SOON.

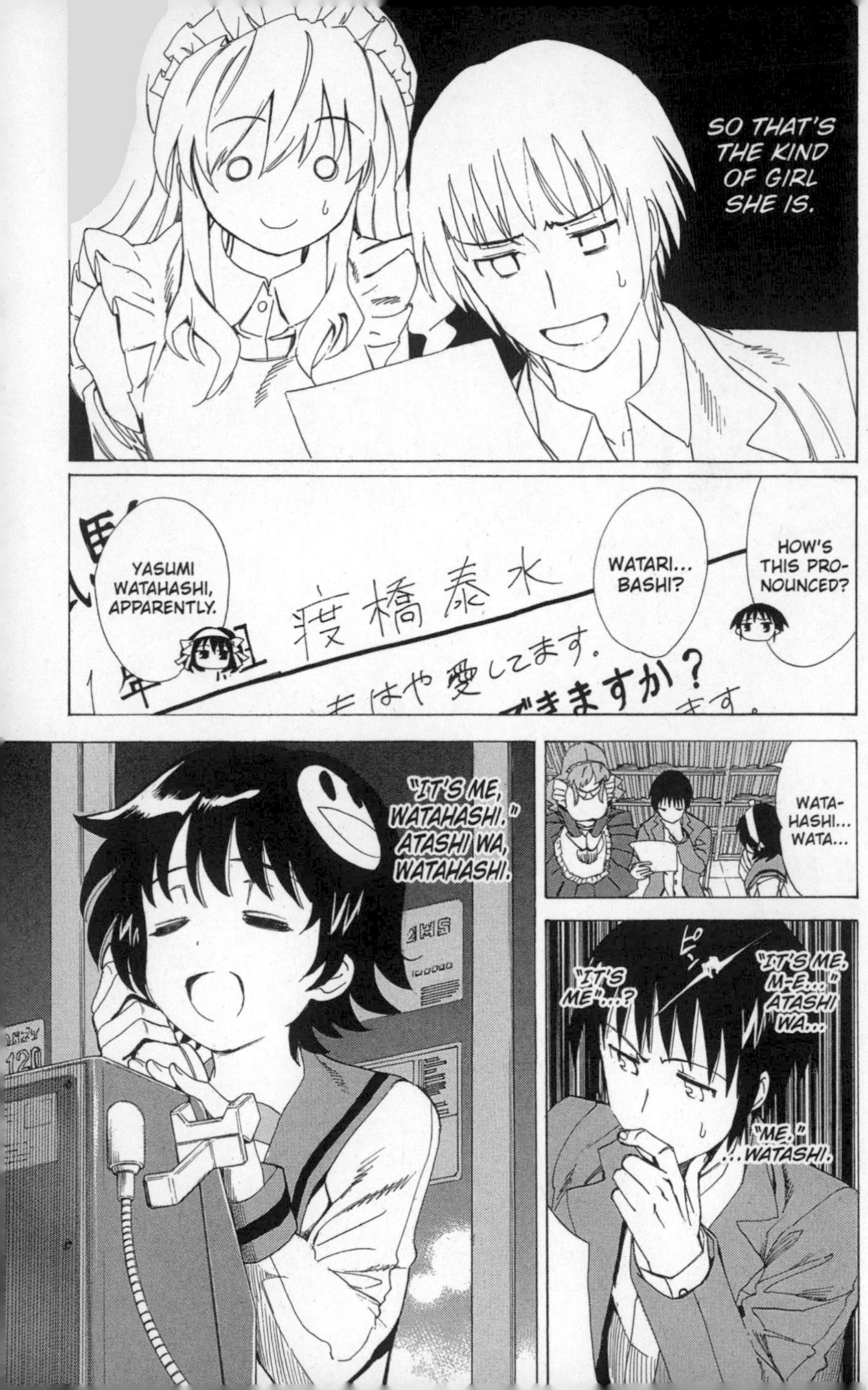
SO THAT'S THE KIND OF GIRL SHE IS.
HOW'S THIS PRONOUNCED?
WATARI... BASHI?
YASUMI WATAHASHI, APPARENTLY.
もはや愛してます。
できますか？
WATA-HASHI... WATA...
"IT'S ME, M-E..." ATASHI WA...
"IT'S ME"...?
"ME." ...WATASHI.
"IT'S ME, WATAHASHI." ATASHI WA, WATAHASHI.

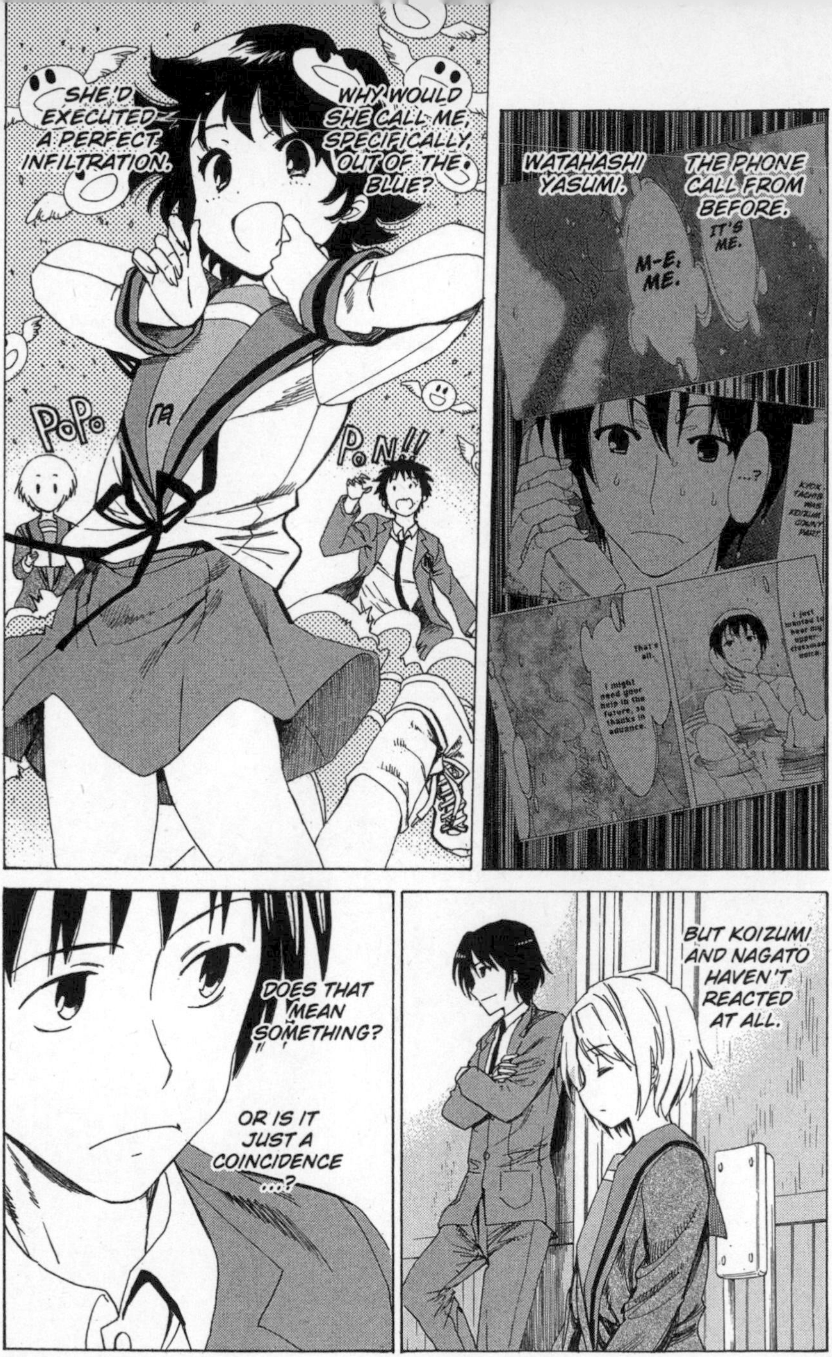
THE PHONE CALL FROM BEFORE.
WATAHASHI YASUMI.
IT'S ME.
M-E, ME.
...?
I just wanted to hear my upperclassman voice.
That's all.
I might need your help in the future, so thanks in advance.
WHY WOULD SHE CALL ME, SPECIFICALLY, OUT OF THE BLUE?
SHE'D EXECUTED A PERFECT INFILTRATION.
PoPo
PoN!!
BUT KOIZUMI AND NAGATO HAVEN'T REACTED AT ALL.
DOES THAT MEAN SOMETHING?
OR IS IT JUST A COINCIDENCE ...?

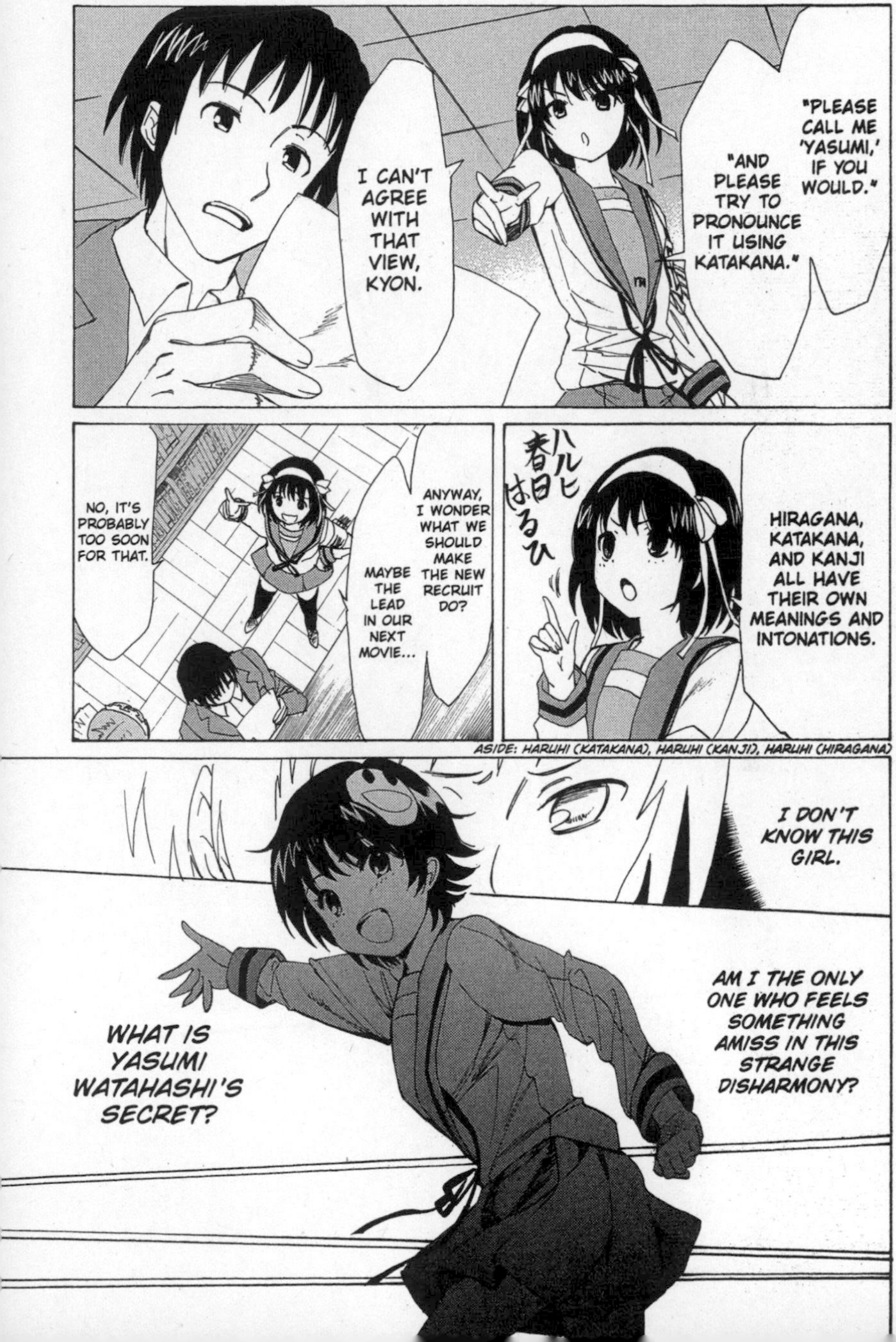
"PLEASE CALL ME 'YASUMI,' IF YOU WOULD."
"AND PLEASE TRY TO PRONOUNCE IT USING KATAKANA."
I CAN'T AGREE WITH THAT VIEW, KYON.
HIRAGANA, KATAKANA, AND KANJI ALL HAVE THEIR OWN MEANINGS AND INTONATIONS.
ハルヒ
春日
はるひ
ANYWAY, I WONDER WHAT WE SHOULD MAKE THE NEW RECRUIT DO?
MAYBE THE LEAD IN OUR NEXT MOVIE...
NO, IT'S PROBABLY TOO SOON FOR THAT.
ASIDE: HARUHI (KATAKANA), HARUHI (KANJI), HARUHI (HIRAGANA)
I DON'T KNOW THIS GIRL.
AM I THE ONLY ONE WHO FEELS SOMETHING AMISS IN THIS STRANGE DISHARMONY?
WHAT IS YASUMI WATAHASHI'S SECRET?

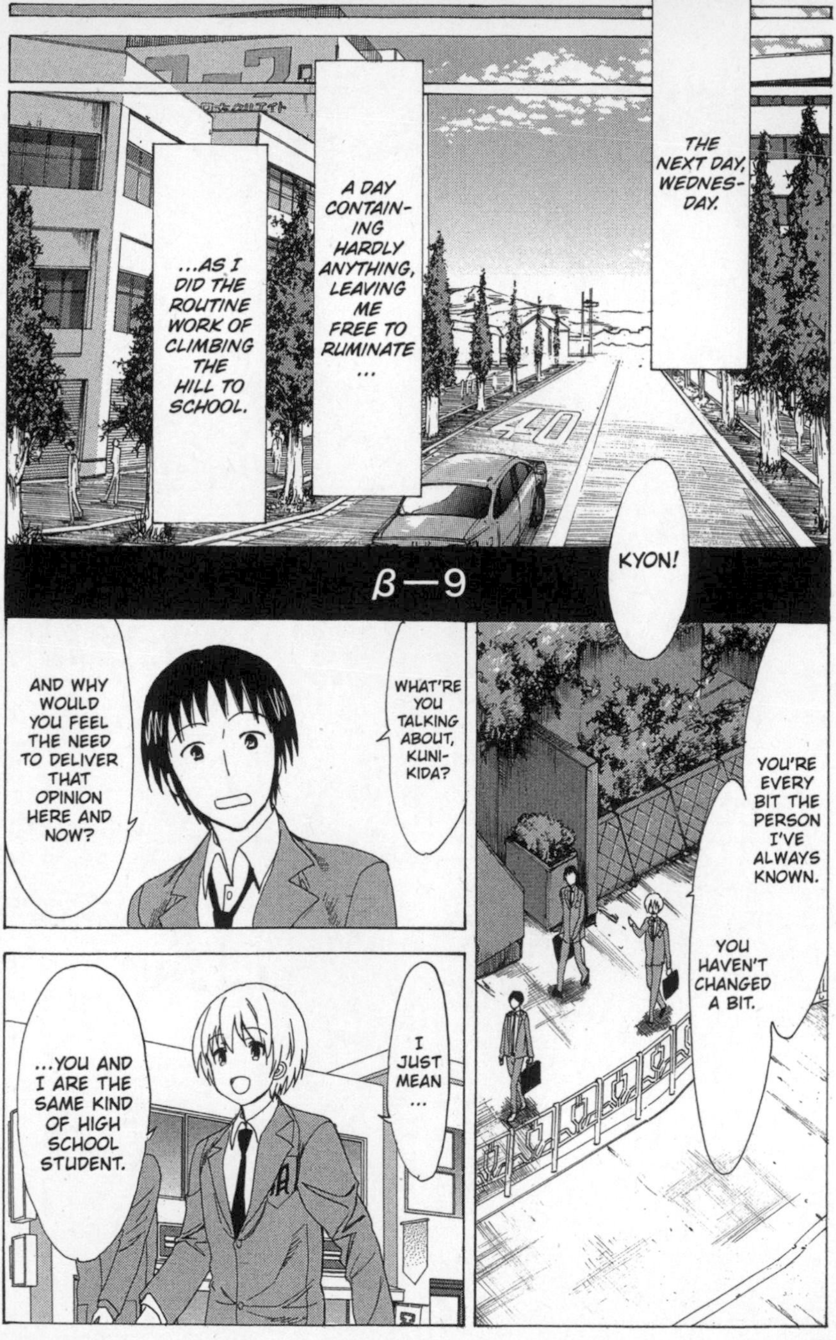
THE NEXT DAY, WEDNESDAY.
A DAY CONTAINING HARDLY ANYTHING, LEAVING ME FREE TO RUMINATE...
...AS I DID THE ROUTINE WORK OF CLIMBING THE HILL TO SCHOOL.
β—9
KYON!
YOU'RE EVERY BIT THE PERSON I'VE ALWAYS KNOWN.
YOU HAVEN'T CHANGED A BIT.
WHAT'RE YOU TALKING ABOUT, KUNIKIDA?
AND WHY WOULD YOU FEEL THE NEED TO DELIVER THAT OPINION HERE AND NOW?
I JUST MEAN...
...YOU AND I ARE THE SAME KIND OF HIGH SCHOOL STUDENT.

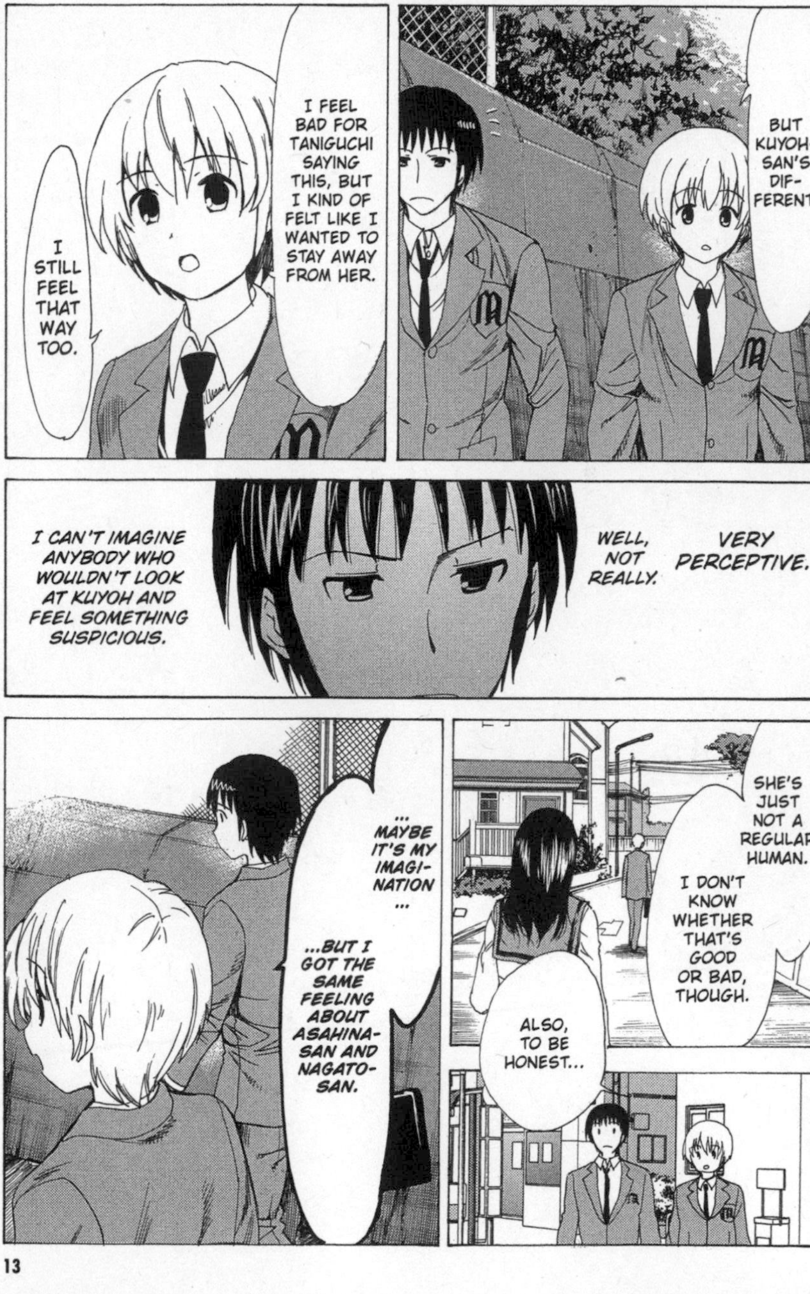
BUT KUYOH-SAN'S DIFFERENT.
I FEEL BAD FOR TANIGUCHI SAYING THIS, BUT I KIND OF FELT LIKE I WANTED TO STAY AWAY FROM HER.
I STILL FEEL THAT WAY TOO.
VERY PERCEPTIVE.
WELL, NOT REALLY.
I CAN'T IMAGINE ANYBODY WHO WOULDN'T LOOK AT KUYOH AND FEEL SOMETHING SUSPICIOUS.
SHE'S JUST NOT A REGULAR HUMAN.
I DON'T KNOW WHETHER THAT'S GOOD OR BAD, THOUGH.
ALSO, TO BE HONEST...
...MAYBE IT'S MY IMAGINATION...
...BUT I GOT THE SAME FEELING ABOUT ASAHINA-SAN AND NAGATO-SAN.

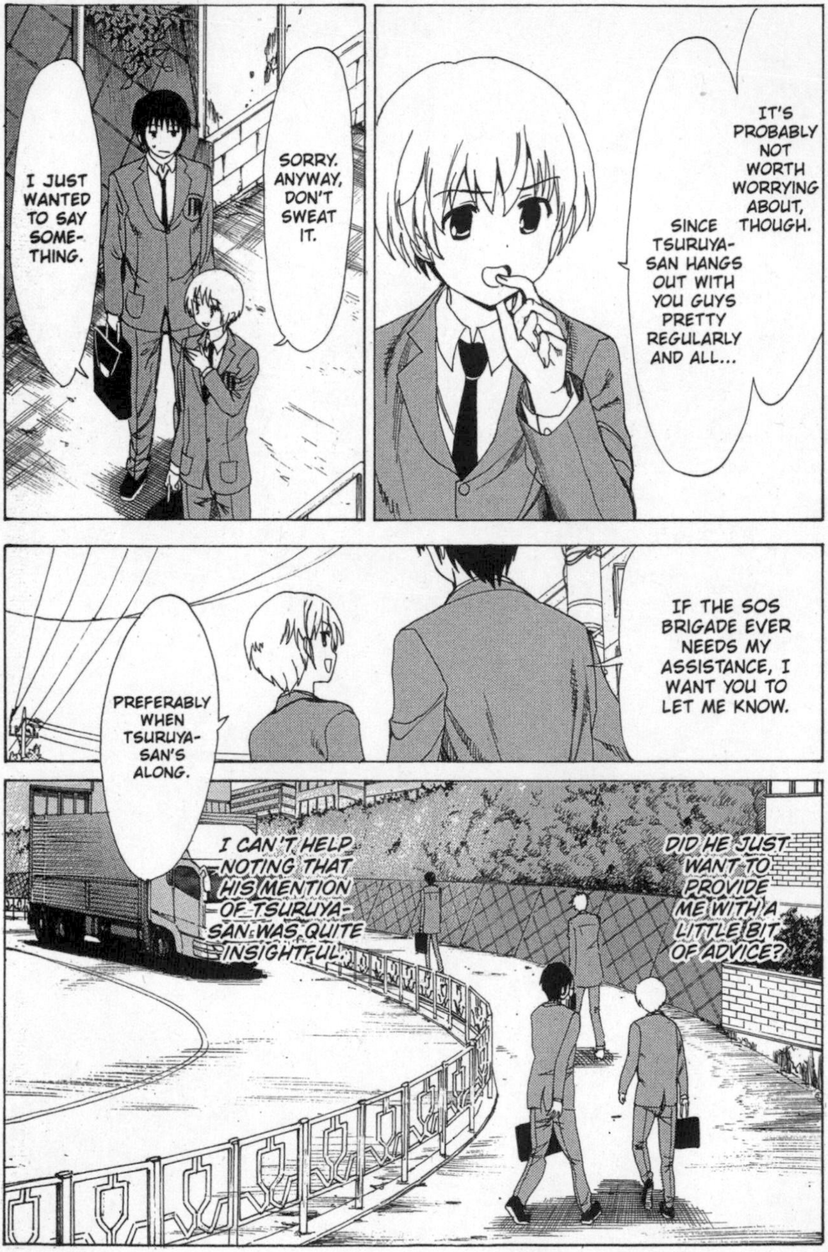
IT'S PROBABLY NOT WORTH WORRYING ABOUT, THOUGH.
SINCE TSURUYA-SAN HANGS OUT WITH YOU GUYS PRETTY REGULARLY AND ALL...
SORRY. ANYWAY, DON'T SWEAT IT.
I JUST WANTED TO SAY SOME-THING.
IF THE SOS BRIGADE EVER NEEDS MY ASSISTANCE, I WANT YOU TO LET ME KNOW.
PREFERABLY WHEN TSURUYA-SAN'S ALONG.
DID HE JUST WANT TO PROVIDE ME WITH A LITTLE BIT OF ADVICE?
I CAN'T HELP NOTING THAT HIS MENTION OF TSURUYA-SAN WAS QUITE INSIGHTFUL.

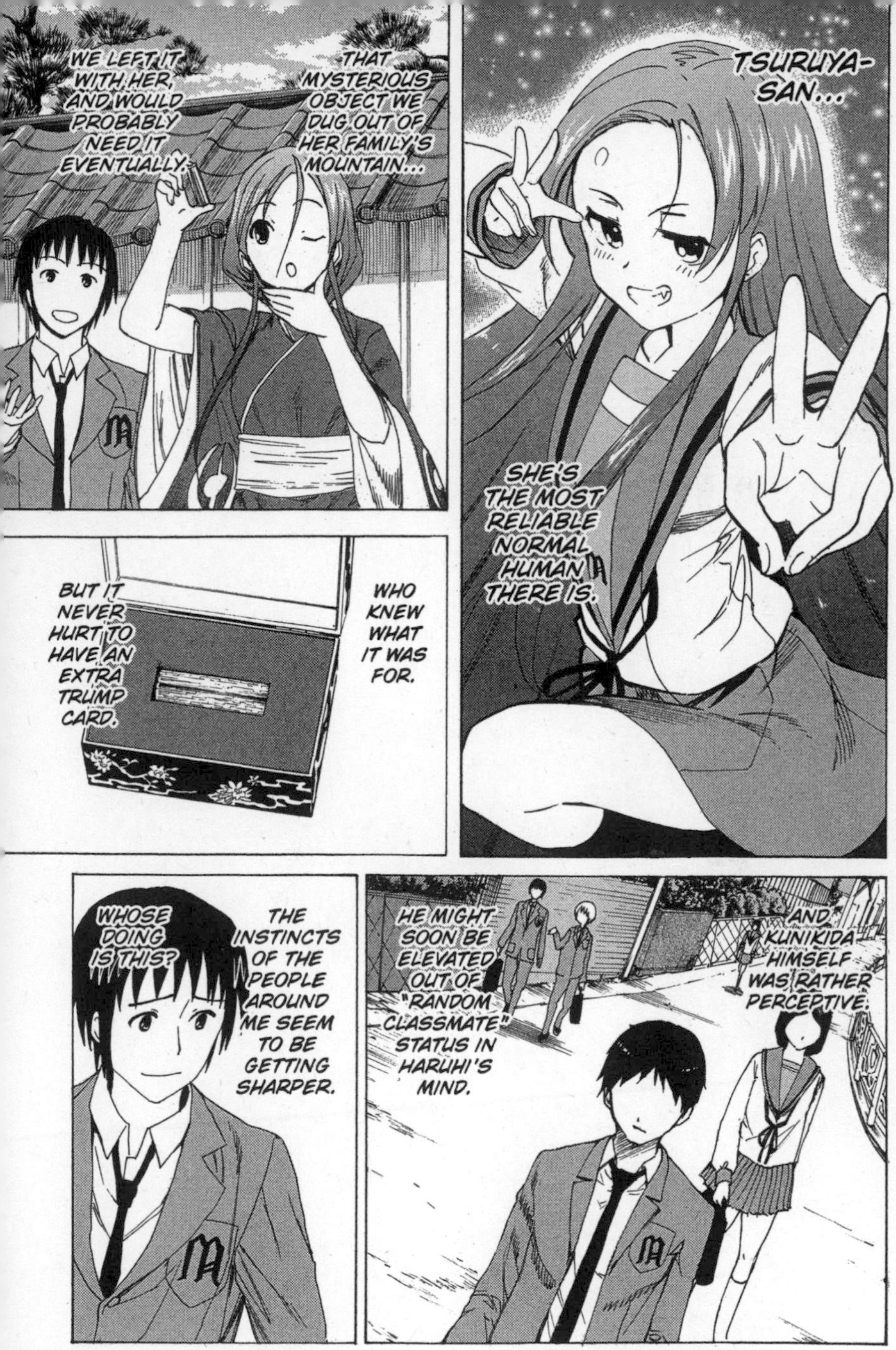
TSURUYA-SAN...
SHE'S THE MOST RELIABLE NORMAL HUMAN THERE IS.
THAT MYSTERIOUS OBJECT WE DUG OUT OF HER FAMILY'S MOUNTAIN...
WE LEFT IT WITH HER, AND WOULD PROBABLY NEED IT EVENTUALLY.
WHO KNEW WHAT IT WAS FOR.
BUT IT NEVER HURT TO HAVE AN EXTRA TRUMP CARD.
AND KUNIKIDA HIMSELF WAS RATHER PERCEPTIVE.
HE MIGHT SOON BE ELEVATED OUT OF "RANDOM CLASSMATE" STATUS IN HARUHI'S MIND.
THE INSTINCTS OF THE PEOPLE AROUND ME SEEM TO BE GETTING SHARPER.
WHOSE DOING IS THIS?

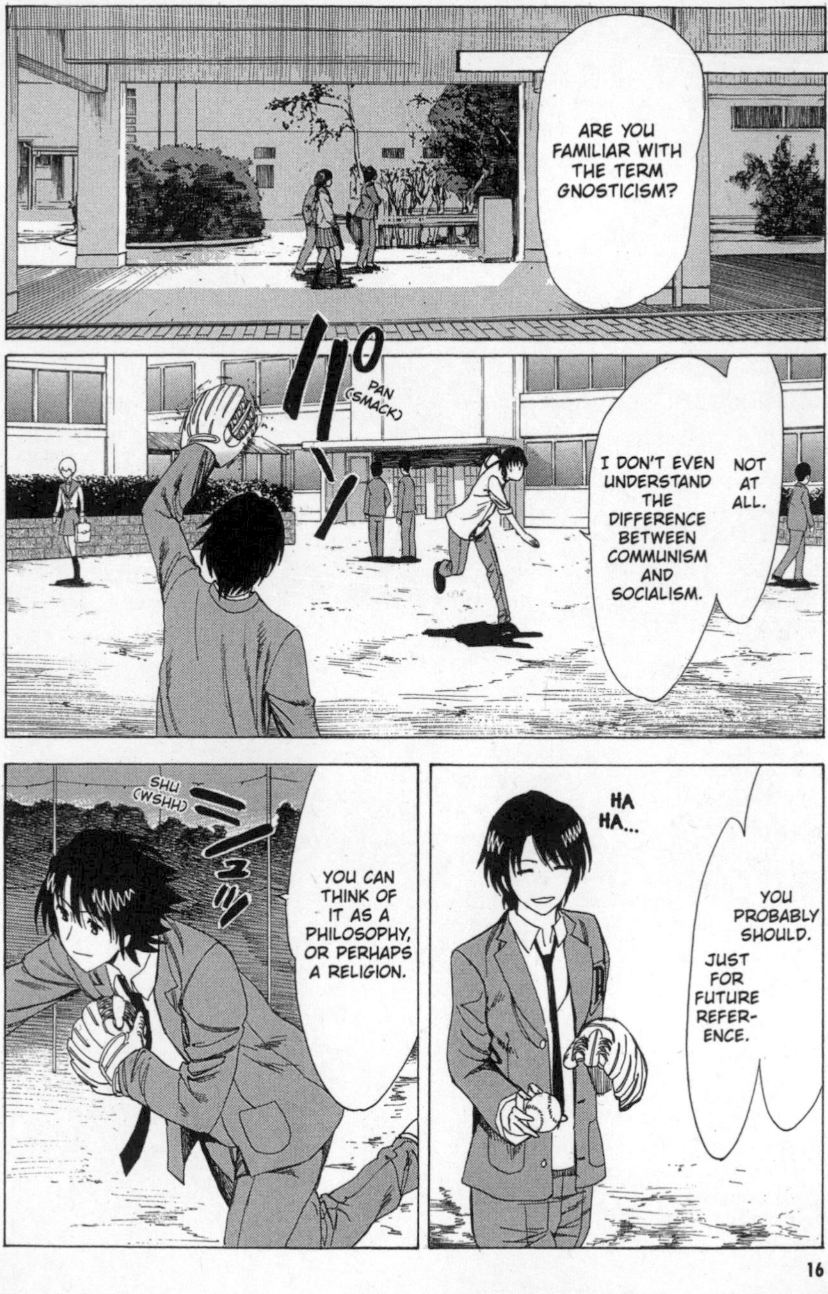
ARE YOU FAMILIAR WITH THE TERM GNOSTICISM?
PAN (SMACK)
NOT AT ALL.
I DON'T EVEN UNDERSTAND THE DIFFERENCE BETWEEN COMMUNISM AND SOCIALISM.
HA HA...
YOU PROBABLY SHOULD.
JUST FOR FUTURE REFERENCE.
SHU (WSHH)
YOU CAN THINK OF IT AS A PHILOSOPHY, OR PERHAPS A RELIGION.

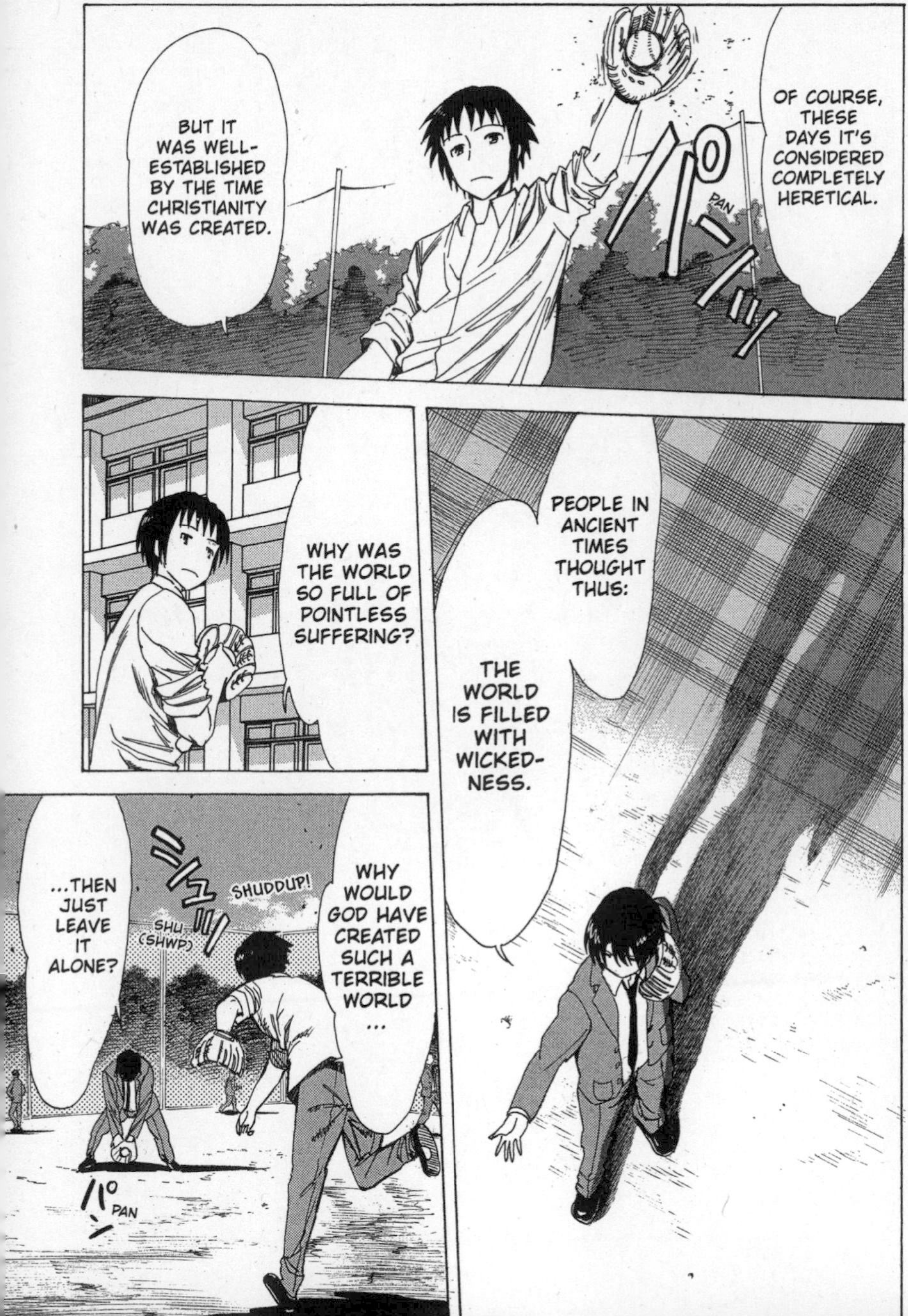

OF COURSE, THESE DAYS IT'S CONSIDERED COMPLETELY HERETICAL.
PAN
BUT IT WAS WELL-ESTABLISHED BY THE TIME CHRISTIANITY WAS CREATED.
PEOPLE IN ANCIENT TIMES THOUGHT THUS:
THE WORLD IS FILLED WITH WICKED-NESS.
WHY WAS THE WORLD SO FULL OF POINTLESS SUFFERING?
WHY WOULD GOD HAVE CREATED SUCH A TERRIBLE WORLD ...
SHUDDUP!
SHU (SHWP)
...THEN JUST LEAVE IT ALONE?
PAN

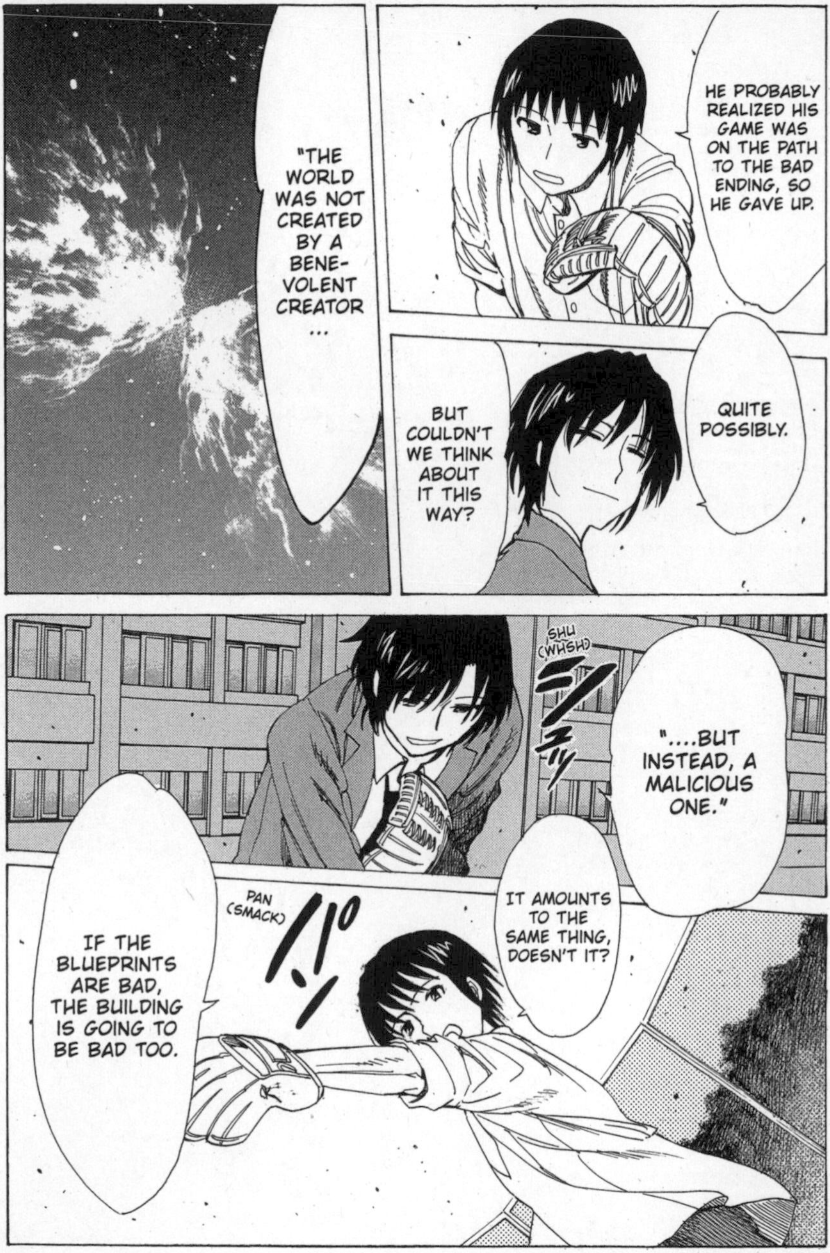
HE PROBABLY REALIZED HIS GAME WAS ON THE PATH TO THE BAD ENDING, SO HE GAVE UP.
QUITE POSSIBLY.
BUT COULDN'T WE THINK ABOUT IT THIS WAY?
"THE WORLD WAS NOT CREATED BY A BENE- VOLENT CREATOR ...
SHU (WHSH)
"....BUT INSTEAD, A MALICIOUS ONE."
IT AMOUNTS TO THE SAME THING, DOESN'T IT?
PAN (SMACK)
IF THE BLUEPRINTS ARE BAD, THE BUILDING IS GOING TO BE BAD TOO.

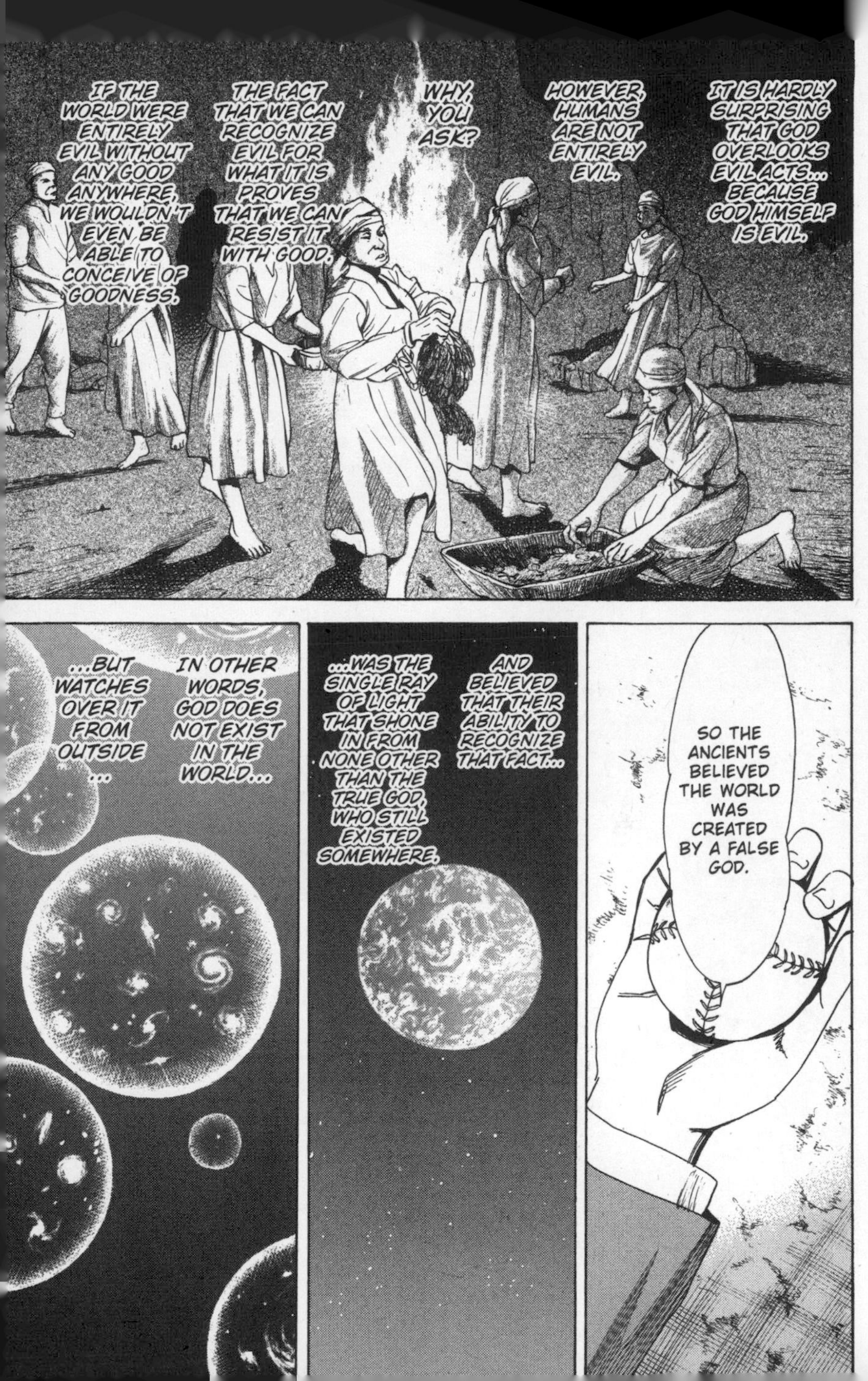
IT IS HARDLY SURPRISING THAT GOD OVERLOOKS EVIL ACTS... BECAUSE GOD HIMSELF IS EVIL.
HOWEVER, HUMANS ARE NOT ENTIRELY EVIL.
WHY, YOU ASK?
THE FACT THAT WE CAN RECOGNIZE EVIL FOR WHAT IT IS PROVES THAT WE CAN RESIST IT WITH GOOD.
IF THE WORLD WERE ENTIRELY EVIL WITHOUT ANY GOOD ANYWHERE, WE WOULDN'T EVEN BE ABLE TO CONCEIVE OF GOODNESS.
SO THE ANCIENTS BELIEVED THE WORLD WAS CREATED BY A FALSE GOD.
AND BELIEVED THAT THEIR ABILITY TO RECOGNIZE THAT FACT...
...WAS THE SINGLE RAY OF LIGHT THAT SHONE IN FROM NONE OTHER THAN THE TRUE GOD, WHO STILL EXISTED SOMEWHERE.
IN OTHER WORDS, GOD DOES NOT EXIST IN THE WORLD...
...BUT WATCHES OVER IT FROM OUTSIDE...

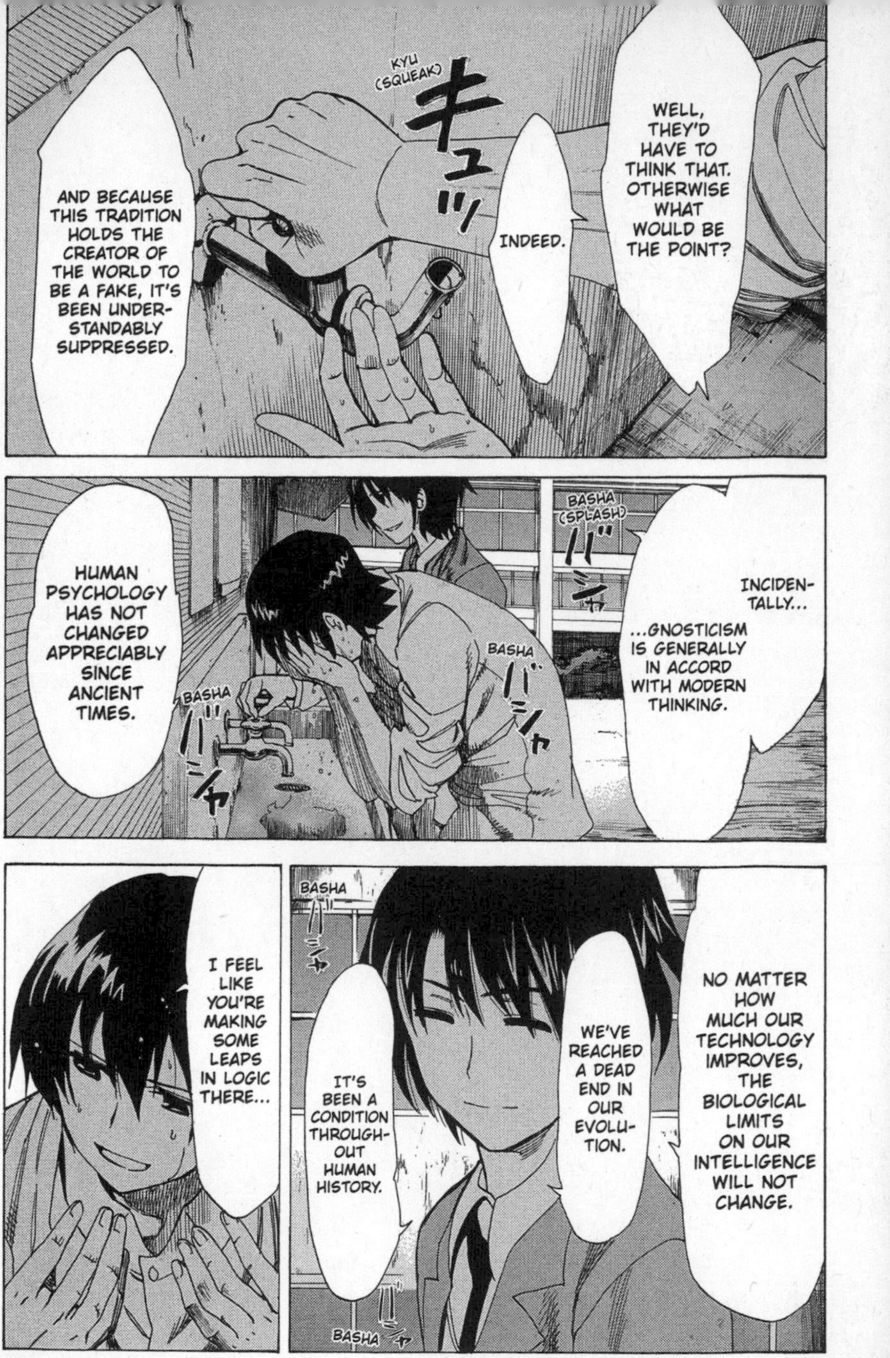
WELL, THEY'D HAVE TO THINK THAT. OTHERWISE WHAT WOULD BE THE POINT?
KYU (SQUEAK)
キュッ
INDEED.
AND BECAUSE THIS TRADITION HOLDS THE CREATOR OF THE WORLD TO BE A FAKE, IT'S BEEN UNDER-STANDABLY SUPPRESSED.
INCIDEN-TALLY...
...GNOSTICISM IS GENERALLY IN ACCORD WITH MODERN THINKING.
BASHA (SPLASH)
バシャ
BASHA
バシャ
BASHA
バシャ
HUMAN PSYCHOLOGY HAS NOT CHANGED APPRECIABLY SINCE ANCIENT TIMES.
NO MATTER HOW MUCH OUR TECHNOLOGY IMPROVES, THE BIOLOGICAL LIMITS ON OUR INTELLIGENCE WILL NOT CHANGE.
WE'VE REACHED A DEAD END IN OUR EVOLU-TION.
IT'S BEEN A CONDITION THROUGH-OUT HUMAN HISTORY.
BASHA
バシャ
BASHA
バシャ
I FEEL LIKE YOU'RE MAKING SOME LEAPS IN LOGIC THERE...

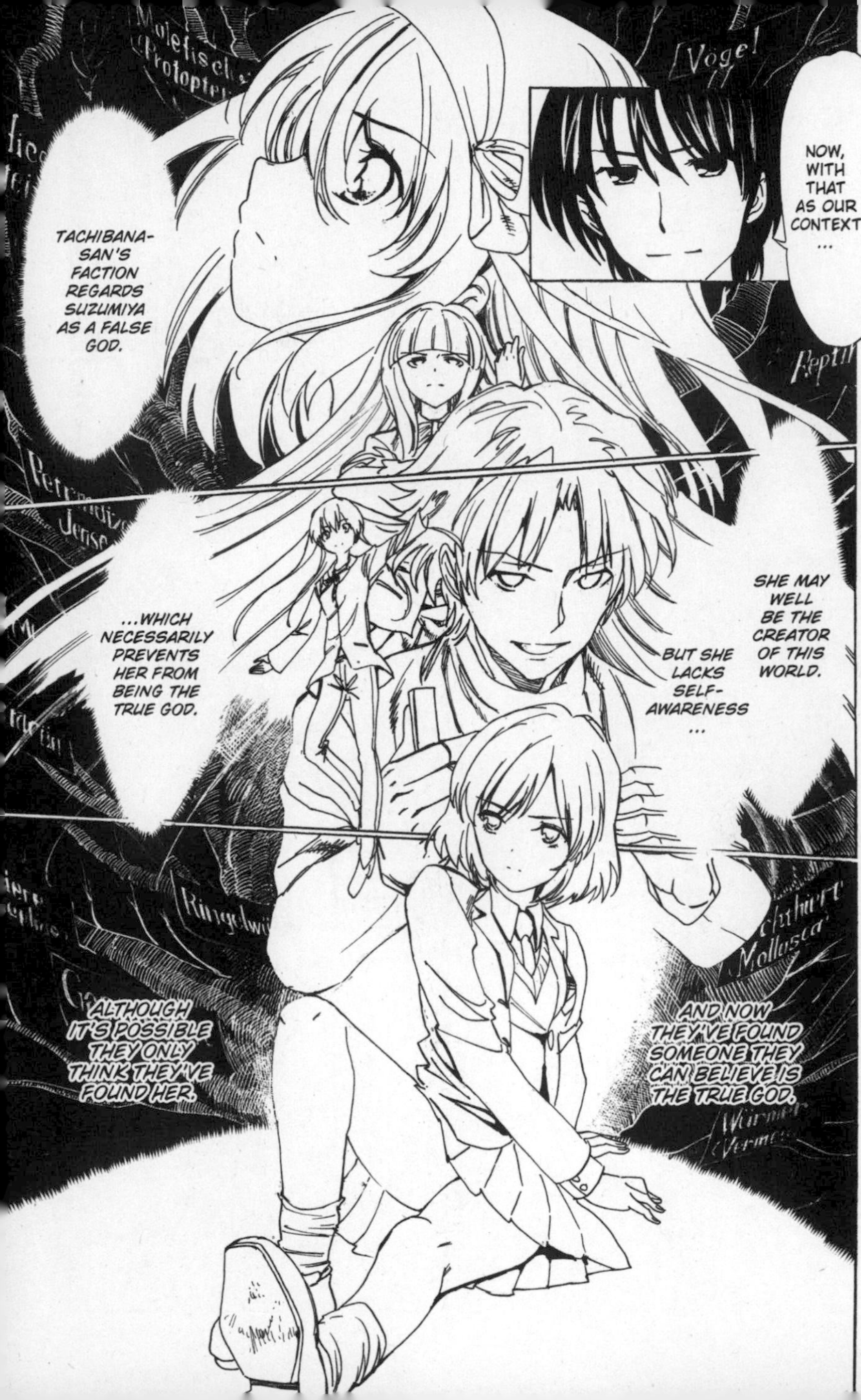
NOW, WITH THAT AS OUR CONTEXT...
TACHIBANA-SAN'S FACTION REGARDS SUZUMIYA AS A FALSE GOD.
SHE MAY WELL BE THE CREATOR OF THIS WORLD.
BUT SHE LACKS SELF-AWARENESS...
...WHICH NECESSARILY PREVENTS HER FROM BEING THE TRUE GOD.
AND NOW THEY'VE FOUND SOMEONE THEY CAN BELIEVE IS THE TRUE GOD.
ALTHOUGH IT'S POSSIBLE THEY ONLY THINK THEY'VE FOUND HER.

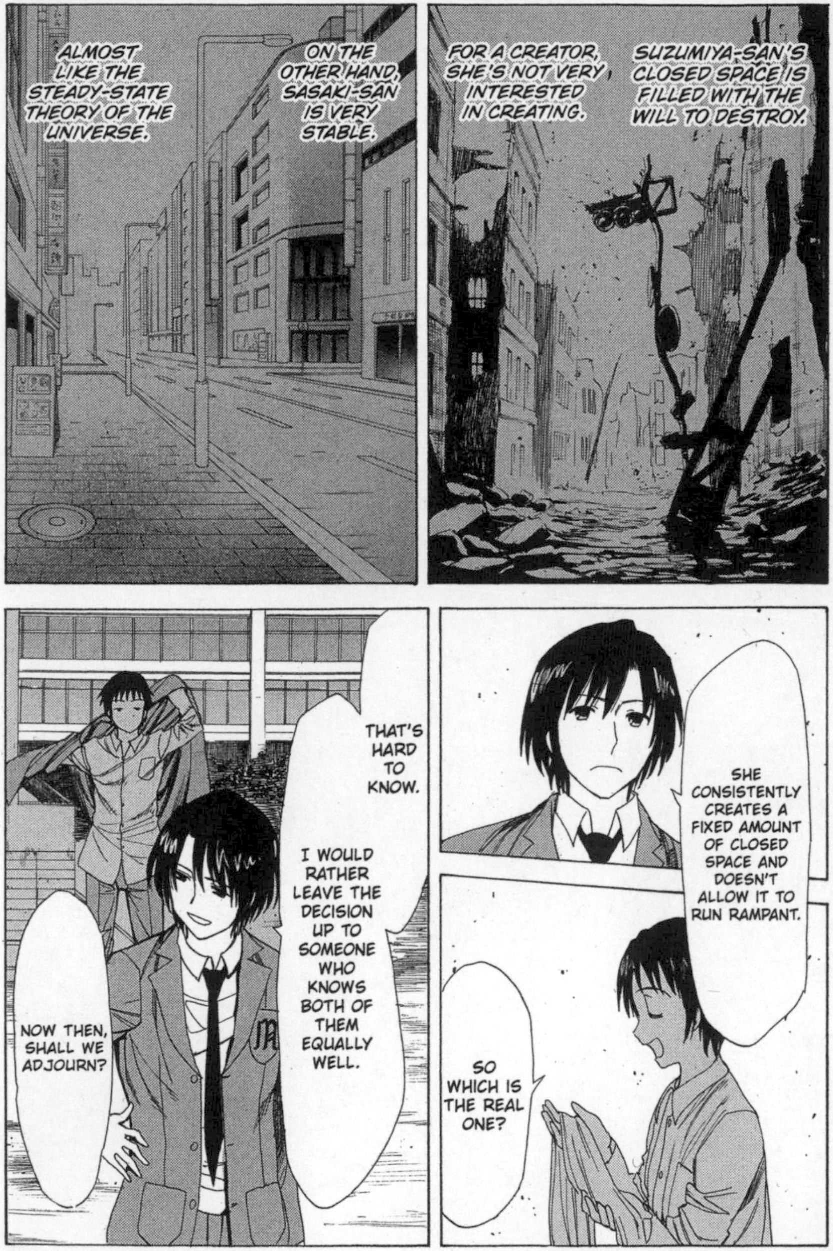
SUZUMIYA-SAN'S CLOSED SPACE IS FILLED WITH THE WILL TO DESTROY.
FOR A CREATOR, SHE'S NOT VERY INTERESTED IN CREATING.
ON THE OTHER HAND, SASAKI-SAN IS VERY STABLE.
ALMOST LIKE THE STEADY-STATE THEORY OF THE UNIVERSE.
SHE CONSISTENTLY CREATES A FIXED AMOUNT OF CLOSED SPACE AND DOESN'T ALLOW IT TO RUN RAMPANT.
SO WHICH IS THE REAL ONE?
THAT'S HARD TO KNOW.
I WOULD RATHER LEAVE THE DECISION UP TO SOMEONE WHO KNOWS BOTH OF THEM EQUALLY WELL.
NOW THEN, SHALL WE ADJOURN?

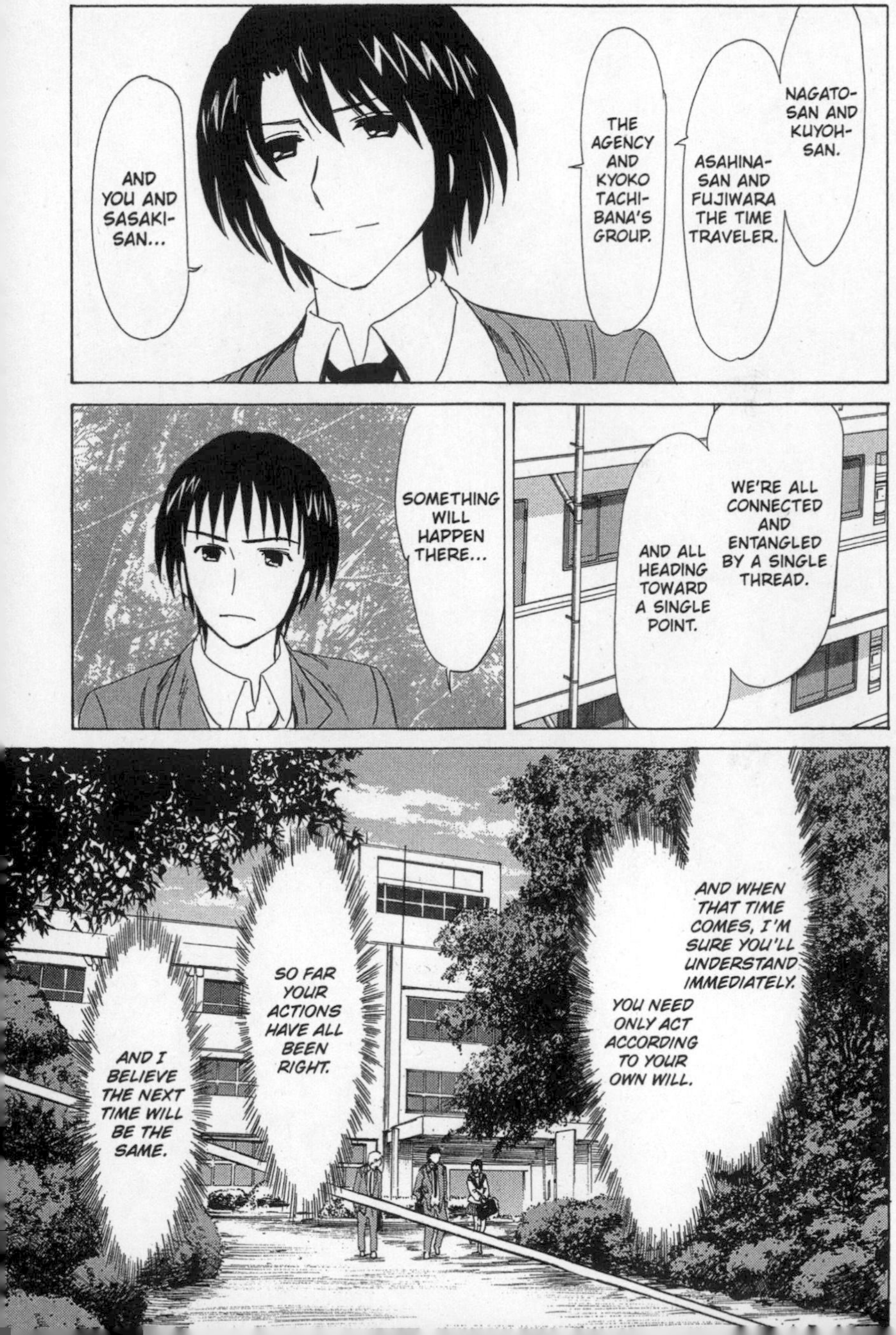
NAGATO-SAN AND KUYOH-SAN.
ASAHINA-SAN AND FUJIWARA THE TIME TRAVELER.
THE AGENCY AND KYOKO TACHIBANA'S GROUP.
AND YOU AND SASAKI-SAN...
WE'RE ALL CONNECTED AND ENTANGLED BY A SINGLE THREAD.
AND ALL HEADING TOWARD A SINGLE POINT.
SOMETHING WILL HAPPEN THERE...
AND WHEN THAT TIME COMES, I'M SURE YOU'LL UNDERSTAND IMMEDIATELY.
YOU NEED ONLY ACT ACCORDING TO YOUR OWN WILL.
SO FAR YOUR ACTIONS HAVE ALL BEEN RIGHT.
AND I BELIEVE THE NEXT TIME WILL BE THE SAME.

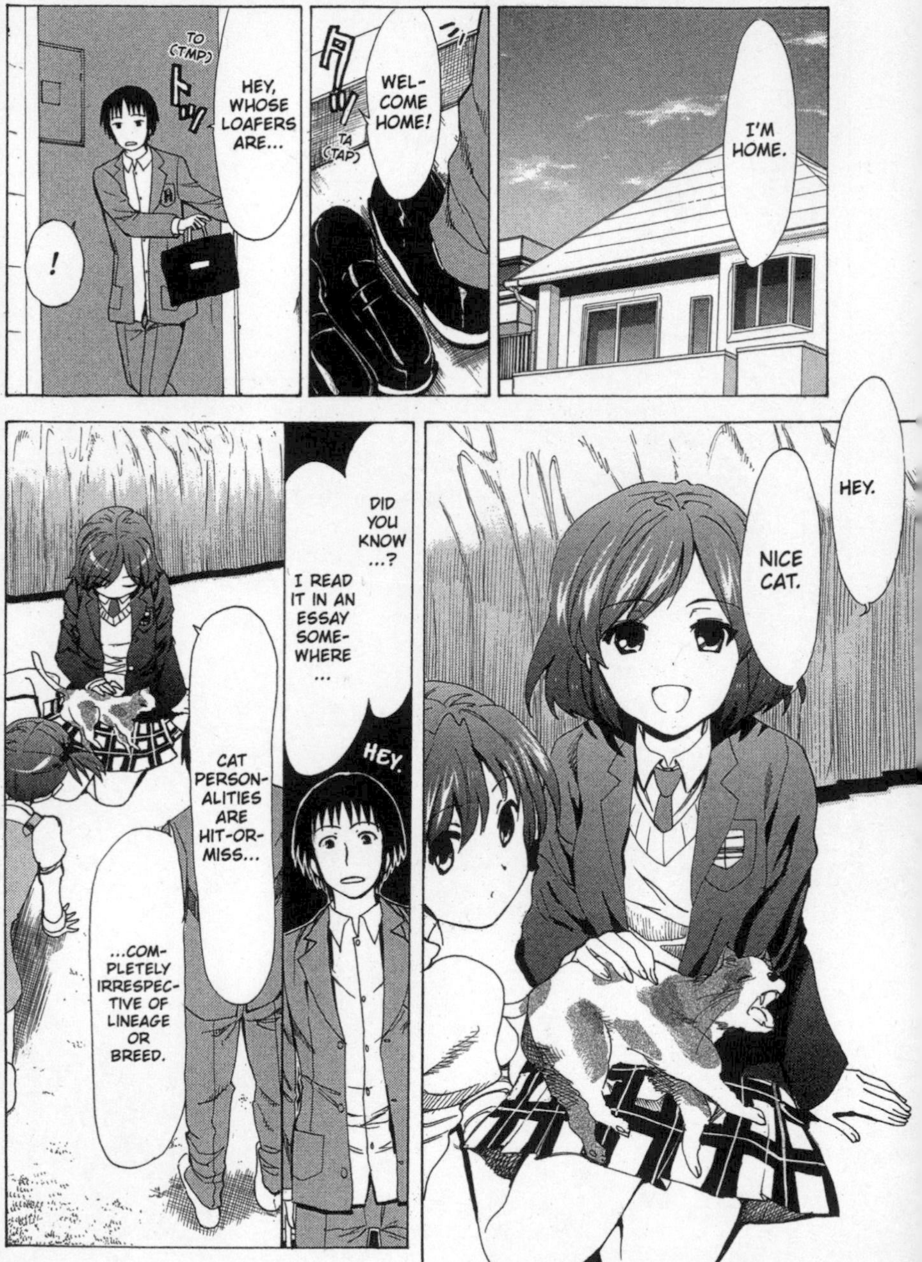
I'M HOME.
WEL-COME HOME!
TA (TAP)
TO (TMP)
HEY, WHOSE LOAFERS ARE...
!
HEY.
NICE CAT.
DID YOU KNOW ...?
I READ IT IN AN ESSAY SOME-WHERE ...
HEY.
CAT PERSON-ALITIES ARE HIT-OR-MISS...
...COM-PLETELY IRRESPEC-TIVE OF LINEAGE OR BREED.

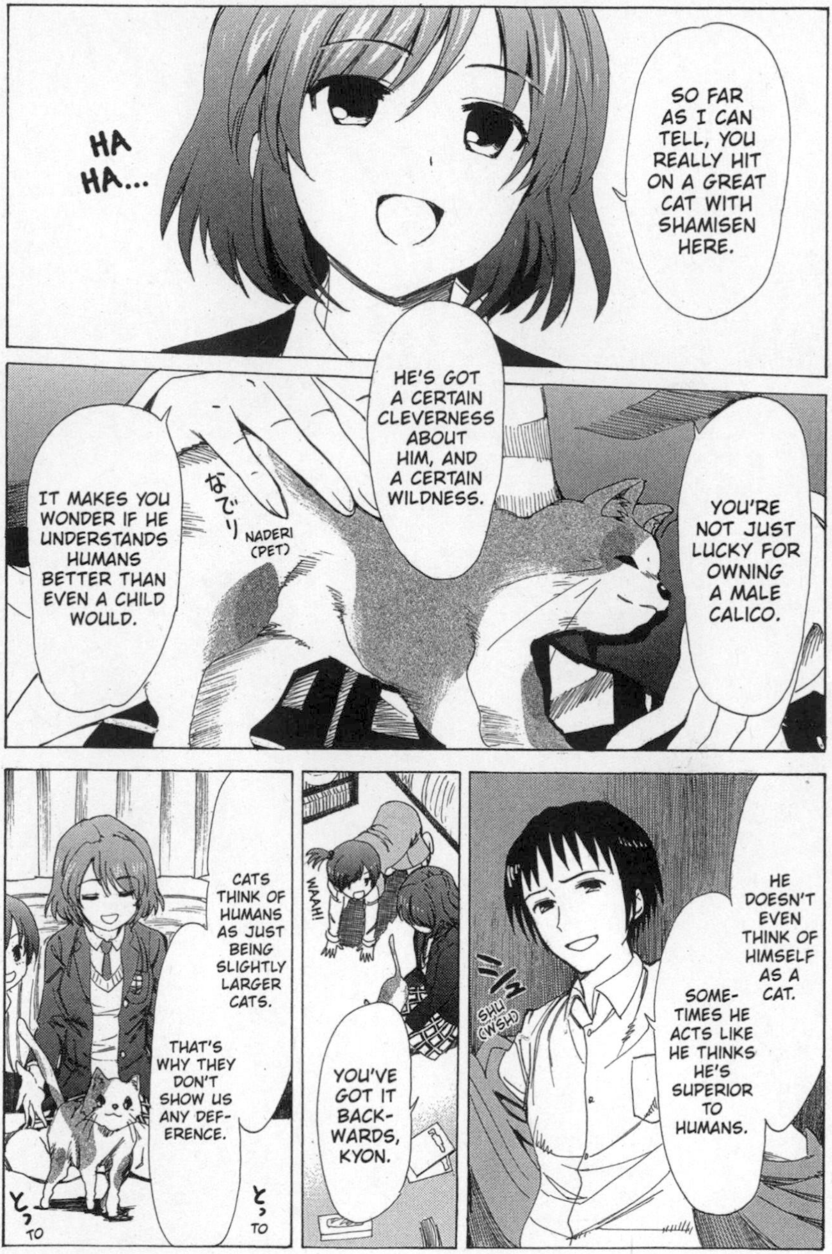
SO FAR AS I CAN TELL, YOU REALLY HIT ON A GREAT CAT WITH SHAMISEN HERE.
HA HA...
YOU'RE NOT JUST LUCKY FOR OWNING A MALE CALICO.
HE'S GOT A CERTAIN CLEVERNESS ABOUT HIM, AND A CERTAIN WILDNESS.
なでり
NADERI (PET)
IT MAKES YOU WONDER IF HE UNDERSTANDS HUMANS BETTER THAN EVEN A CHILD WOULD.
HE DOESN'T EVEN THINK OF HIMSELF AS A CAT.
SOME-TIMES HE ACTS LIKE HE THINKS HE'S SUPERIOR TO HUMANS.
SHU (WSH)
WAAH!
YOU'VE GOT IT BACK-WARDS, KYON.
CATS THINK OF HUMANS AS JUST BEING SLIGHTLY LARGER CATS.
THAT'S WHY THEY DON'T SHOW US ANY DEF-ERENCE.
とっ
TO
とっ
TO

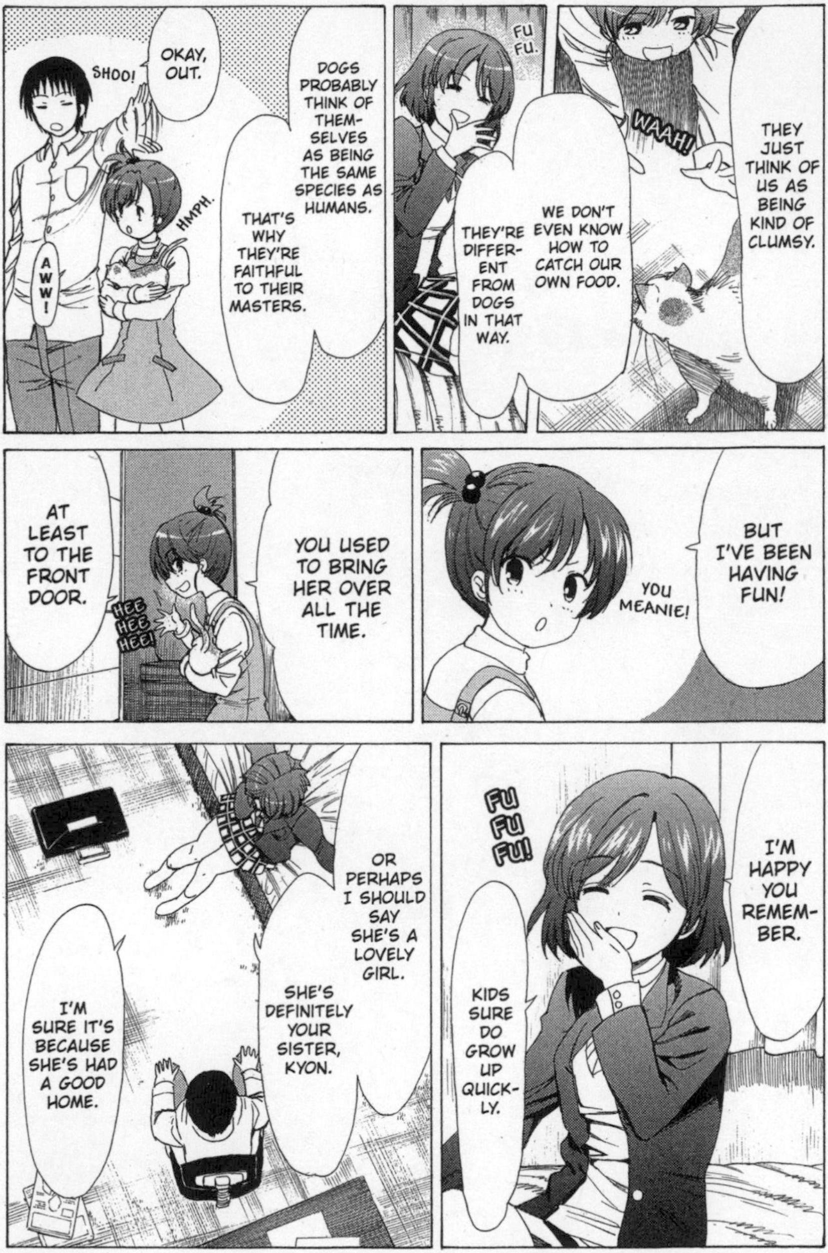
WAAH!
THEY JUST THINK OF US AS BEING KIND OF CLUMSY.
FU FU.
WE DON'T EVEN KNOW HOW TO CATCH OUR OWN FOOD.
THEY'RE DIFFERENT FROM DOGS IN THAT WAY.
DOGS PROBABLY THINK OF THEMSELVES AS BEING THE SAME SPECIES AS HUMANS.
THAT'S WHY THEY'RE FAITHFUL TO THEIR MASTERS.
OKAY, OUT.
SHOO!
HMPH.
AWW!
BUT I'VE BEEN HAVING FUN!
YOU MEANIE!
YOU USED TO BRING HER OVER ALL THE TIME.
AT LEAST TO THE FRONT DOOR.
HEE HEE HEE!
FU FU FU!
I'M HAPPY YOU REMEMBER.
KIDS SURE DO GROW UP QUICKLY.
SHE'S DEFINITELY YOUR SISTER, KYON.
OR PERHAPS I SHOULD SAY SHE'S A LOVELY GIRL.
I'M SURE IT'S BECAUSE SHE'S HAD A GOOD HOME.

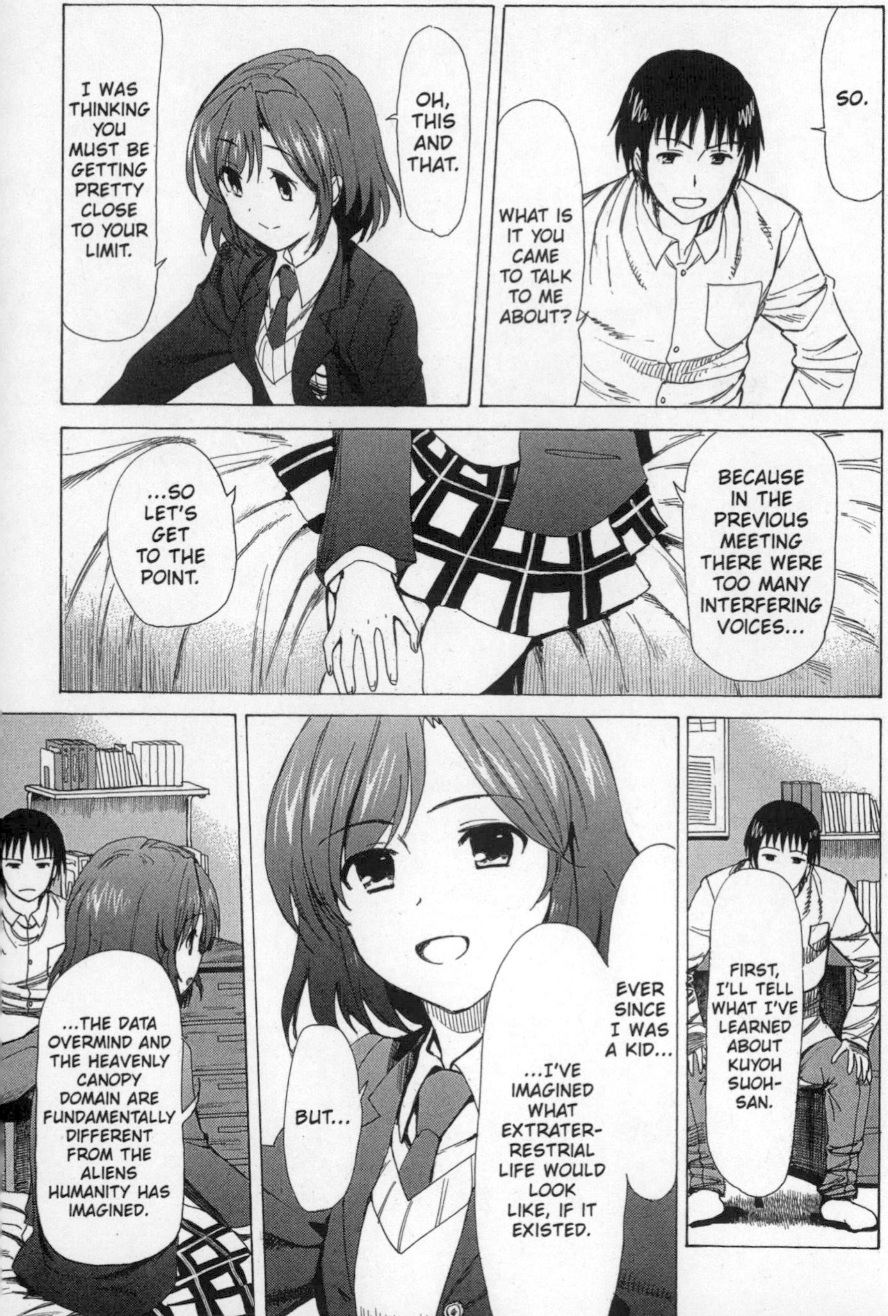
SO.
WHAT IS IT YOU CAME TO TALK TO ME ABOUT?
OH, THIS AND THAT.
I WAS THINKING YOU MUST BE GETTING PRETTY CLOSE TO YOUR LIMIT.
BECAUSE IN THE PREVIOUS MEETING THERE WERE TOO MANY INTERFERING VOICES...
...SO LET'S GET TO THE POINT.
FIRST, I'LL TELL WHAT I'VE LEARNED ABOUT KUYOH SUOH-SAN.
EVER SINCE I WAS A KID...
...I'VE IMAGINED WHAT EXTRATER-RESTRIAL LIFE WOULD LOOK LIKE, IF IT EXISTED.
BUT...
...THE DATA OVERMIND AND THE HEAVENLY CANOPY DOMAIN ARE FUNDAMENTALLY DIFFERENT FROM THE ALIENS HUMANITY HAS IMAGINED.

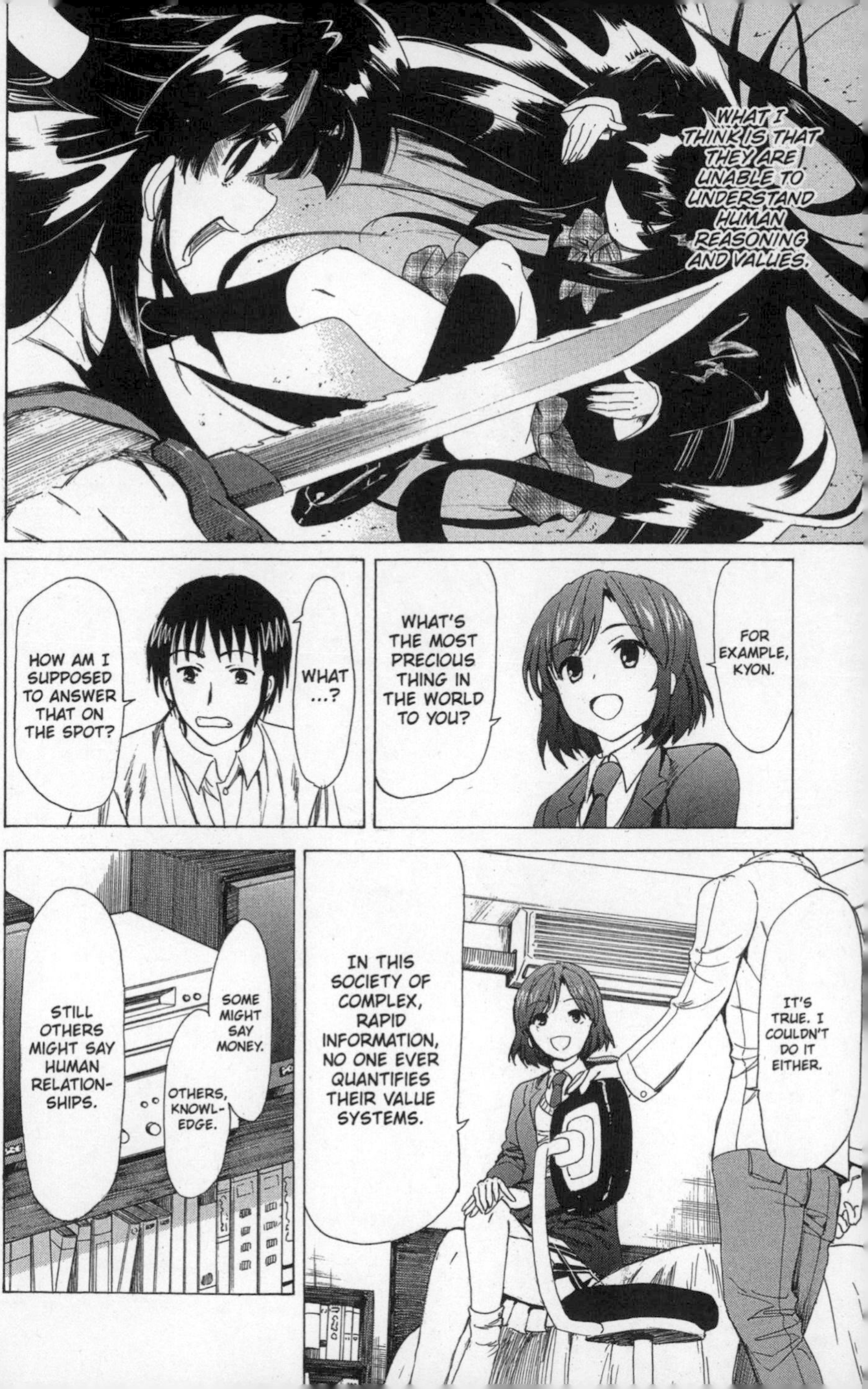
WHAT I THINK IS THAT THEY ARE UNABLE TO UNDERSTAND HUMAN REASONING AND VALUES.
FOR EXAMPLE, KYON.
WHAT'S THE MOST PRECIOUS THING IN THE WORLD TO YOU?
WHAT ...?
HOW AM I SUPPOSED TO ANSWER THAT ON THE SPOT?
IT'S TRUE. I COULDN'T DO IT EITHER.
IN THIS SOCIETY OF COMPLEX, RAPID INFORMATION, NO ONE EVER QUANTIFIES THEIR VALUE SYSTEMS.
SOME MIGHT SAY MONEY.
OTHERS, KNOWLEDGE.
STILL OTHERS MIGHT SAY HUMAN RELATION-SHIPS.

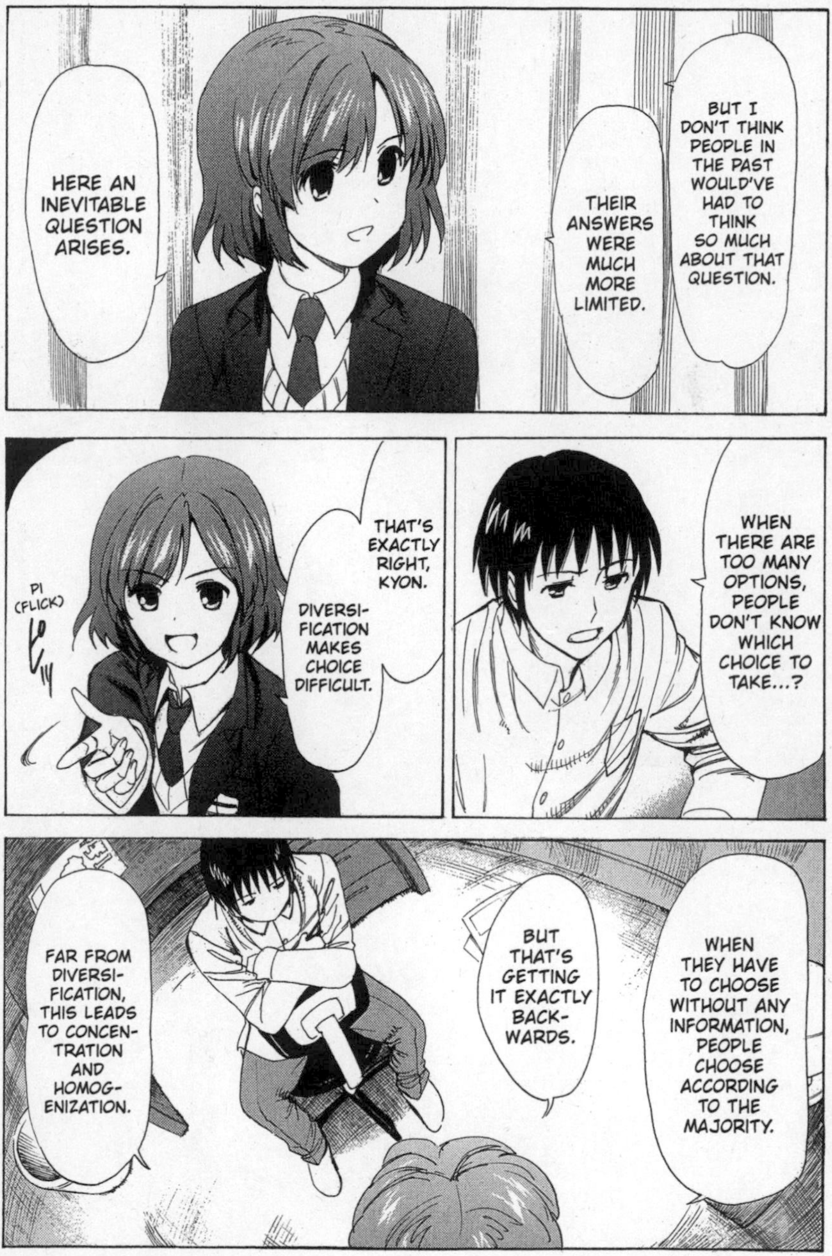
BUT I DON'T THINK PEOPLE IN THE PAST WOULD'VE HAD TO THINK SO MUCH ABOUT THAT QUESTION.
THEIR ANSWERS WERE MUCH MORE LIMITED.
HERE AN INEVITABLE QUESTION ARISES.
WHEN THERE ARE TOO MANY OPTIONS, PEOPLE DON'T KNOW WHICH CHOICE TO TAKE...?
THAT'S EXACTLY RIGHT, KYON.
DIVERSI-FICATION MAKES CHOICE DIFFICULT.
PI (FLICK)
WHEN THEY HAVE TO CHOOSE WITHOUT ANY INFORMATION, PEOPLE CHOOSE ACCORDING TO THE MAJORITY.
BUT THAT'S GETTING IT EXACTLY BACK-WARDS.
FAR FROM DIVERSI-FICATION, THIS LEADS TO CONCEN-TRATION AND HOMOG-ENIZATION.

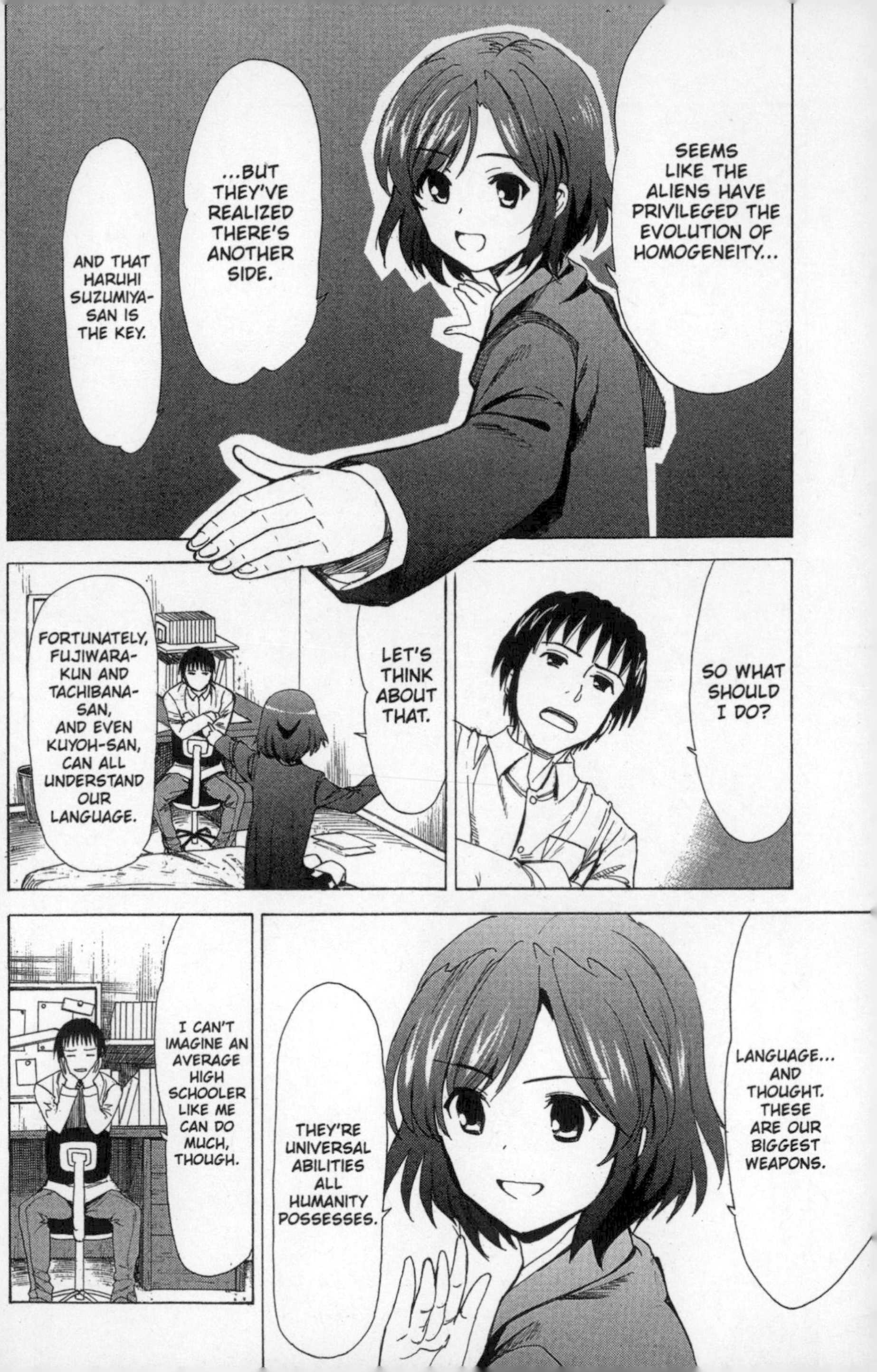
SEEMS LIKE THE ALIENS HAVE PRIVILEGED THE EVOLUTION OF HOMOGENEITY...
...BUT THEY'VE REALIZED THERE'S ANOTHER SIDE.
AND THAT HARUHI SUZUMIYA-SAN IS THE KEY.
SO WHAT SHOULD I DO?
LET'S THINK ABOUT THAT.
FORTUNATELY, FUJIWARA-KUN AND TACHIBANA-SAN, AND EVEN KUYOH-SAN, CAN ALL UNDERSTAND OUR LANGUAGE.
LANGUAGE... AND THOUGHT. THESE ARE OUR BIGGEST WEAPONS.
THEY'RE UNIVERSAL ABILITIES ALL HUMANITY POSSESSES.
I CAN'T IMAGINE AN AVERAGE HIGH SCHOOLER LIKE ME CAN DO MUCH, THOUGH.

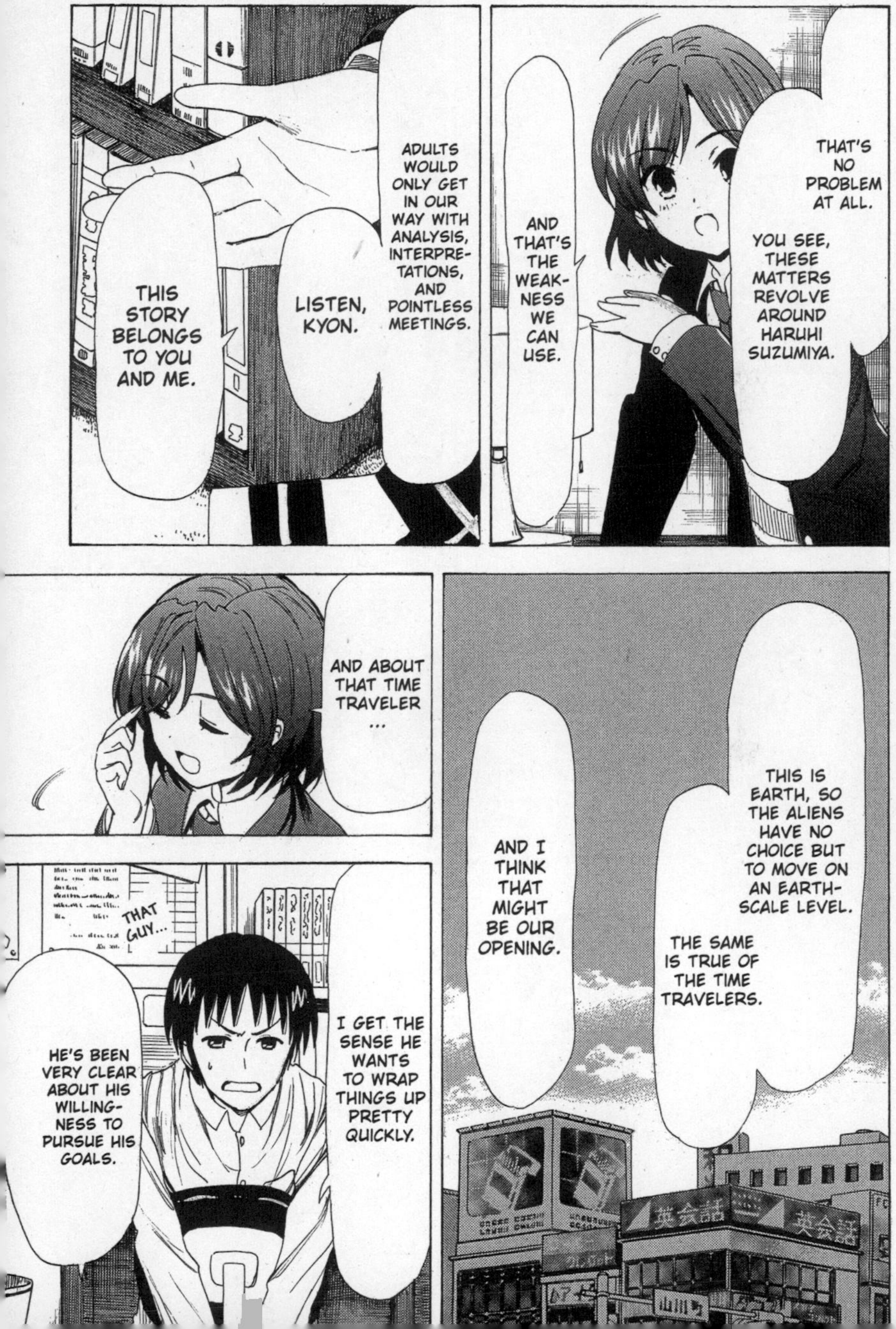
THAT'S NO PROBLEM AT ALL.
YOU SEE, THESE MATTERS REVOLVE AROUND HARUHI SUZUMIYA.
AND THAT'S THE WEAKNESS WE CAN USE.
ADULTS WOULD ONLY GET IN OUR WAY WITH ANALYSIS, INTERPRETATIONS, AND POINTLESS MEETINGS.
LISTEN, KYON.
THIS STORY BELONGS TO YOU AND ME.
THIS IS EARTH, SO THE ALIENS HAVE NO CHOICE BUT TO MOVE ON AN EARTH-SCALE LEVEL.
THE SAME IS TRUE OF THE TIME TRAVELERS.
AND I THINK THAT MIGHT BE OUR OPENING.
英会話
英会話
AND ABOUT THAT TIME TRAVELER...
THAT GUY...
I GET THE SENSE HE WANTS TO WRAP THINGS UP PRETTY QUICKLY.
HE'S BEEN VERY CLEAR ABOUT HIS WILLINGNESS TO PURSUE HIS GOALS.

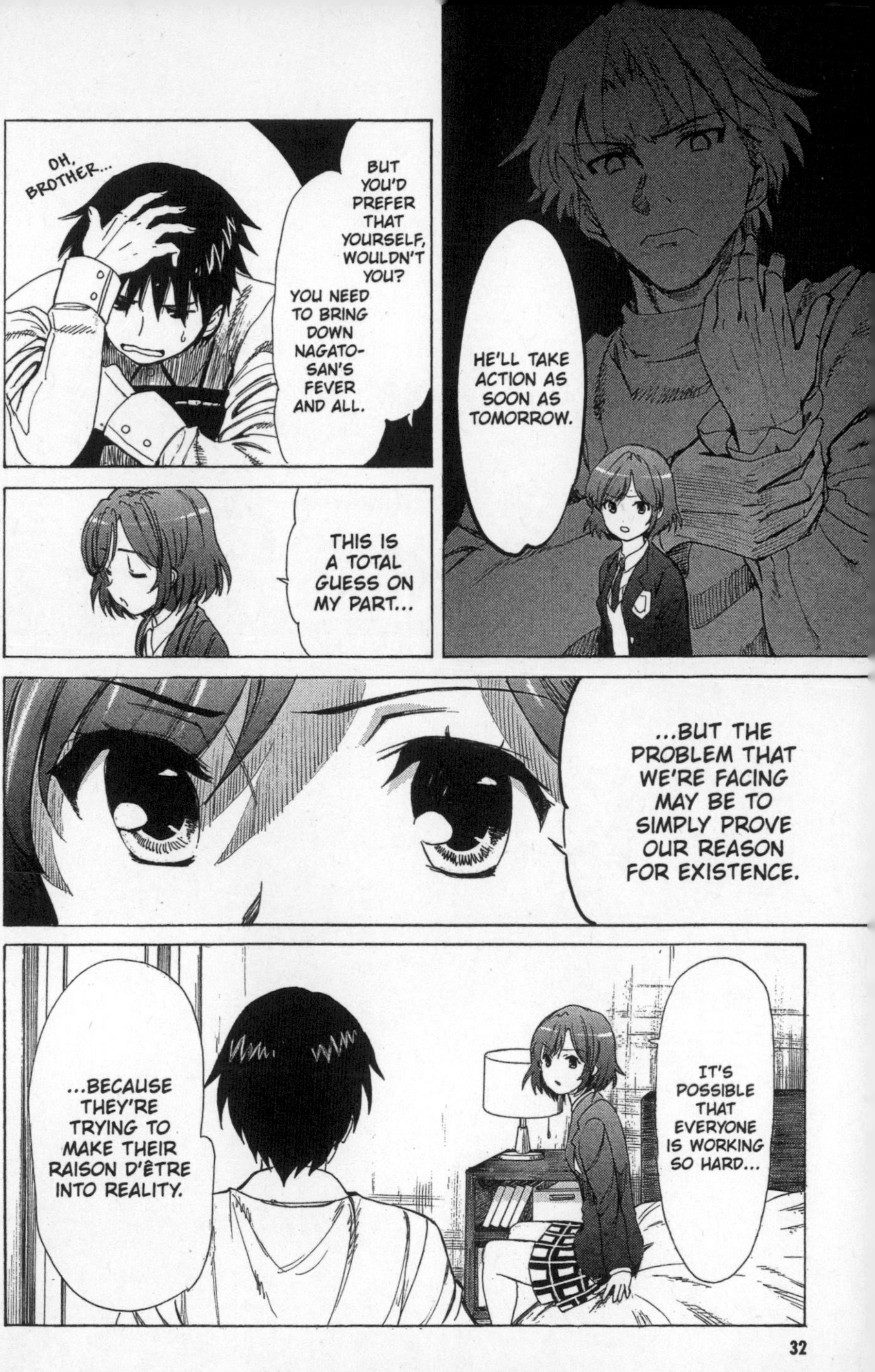
HE'LL TAKE ACTION AS SOON AS TOMORROW.
BUT YOU'D PREFER THAT YOURSELF, WOULDN'T YOU?
YOU NEED TO BRING DOWN NAGATO-SAN'S FEVER AND ALL.
OH, BROTHER...
THIS IS A TOTAL GUESS ON MY PART...
...BUT THE PROBLEM THAT WE'RE FACING MAY BE TO SIMPLY PROVE OUR REASON FOR EXISTENCE.
IT'S POSSIBLE THAT EVERYONE IS WORKING SO HARD...
...BECAUSE THEY'RE TRYING TO MAKE THEIR RAISON D'ÊTRE INTO REALITY.

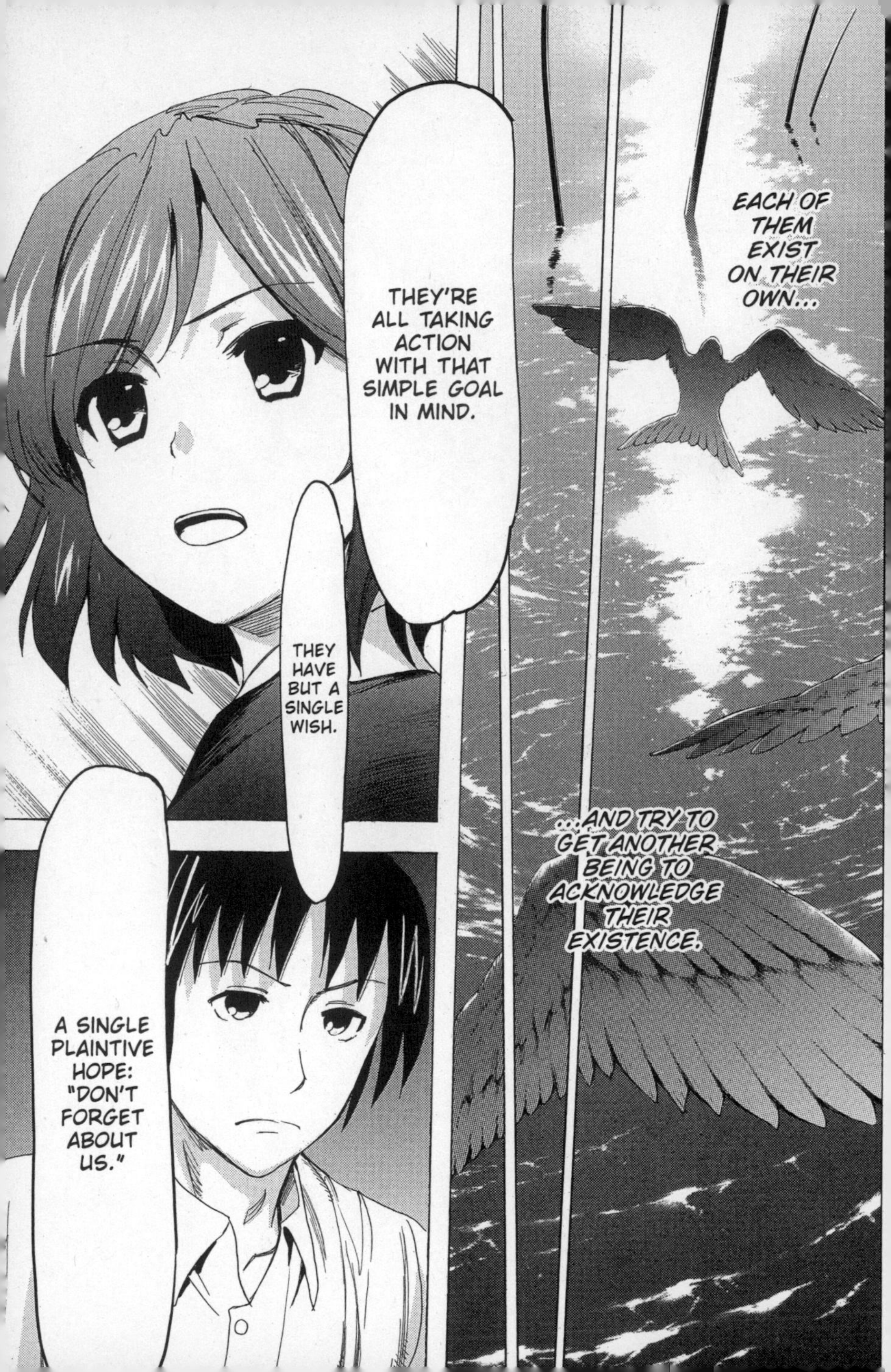
EACH OF THEM EXIST ON THEIR OWN...
...AND TRY TO GET ANOTHER BEING TO ACKNOWLEDGE THEIR EXISTENCE.
THEY'RE ALL TAKING ACTION WITH THAT SIMPLE GOAL IN MIND.
THEY HAVE BUT A SINGLE WISH.
A SINGLE PLAINTIVE HOPE: "DON'T FORGET ABOUT US."

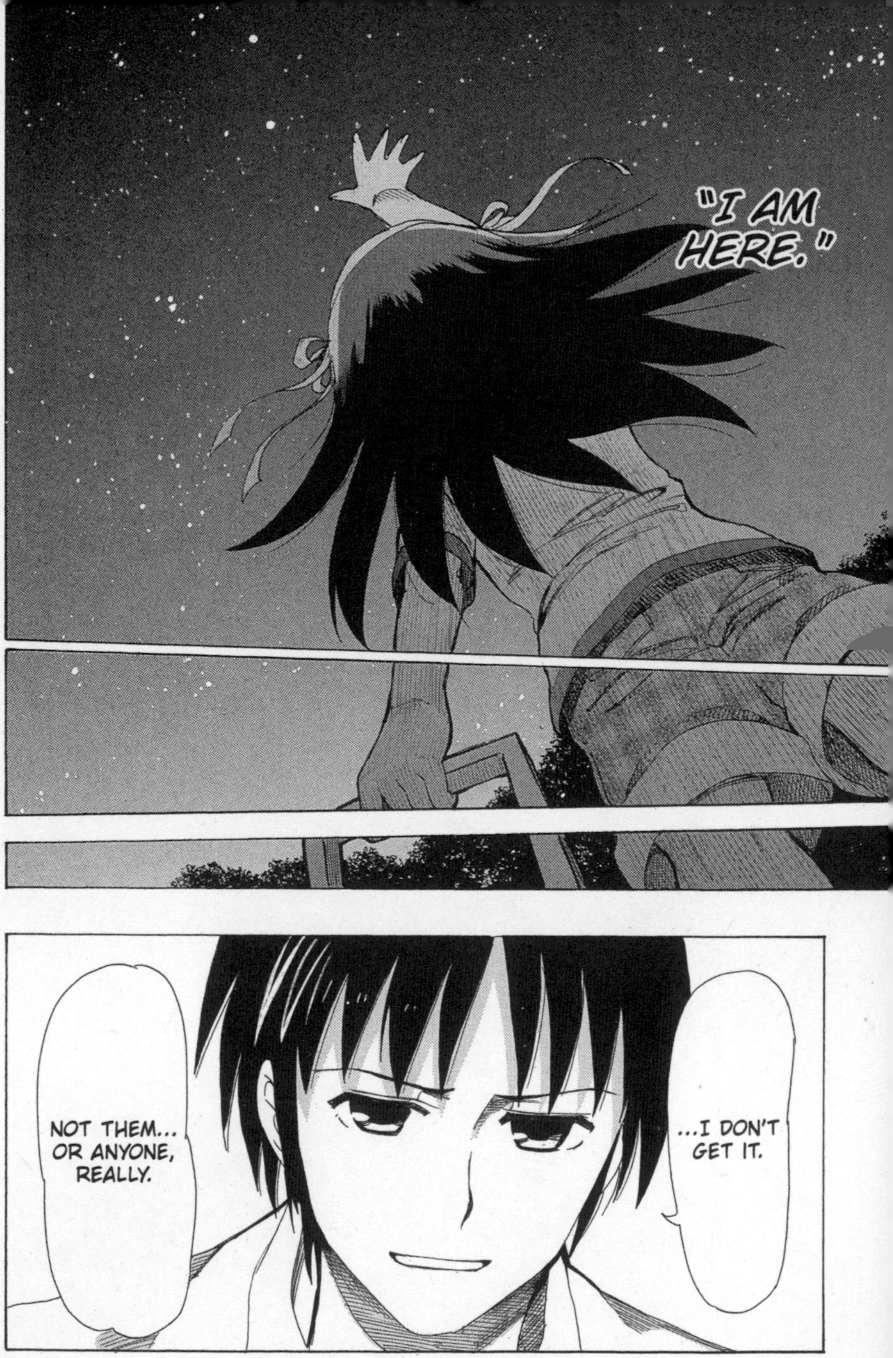
"I AM HERE."
...I DON'T GET IT.
NOT THEM... OR ANYONE, REALLY.

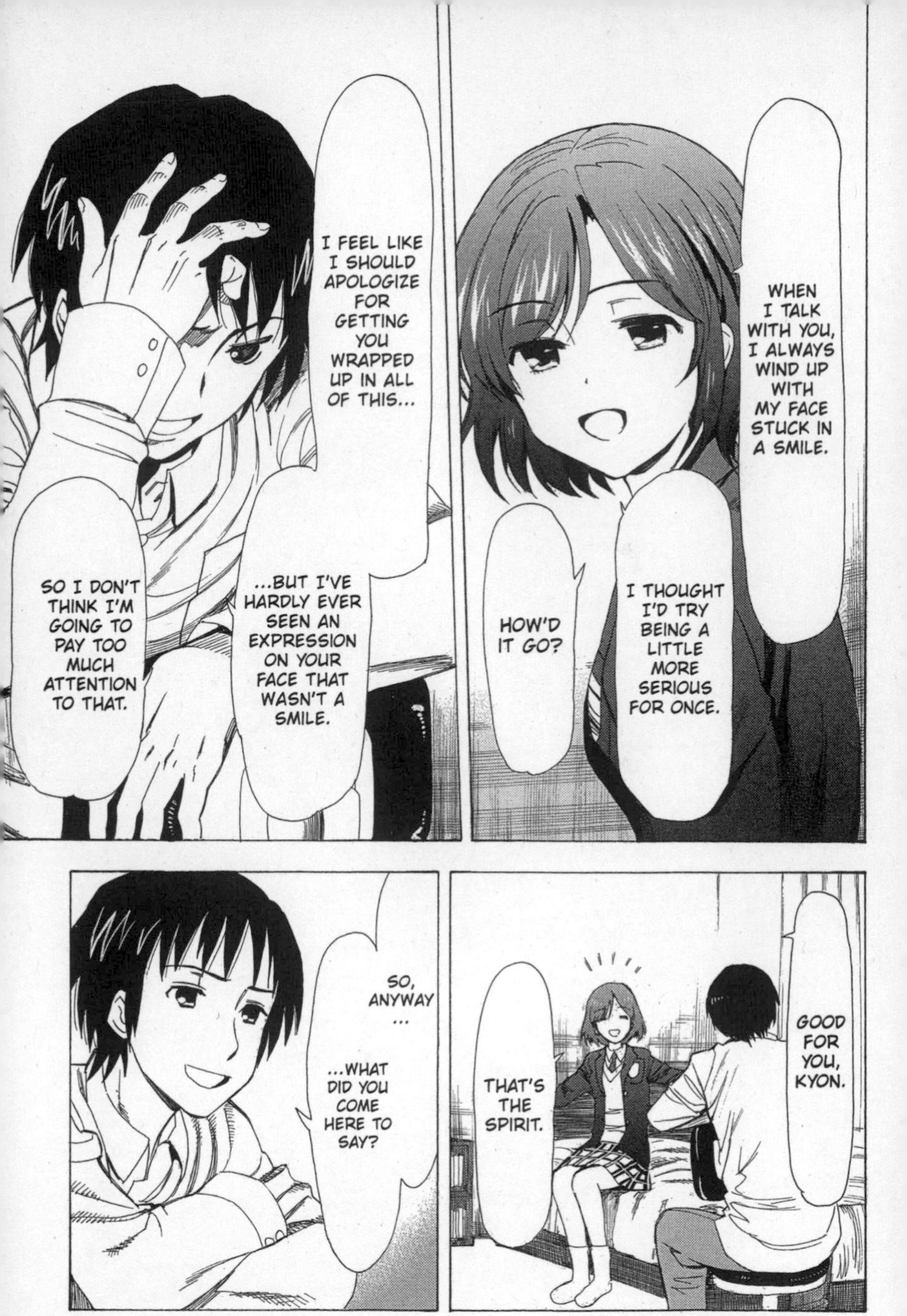
WHEN I TALK WITH YOU, I ALWAYS WIND UP WITH MY FACE STUCK IN A SMILE.
I THOUGHT I'D TRY BEING A LITTLE MORE SERIOUS FOR ONCE.
HOW'D IT GO?
I FEEL LIKE I SHOULD APOLOGIZE FOR GETTING YOU WRAPPED UP IN ALL OF THIS...
...BUT I'VE HARDLY EVER SEEN AN EXPRESSION ON YOUR FACE THAT WASN'T A SMILE.
SO I DON'T THINK I'M GOING TO PAY TOO MUCH ATTENTION TO THAT.
GOOD FOR YOU, KYON.
THAT'S THE SPIRIT.
SO, ANYWAY ...
...WHAT DID YOU COME HERE TO SAY?

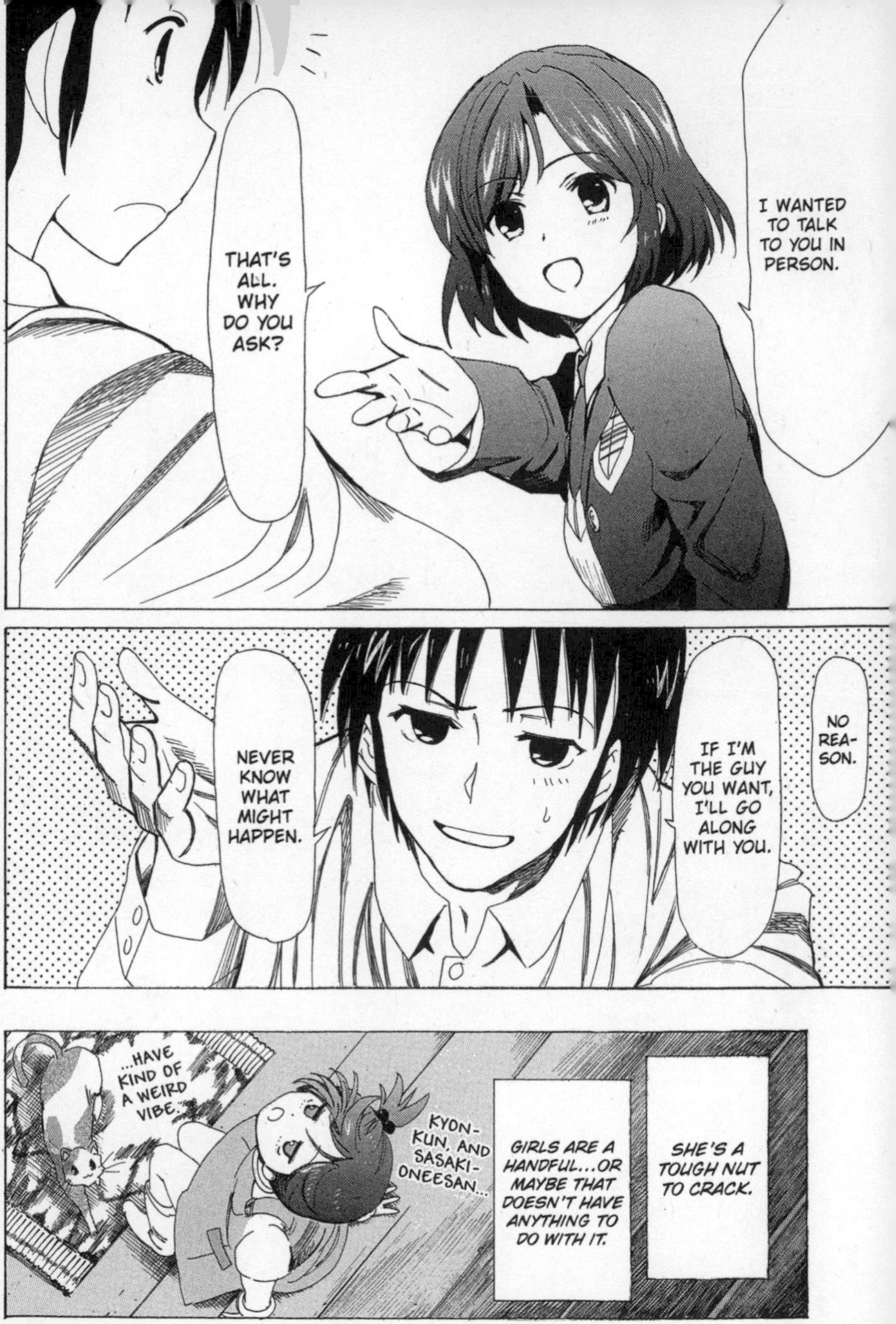
I WANTED TO TALK TO YOU IN PERSON.
THAT'S ALL. WHY DO YOU ASK?
NO REASON.
IF I'M THE GUY YOU WANT, I'LL GO ALONG WITH YOU.
NEVER KNOW WHAT MIGHT HAPPEN.
SHE'S A TOUGH NUT TO CRACK.
GIRLS ARE A HANDFUL...OR MAYBE THAT DOESN'T HAVE ANYTHING TO DO WITH IT.
KYON-KUN, AND SASAKI-ONEESAN...
...HAVE KIND OF A WEIRD VIBE.

THE SURPRISE OF HARUHI SUZUMIYA VII : END

THE MELANCHOLY OF HARUHI SUZUMIYA

# THE SURPRISE OF HARUHI SUZUMIYA VIII

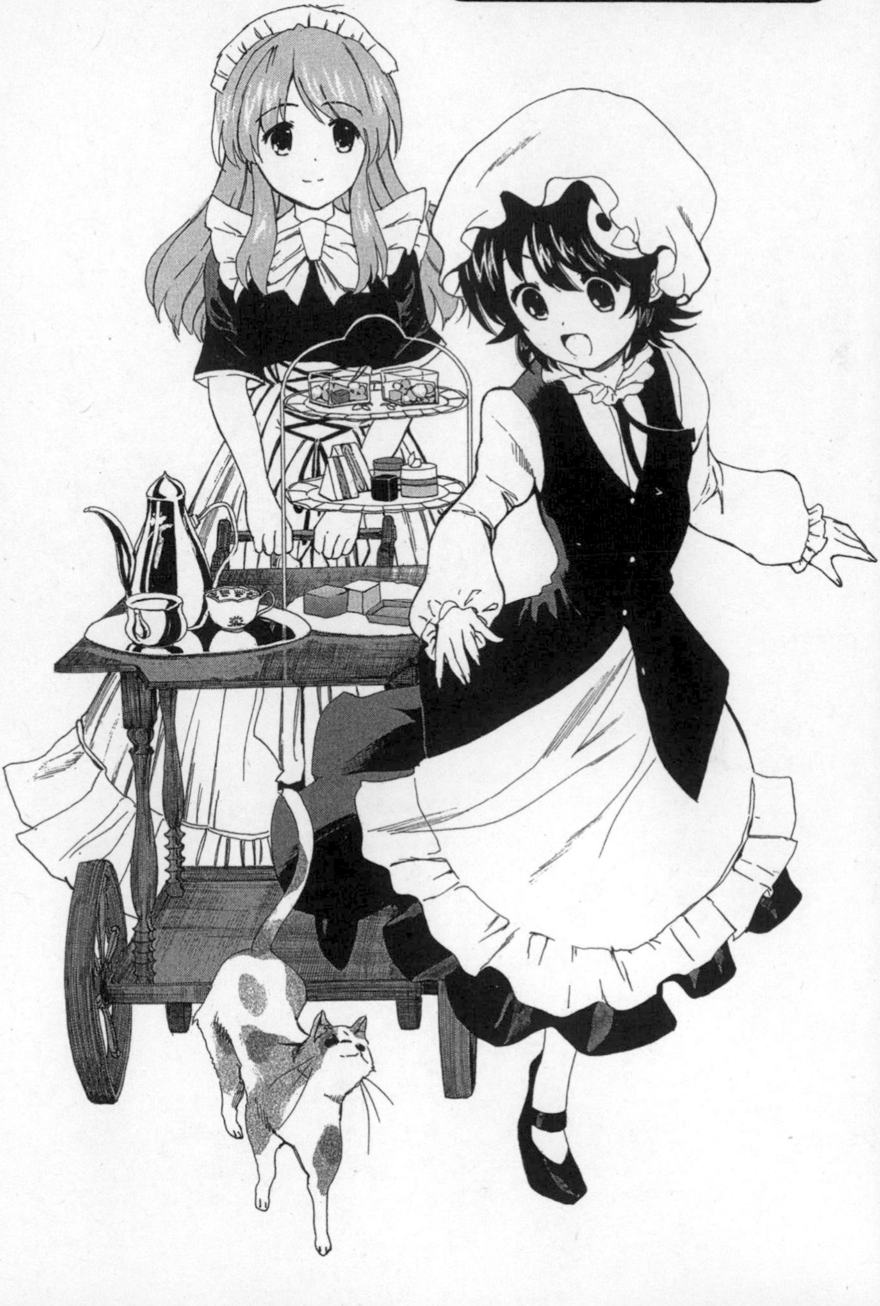

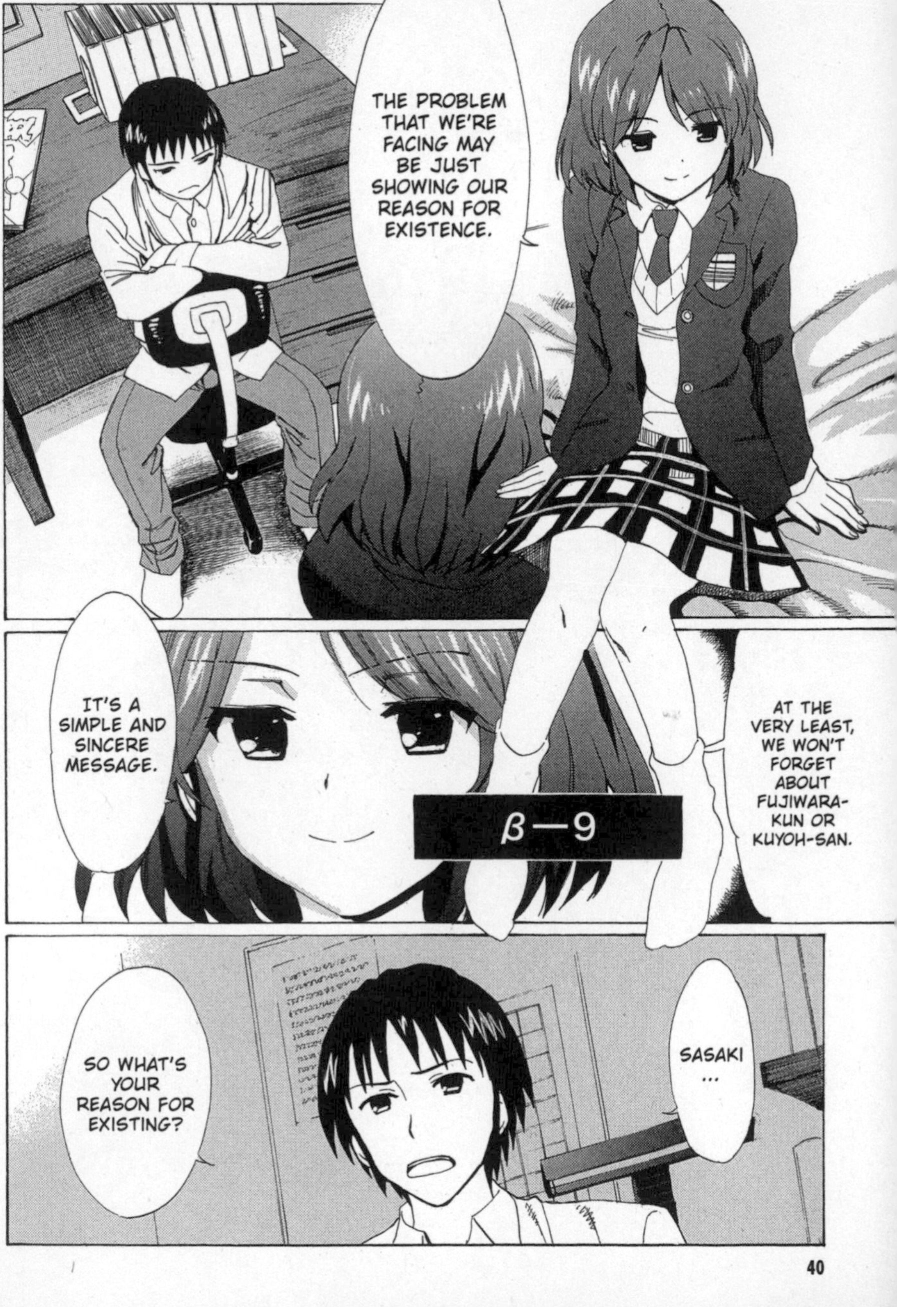
THE PROBLEM THAT WE'RE FACING MAY BE JUST SHOWING OUR REASON FOR EXISTENCE.
AT THE VERY LEAST, WE WON'T FORGET ABOUT FUJIWARA-KUN OR KUYOH-SAN.
β—9
IT'S A SIMPLE AND SINCERE MESSAGE.
SASAKI ...
SO WHAT'S YOUR REASON FOR EXISTING?

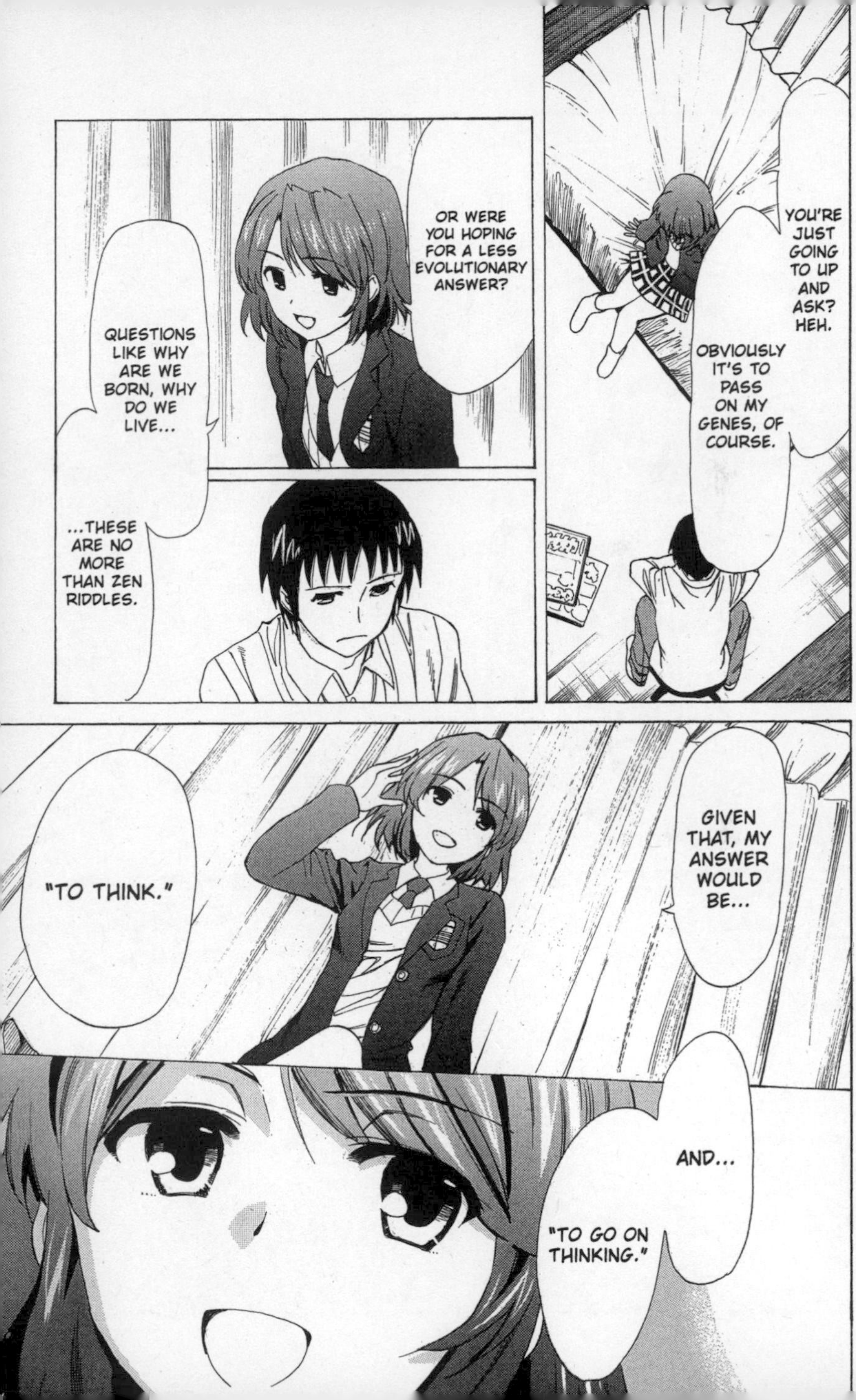
YOU'RE JUST GOING TO UP AND ASK? HEH.
OBVIOUSLY IT'S TO PASS ON MY GENES, OF COURSE.
OR WERE YOU HOPING FOR A LESS EVOLUTIONARY ANSWER?
QUESTIONS LIKE WHY ARE WE BORN, WHY DO WE LIVE...
...THESE ARE NO MORE THAN ZEN RIDDLES.
GIVEN THAT, MY ANSWER WOULD BE...
"TO THINK."
AND...
"TO GO ON THINKING."
....

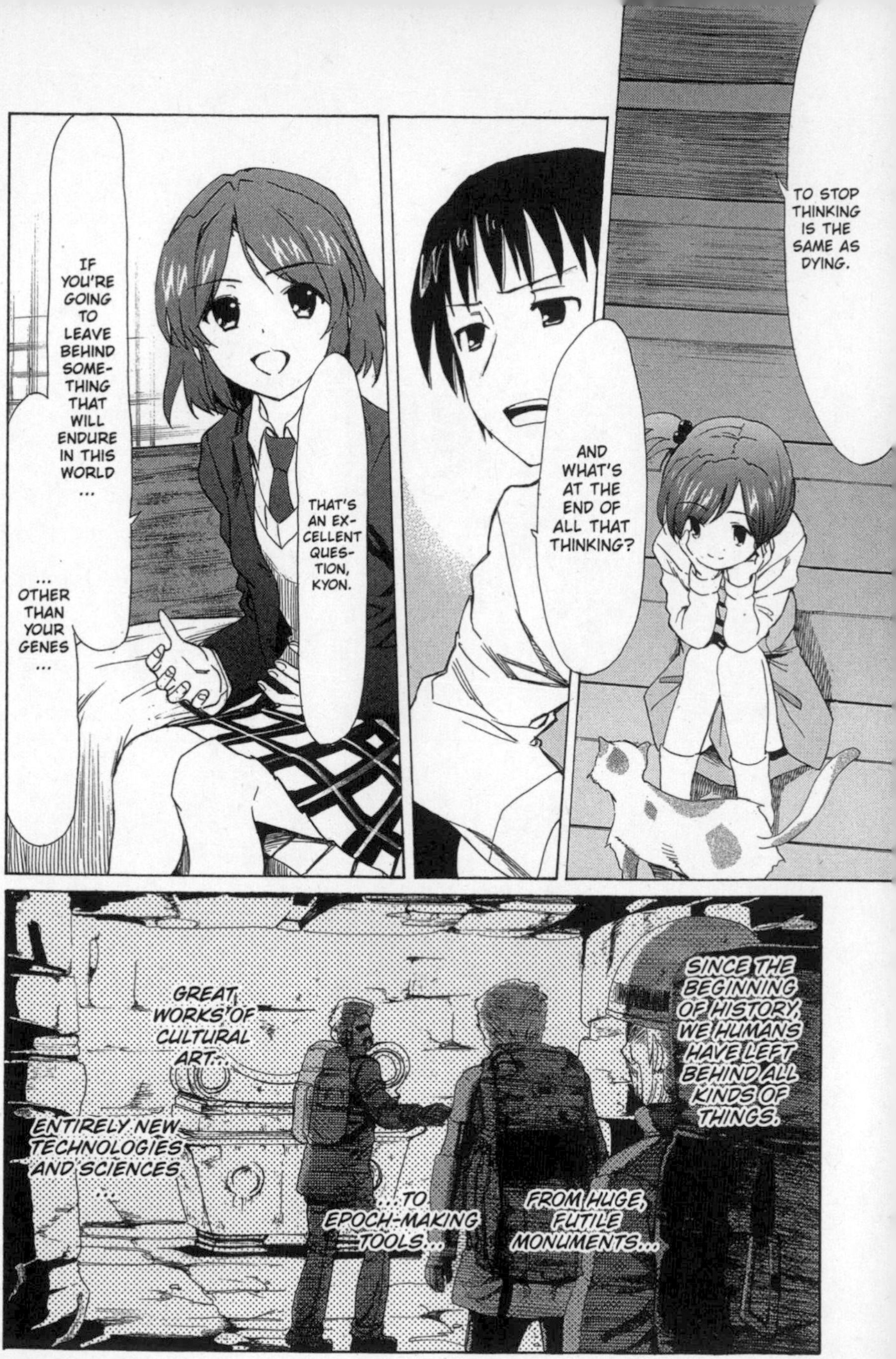
TO STOP THINKING IS THE SAME AS DYING.
AND WHAT'S AT THE END OF ALL THAT THINKING?
THAT'S AN EXCELLENT QUESTION, KYON.
IF YOU'RE GOING TO LEAVE BEHIND SOMETHING THAT WILL ENDURE IN THIS WORLD ...
... OTHER THAN YOUR GENES ...
SINCE THE BEGINNING OF HISTORY, WE HUMANS HAVE LEFT BEHIND ALL KINDS OF THINGS.
FROM HUGE, FUTILE MONUMENTS...
...TO EPOCH-MAKING TOOLS...
GREAT WORKS OF CULTURAL ART...
ENTIRELY NEW TECHNOLOGIES AND SCIENCES ...

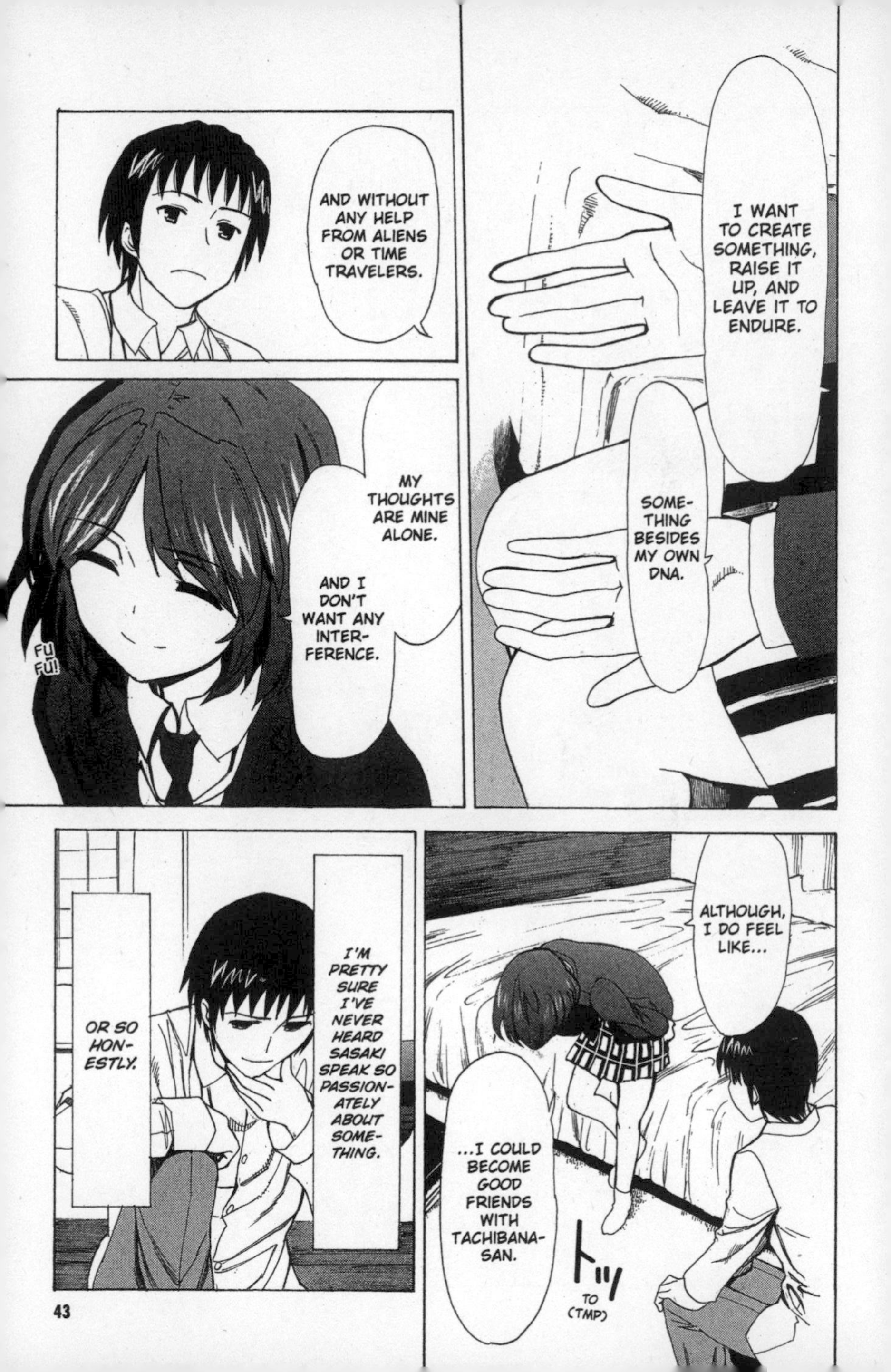

I WANT TO CREATE SOMETHING, RAISE IT UP, AND LEAVE IT TO ENDURE.
SOMETHING BESIDES MY OWN DNA.
AND WITHOUT ANY HELP FROM ALIENS OR TIME TRAVELERS.
MY THOUGHTS ARE MINE ALONE.
AND I DON'T WANT ANY INTERFERENCE.
FU FU!
ALTHOUGH, I DO FEEL LIKE...
...I COULD BECOME GOOD FRIENDS WITH TACHIBANA-SAN.
トッ
TO (TMP)
I'M PRETTY SURE I'VE NEVER HEARD SASAKI SPEAK SO PASSIONATELY ABOUT SOMETHING.
OR SO HONESTLY.

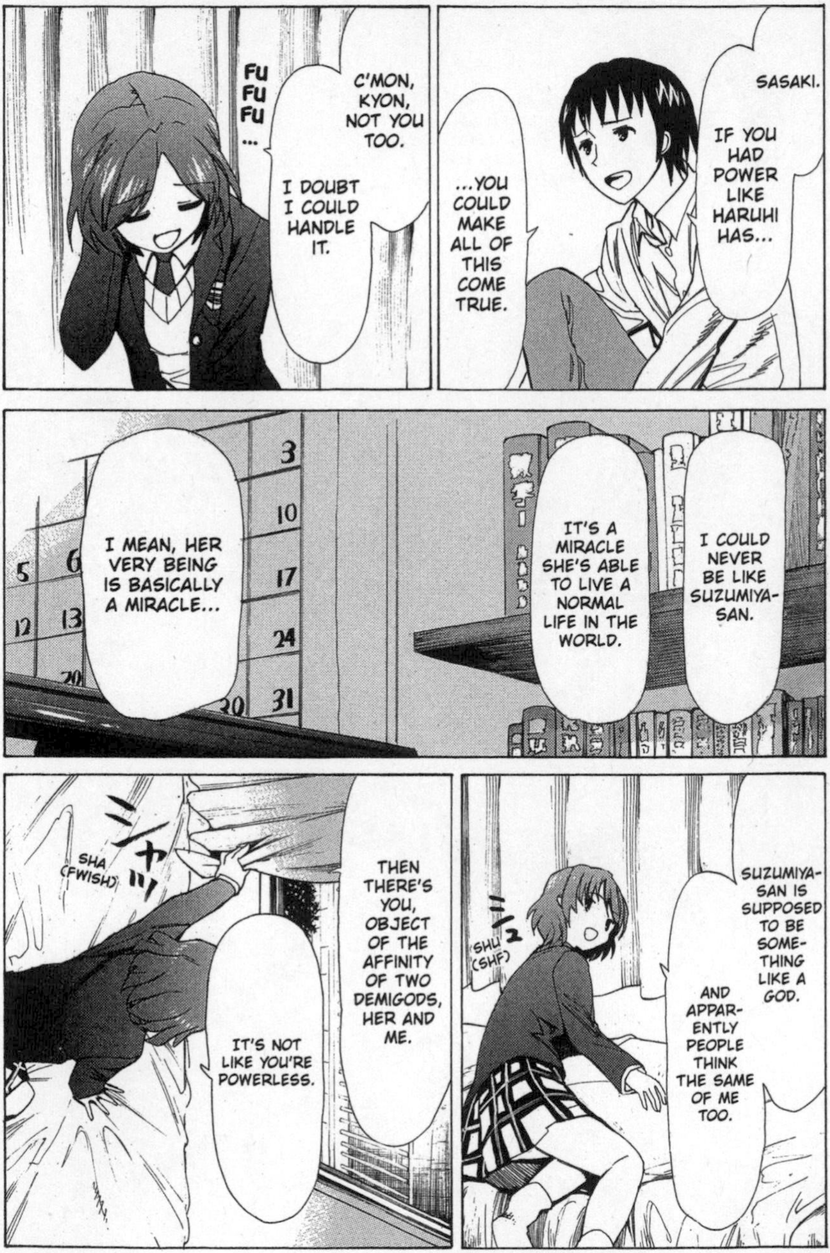
SASAKI.
IF YOU HAD POWER LIKE HARUHI HAS...
...YOU COULD MAKE ALL OF THIS COME TRUE.
C'MON, KYON, NOT YOU TOO.
I DOUBT I COULD HANDLE IT.
FU FU FU ...
I COULD NEVER BE LIKE SUZUMIYA-SAN.
IT'S A MIRACLE SHE'S ABLE TO LIVE A NORMAL LIFE IN THE WORLD.
I MEAN, HER VERY BEING IS BASICALLY A MIRACLE...
SUZUMIYA-SAN IS SUPPOSED TO BE SOME-THING LIKE A GOD.
AND APPAR-ENTLY PEOPLE THINK THE SAME OF ME TOO.
SHU (SHF)
THEN THERE'S YOU, OBJECT OF THE AFFINITY OF TWO DEMIGODS, HER AND ME.
IT'S NOT LIKE YOU'RE POWERLESS.
SHA (FWISH)

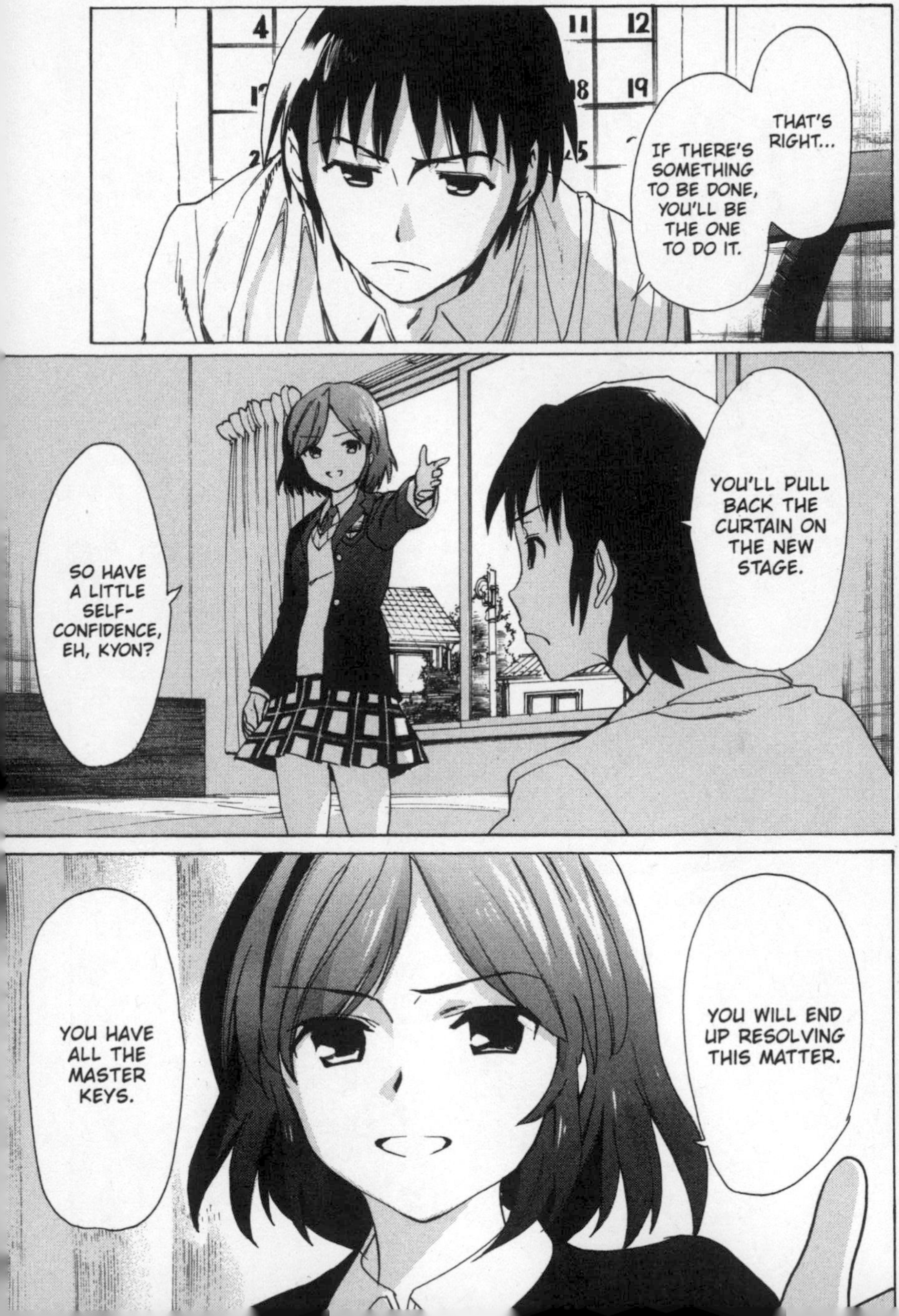
THAT'S RIGHT...
IF THERE'S SOMETHING TO BE DONE, YOU'LL BE THE ONE TO DO IT.
YOU'LL PULL BACK THE CURTAIN ON THE NEW STAGE.
SO HAVE A LITTLE SELF-CONFIDENCE, EH, KYON?
YOU WILL END UP RESOLVING THIS MATTER.
YOU HAVE ALL THE MASTER KEYS.

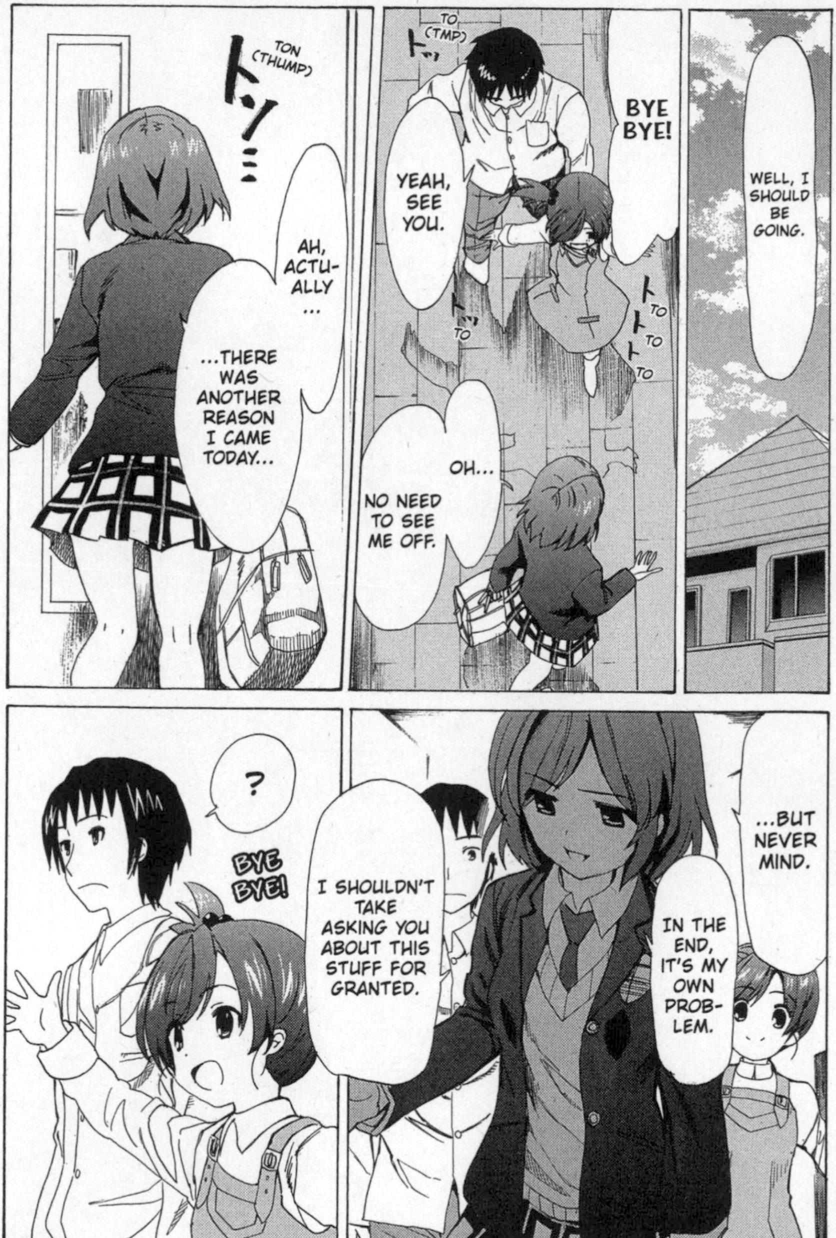
WELL, I SHOULD BE GOING.
BYE BYE!
TO (TMP)
YEAH, SEE YOU.
TO TO TO
TO
OH...
NO NEED TO SEE ME OFF.
TON (THUMP)
AH, ACTU-ALLY ...
...THERE WAS ANOTHER REASON I CAME TODAY...
...BUT NEVER MIND.
IN THE END, IT'S MY OWN PROB-LEM.
I SHOULDN'T TAKE ASKING YOU ABOUT THIS STUFF FOR GRANTED.
?
BYE BYE!

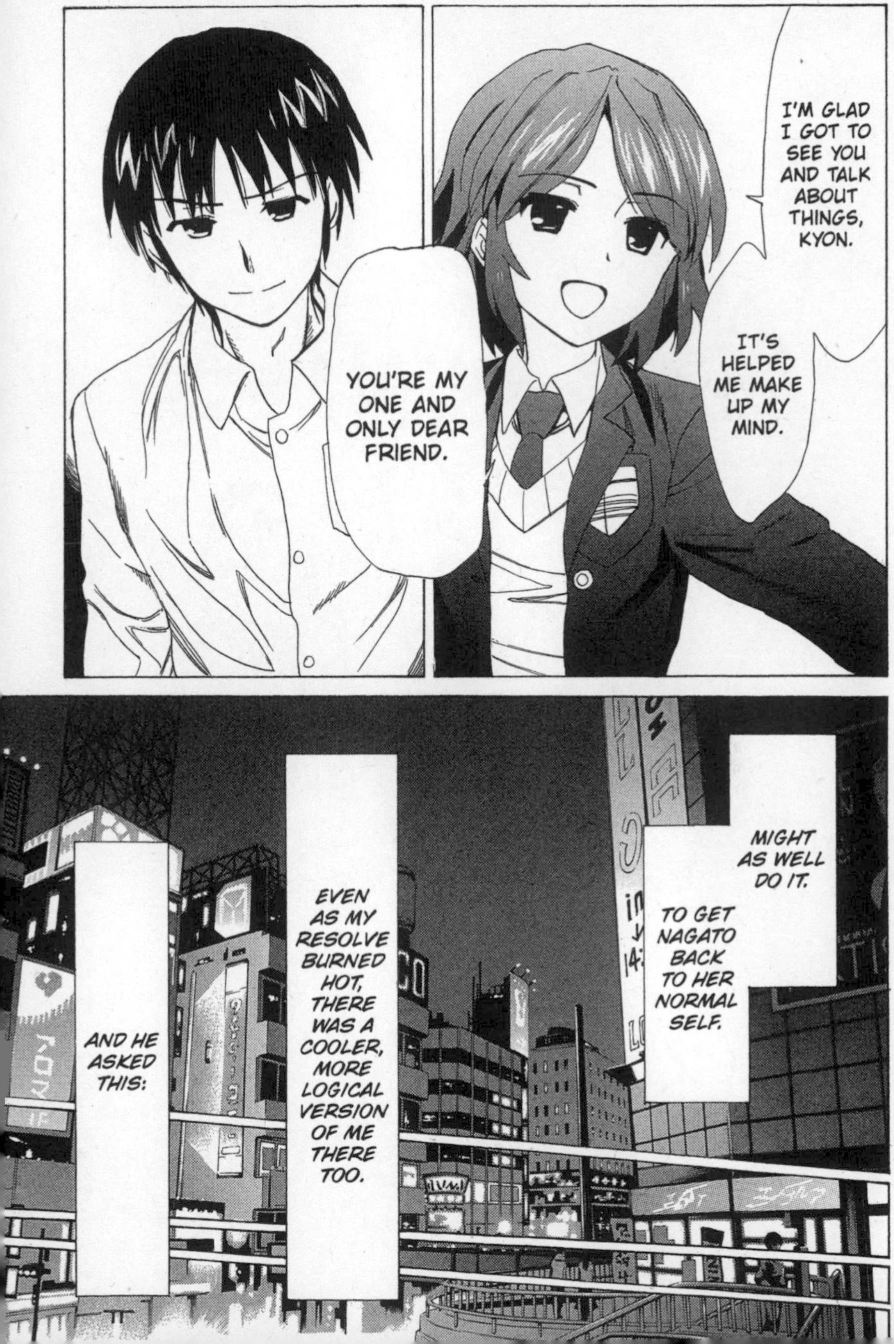
I'M GLAD I GOT TO SEE YOU AND TALK ABOUT THINGS, KYON.
IT'S HELPED ME MAKE UP MY MIND.
YOU'RE MY ONE AND ONLY DEAR FRIEND.
MIGHT AS WELL DO IT.
TO GET NAGATO BACK TO HER NORMAL SELF.
EVEN AS MY RESOLVE BURNED HOT, THERE WAS A COOLER, MORE LOGICAL VERSION OF ME THERE TOO.
AND HE ASKED THIS:

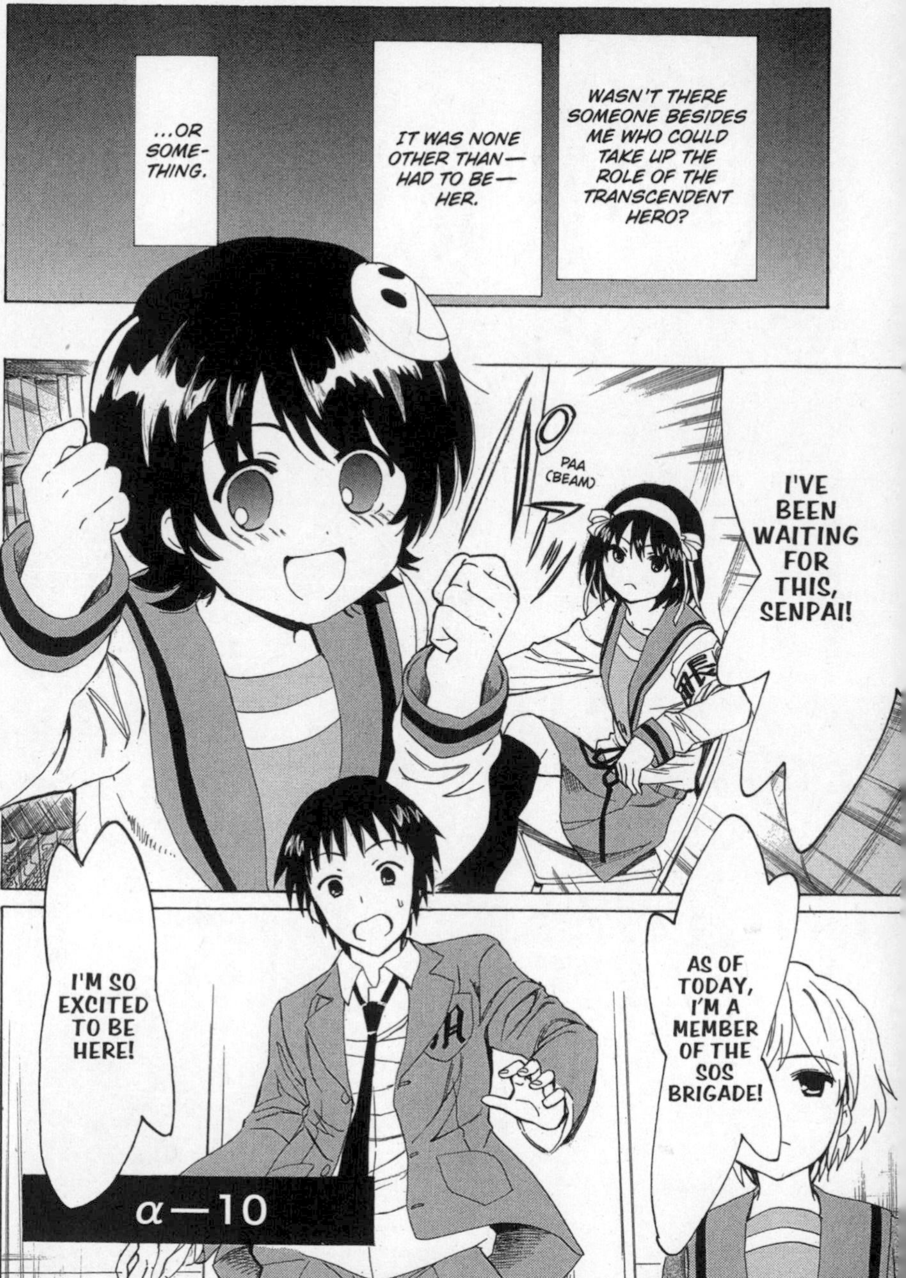
WASN'T THERE SOMEONE BESIDES ME WHO COULD TAKE UP THE ROLE OF THE TRANSCENDENT HERO?
IT WAS NONE OTHER THAN— HAD TO BE— HER.
...OR SOME-THING.
I'VE BEEN WAITING FOR THIS, SENPAI!
PAA (BEAM)
AS OF TODAY, I'M A MEMBER OF THE SOS BRIGADE!
I'M SO EXCITED TO BE HERE!
α—10

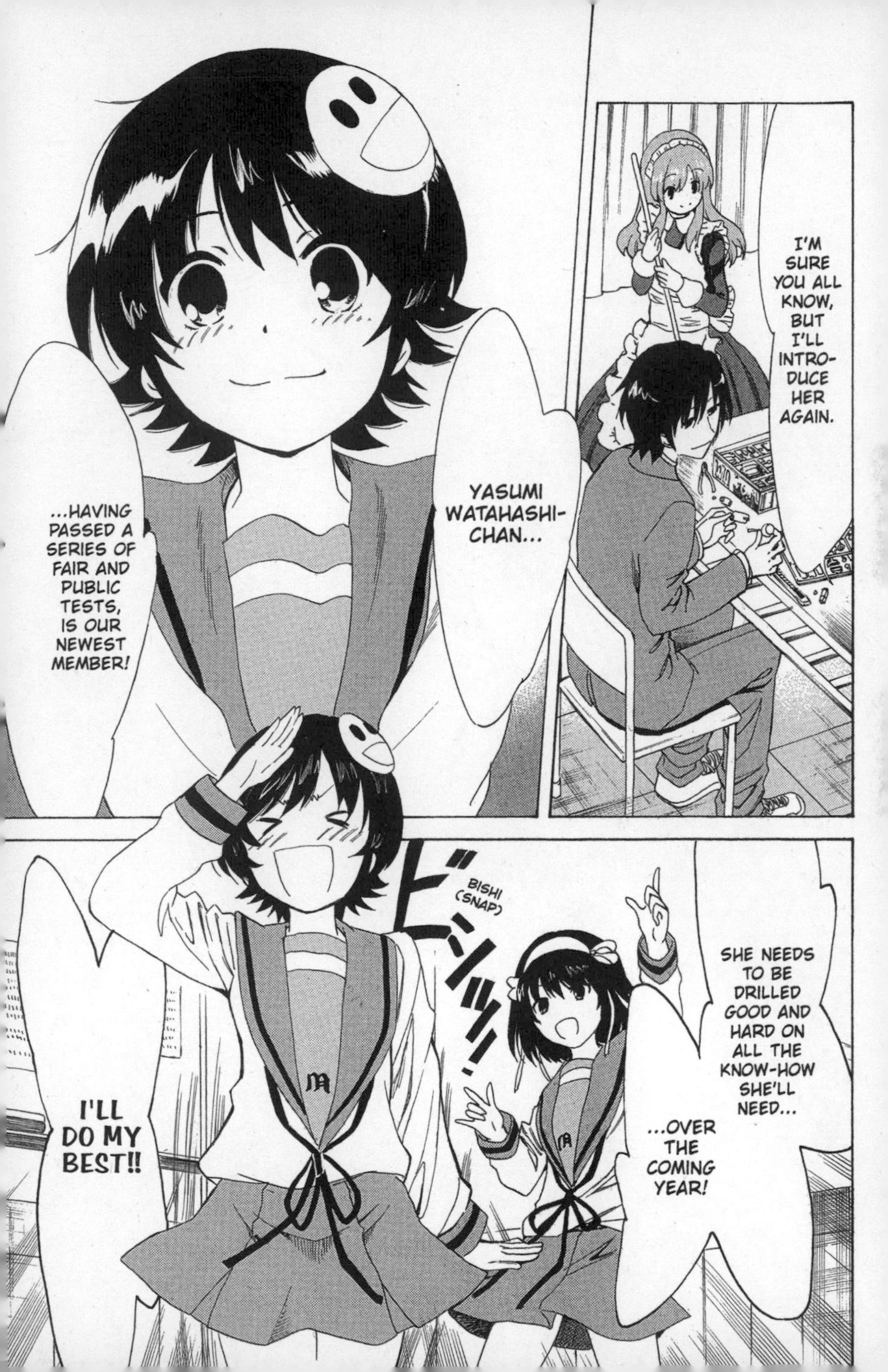

I'M SURE YOU ALL KNOW, BUT I'LL INTRODUCE HER AGAIN.
YASUMI WATAHASHI-CHAN...
...HAVING PASSED A SERIES OF FAIR AND PUBLIC TESTS, IS OUR NEWEST MEMBER!
SHE NEEDS TO BE DRILLED GOOD AND HARD ON ALL THE KNOW-HOW SHE'LL NEED...
BISHI (SNAP)
...OVER THE COMING YEAR!
I'LL DO MY BEST!!

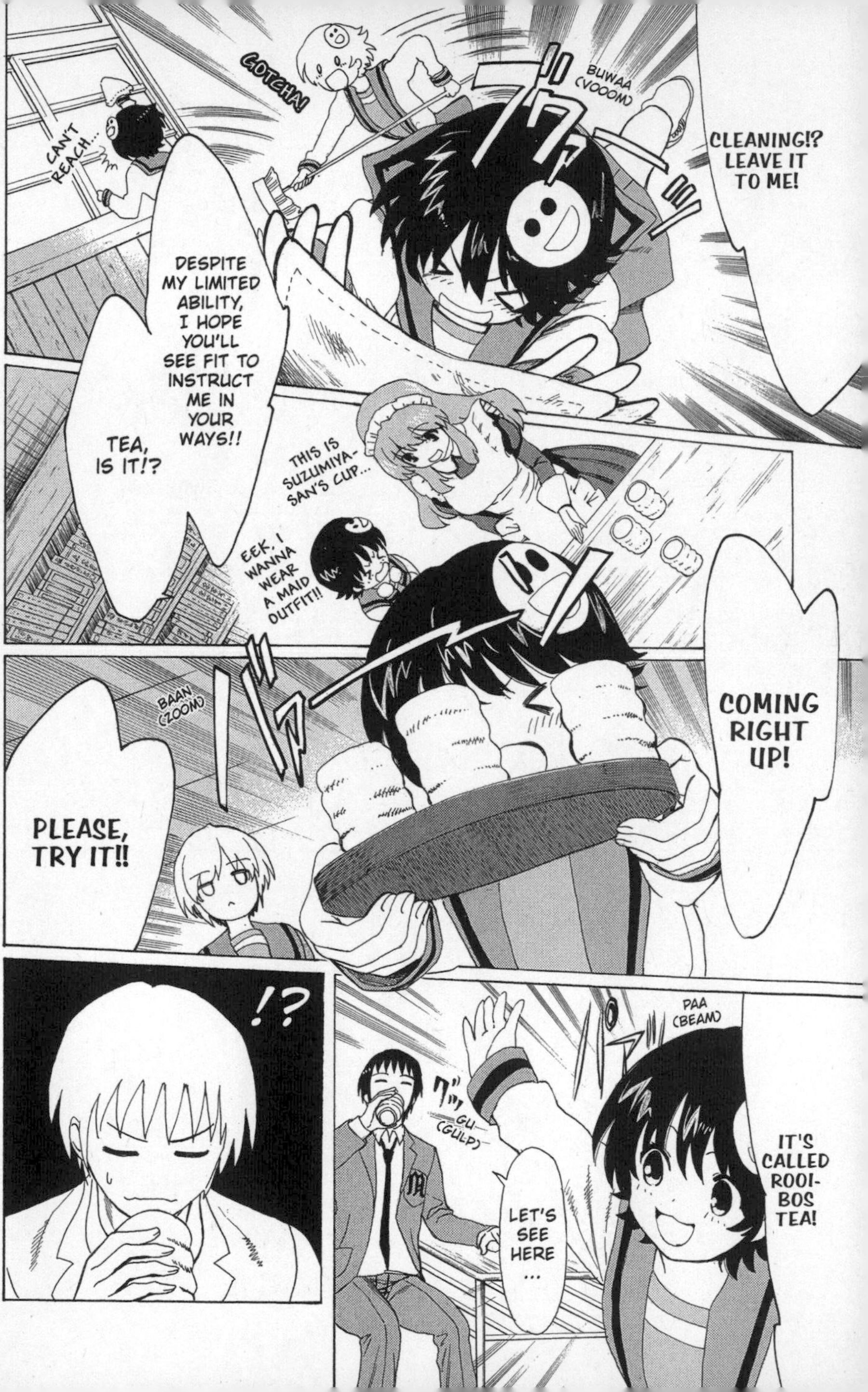
CLEANING!? LEAVE IT TO ME!
BUWAA (VOOOM)
GOTCHA!
CAN'T REACH...
DESPITE MY LIMITED ABILITY, I HOPE YOU'LL SEE FIT TO INSTRUCT ME IN YOUR WAYS!!
TEA, IS IT!?
THIS IS SUZUMIYA-SAN'S CUP...
EEK, I WANNA WEAR A MAID OUTFIT!!
COMING RIGHT UP!
BAAN (ZOOM)
PLEASE, TRY IT!!
PAA (BEAM)
IT'S CALLED ROOI-BOS TEA!
GU (GULP)
LET'S SEE HERE ...
!?

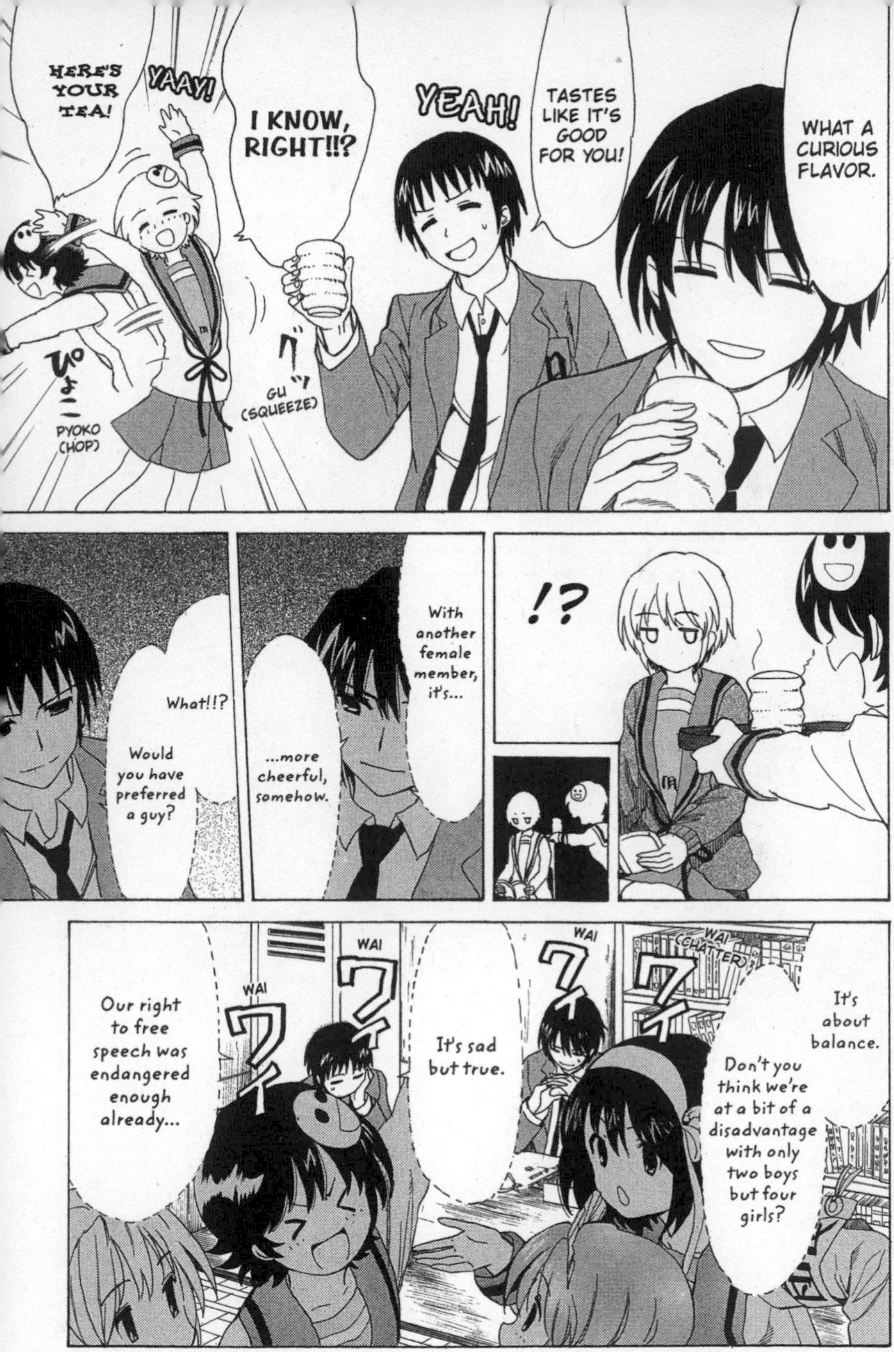
WHAT A CURIOUS FLAVOR.
TASTES LIKE IT'S GOOD FOR YOU!
YEAH!
I KNOW, RIGHT!!?
グッ
GU (SQUEEZE)
YAAY!
HERE'S YOUR TEA!
ぴょこ
PYOKO (HOP)
!?
With another female member, it's...
...more cheerful, somehow.
What!!?
Would you have preferred a guy?
It's about balance.
Don't you think we're at a bit of a disadvantage with only two boys but four girls?
WAI (CHATTER)
WAI
It's sad but true.
WAI
WAI
Our right to free speech was endangered enough already...

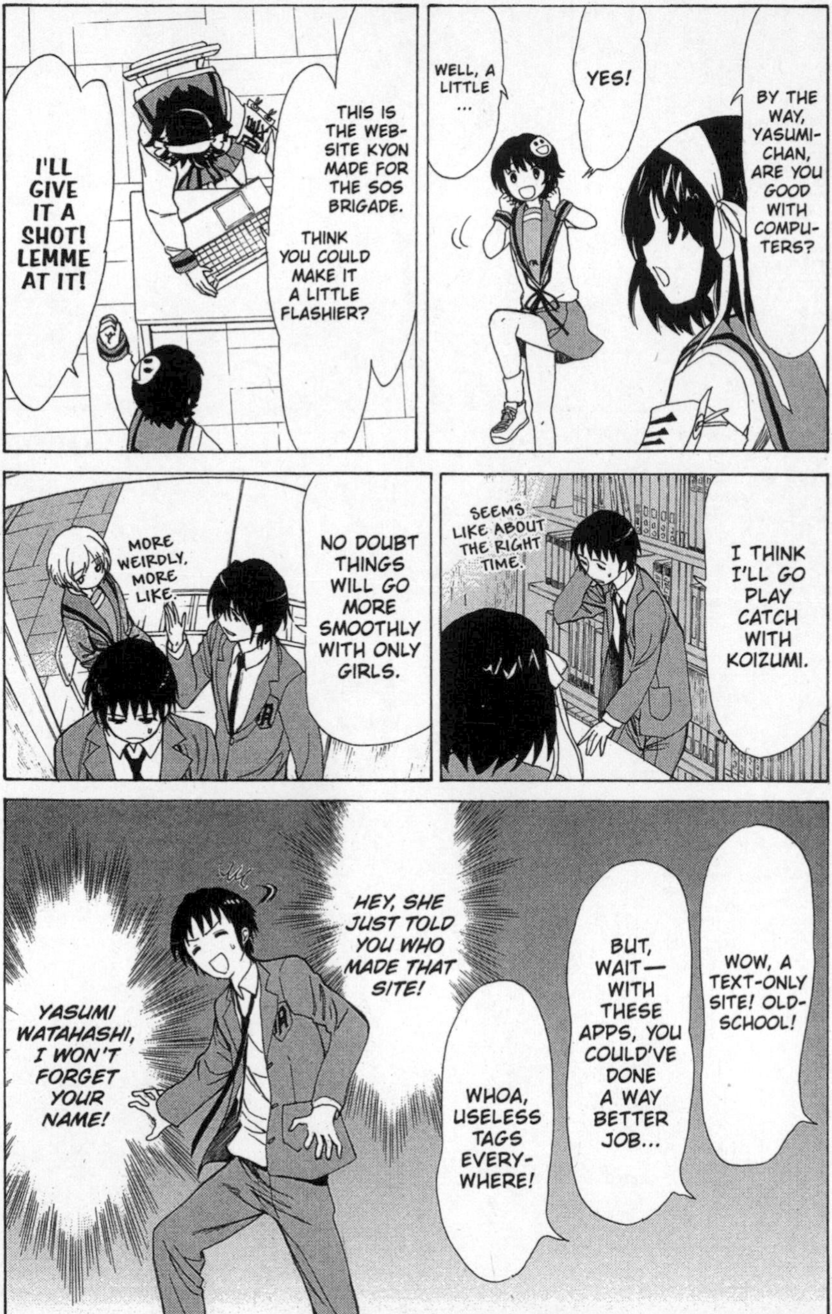
BY THE WAY, YASUMI-CHAN, ARE YOU GOOD WITH COMPU-TERS?
YES!
WELL, A LITTLE ...
THIS IS THE WEB-SITE KYON MADE FOR THE SOS BRIGADE.
THINK YOU COULD MAKE IT A LITTLE FLASHIER?
I'LL GIVE IT A SHOT! LEMME AT IT!
I THINK I'LL GO PLAY CATCH WITH KOIZUMI.
SEEMS LIKE ABOUT THE RIGHT TIME.
NO DOUBT THINGS WILL GO MORE SMOOTHLY WITH ONLY GIRLS.
MORE WEIRDLY, MORE LIKE.
WOW, A TEXT-ONLY SITE! OLD-SCHOOL!
BUT, WAIT— WITH THESE APPS, YOU COULD'VE DONE A WAY BETTER JOB...
WHOA, USELESS TAGS EVERY-WHERE!
HEY, SHE JUST TOLD YOU WHO MADE THAT SITE!
YASUMI WATAHASHI, I WON'T FORGET YOUR NAME!

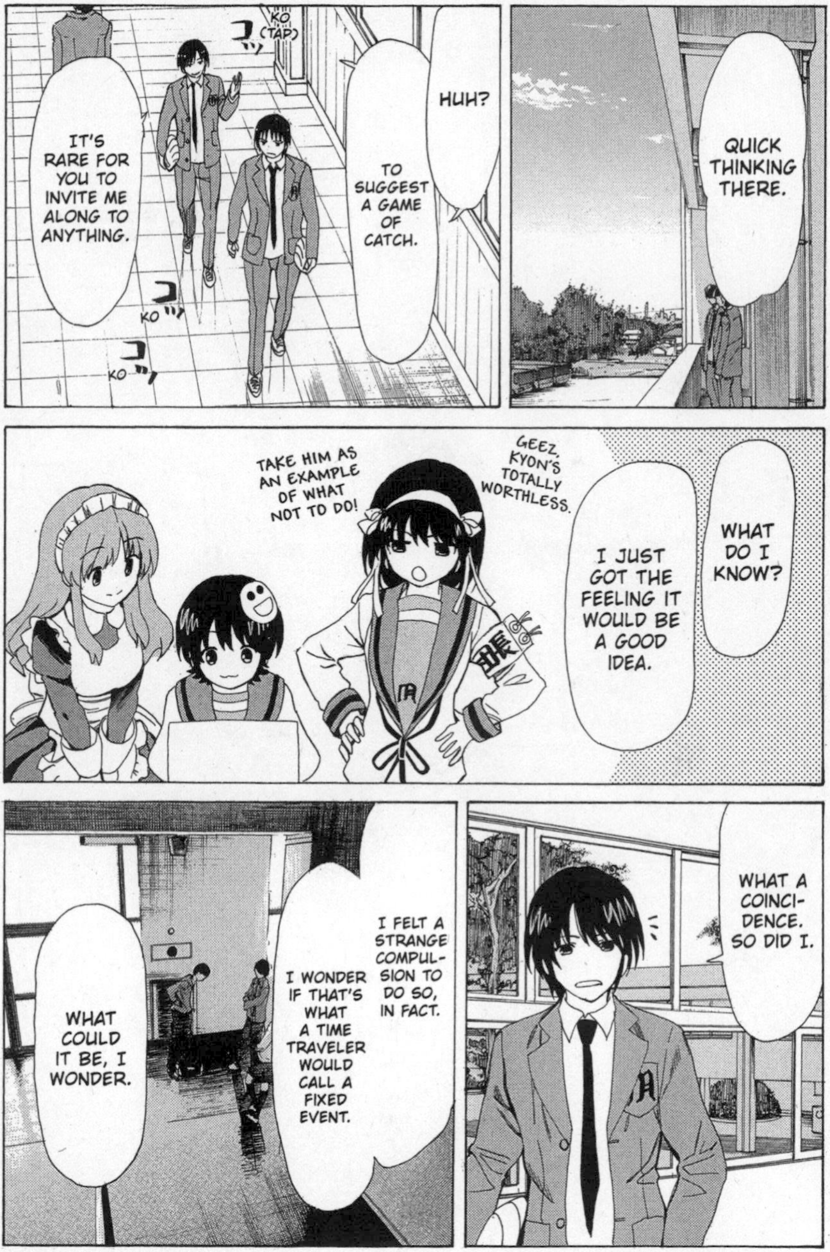
QUICK THINKING THERE.
HUH?
TO SUGGEST A GAME OF CATCH.
KO (TAP)
IT'S RARE FOR YOU TO INVITE ME ALONG TO ANYTHING.
KO
KO
WHAT DO I KNOW?
I JUST GOT THE FEELING IT WOULD BE A GOOD IDEA.
GEEZ, KYON'S TOTALLY WORTHLESS.
TAKE HIM AS AN EXAMPLE OF WHAT NOT TO DO!
WHAT A COINCIDENCE. SO DID I.
I FELT A STRANGE COMPULSION TO DO SO, IN FACT.
I WONDER IF THAT'S WHAT A TIME TRAVELER WOULD CALL A FIXED EVENT.
WHAT COULD IT BE, I WONDER.

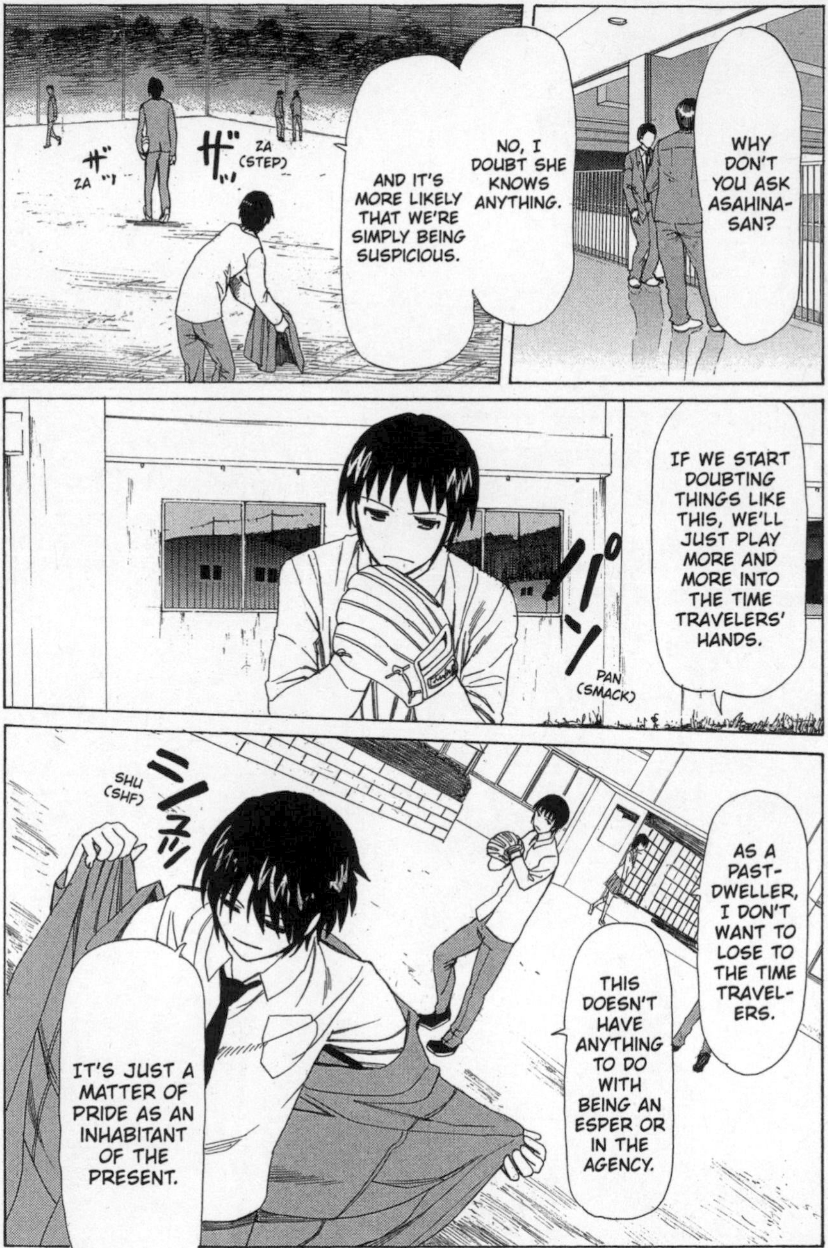
WHY DON'T YOU ASK ASAHINA-SAN?
NO, I DOUBT SHE KNOWS ANYTHING.
AND IT'S MORE LIKELY THAT WE'RE SIMPLY BEING SUSPICIOUS.
ZA (STEP)
ZA
IF WE START DOUBTING THINGS LIKE THIS, WE'LL JUST PLAY MORE AND MORE INTO THE TIME TRAVELERS' HANDS.
PAN (SMACK)
AS A PAST-DWELLER, I DON'T WANT TO LOSE TO THE TIME TRAVEL-ERS.
THIS DOESN'T HAVE ANYTHING TO DO WITH BEING AN ESPER OR IN THE AGENCY.
SHU (SHF)
IT'S JUST A MATTER OF PRIDE AS AN INHABITANT OF THE PRESENT.

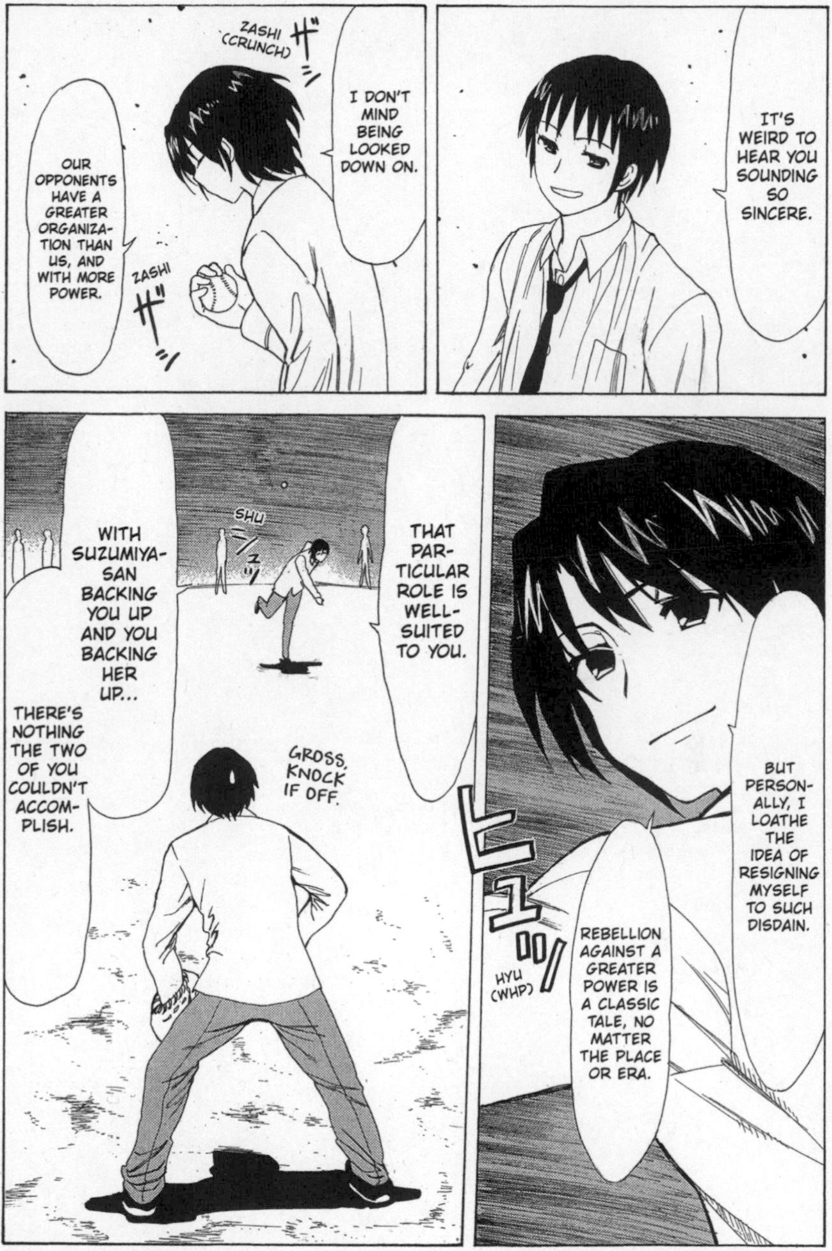
IT'S WEIRD TO HEAR YOU SOUNDING SO SINCERE.
ZASHI (CRUNCH)
I DON'T MIND BEING LOOKED DOWN ON.
OUR OPPONENTS HAVE A GREATER ORGANIZATION THAN US, AND WITH MORE POWER.
ZASHI
BUT PERSONALLY, I LOATHE THE IDEA OF RESIGNING MYSELF TO SUCH DISDAIN.
REBELLION AGAINST A GREATER POWER IS A CLASSIC TALE, NO MATTER THE PLACE OR ERA.
HYU (WHP)
THAT PARTICULAR ROLE IS WELL-SUITED TO YOU.
SHU
WITH SUZUMIYA-SAN BACKING YOU UP AND YOU BACKING HER UP...
GROSS, KNOCK IF OFF.
THERE'S NOTHING THE TWO OF YOU COULDN'T ACCOMPLISH.

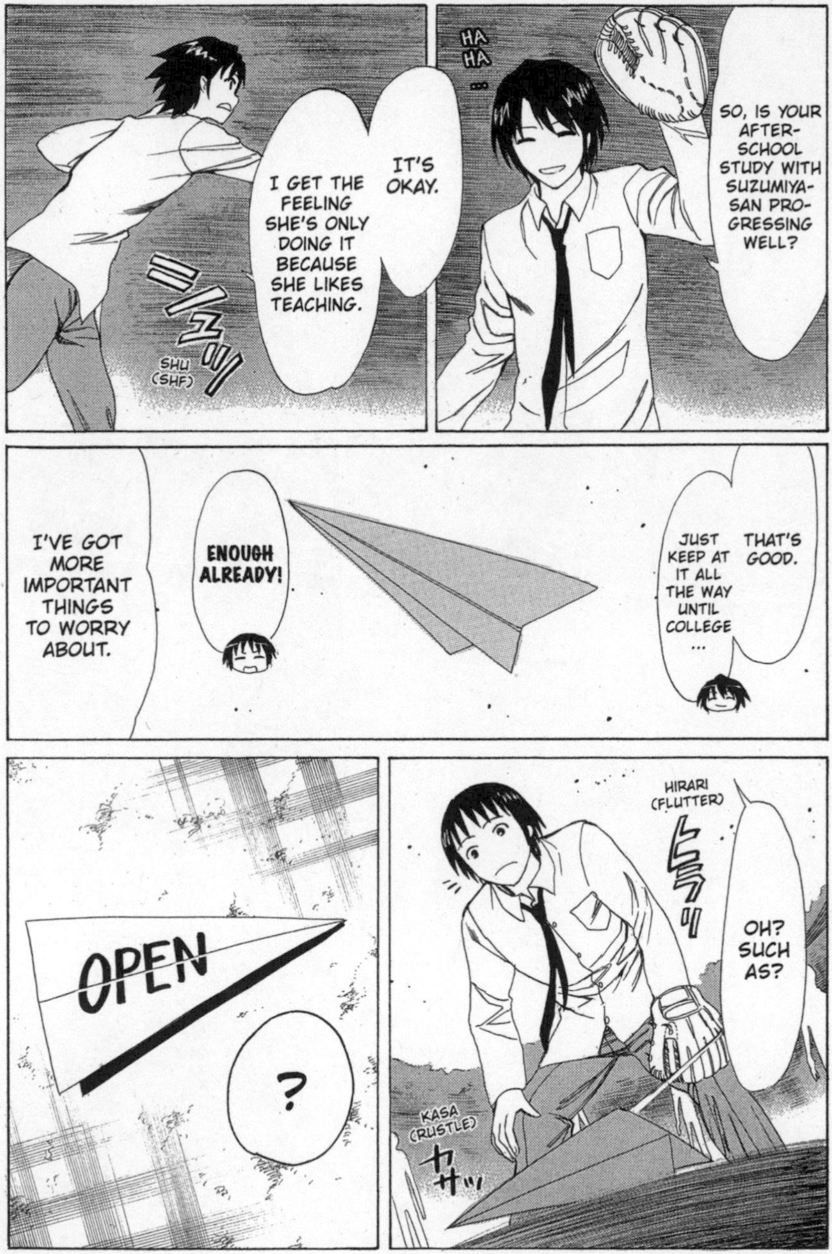
SO, IS YOUR AFTER-SCHOOL STUDY WITH SUZUMIYA-SAN PROGRESSING WELL?
HA HA ...
IT'S OKAY.
I GET THE FEELING SHE'S ONLY DOING IT BECAUSE SHE LIKES TEACHING.
SHU (SHF)
THAT'S GOOD.
JUST KEEP AT IT ALL THE WAY UNTIL COLLEGE ...
ENOUGH ALREADY!
I'VE GOT MORE IMPORTANT THINGS TO WORRY ABOUT.
OH? SUCH AS?
HIRARI (FLUTTER)
KASA (RUSTLE)
OPEN
?

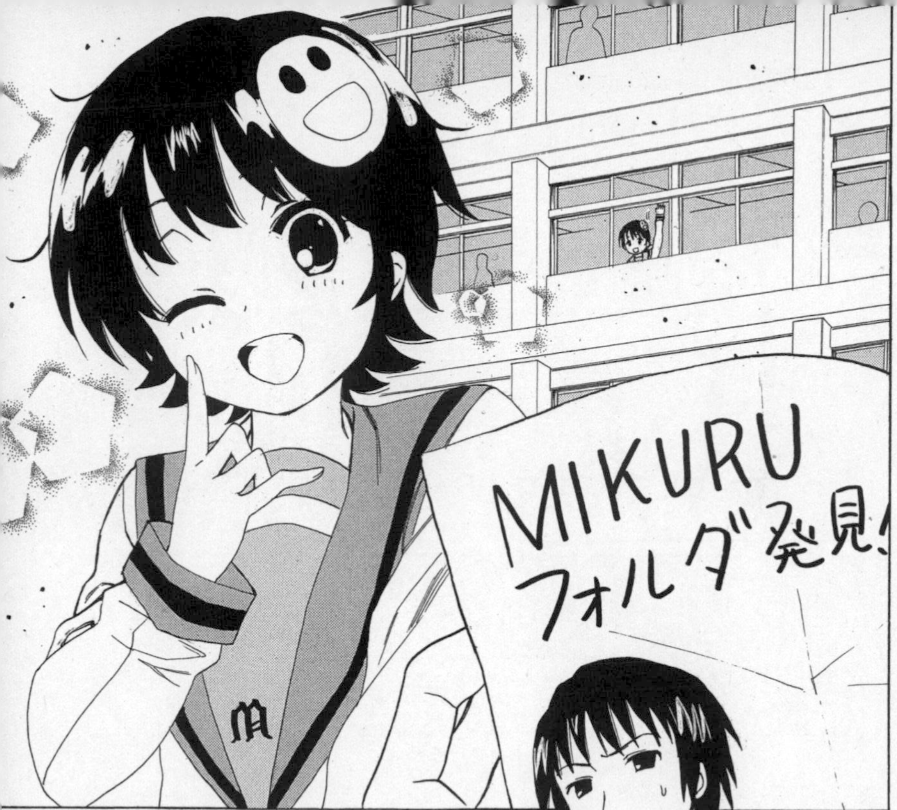
MIKURU
フォルダ発見!

PAPER: I FOUND THE MIKURU FOLDER!

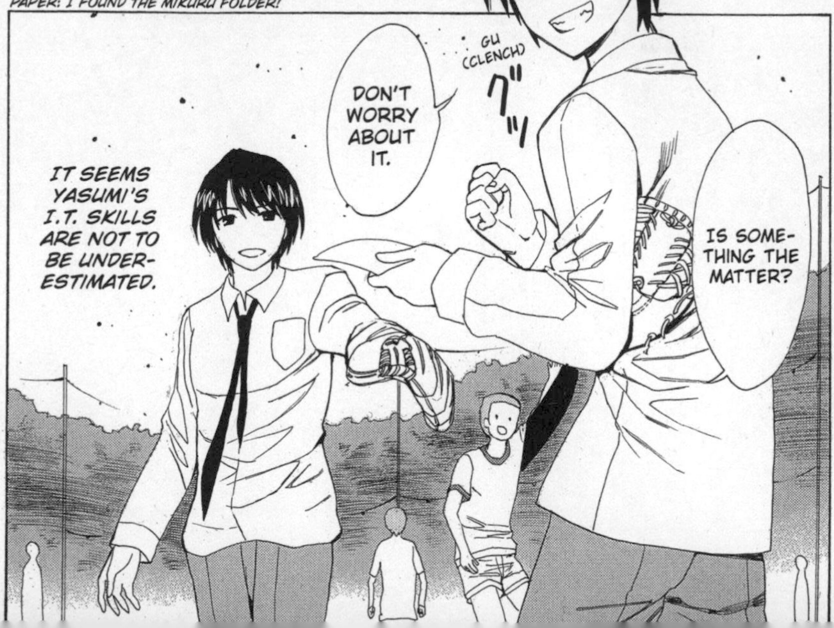
IS SOME-THING THE MATTER?
GU (CLENCH)
グッ
DON'T WORRY ABOUT IT.
IT SEEMS YASUMI'S I.T. SKILLS ARE NOT TO BE UNDER-ESTIMATED.

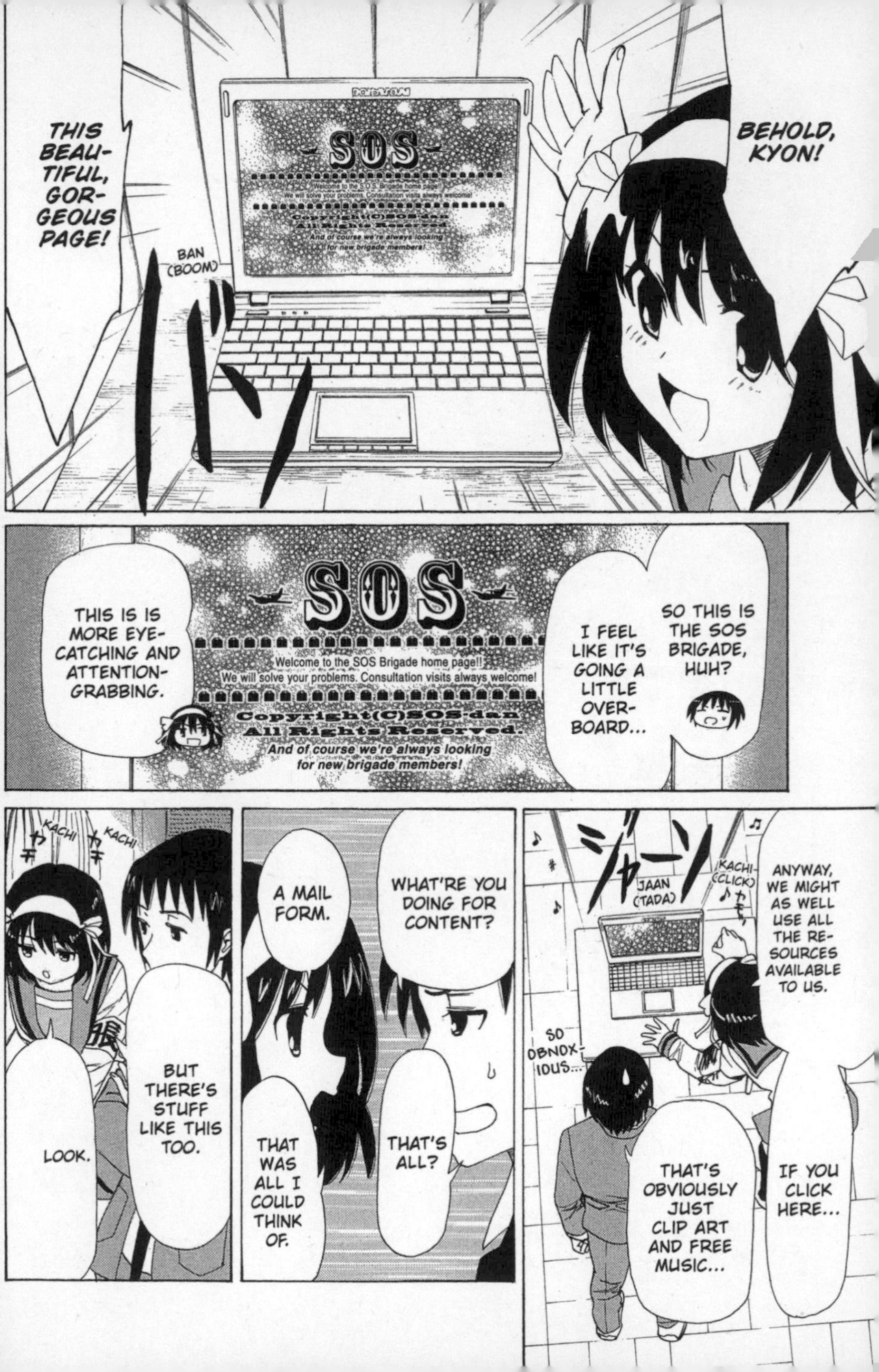
BEHOLD, KYON!
THIS BEAUTIFUL, GORGEOUS PAGE!
BAN (BOOM)
SO THIS IS THE SOS BRIGADE, HUH?
I FEEL LIKE IT'S GOING A LITTLE OVERBOARD...
SOS
Welcome to the SOS Brigade home page!!
We will solve your problems. Consultation visits always welcome!
Copyright(C)SOS-dan
All Rights Reserved.
And of course we're always looking for new brigade members!
THIS IS IS MORE EYE-CATCHING AND ATTENTION-GRABBING.
ANYWAY, WE MIGHT AS WELL USE ALL THE RESOURCES AVAILABLE TO US.
KACHI (CLICK)
JAAN (TADA)
SO OBNOXIOUS...
IF YOU CLICK HERE...
THAT'S OBVIOUSLY JUST CLIP ART AND FREE MUSIC...
WHAT'RE YOU DOING FOR CONTENT?
A MAIL FORM.
THAT'S ALL?
THAT WAS ALL I COULD THINK OF.
KACHI
KACHI
BUT THERE'S STUFF LIKE THIS TOO.
LOOK.

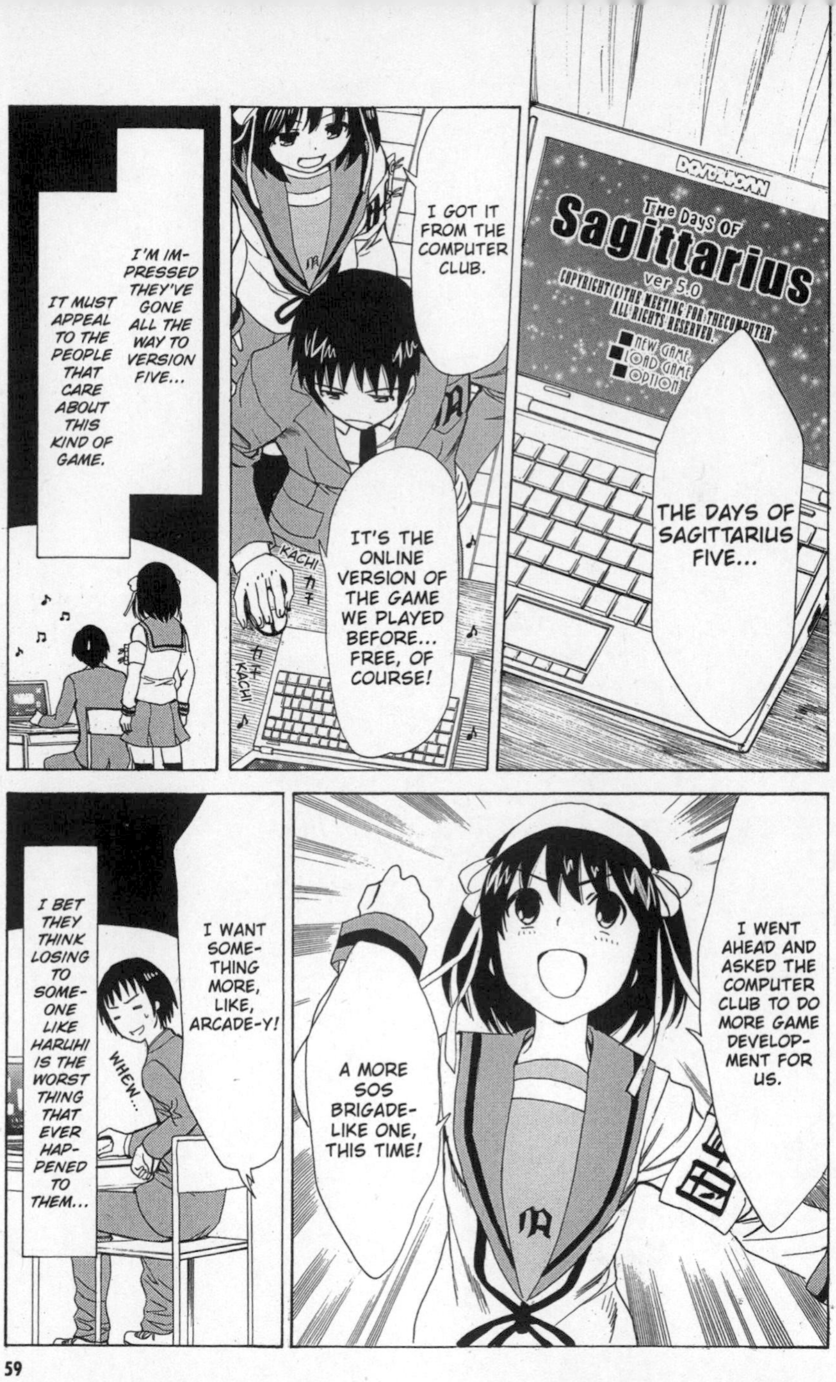

The Days OF
Sagittarius
ver 5.0
COPYRIGHT(C)THE MEETING FOR THECOMPUTER ALL RIGHTS RESERVED.
NEW GAME
LOAD GAME
OPTION
THE DAYS OF SAGITTARIUS FIVE...
I GOT IT FROM THE COMPUTER CLUB.
IT'S THE ONLINE VERSION OF THE GAME WE PLAYED BEFORE... FREE, OF COURSE!
KACHI
KACHI
I'M IMPRESSED THEY'VE GONE ALL THE WAY TO VERSION FIVE...
IT MUST APPEAL TO THE PEOPLE THAT CARE ABOUT THIS KIND OF GAME.
I WENT AHEAD AND ASKED THE COMPUTER CLUB TO DO MORE GAME DEVELOPMENT FOR US.
A MORE SOS BRIGADE-LIKE ONE, THIS TIME!
I WANT SOMETHING MORE, LIKE, ARCADE-Y!
WHEW...
I BET THEY THINK LOSING TO SOMEONE LIKE HARUHI IS THE WORST THING THAT EVER HAPPENED TO THEM...

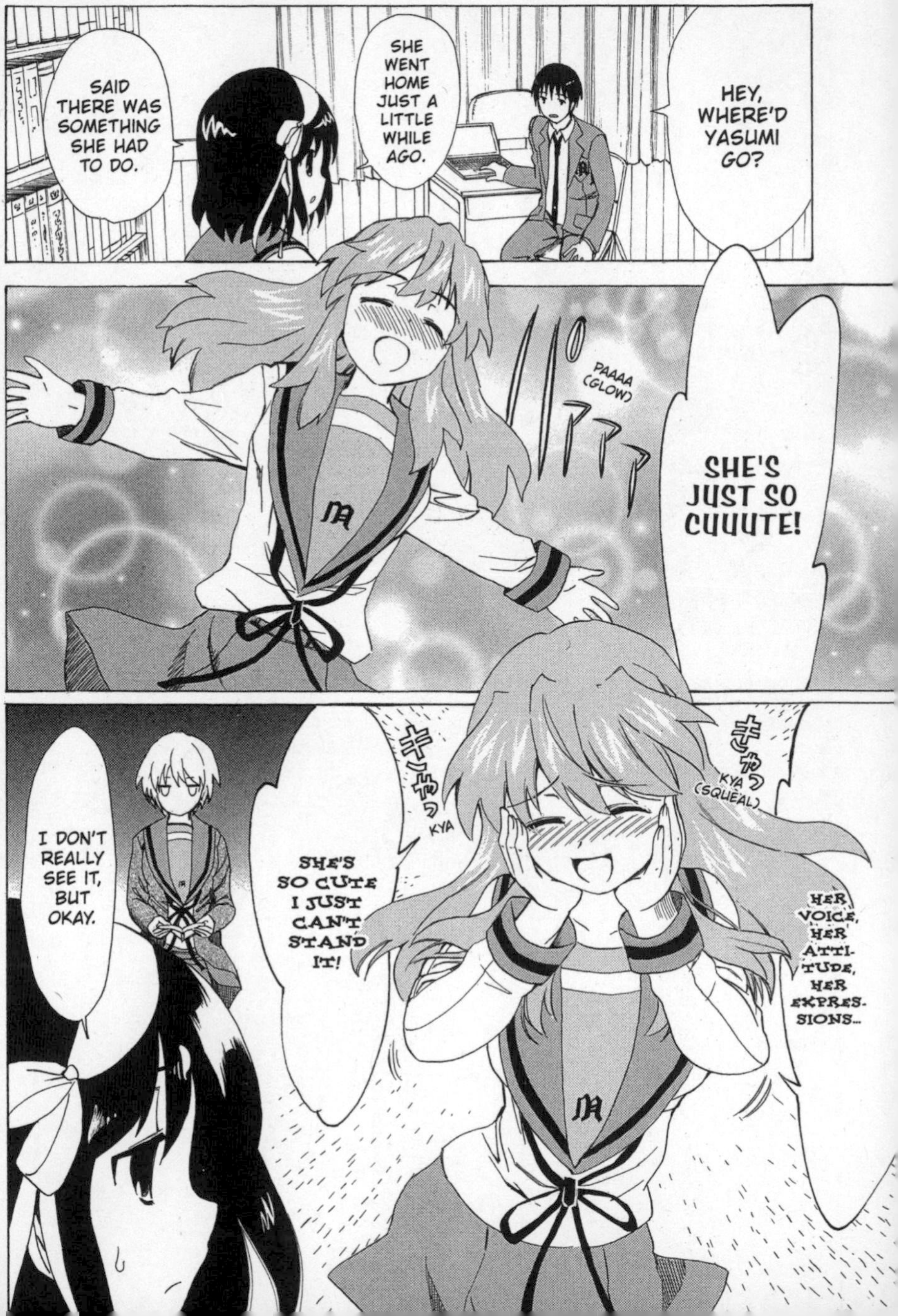

HEY, WHERE'D YASUMI GO?
SHE WENT HOME JUST A LITTLE WHILE AGO.
SAID THERE WAS SOMETHING SHE HAD TO DO.
SHE'S JUST SO CUUUTE!
PAAAA (GLOW)
HER VOICE, HER ATTITUDE, HER EXPRESSIONS...
KYA (SQUEAL)
KYA
SHE'S SO CUTE I JUST CAN'T STAND IT!
I DON'T REALLY SEE IT, BUT OKAY.

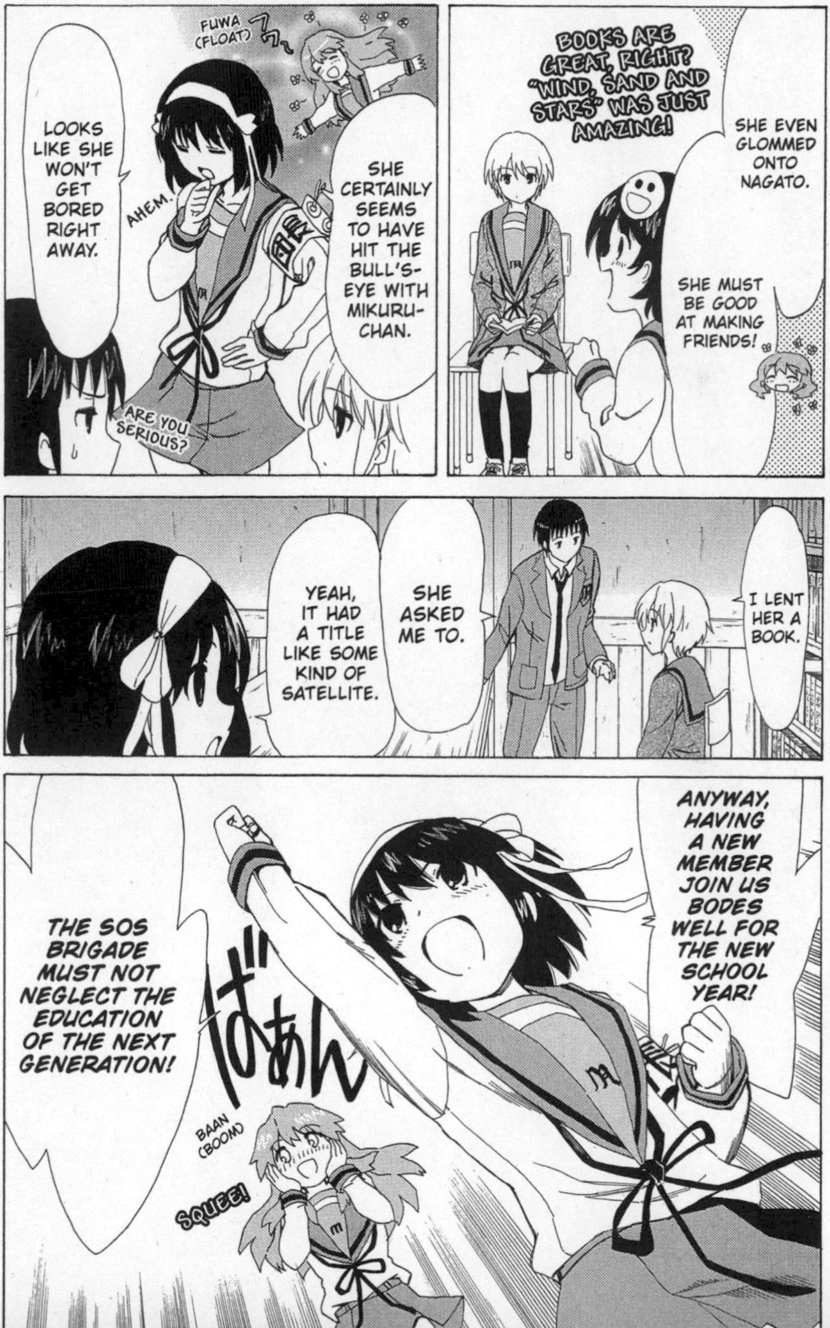
BOOKS ARE GREAT, RIGHT? "WIND, SAND AND STARS" WAS JUST AMAZING!
SHE EVEN GLOMMED ONTO NAGATO.
SHE MUST BE GOOD AT MAKING FRIENDS!
FUWA (FLOAT)
SHE CERTAINLY SEEMS TO HAVE HIT THE BULL'S-EYE WITH MIKURU-CHAN.
AHEM.
LOOKS LIKE SHE WON'T GET BORED RIGHT AWAY.
ARE YOU SERIOUS?
I LENT HER A BOOK.
SHE ASKED ME TO.
YEAH, IT HAD A TITLE LIKE SOME KIND OF SATELLITE.
ANYWAY, HAVING A NEW MEMBER JOIN US BODES WELL FOR THE NEW SCHOOL YEAR!
ばあん
BAAN (BOOM)
THE SOS BRIGADE MUST NOT NEGLECT THE EDUCATION OF THE NEXT GENERATION!
SQUEE!

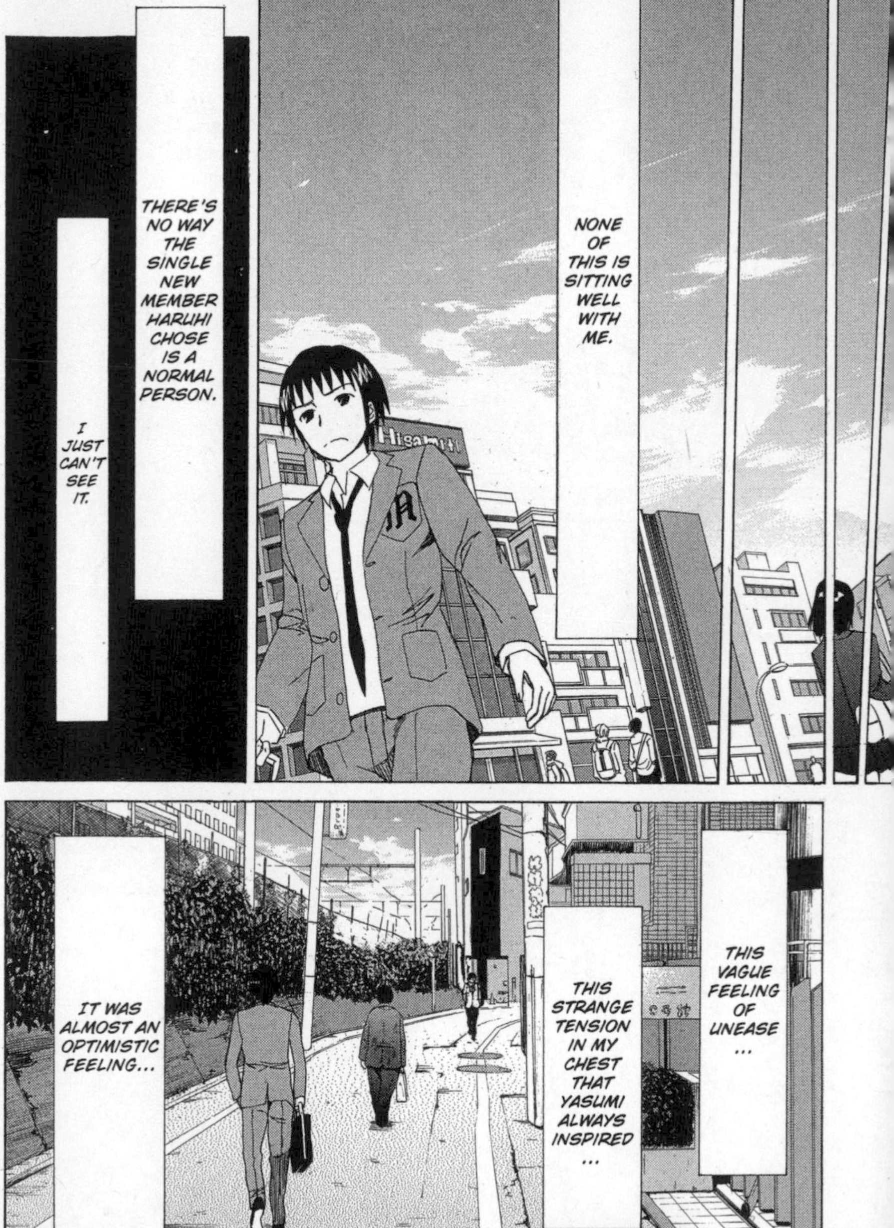
NONE OF THIS IS SITTING WELL WITH ME.
THERE'S NO WAY THE SINGLE NEW MEMBER HARUHI CHOSE IS A NORMAL PERSON.
I JUST CAN'T SEE IT.
THIS VAGUE FEELING OF UNEASE...
THIS STRANGE TENSION IN MY CHEST THAT YASUMI ALWAYS INSPIRED...
IT WAS ALMOST AN OPTIMISTIC FEELING...

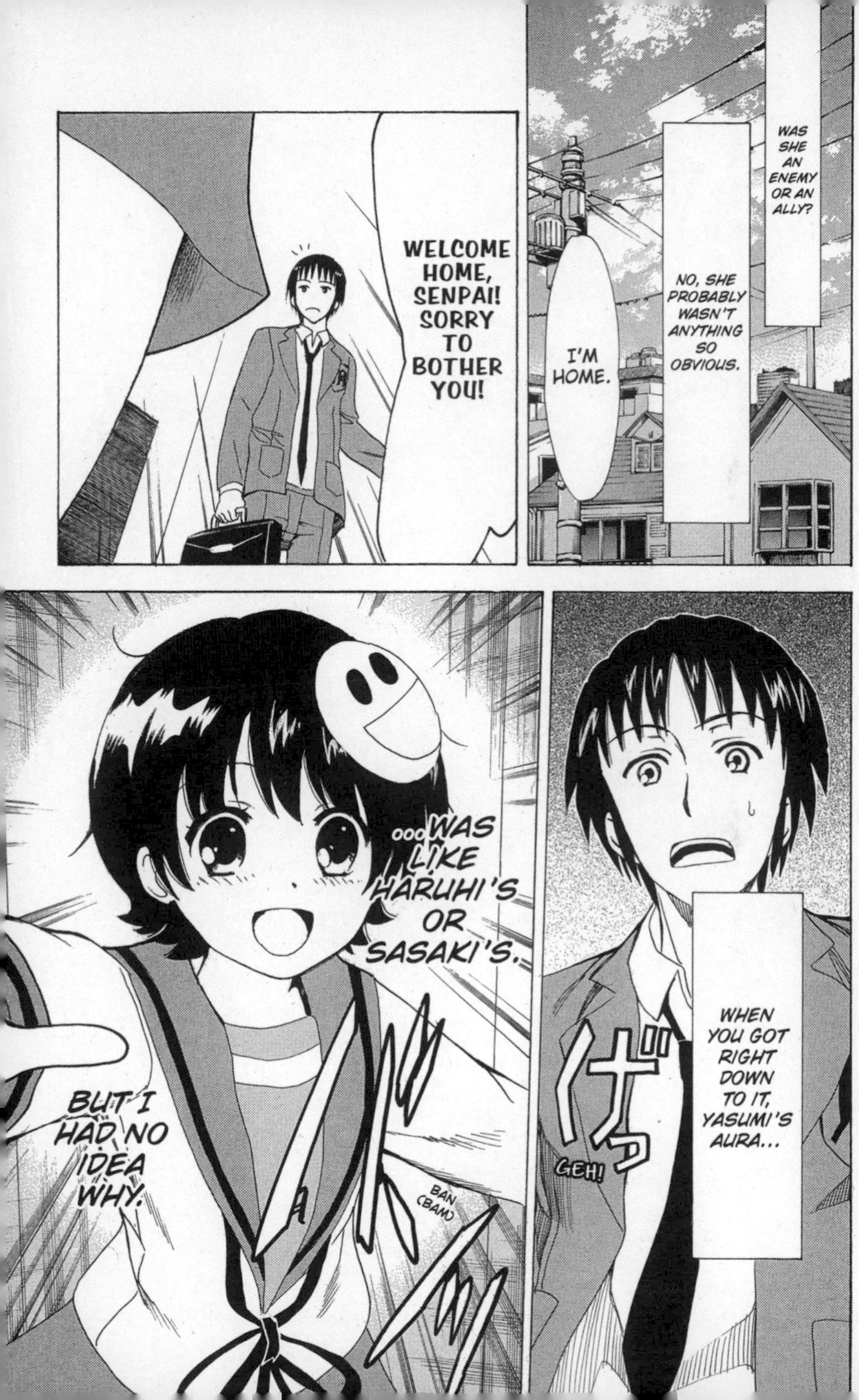
WAS SHE AN ENEMY OR AN ALLY?
NO, SHE PROBABLY WASN'T ANYTHING SO OBVIOUS.
I'M HOME.
WELCOME HOME, SENPAI! SORRY TO BOTHER YOU!
WHEN YOU GOT RIGHT DOWN TO IT, YASUMI'S AURA...
GEH!
...WAS LIKE HARUHI'S OR SASAKI'S.
BAN (BAM)
BUT I HAD NO IDEA WHY.

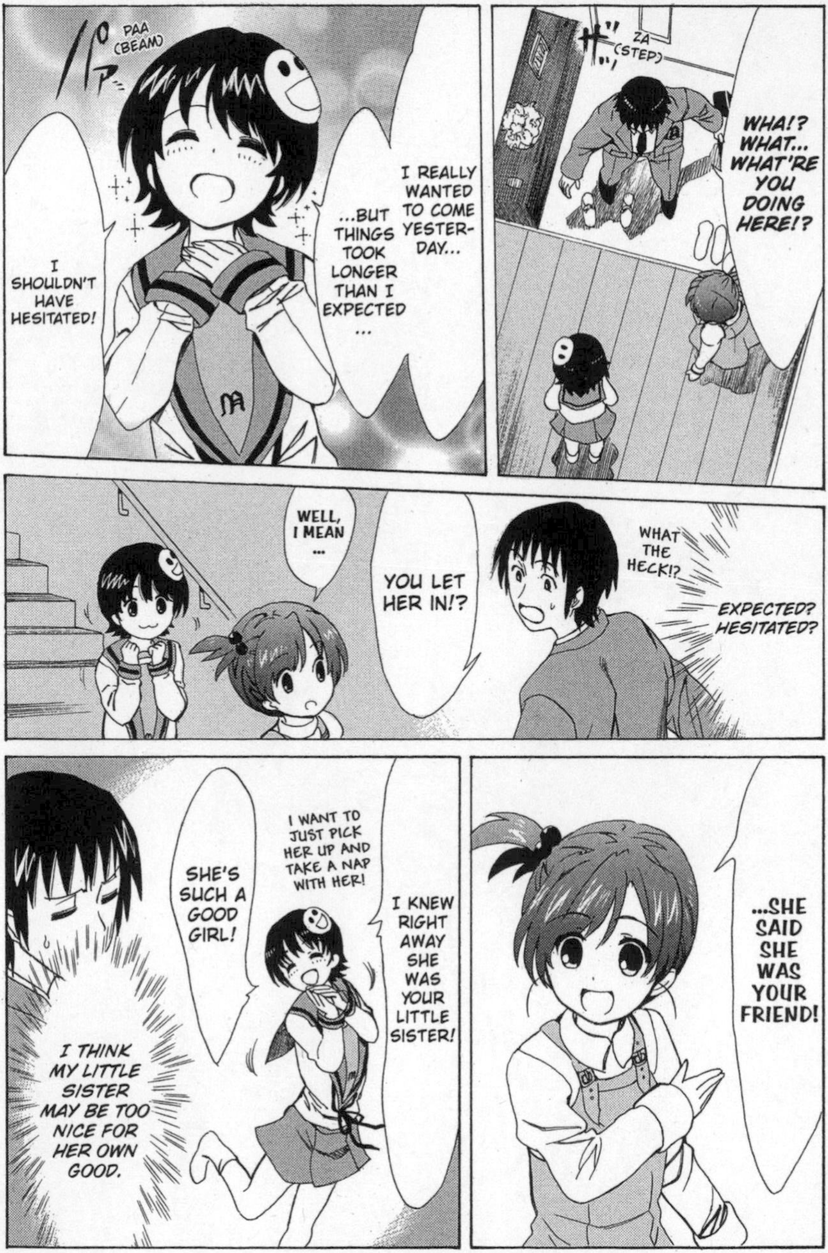
ZA (STEP)
WHA!? WHAT... WHAT'RE YOU DOING HERE!?
PAA (BEAM)
I REALLY WANTED TO COME YESTER-DAY...
...BUT THINGS TOOK LONGER THAN I EXPECTED ...
I SHOULDN'T HAVE HESITATED!
WHAT THE HECK!?
EXPECTED? HESITATED?
YOU LET HER IN!?
WELL, I MEAN ...
...SHE SAID SHE WAS YOUR FRIEND!
I KNEW RIGHT AWAY SHE WAS YOUR LITTLE SISTER!
I WANT TO JUST PICK HER UP AND TAKE A NAP WITH HER!
SHE'S SUCH A GOOD GIRL!
I THINK MY LITTLE SISTER MAY BE TOO NICE FOR HER OWN GOOD.

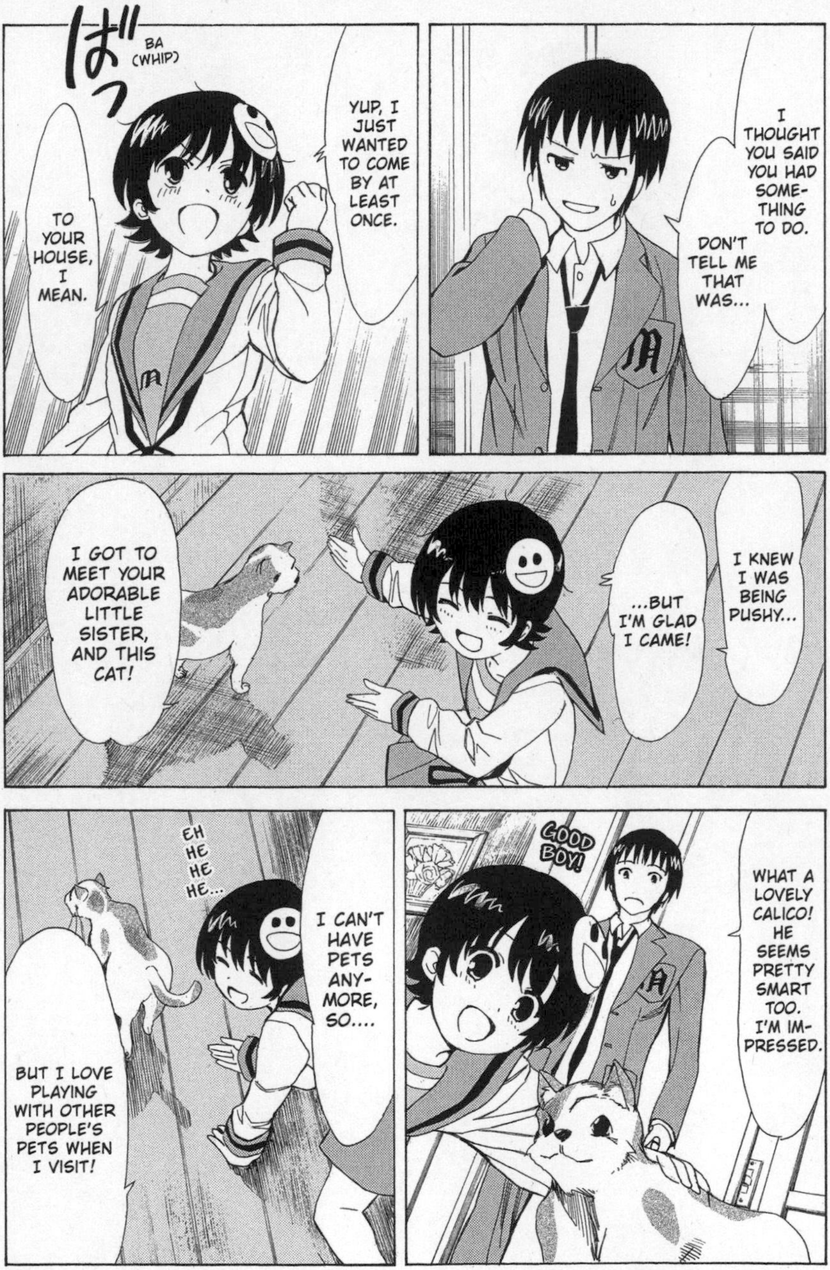
I THOUGHT YOU SAID YOU HAD SOME-THING TO DO.
DON'T TELL ME THAT WAS...
YUP, I JUST WANTED TO COME BY AT LEAST ONCE.
ばっ
BA (WHIP)
TO YOUR HOUSE, I MEAN.
I KNEW I WAS BEING PUSHY...
...BUT I'M GLAD I CAME!
I GOT TO MEET YOUR ADORABLE LITTLE SISTER, AND THIS CAT!
WHAT A LOVELY CALICO! HE SEEMS PRETTY SMART TOO. I'M IM-PRESSED.
GOOD BOY!
I CAN'T HAVE PETS ANY-MORE, SO....
EH HE HE HE...
BUT I LOVE PLAYING WITH OTHER PEOPLE'S PETS WHEN I VISIT!

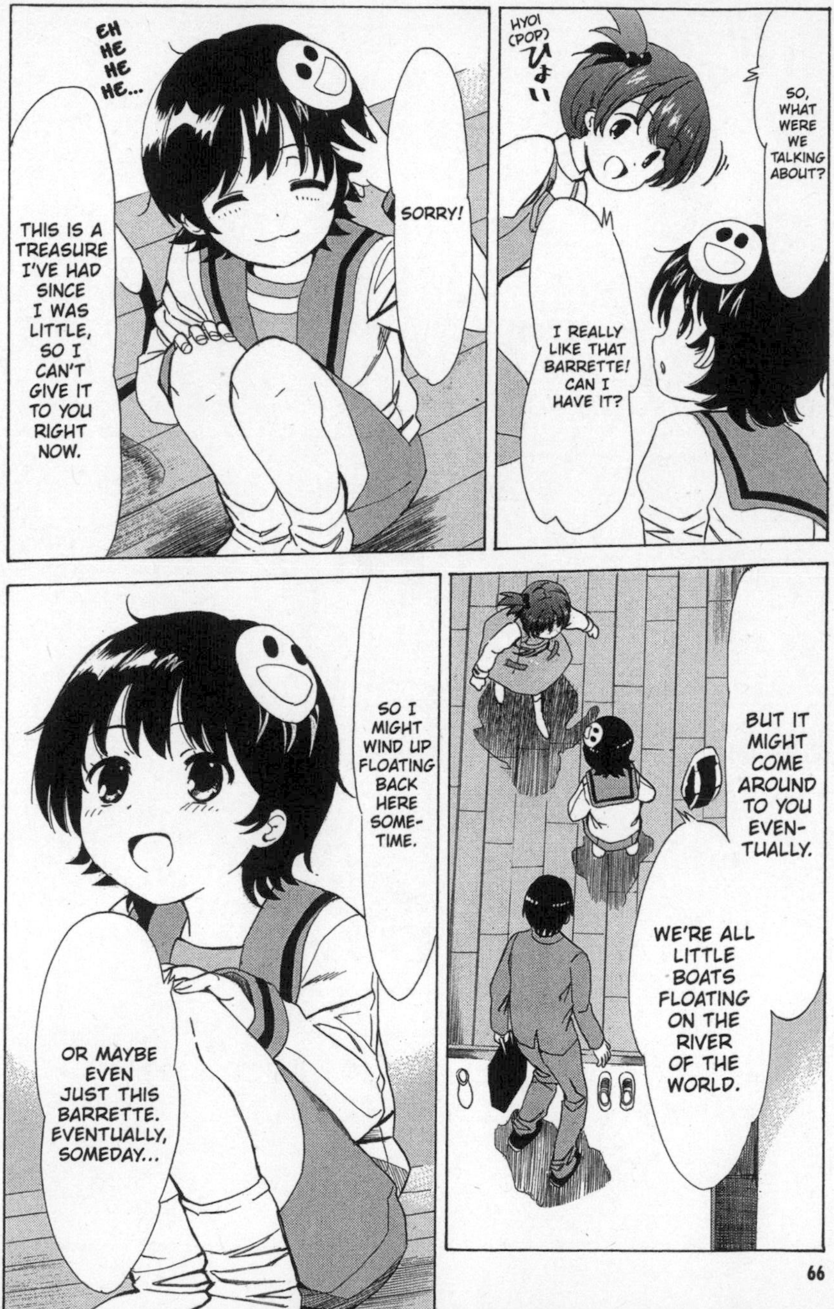
HYOI (POP) ひょい
SO, WHAT WERE WE TALKING ABOUT?
I REALLY LIKE THAT BARRETTE! CAN I HAVE IT?
EH HE HE HE...
SORRY!
THIS IS A TREASURE I'VE HAD SINCE I WAS LITTLE, SO I CAN'T GIVE IT TO YOU RIGHT NOW.
BUT IT MIGHT COME AROUND TO YOU EVENTUALLY.
WE'RE ALL LITTLE BOATS FLOATING ON THE RIVER OF THE WORLD.
SO I MIGHT WIND UP FLOATING BACK HERE SOMETIME.
OR MAYBE EVEN JUST THIS BARRETTE. EVENTUALLY, SOMEDAY...

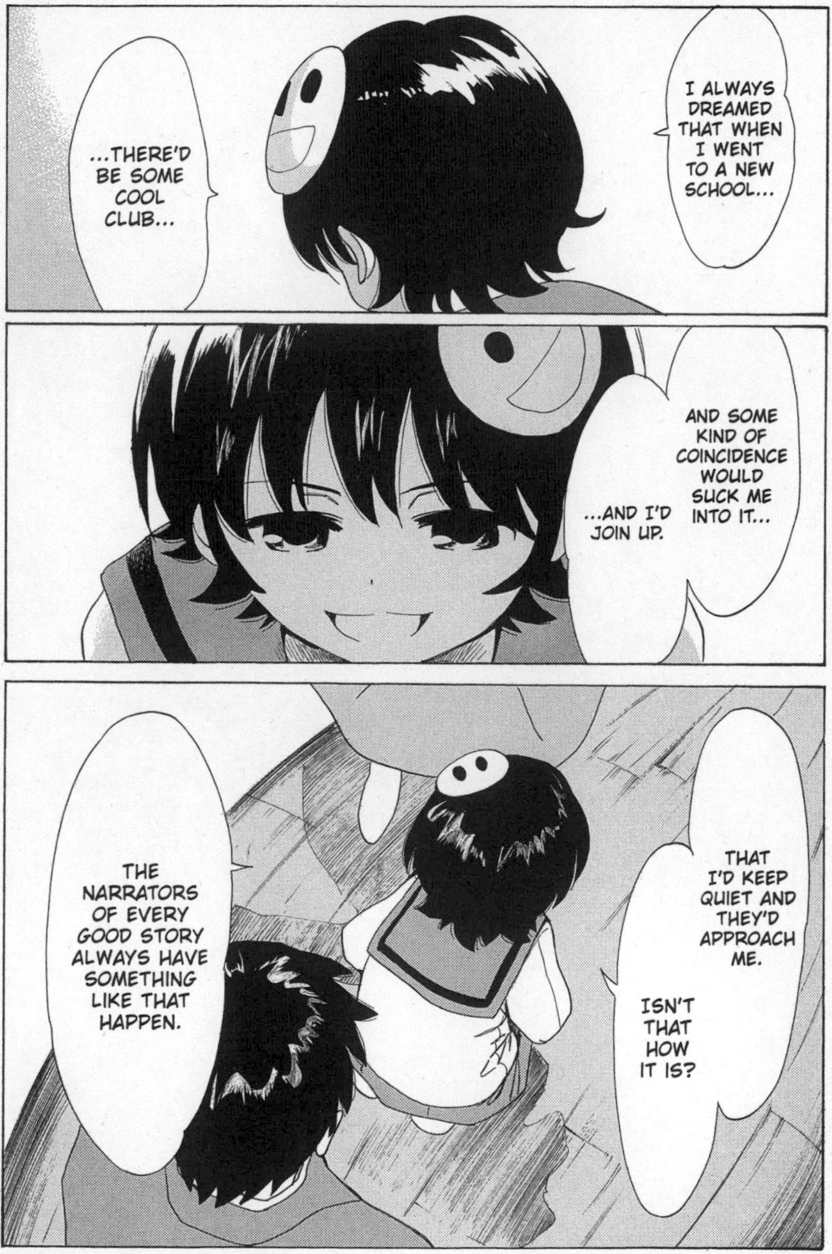
I ALWAYS DREAMED THAT WHEN I WENT TO A NEW SCHOOL...
...THERE'D BE SOME COOL CLUB...
AND SOME KIND OF COINCIDENCE WOULD SUCK ME INTO IT...
...AND I'D JOIN UP.
THAT I'D KEEP QUIET AND THEY'D APPROACH ME.
ISN'T THAT HOW IT IS?
THE NARRATORS OF EVERY GOOD STORY ALWAYS HAVE SOMETHING LIKE THAT HAPPEN.

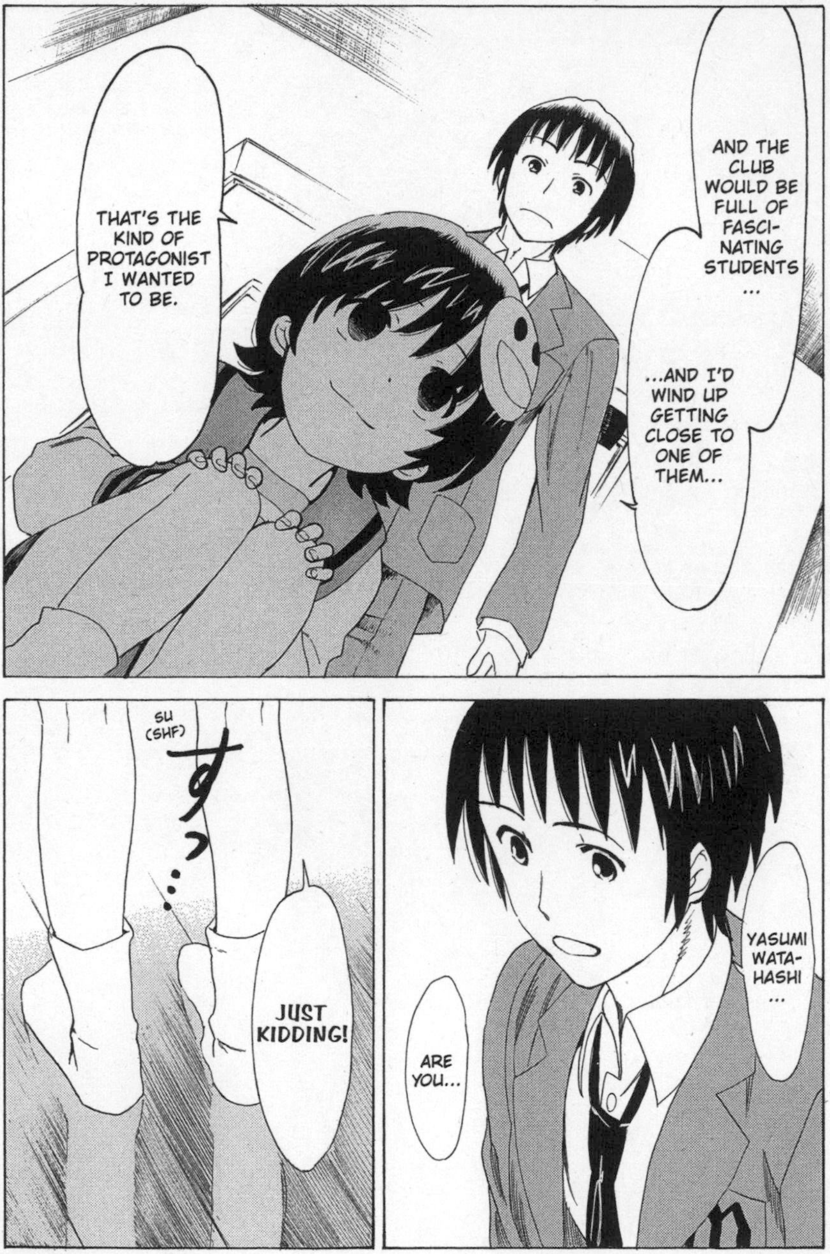
AND THE CLUB WOULD BE FULL OF FASCI-NATING STUDENTS ...
...AND I'D WIND UP GETTING CLOSE TO ONE OF THEM...
THAT'S THE KIND OF PROTAGONIST I WANTED TO BE.
YASUMI WATA-HASHI ...
ARE YOU...
SU (SHF)
すっ…
JUST KIDDING!

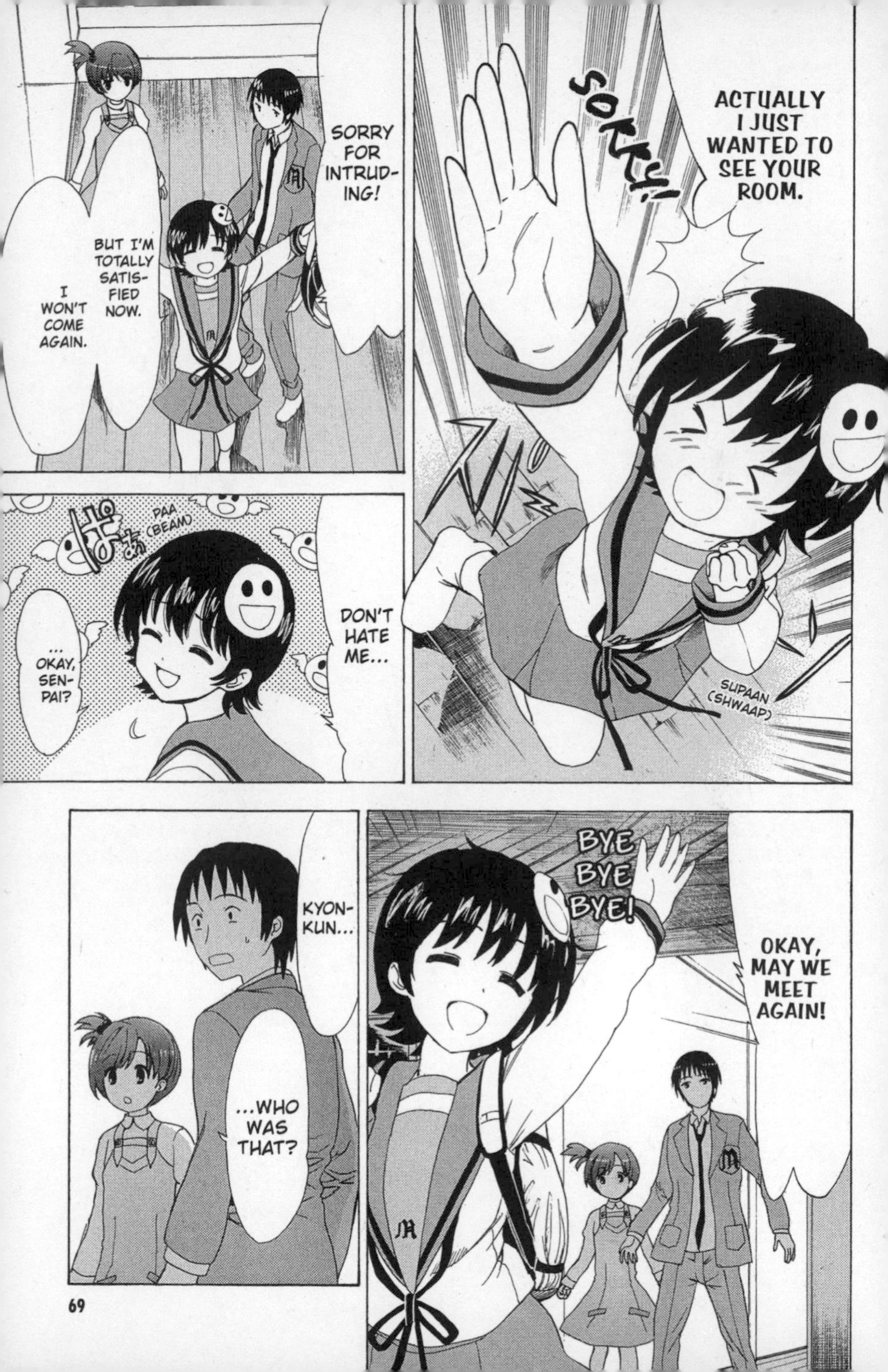
ACTUALLY I JUST WANTED TO SEE YOUR ROOM.
SOKKY!!
SUPAAN (SHWAAP)
SORRY FOR INTRUD-ING!
BUT I'M TOTALLY SATIS-FIED NOW.
I WON'T COME AGAIN.
PAA (BEAM)
DON'T HATE ME...
...OKAY, SEN-PAI?
BYE BYE BYE!
OKAY, MAY WE MEET AGAIN!
KYON-KUN...
...WHO WAS THAT?

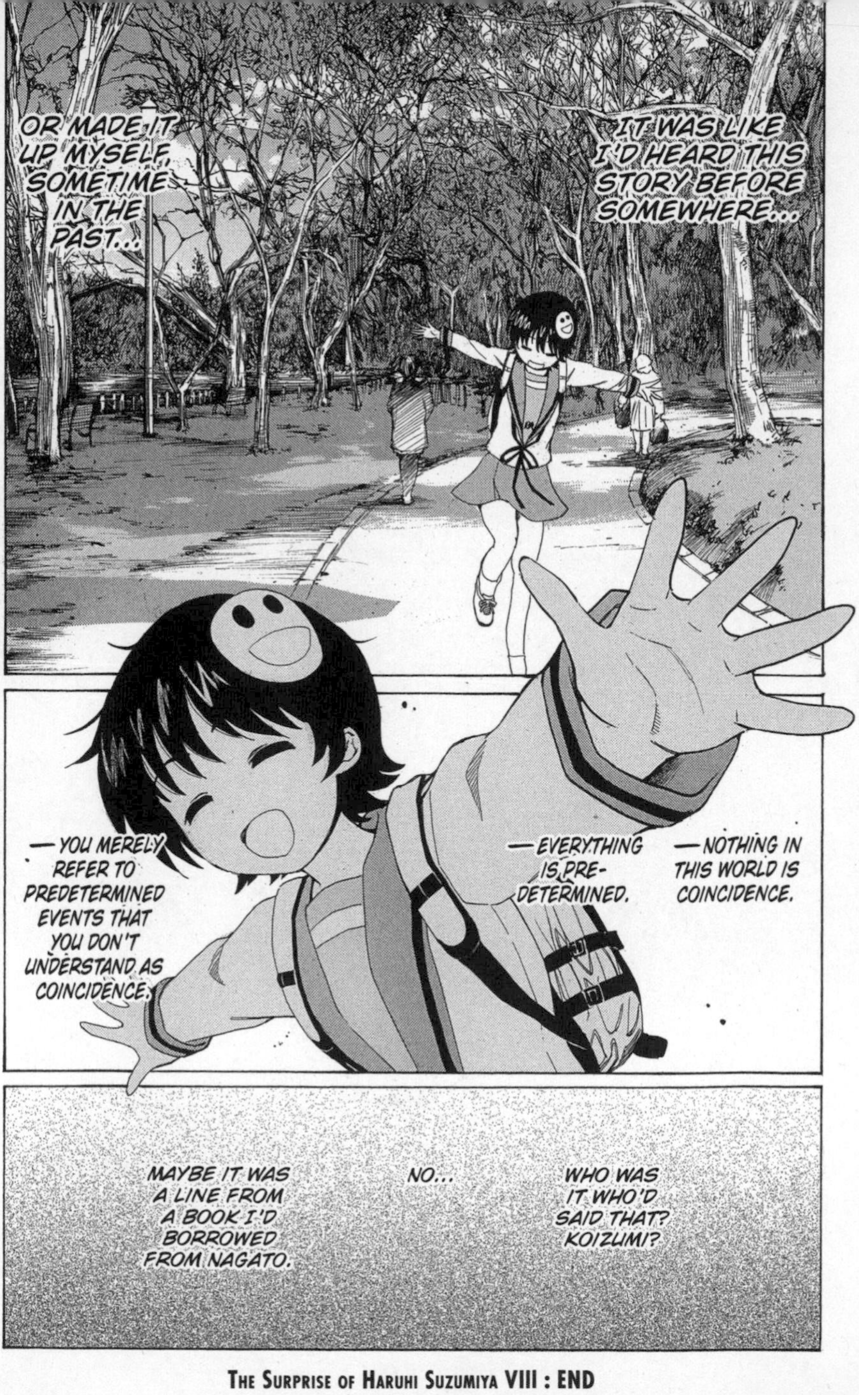
IT WAS LIKE I'D HEARD THIS STORY BEFORE SOMEWHERE...
OR MADE IT UP MYSELF, SOMETIME IN THE PAST...
—NOTHING IN THIS WORLD IS COINCIDENCE.
—EVERYTHING IS PRE-DETERMINED.
—YOU MERELY REFER TO PREDETERMINED EVENTS THAT YOU DON'T UNDERSTAND AS COINCIDENCE.
WHO WAS IT WHO'D SAID THAT? KOIZUMI?
NO...
MAYBE IT WAS A LINE FROM A BOOK I'D BORROWED FROM NAGATO.

**The Surprise of Haruhi Suzumiya VIII : END**

THE MELANCHOLY OF HARUHI SUZUMIYA

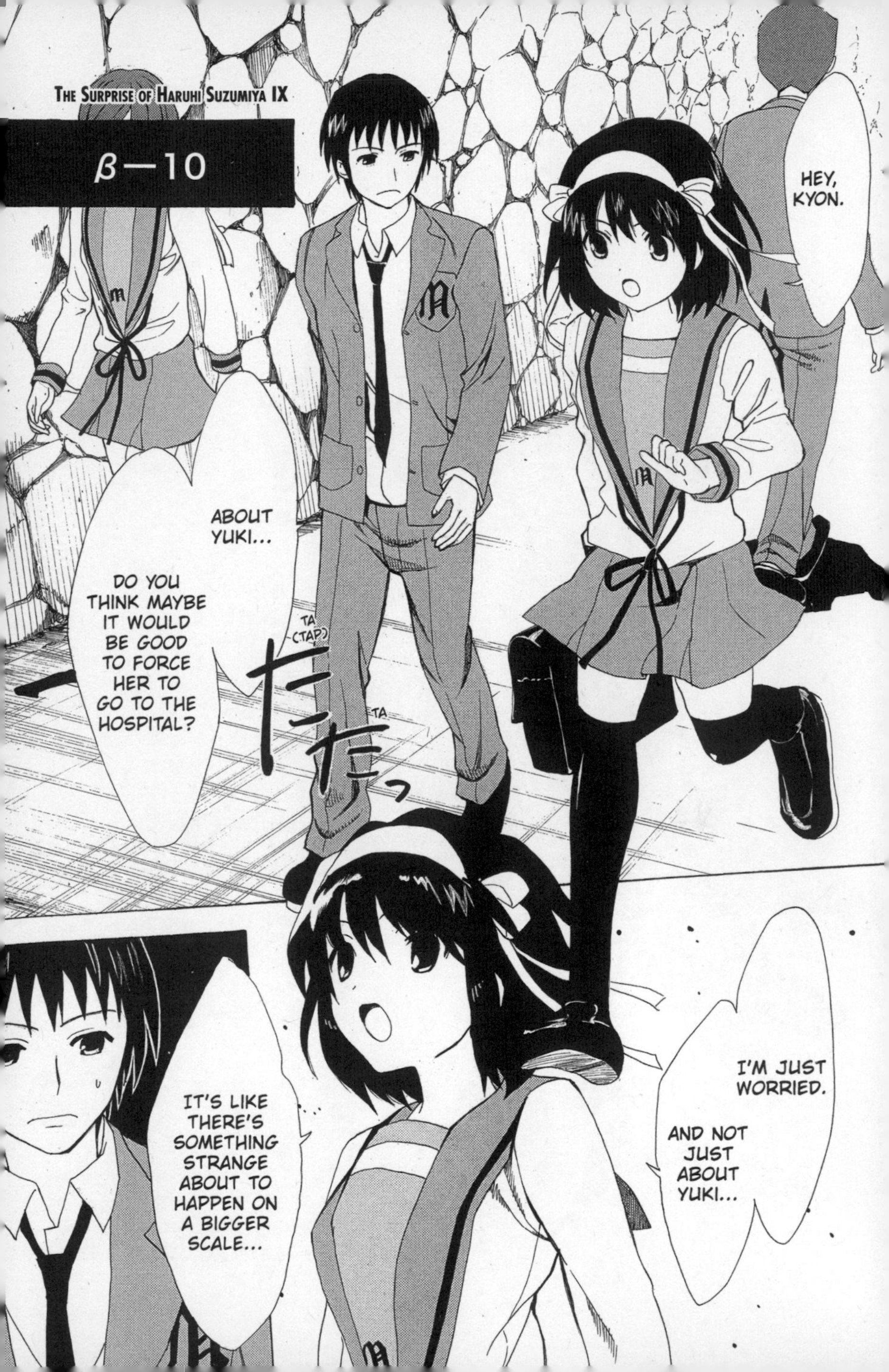
THE SURPRISE OF HARUHI SUZUMIYA IX
β—10
HEY, KYON.
TA (TAP) TA
ABOUT YUKI...
DO YOU THINK MAYBE IT WOULD BE GOOD TO FORCE HER TO GO TO THE HOSPITAL?
I'M JUST WORRIED.
AND NOT JUST ABOUT YUKI...
IT'S LIKE THERE'S SOMETHING STRANGE ABOUT TO HAPPEN ON A BIGGER SCALE...

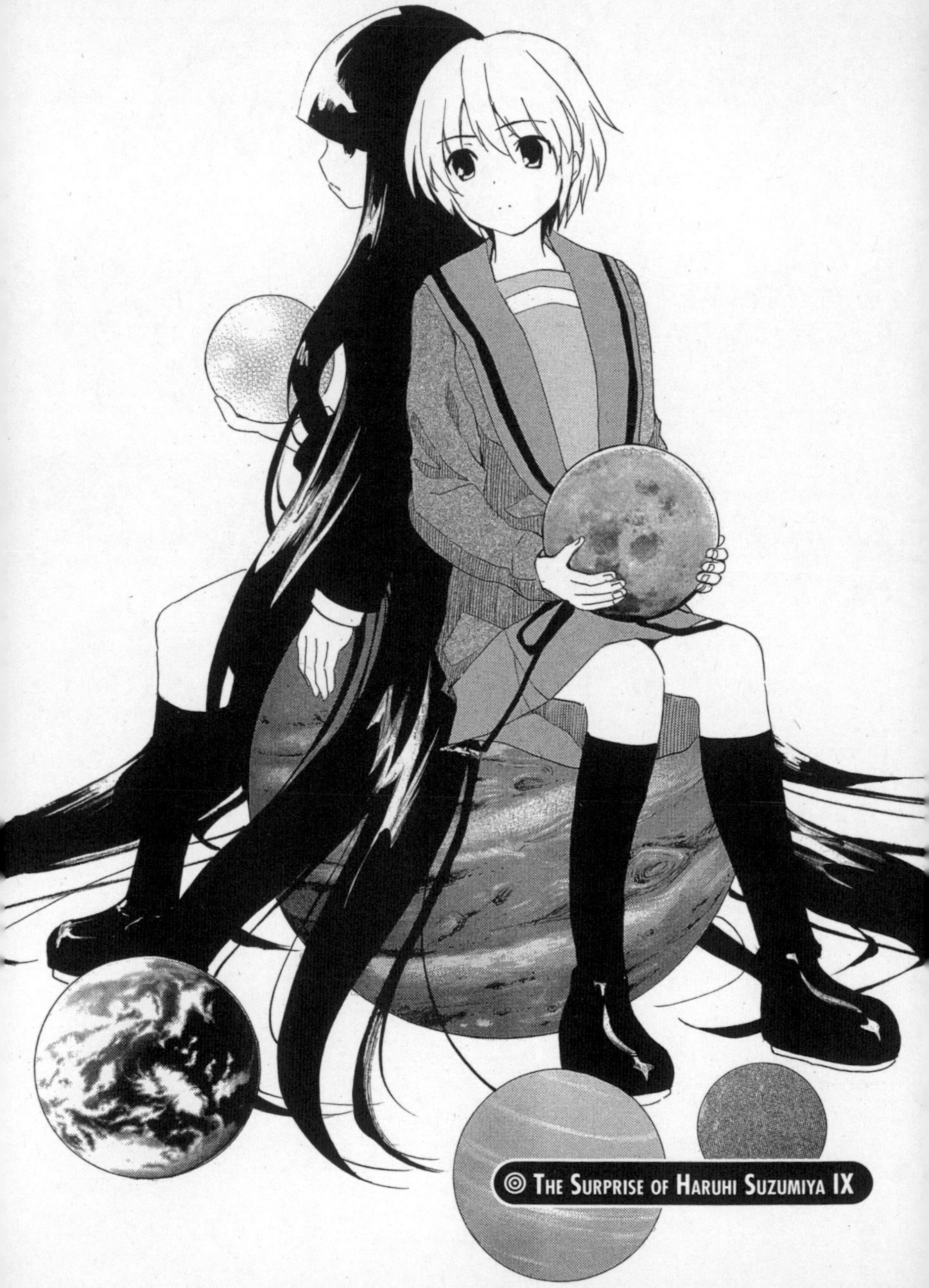

## ◎ The Surprise of Haruhi Suzumiya IX

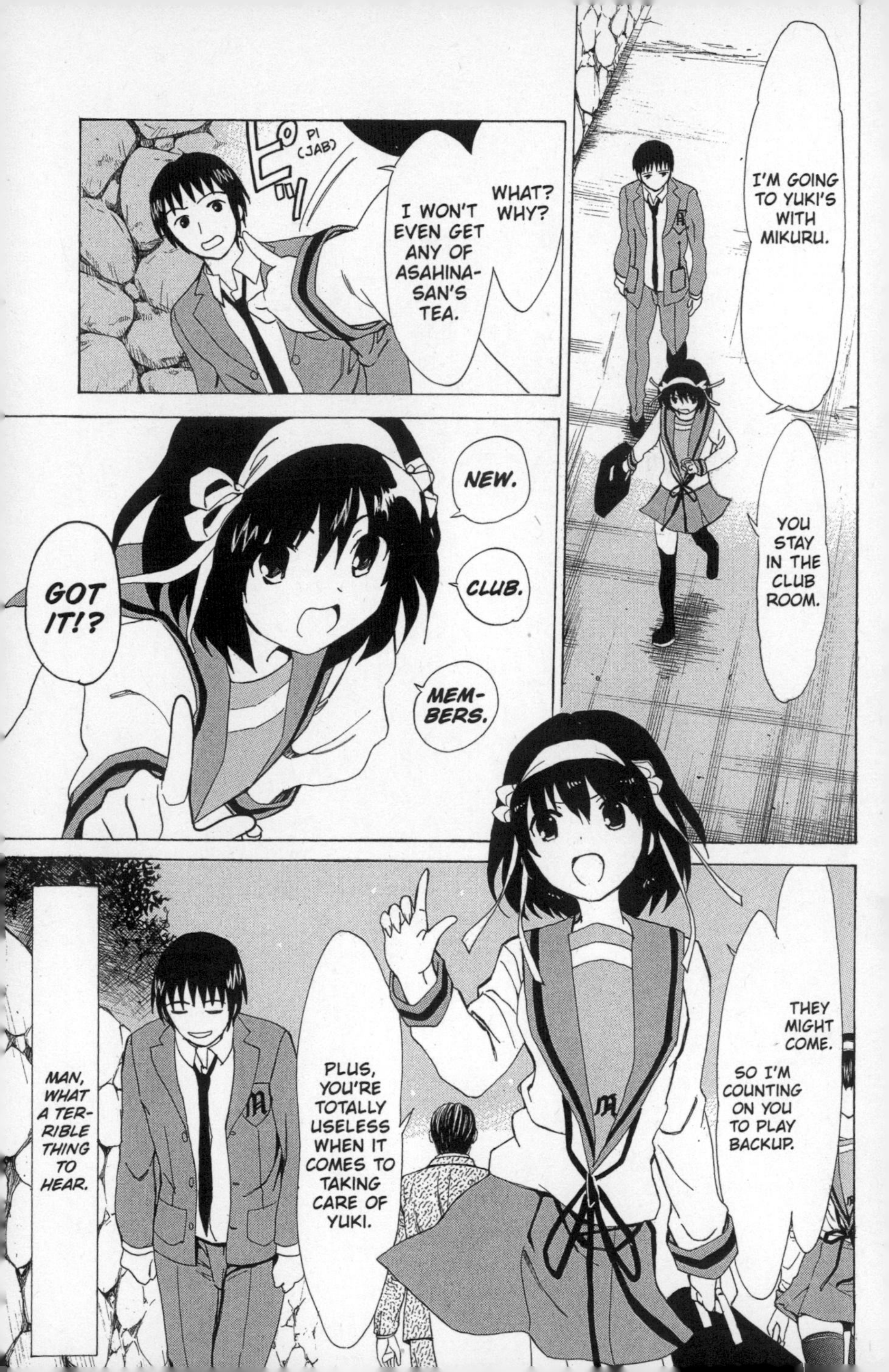
I'M GOING TO YUKI'S WITH MIKURU.
YOU STAY IN THE CLUB ROOM.
WHAT? WHY?
I WON'T EVEN GET ANY OF ASAHINA-SAN'S TEA.
PI (JAB)
NEW.
CLUB.
MEMBERS.
GOT IT!?
THEY MIGHT COME.
SO I'M COUNTING ON YOU TO PLAY BACKUP.
PLUS, YOU'RE TOTALLY USELESS WHEN IT COMES TO TAKING CARE OF YUKI.
MAN, WHAT A TERRIBLE THING TO HEAR.

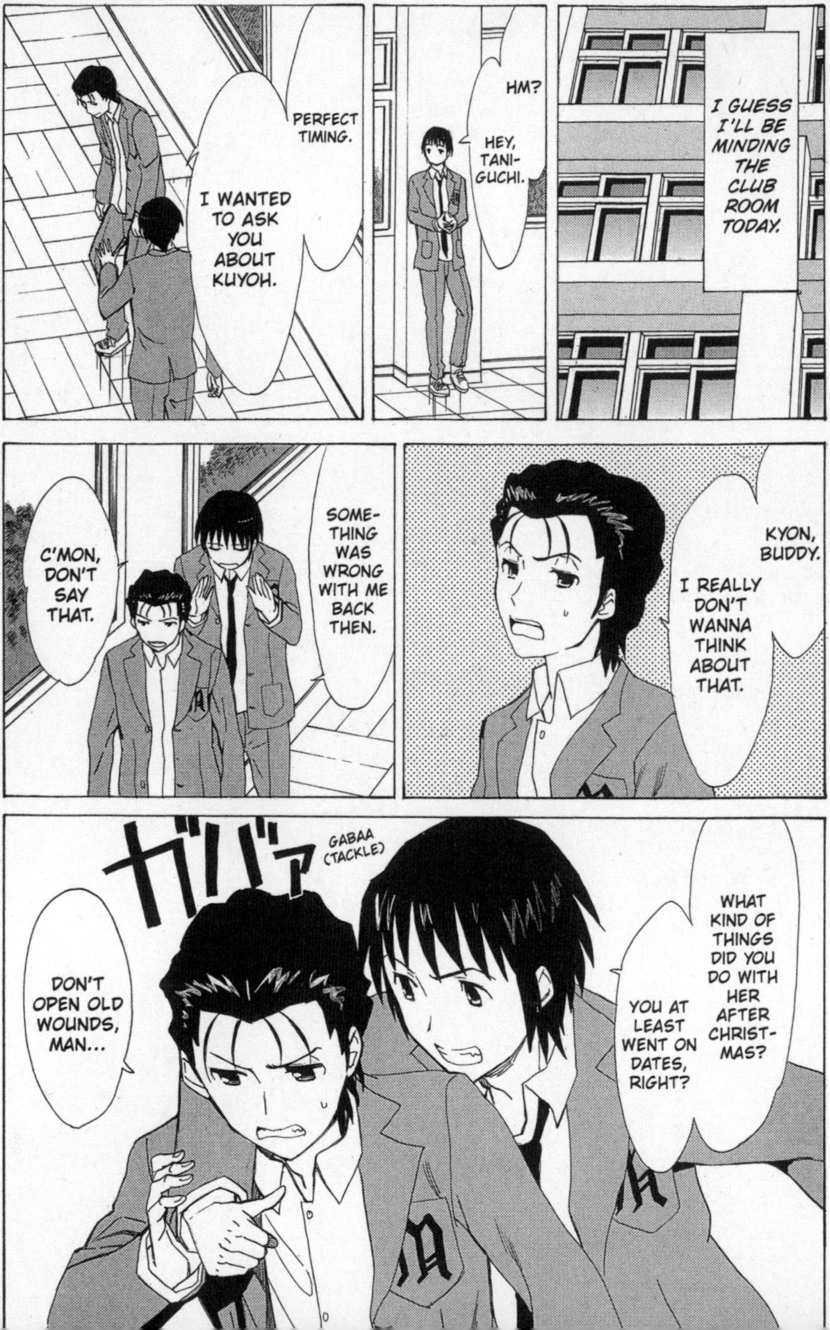
I GUESS I'LL BE MINDING THE CLUB ROOM TODAY.
HM?
HEY, TANI-GUCHI.
PERFECT TIMING.
I WANTED TO ASK YOU ABOUT KUYOH.
KYON, BUDDY.
I REALLY DON'T WANNA THINK ABOUT THAT.
SOME-THING WAS WRONG WITH ME BACK THEN.
C'MON, DON'T SAY THAT.
WHAT KIND OF THINGS DID YOU DO WITH HER AFTER CHRIST-MAS?
YOU AT LEAST WENT ON DATES, RIGHT?
ガバァ
GABAA (TACKLE)
DON'T OPEN OLD WOUNDS, MAN...

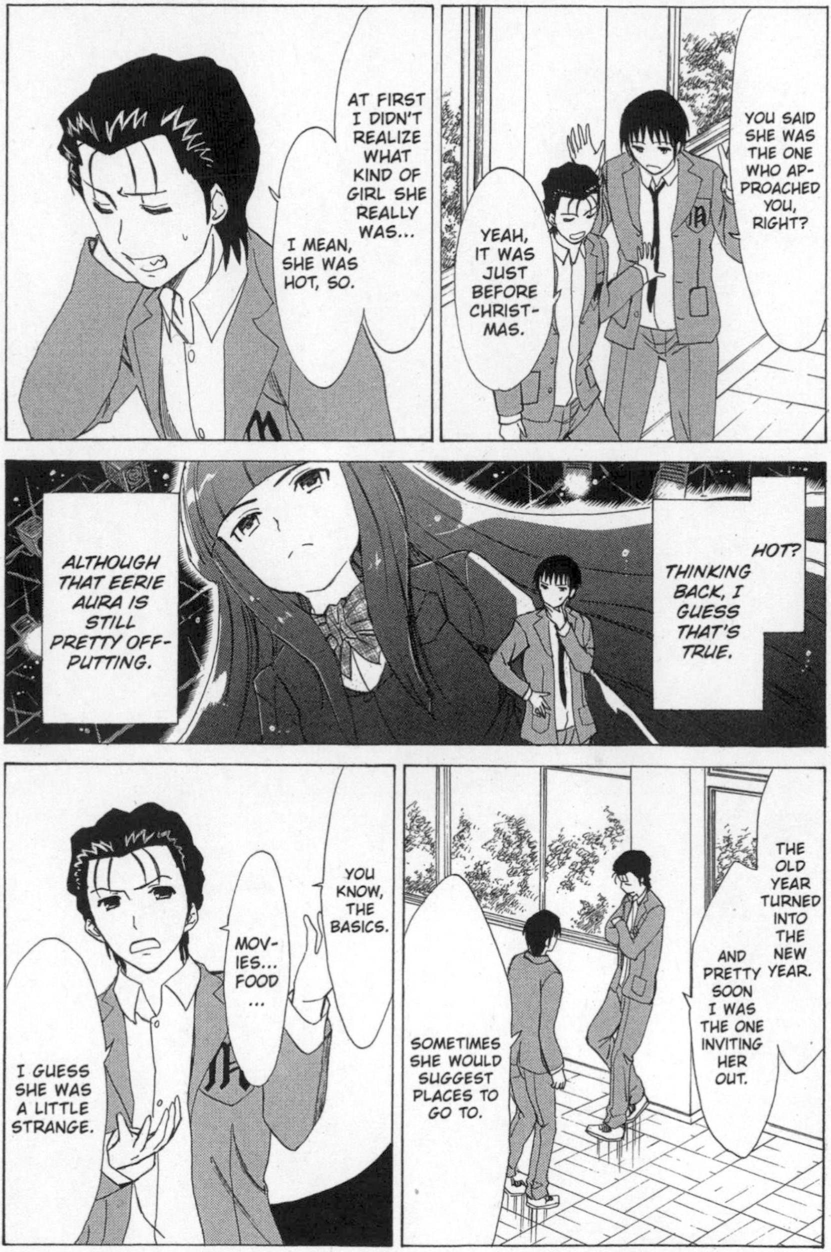
YOU SAID SHE WAS THE ONE WHO APPROACHED YOU, RIGHT?
YEAH, IT WAS JUST BEFORE CHRISTMAS.
AT FIRST I DIDN'T REALIZE WHAT KIND OF GIRL SHE REALLY WAS...
I MEAN, SHE WAS HOT, SO.
HOT? THINKING BACK, I GUESS THAT'S TRUE.
ALTHOUGH THAT EERIE AURA IS STILL PRETTY OFF-PUTTING.
THE OLD YEAR TURNED INTO THE NEW YEAR.
AND PRETTY SOON I WAS THE ONE INVITING HER OUT.
SOMETIMES SHE WOULD SUGGEST PLACES TO GO TO.
YOU KNOW, THE BASICS.
MOVIES... FOOD...
I GUESS SHE WAS A LITTLE STRANGE.

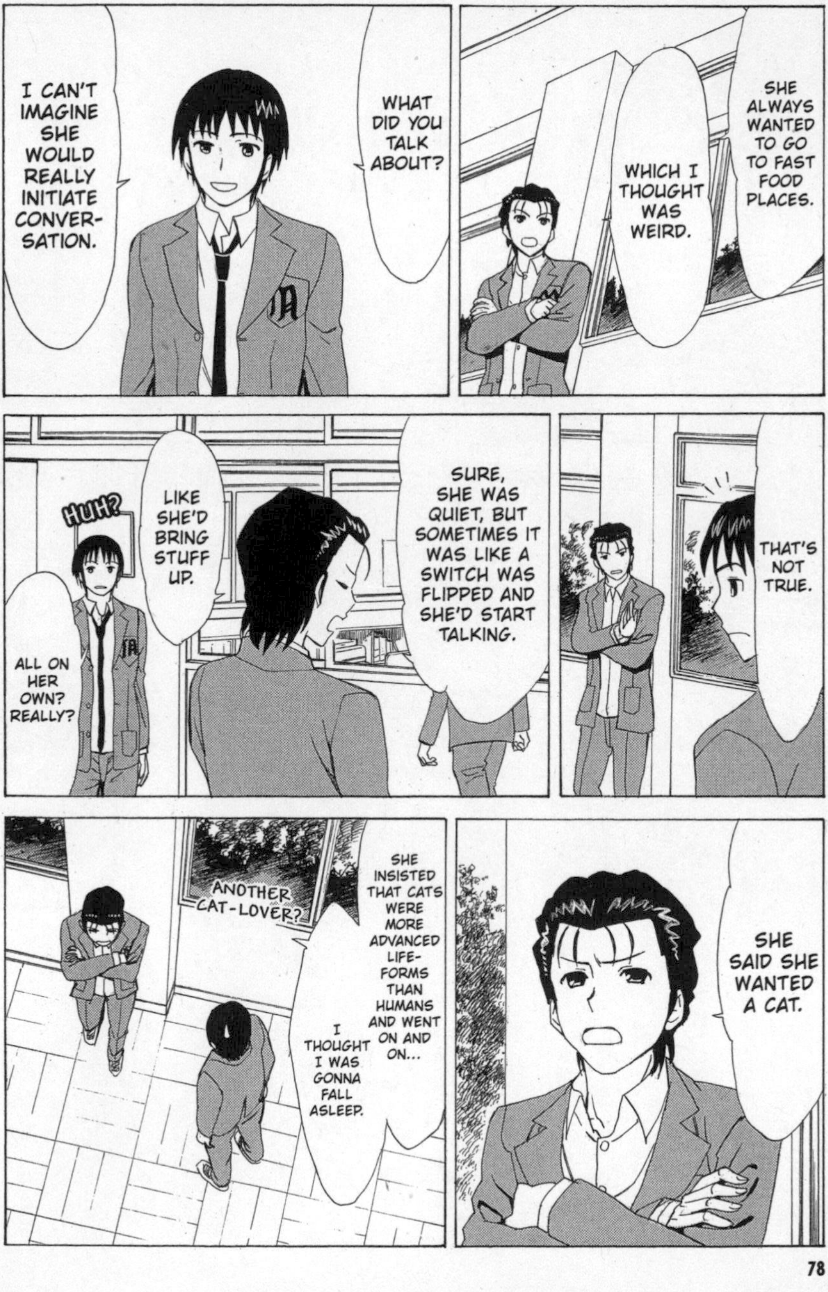
SHE ALWAYS WANTED TO GO TO FAST FOOD PLACES.
WHICH I THOUGHT WAS WEIRD.
WHAT DID YOU TALK ABOUT?
I CAN'T IMAGINE SHE WOULD REALLY INITIATE CONVER-SATION.
THAT'S NOT TRUE.
SURE, SHE WAS QUIET, BUT SOMETIMES IT WAS LIKE A SWITCH WAS FLIPPED AND SHE'D START TALKING.
LIKE SHE'D BRING STUFF UP.
HUH?
ALL ON HER OWN? REALLY?
SHE SAID SHE WANTED A CAT.
SHE INSISTED THAT CATS WERE MORE ADVANCED LIFE-FORMS THAN HUMANS AND WENT ON AND ON...
I THOUGHT I WAS GONNA FALL ASLEEP.
ANOTHER CAT-LOVER?

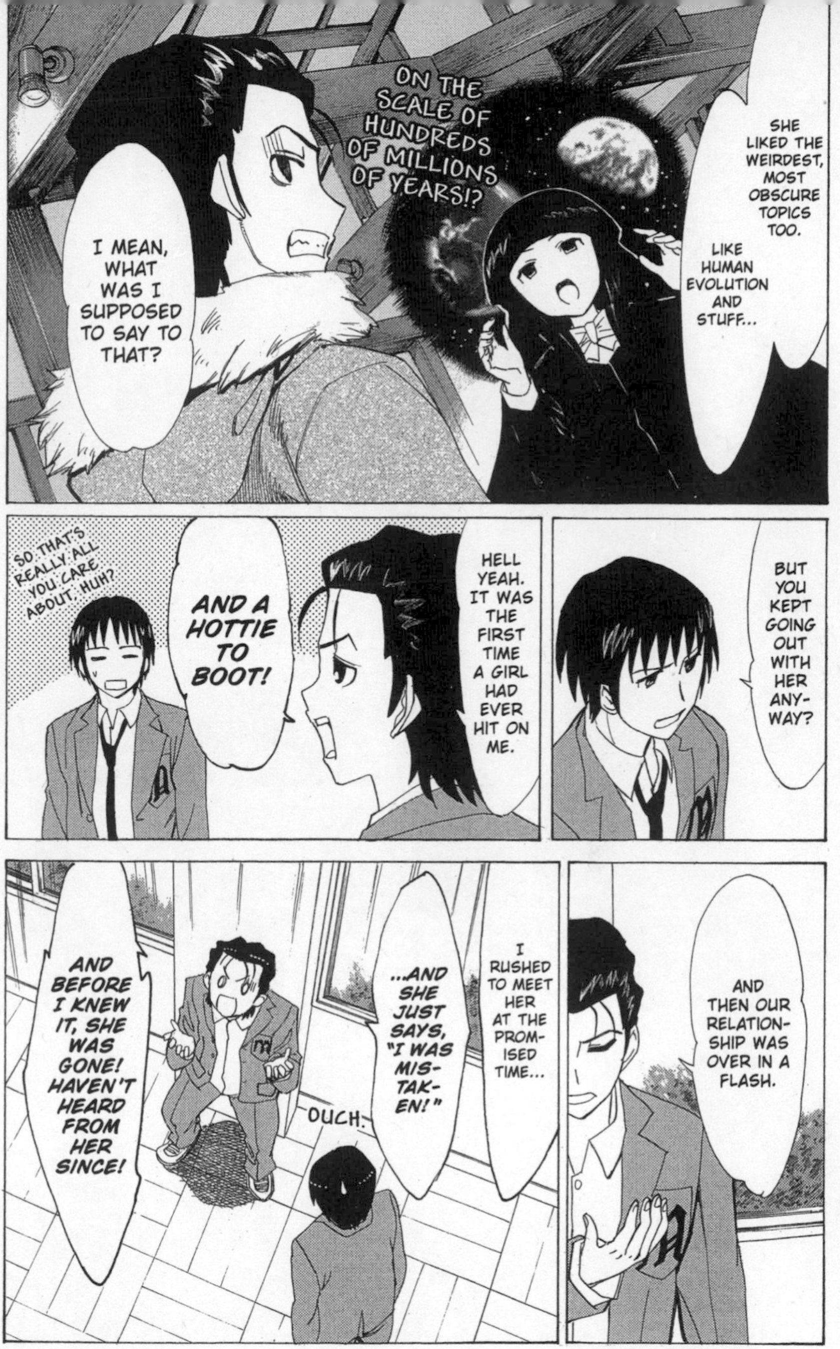
SHE LIKED THE WEIRDEST, MOST OBSCURE TOPICS TOO.
LIKE HUMAN EVOLUTION AND STUFF...
ON THE SCALE OF HUNDREDS OF MILLIONS OF YEARS!?
I MEAN, WHAT WAS I SUPPOSED TO SAY TO THAT?
BUT YOU KEPT GOING OUT WITH HER ANYWAY?
HELL YEAH. IT WAS THE FIRST TIME A GIRL HAD EVER HIT ON ME.
AND A HOTTIE TO BOOT!
SO THAT'S REALLY ALL YOU CARE ABOUT, HUH?
AND THEN OUR RELATIONSHIP WAS OVER IN A FLASH.
I RUSHED TO MEET HER AT THE PROMISED TIME...
...AND SHE JUST SAYS, "I WAS MISTAKEN!"
OUCH.
AND BEFORE I KNEW IT, SHE WAS GONE! HAVEN'T HEARD FROM HER SINCE!

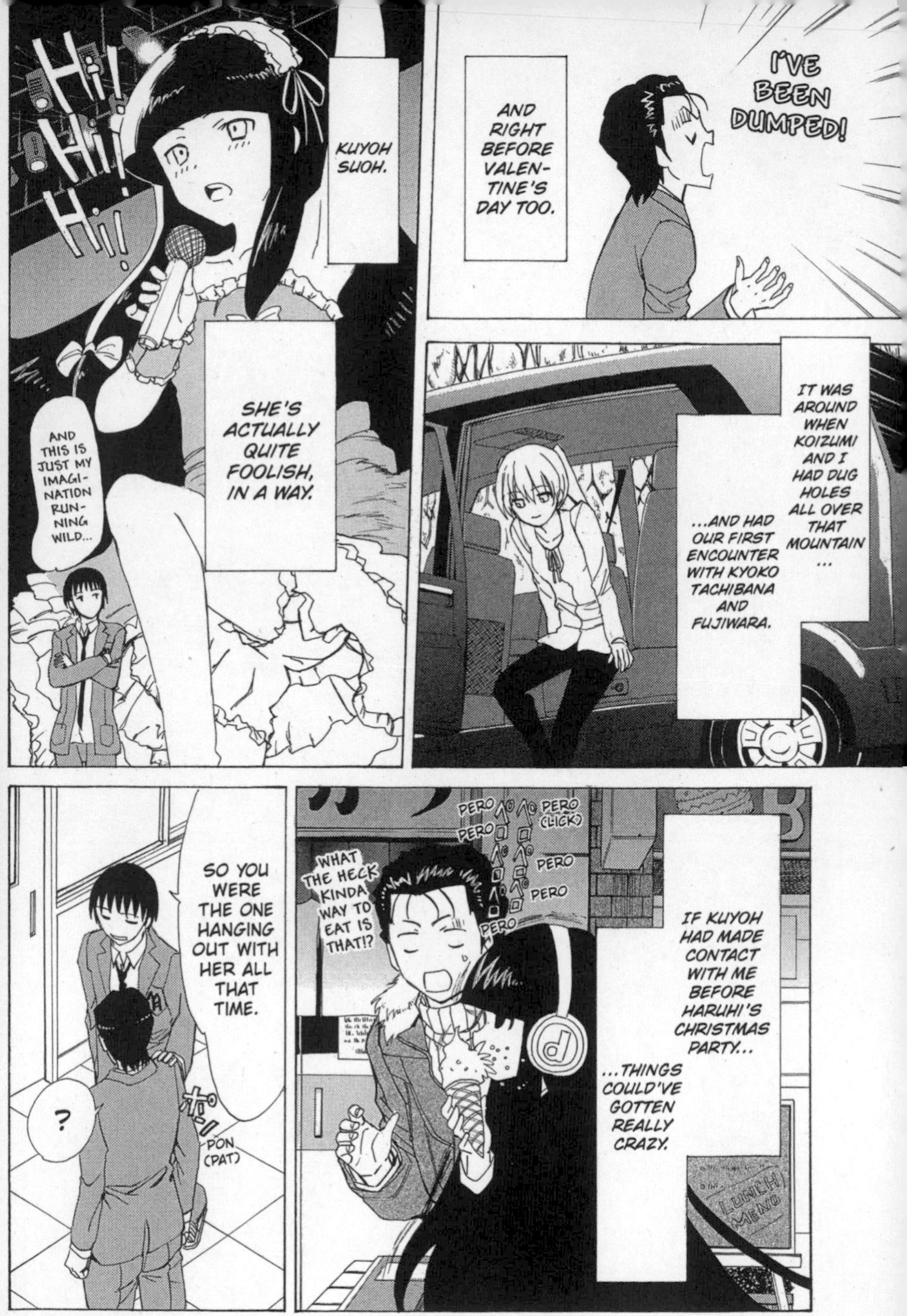
I'VE BEEN DUMPED!
AND RIGHT BEFORE VALEN-TINE'S DAY TOO.
IT WAS AROUND WHEN KOIZUMI AND I HAD DUG HOLES ALL OVER THAT MOUNTAIN...
...AND HAD OUR FIRST ENCOUNTER WITH KYOKO TACHIBANA AND FUJIWARA.
KUYOH SUOH.
HI! HI! HI!
SHE'S ACTUALLY QUITE FOOLISH, IN A WAY.
AND THIS IS JUST MY IMAGI-NATION RUN-NING WILD...
IF KUYOH HAD MADE CONTACT WITH ME BEFORE HARUHI'S CHRISTMAS PARTY...
...THINGS COULD'VE GOTTEN REALLY CRAZY.
PERO (LICK)
PERO
PERO
PERO
PERO
PERO
WHAT THE HECK KINDA WAY TO EAT IS THAT!?
LUNCH MENU
SO YOU WERE THE ONE HANGING OUT WITH HER ALL THAT TIME.
PON (PAT)
?

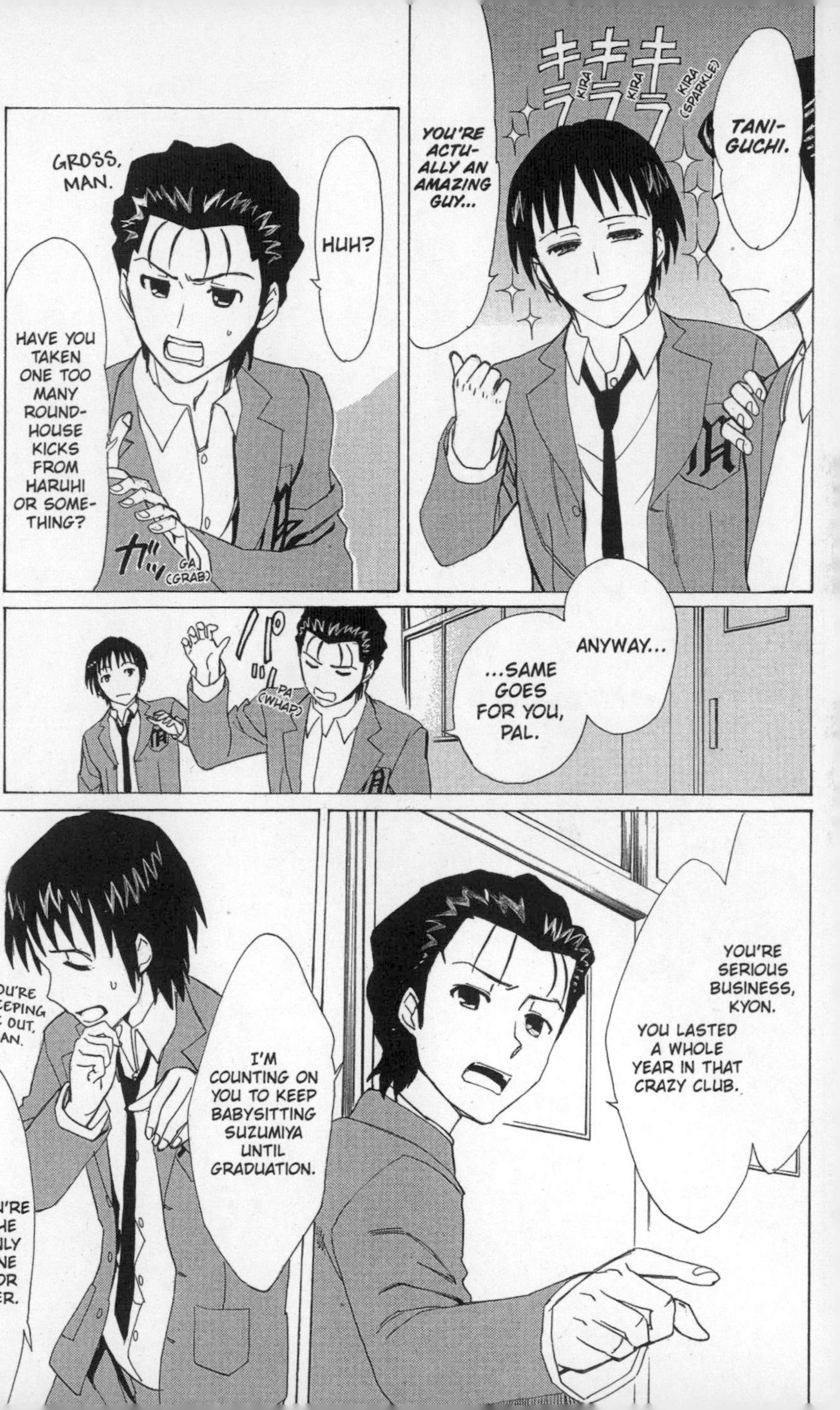
TANI-GUCHI.
キラキラキラ
KIRA KIRA KIRA (SPARKLE)
YOU'RE ACTUALLY AN AMAZING GUY...
HUH?
GROSS, MAN.
HAVE YOU TAKEN ONE TOO MANY ROUNDHOUSE KICKS FROM HARUHI OR SOMETHING?
ガッ
GA (GRAB)
ANYWAY...
...SAME GOES FOR YOU, PAL.
パッ
PA (WHAP)
YOU'RE SERIOUS BUSINESS, KYON.
YOU LASTED A WHOLE YEAR IN THAT CRAZY CLUB.
I'M COUNTING ON YOU TO KEEP BABYSITTING SUZUMIYA UNTIL GRADUATION.
YOU'RE CREEPING ME OUT, MAN.
YOU'RE THE ONLY ONE FOR HER.

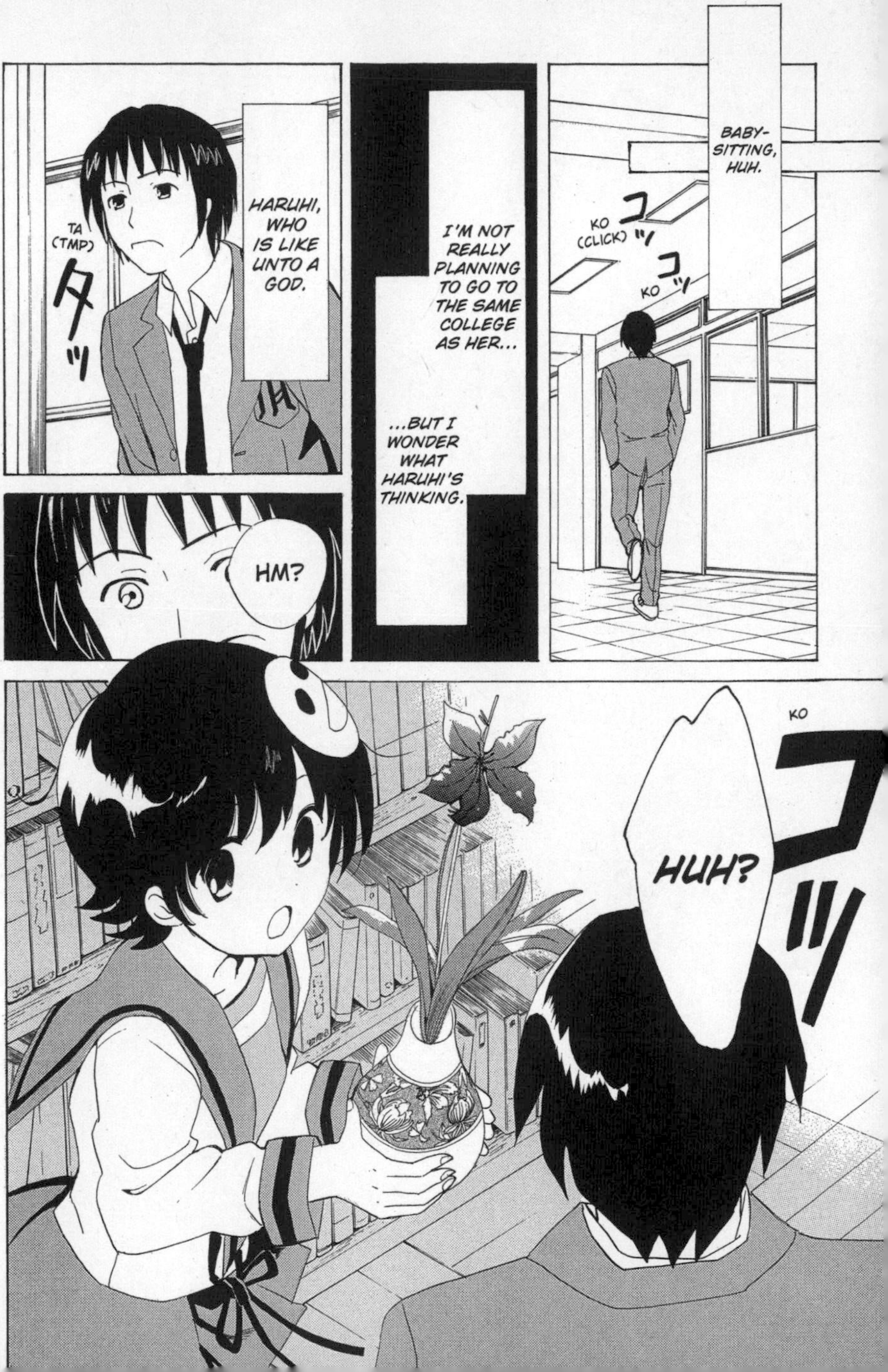
BABY-SITTING, HUH.
KO (CLICK)
KO
I'M NOT REALLY PLANNING TO GO TO THE SAME COLLEGE AS HER...
...BUT I WONDER WHAT HARUHI'S THINKING.
HARUHI, WHO IS LIKE UNTO A GOD.
TA (TMP)
HM?
KO
HUH?

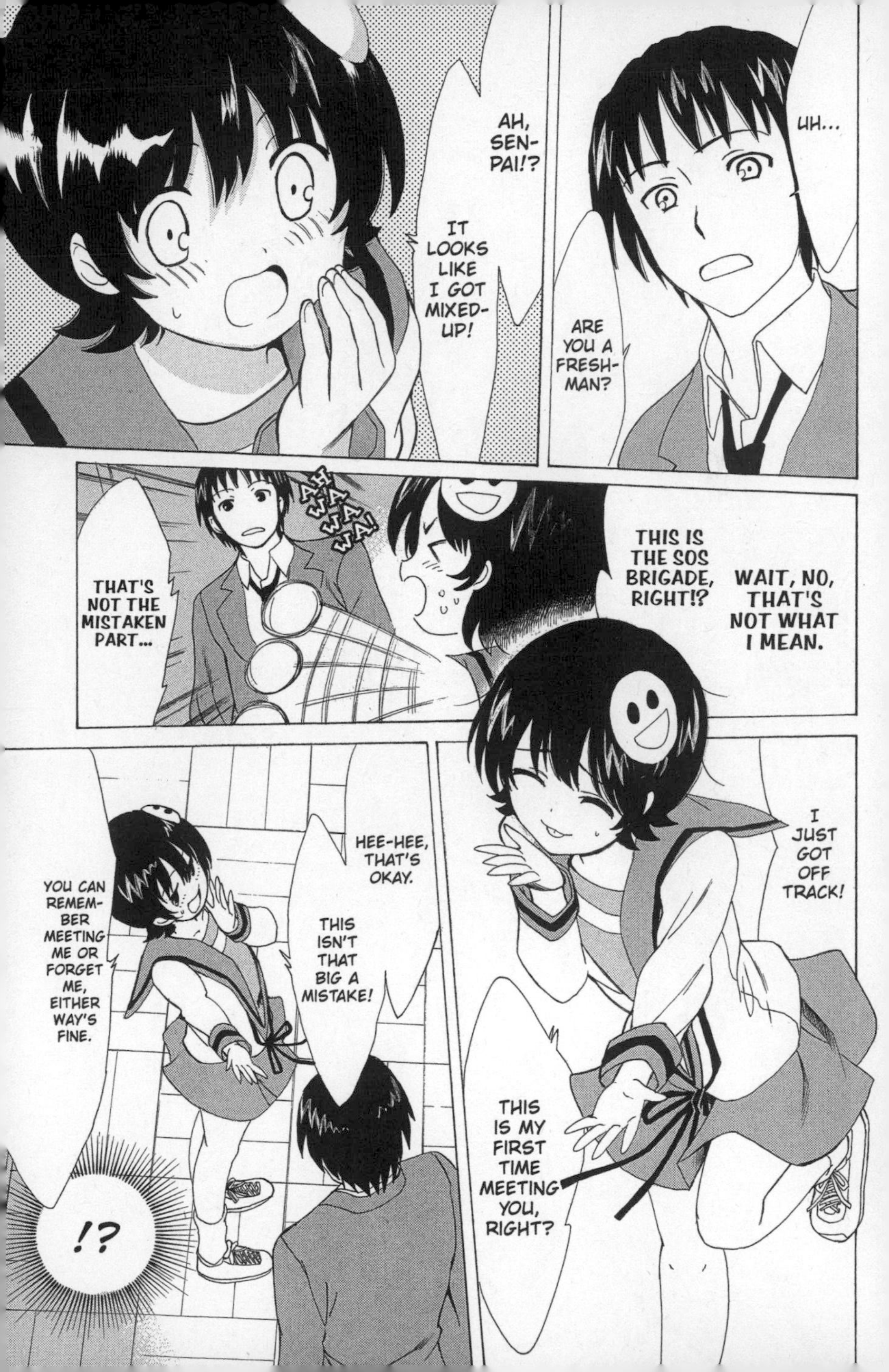
UH...
ARE YOU A FRESHMAN?
AH, SENPAI!?
IT LOOKS LIKE I GOT MIXED-UP!
WAIT, NO, THAT'S NOT WHAT I MEAN.
THIS IS THE SOS BRIGADE, RIGHT!?
THAT'S NOT THE MISTAKEN PART...
I JUST GOT OFF TRACK!
THIS IS MY FIRST TIME MEETING YOU, RIGHT?
HEE-HEE, THAT'S OKAY.
THIS ISN'T THAT BIG A MISTAKE!
YOU CAN REMEMBER MEETING ME OR FORGET ME, EITHER WAY'S FINE.
!?

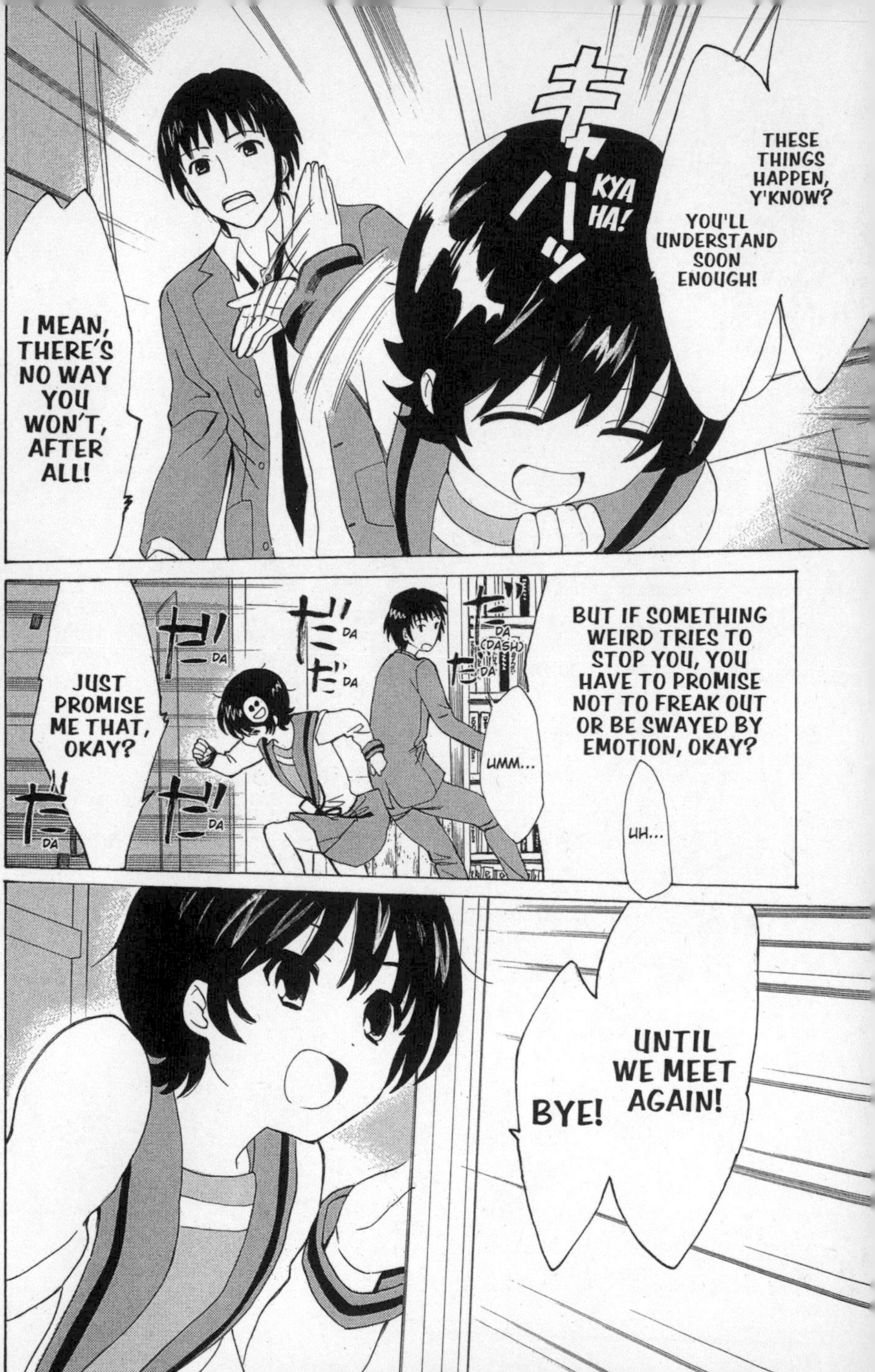
KYA HA!
THESE THINGS HAPPEN, Y'KNOW?
YOU'LL UNDERSTAND SOON ENOUGH!
I MEAN, THERE'S NO WAY YOU WON'T, AFTER ALL!
BUT IF SOMETHING WEIRD TRIES TO STOP YOU, YOU HAVE TO PROMISE NOT TO FREAK OUT OR BE SWAYED BY EMOTION, OKAY?
UH...
DA (DASH) DA
UMM...
DA DA
JUST PROMISE ME THAT, OKAY?
DA DA DA
UNTIL WE MEET AGAIN!
BYE!

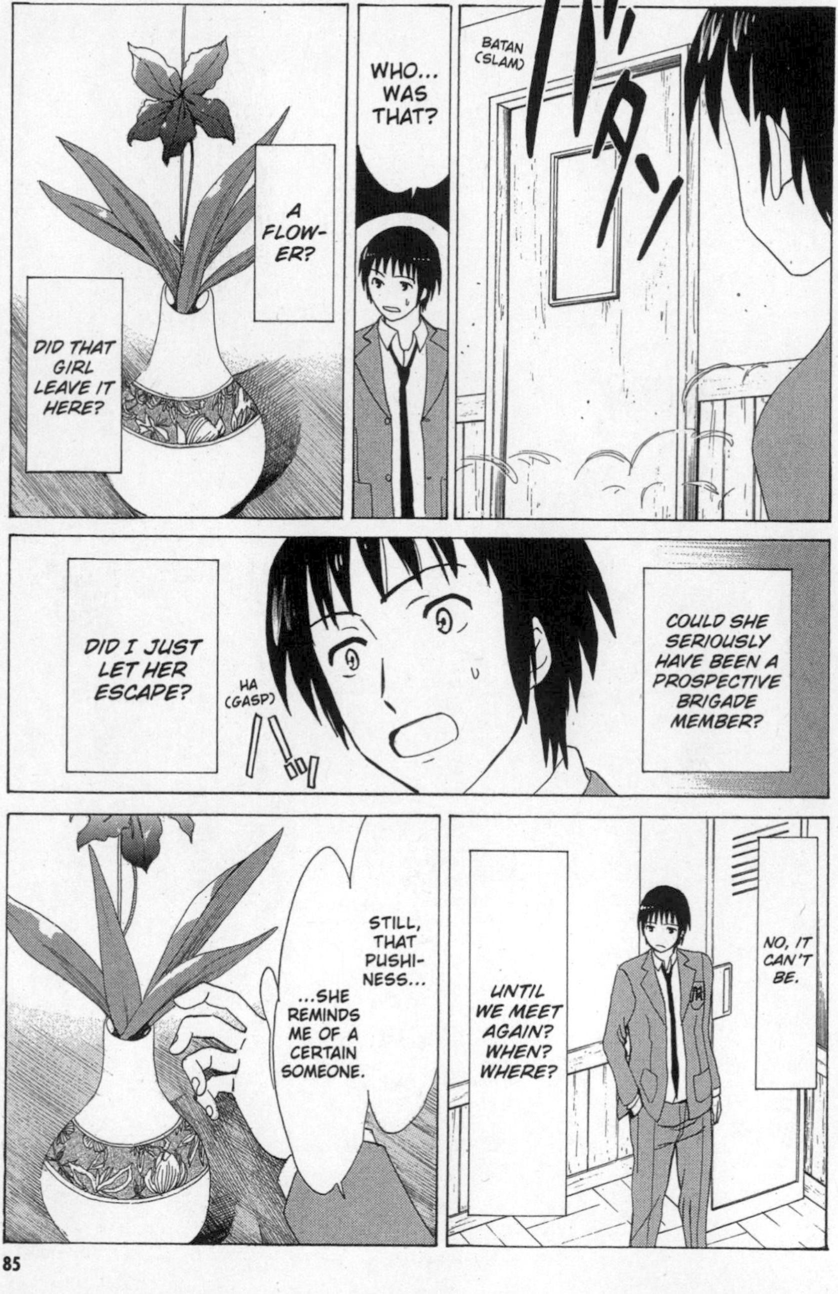
BATAN (SLAM)
WHO... WAS THAT?
A FLOWER?
DID THAT GIRL LEAVE IT HERE?
COULD SHE SERIOUSLY HAVE BEEN A PROSPECTIVE BRIGADE MEMBER?
HA (GASP)
DID I JUST LET HER ESCAPE?
NO, IT CAN'T BE.
UNTIL WE MEET AGAIN? WHEN? WHERE?
STILL, THAT PUSHINESS...
...SHE REMINDS ME OF A CERTAIN SOMEONE.

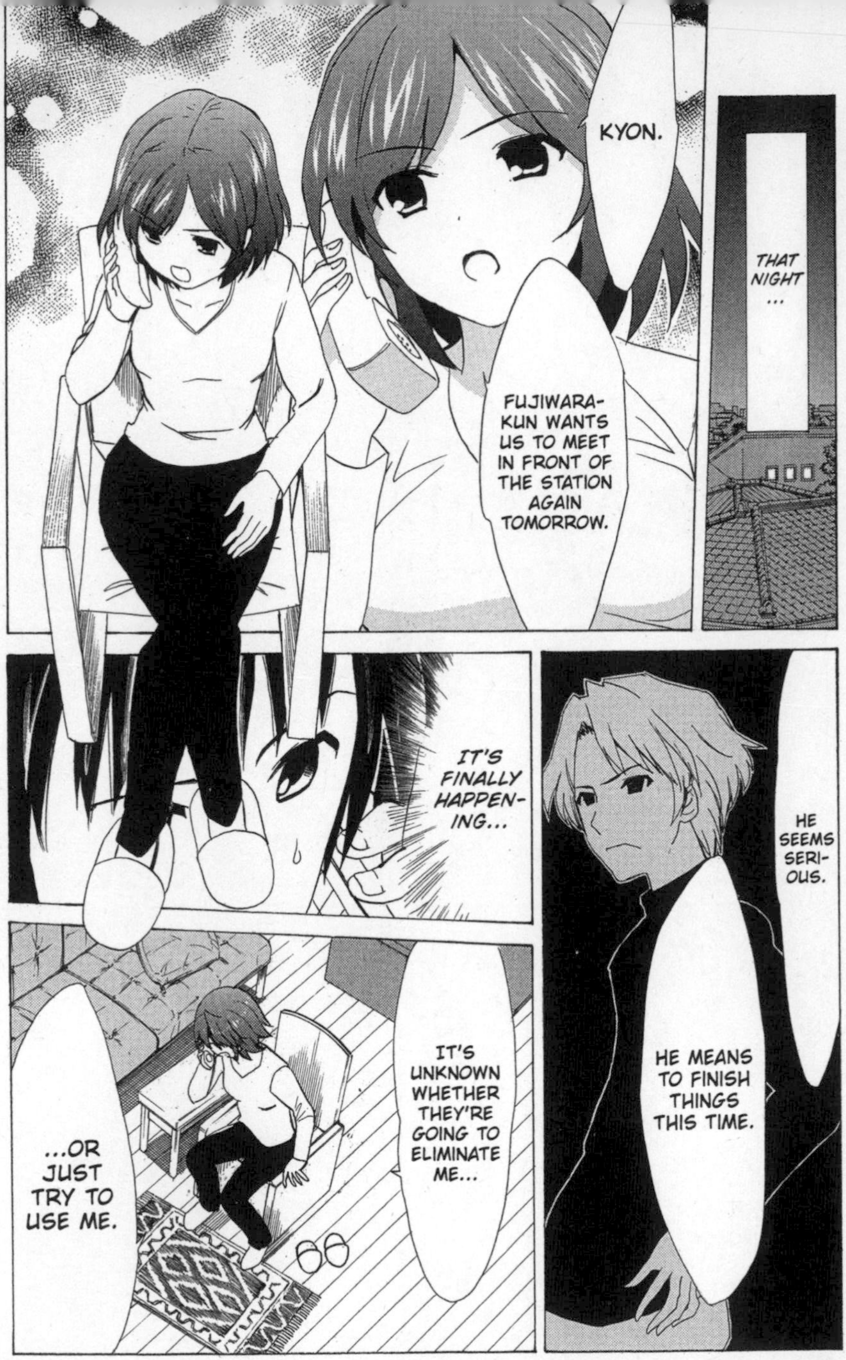
THAT NIGHT...
KYON.
FUJIWARA-KUN WANTS US TO MEET IN FRONT OF THE STATION AGAIN TOMORROW.
HE SEEMS SERIOUS.
HE MEANS TO FINISH THINGS THIS TIME.
IT'S FINALLY HAPPENING...
IT'S UNKNOWN WHETHER THEY'RE GOING TO ELIMINATE ME...
...OR JUST TRY TO USE ME.

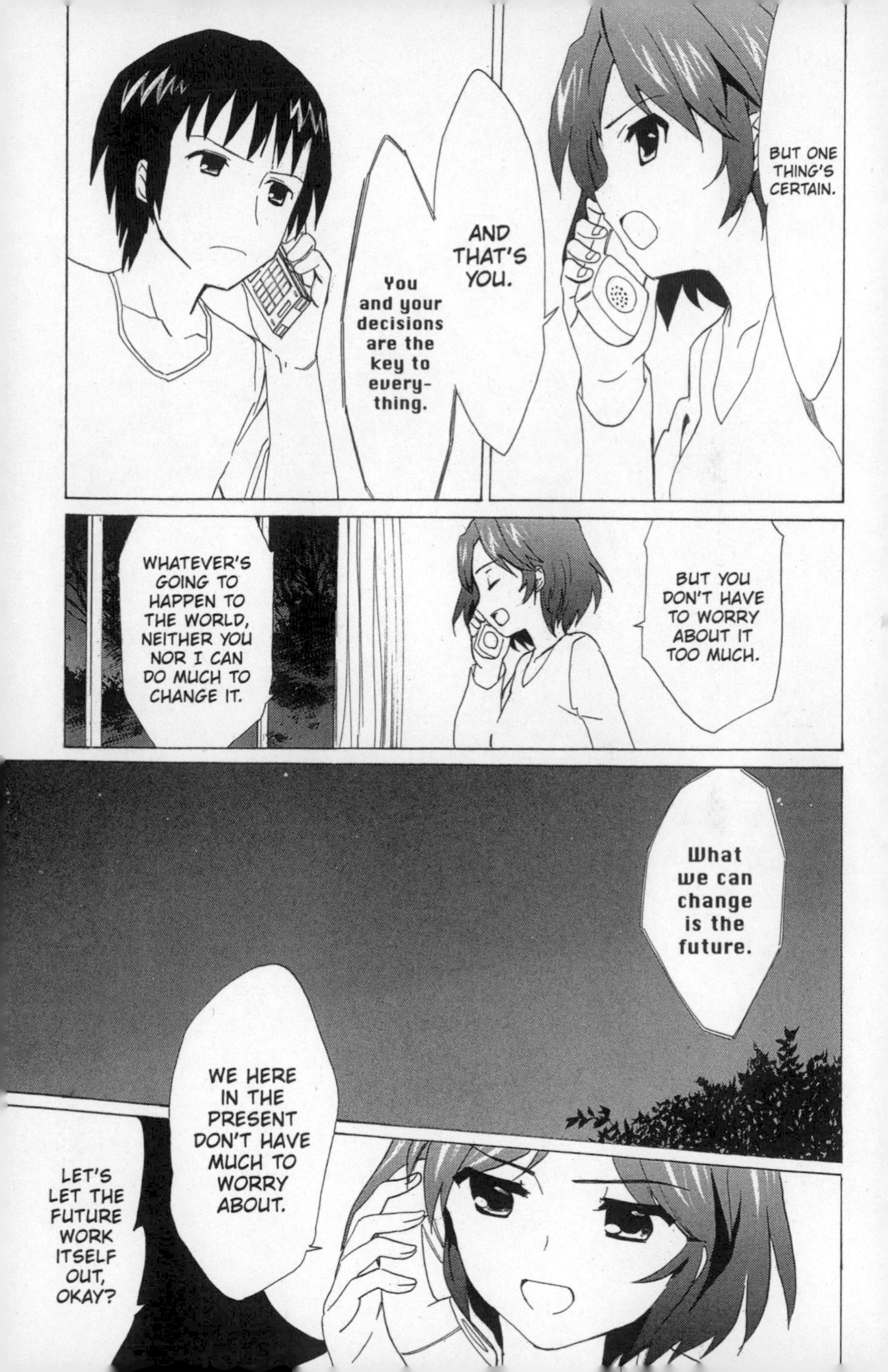
BUT ONE THING'S CERTAIN.
AND THAT'S YOU.
You and your decisions are the key to every-thing.
BUT YOU DON'T HAVE TO WORRY ABOUT IT TOO MUCH.
WHATEVER'S GOING TO HAPPEN TO THE WORLD, NEITHER YOU NOR I CAN DO MUCH TO CHANGE IT.
What we can change is the future.
WE HERE IN THE PRESENT DON'T HAVE MUCH TO WORRY ABOUT.
LET'S LET THE FUTURE WORK ITSELF OUT, OKAY?

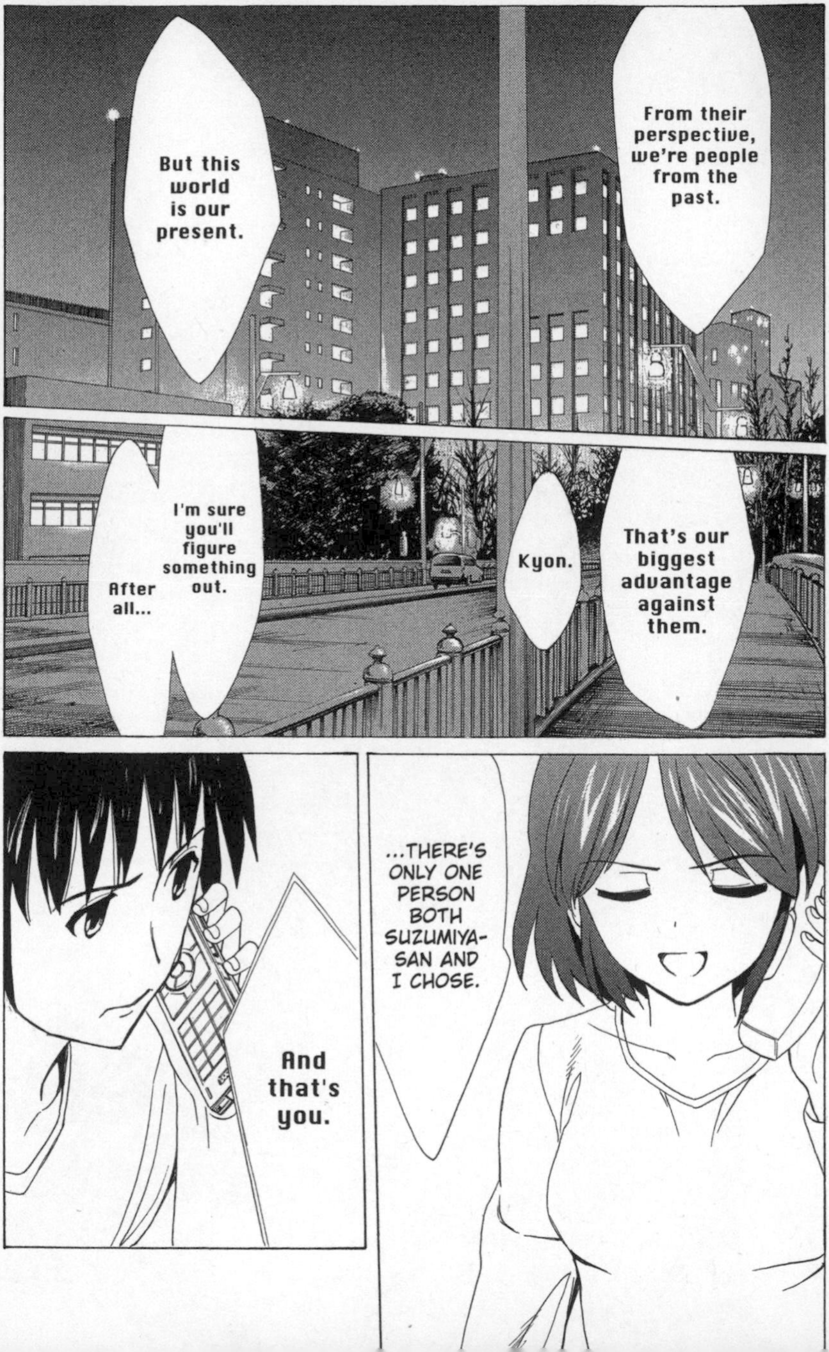
From their perspective, we're people from the past.
But this world is our present.
That's our biggest advantage against them.
Kyon.
I'm sure you'll figure something out.
After all...
...THERE'S ONLY ONE PERSON BOTH SUZUMIYA-SAN AND I CHOSE.
And that's you.

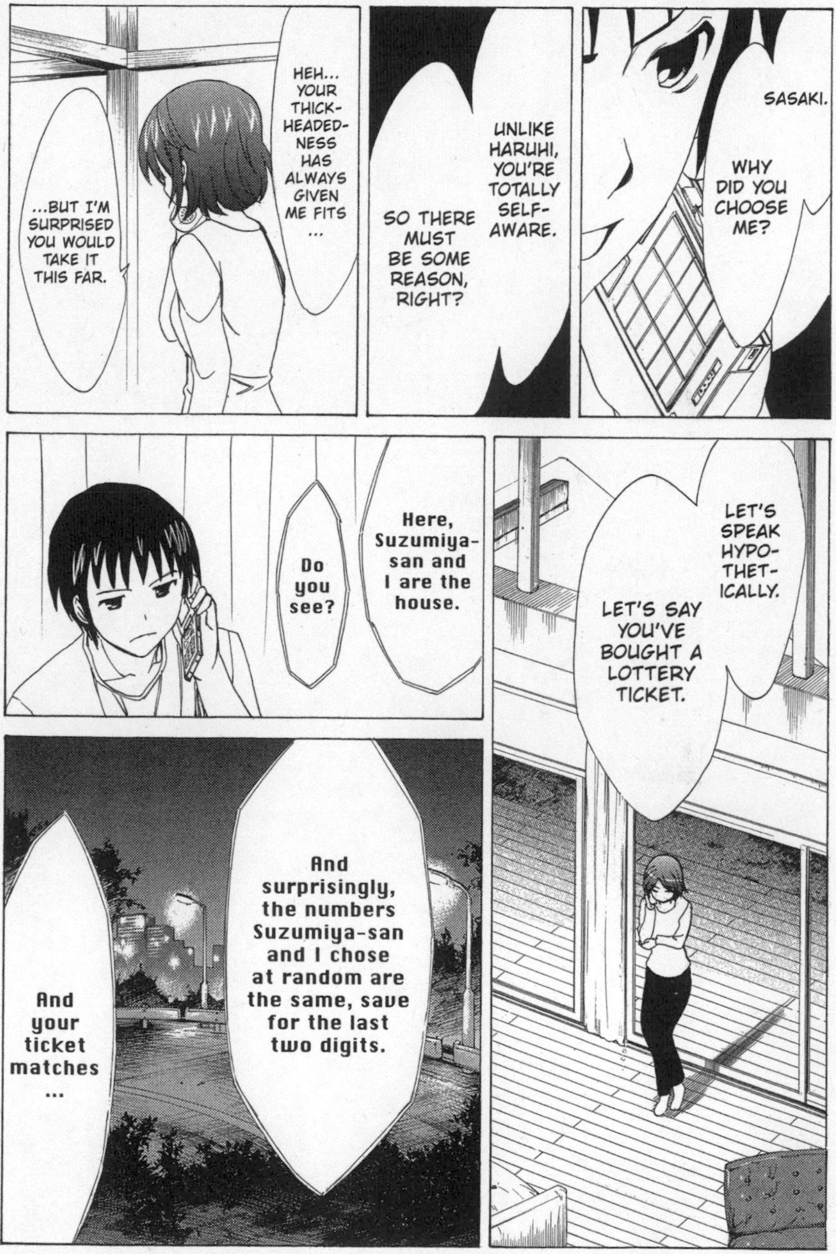
SASAKI.
WHY DID YOU CHOOSE ME?
UNLIKE HARUHI, YOU'RE TOTALLY SELF-AWARE.
SO THERE MUST BE SOME REASON, RIGHT?
HEH... YOUR THICK-HEADED-NESS HAS ALWAYS GIVEN ME FITS...
...BUT I'M SURPRISED YOU WOULD TAKE IT THIS FAR.
LET'S SPEAK HYPO-THET-ICALLY.
LET'S SAY YOU'VE BOUGHT A LOTTERY TICKET.
Here, Suzumiya-san and I are the house.
Do you see?
And surprisingly, the numbers Suzumiya-san and I chose at random are the same, save for the last two digits.
And your ticket matches...

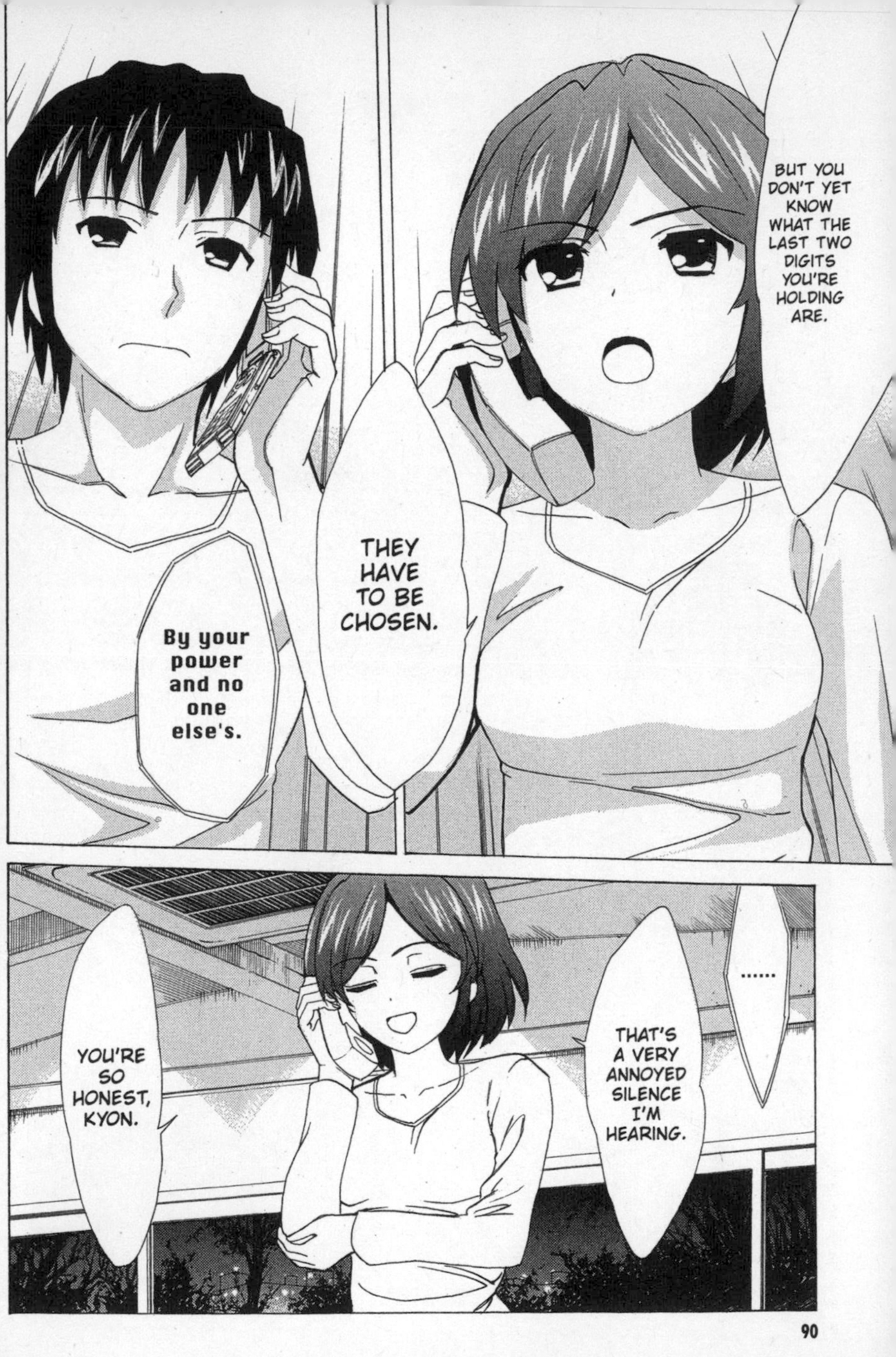
BUT YOU DON'T YET KNOW WHAT THE LAST TWO DIGITS YOU'RE HOLDING ARE.
THEY HAVE TO BE CHOSEN.
By your power and no one else's.
......
THAT'S A VERY ANNOYED SILENCE I'M HEARING.
YOU'RE SO HONEST, KYON.

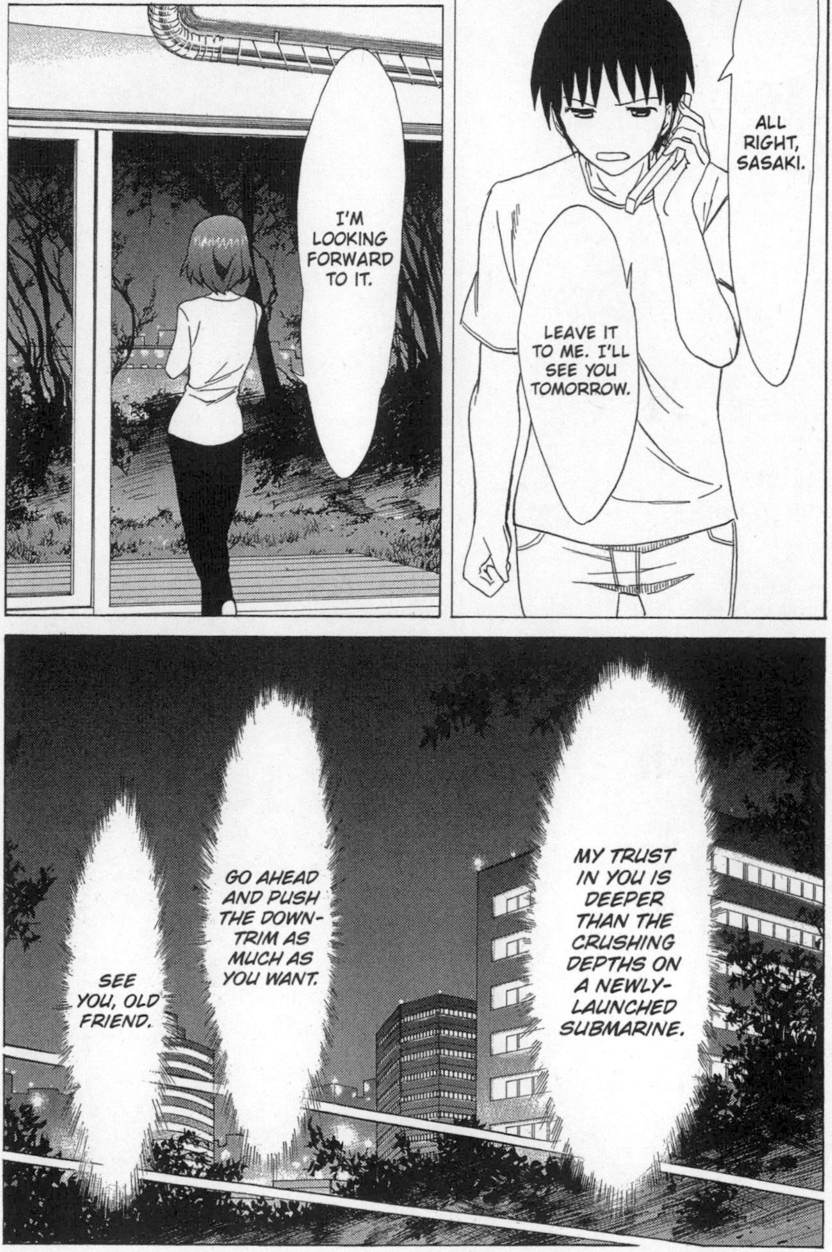
ALL RIGHT, SASAKI.
LEAVE IT TO ME. I'LL SEE YOU TOMORROW.
I'M LOOKING FORWARD TO IT.
MY TRUST IN YOU IS DEEPER THAN THE CRUSHING DEPTHS ON A NEWLY-LAUNCHED SUBMARINE.
GO AHEAD AND PUSH THE DOWN-TRIM AS MUCH AS YOU WANT.
SEE YOU, OLD FRIEND.

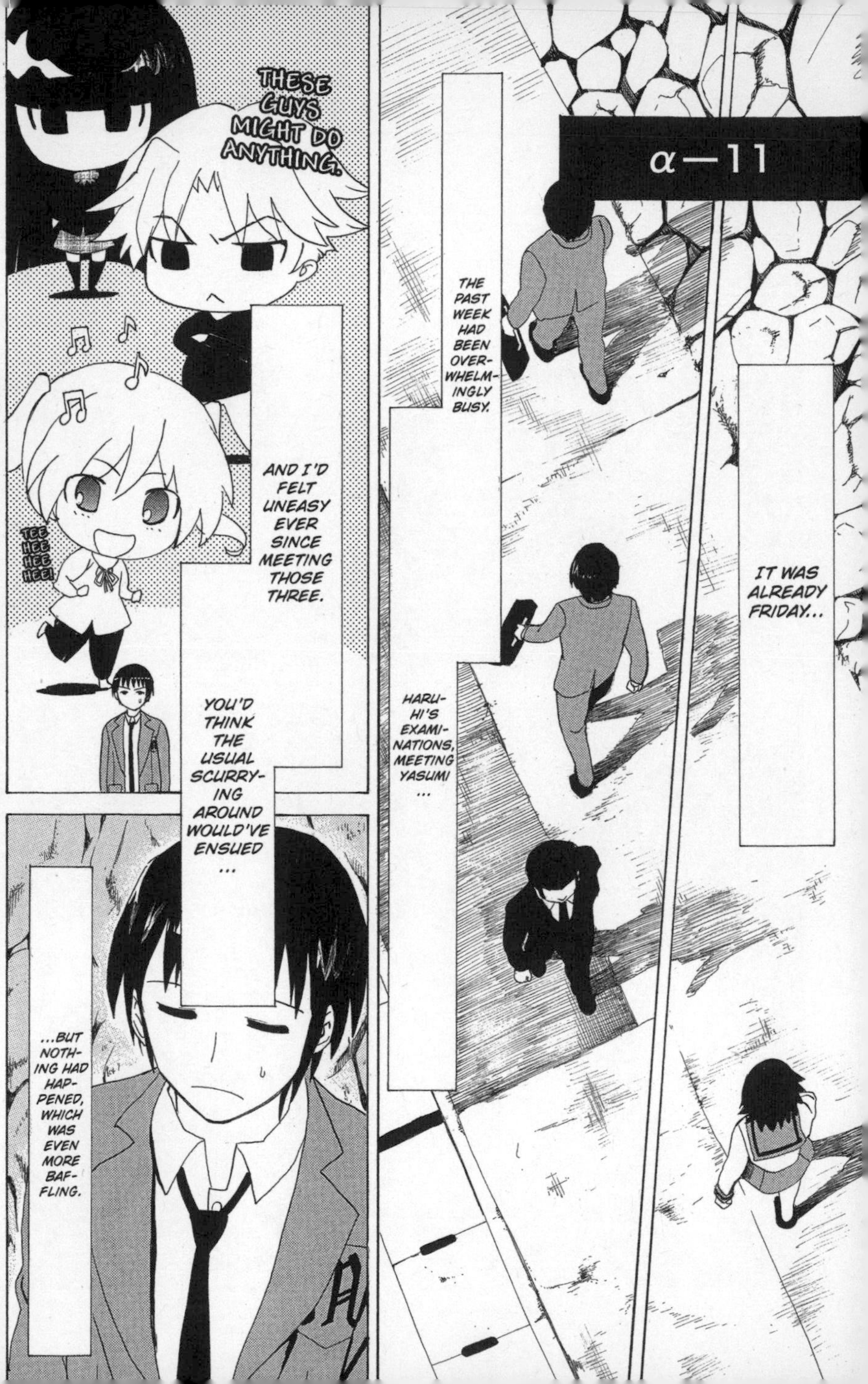
α—11
IT WAS ALREADY FRIDAY...
THE PAST WEEK HAD BEEN OVERWHELMINGLY BUSY.
HARUHI'S EXAMINATIONS, MEETING YASUMI ...
THESE GUYS MIGHT DO ANYTHING.
AND I'D FELT UNEASY EVER SINCE MEETING THOSE THREE.
TEE HEE HEE HEE!
YOU'D THINK THE USUAL SCURRYING AROUND WOULD'VE ENSUED ...
...BUT NOTHING HAD HAPPENED, WHICH WAS EVEN MORE BAFFLING.

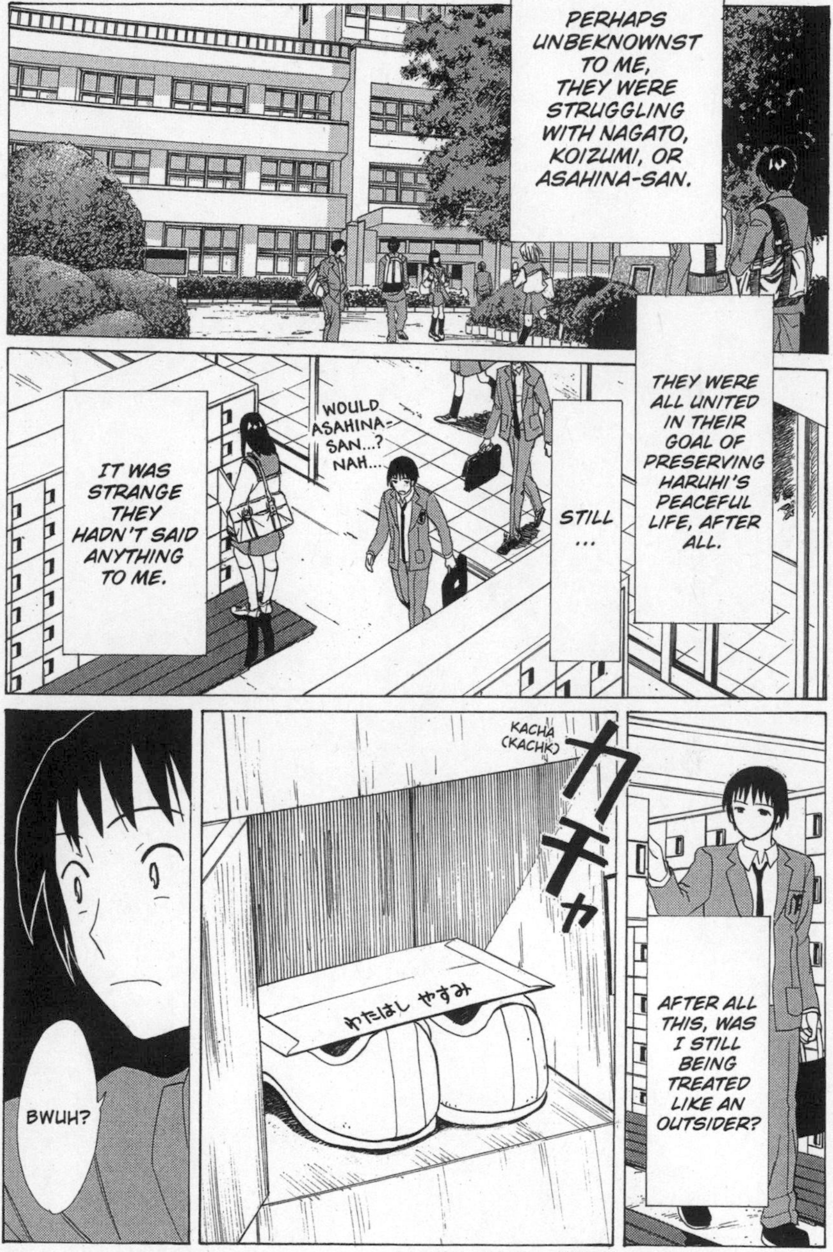
PERHAPS UNBEKNOWNST TO ME, THEY WERE STRUGGLING WITH NAGATO, KOIZUMI, OR ASAHINA-SAN.
THEY WERE ALL UNITED IN THEIR GOAL OF PRESERVING HARUHI'S PEACEFUL LIFE, AFTER ALL.
STILL ...
WOULD ASAHINA-SAN...? NAH...
IT WAS STRANGE THEY HADN'T SAID ANYTHING TO ME.
AFTER ALL THIS, WAS I STILL BEING TREATED LIKE AN OUTSIDER?
カチャ
KACHA (KACHK)
わたはし やすみ
BWUH?



ENVELOPE: YASUMI WATAHASHI

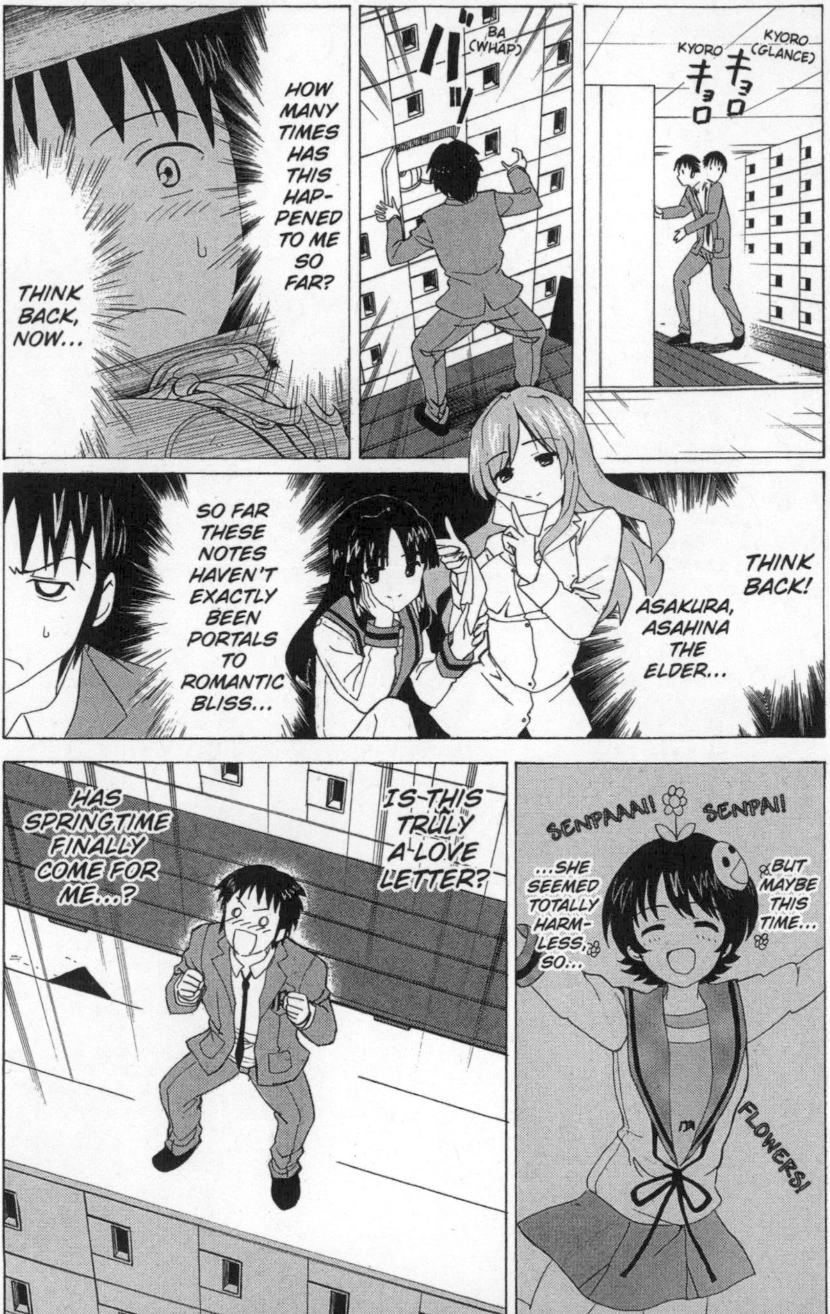
KYORO (GLANCE)
KYORO
キョロ キョロ
BA (WHAP)
バッ
HOW MANY TIMES HAS THIS HAPPENED TO ME SO FAR?
THINK BACK, NOW...
THINK BACK!
ASAKURA, ASAHINA THE ELDER...
SO FAR THESE NOTES HAVEN'T EXACTLY BEEN PORTALS TO ROMANTIC BLISS...
SENPAI!
SENPAAAI!
...SHE SEEMED TOTALLY HARMLESS, SO...
BUT MAYBE THIS TIME...
FLOWERS!
IS THIS TRULY A LOVE LETTER?
HAS SPRINGTIME FINALLY COME FOR ME...?

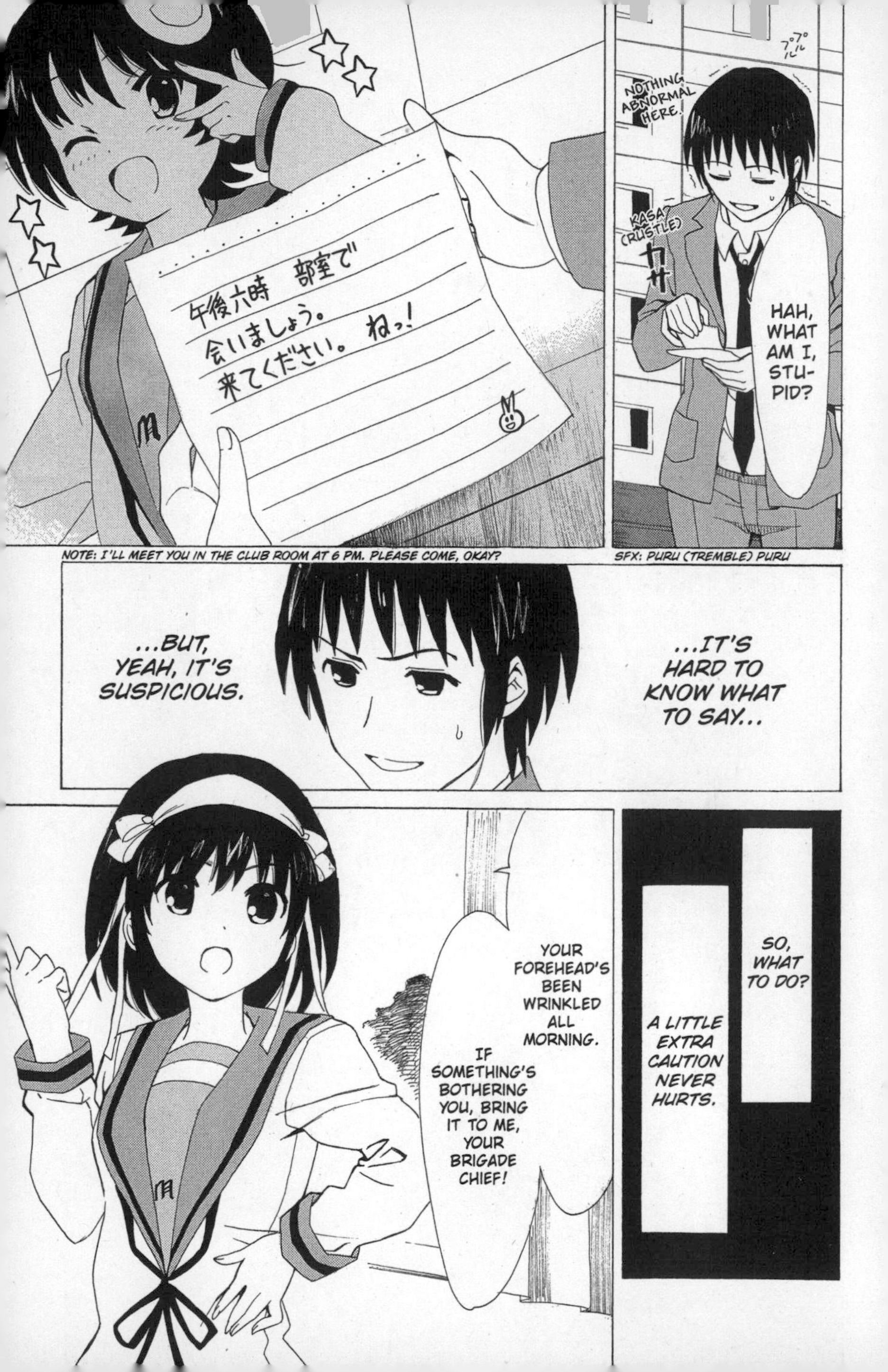
プルプル
NOTHING ABNORMAL HERE.
KASA (RUSTLE)
カサ
HAH, WHAT AM I, STUPID?
午後六時 部室で
会いましょう。
来てください。ねっ!
SFX: PURU (TREMBLE) PURU
NOTE: I'LL MEET YOU IN THE CLUB ROOM AT 6 PM. PLEASE COME, OKAY?
...IT'S HARD TO KNOW WHAT TO SAY...
...BUT, YEAH, IT'S SUSPICIOUS.
SO, WHAT TO DO?
A LITTLE EXTRA CAUTION NEVER HURTS.
YOUR FOREHEAD'S BEEN WRINKLED ALL MORNING.
IF SOMETHING'S BOTHERING YOU, BRING IT TO ME, YOUR BRIGADE CHIEF!

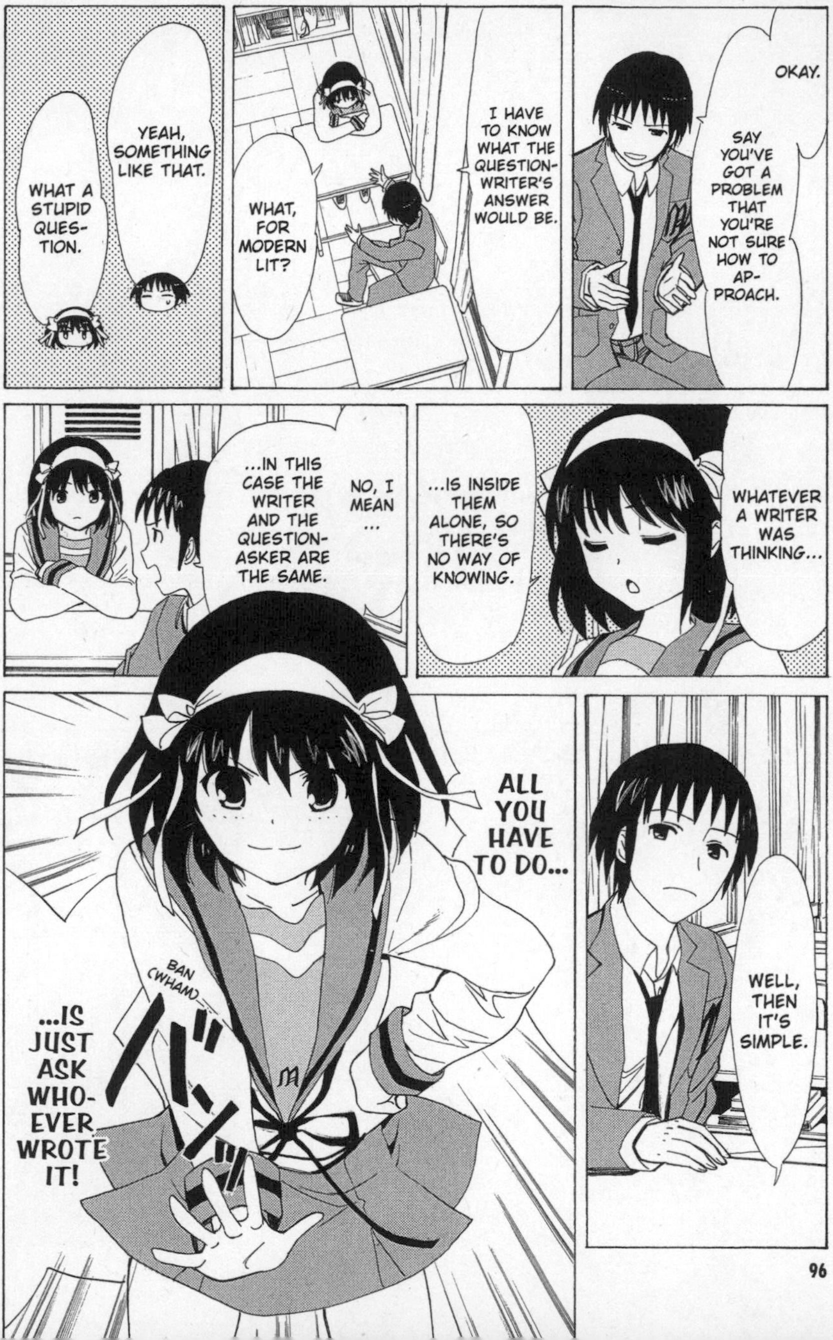
OKAY.
SAY YOU'VE GOT A PROBLEM THAT YOU'RE NOT SURE HOW TO APPROACH.
I HAVE TO KNOW WHAT THE QUESTION-WRITER'S ANSWER WOULD BE.
WHAT, FOR MODERN LIT?
YEAH, SOMETHING LIKE THAT.
WHAT A STUPID QUESTION.
WHATEVER A WRITER WAS THINKING...
...IS INSIDE THEM ALONE, SO THERE'S NO WAY OF KNOWING.
NO, I MEAN...
...IN THIS CASE THE WRITER AND THE QUESTION-ASKER ARE THE SAME.
WELL, THEN IT'S SIMPLE.
ALL YOU HAVE TO DO...
BAN (WHAM)
...IS JUST ASK WHOEVER WROTE IT!

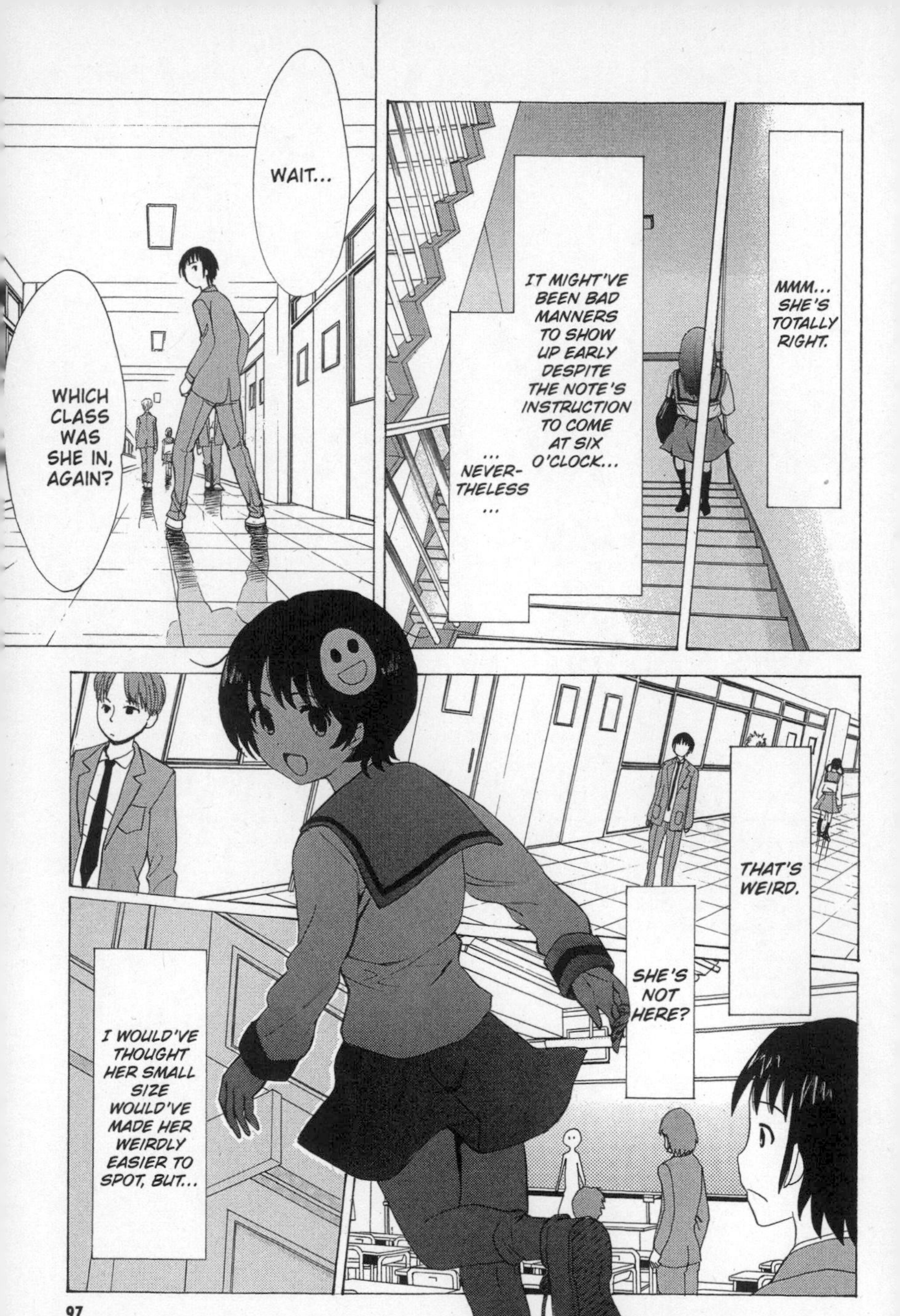
MMM... SHE'S TOTALLY RIGHT.
IT MIGHT'VE BEEN BAD MANNERS TO SHOW UP EARLY DESPITE THE NOTE'S INSTRUCTION TO COME AT SIX O'CLOCK...
...NEVER-THELESS...
WAIT...
WHICH CLASS WAS SHE IN, AGAIN?
THAT'S WEIRD.
SHE'S NOT HERE?
I WOULD'VE THOUGHT HER SMALL SIZE WOULD'VE MADE HER WEIRDLY EASIER TO SPOT, BUT...

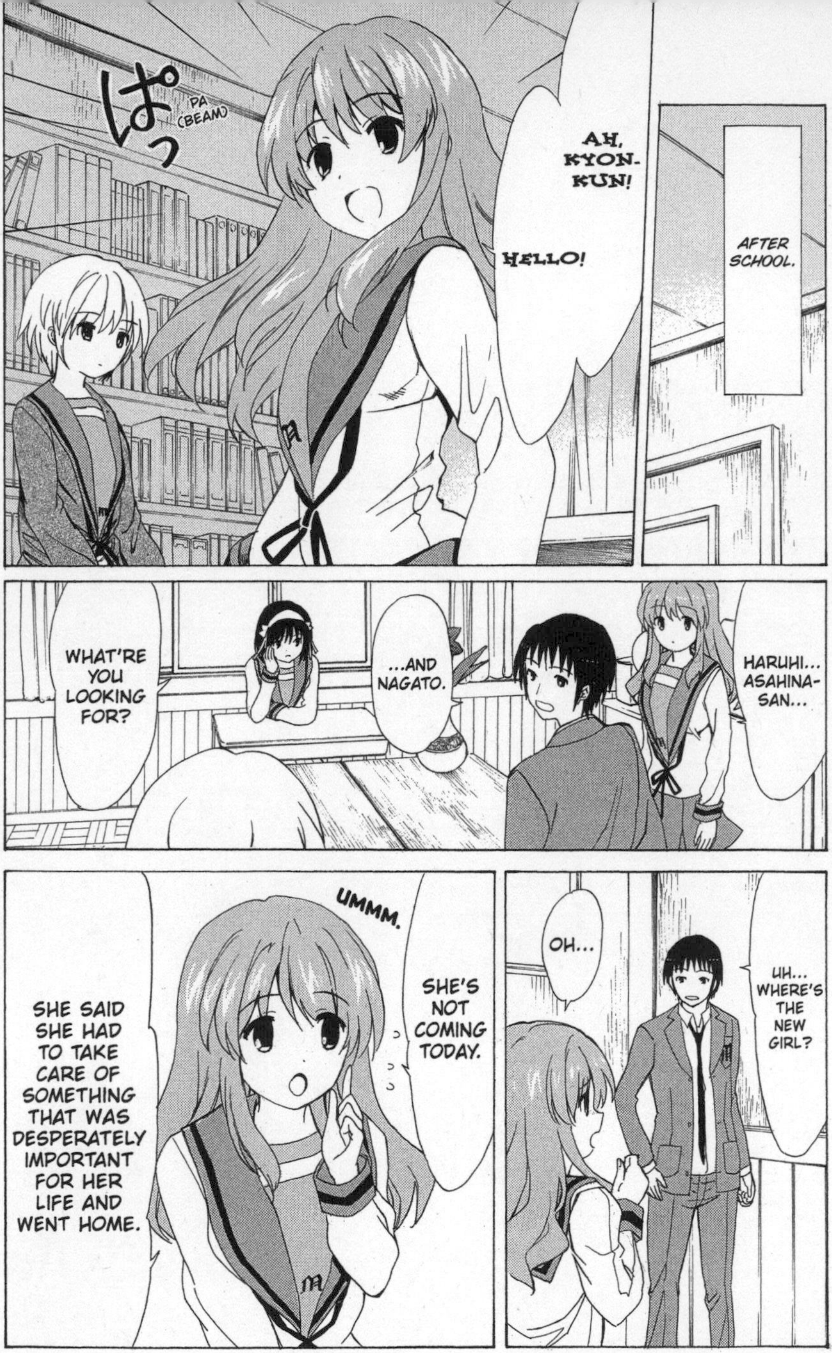

AFTER SCHOOL.
AH, KYON-KUN!
HELLO!
ぱっ
PA (BEAM)
HARUHI... ASAHINA-SAN...
...AND NAGATO.
WHAT'RE YOU LOOKING FOR?
UH... WHERE'S THE NEW GIRL?
OH...
UMMM.
SHE'S NOT COMING TODAY.
SHE SAID SHE HAD TO TAKE CARE OF SOMETHING THAT WAS DESPERATELY IMPORTANT FOR HER LIFE AND WENT HOME.

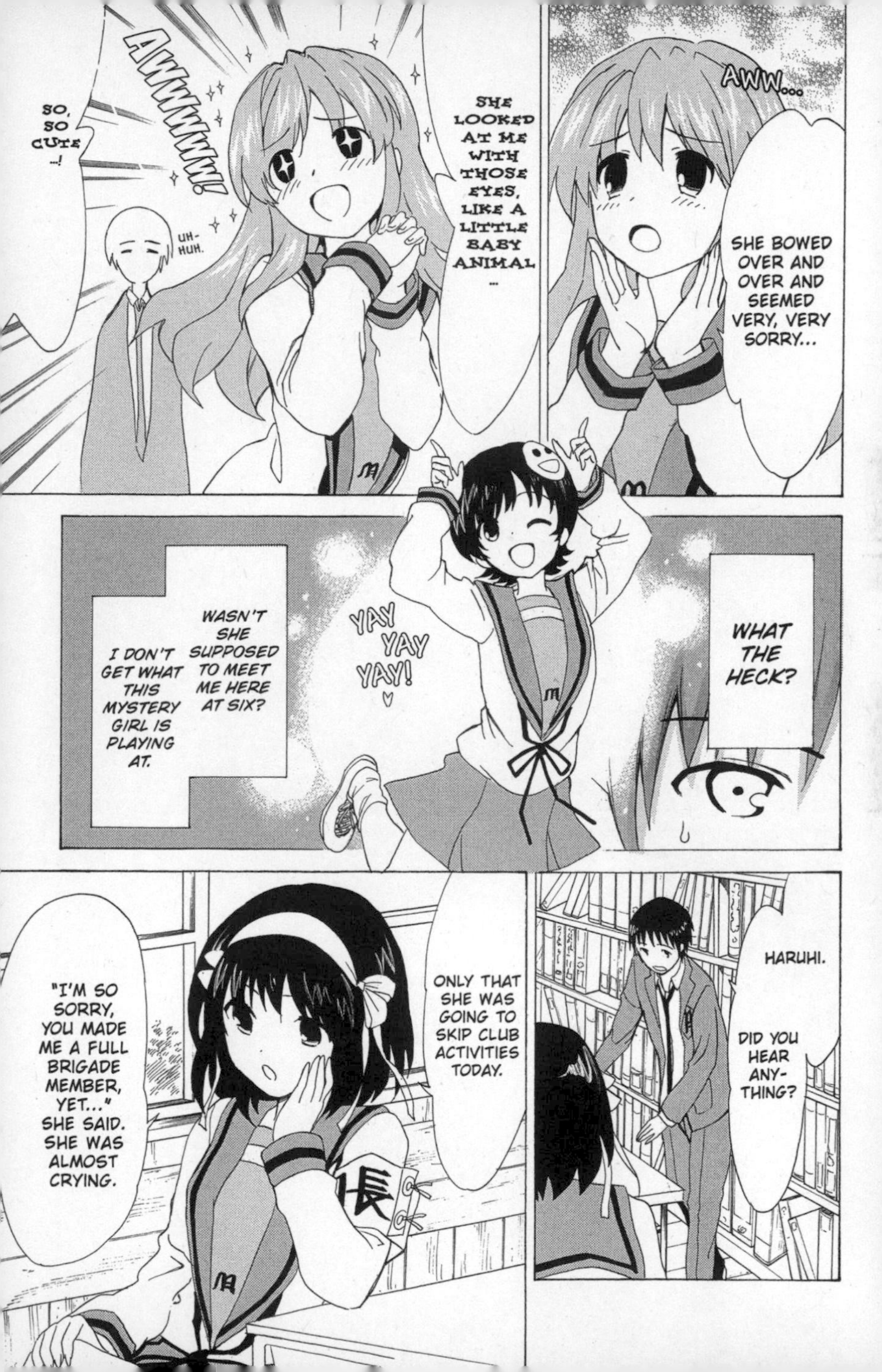
AWW...
SHE BOWED OVER AND OVER AND SEEMED VERY, VERY SORRY...
SHE LOOKED AT ME WITH THOSE EYES, LIKE A LITTLE BABY ANIMAL...
AWWWWWW!
SO, SO CUTE...!
UH-HUH.
WHAT THE HECK?
YAY YAY YAY!
WASN'T SHE SUPPOSED TO MEET ME HERE AT SIX?
I DON'T GET WHAT THIS MYSTERY GIRL IS PLAYING AT.
HARUHI.
DID YOU HEAR ANY-THING?
ONLY THAT SHE WAS GOING TO SKIP CLUB ACTIVITIES TODAY.
"I'M SO SORRY, YOU MADE ME A FULL BRIGADE MEMBER, YET..." SHE SAID. SHE WAS ALMOST CRYING.

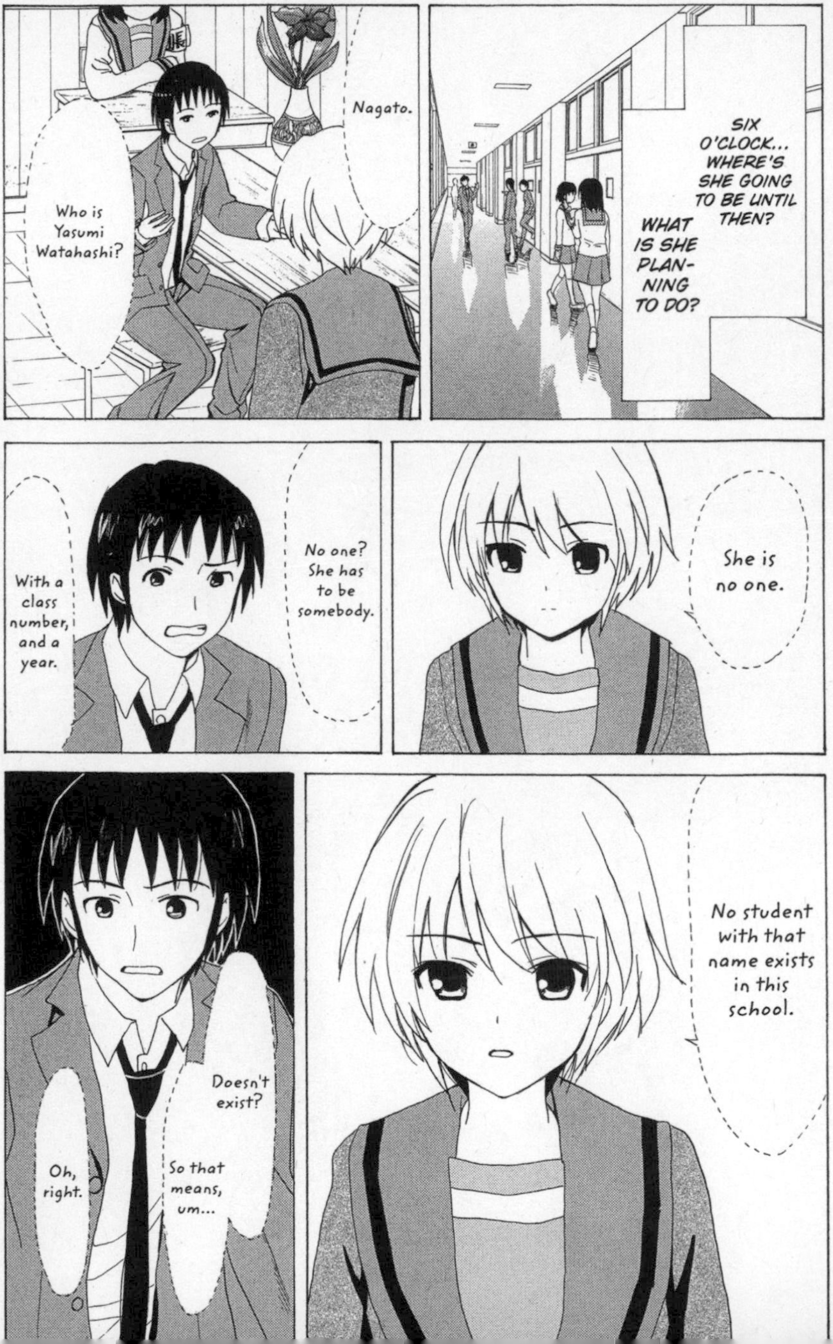
SIX O'CLOCK... WHERE'S SHE GOING TO BE UNTIL THEN?
WHAT IS SHE PLAN-NING TO DO?
Nagato.
Who is Yasumi Watahashi?
She is no one.
No one? She has to be somebody.
With a class number, and a year.
No student with that name exists in this school.
Doesn't exist?
So that means, um...
Oh, right.

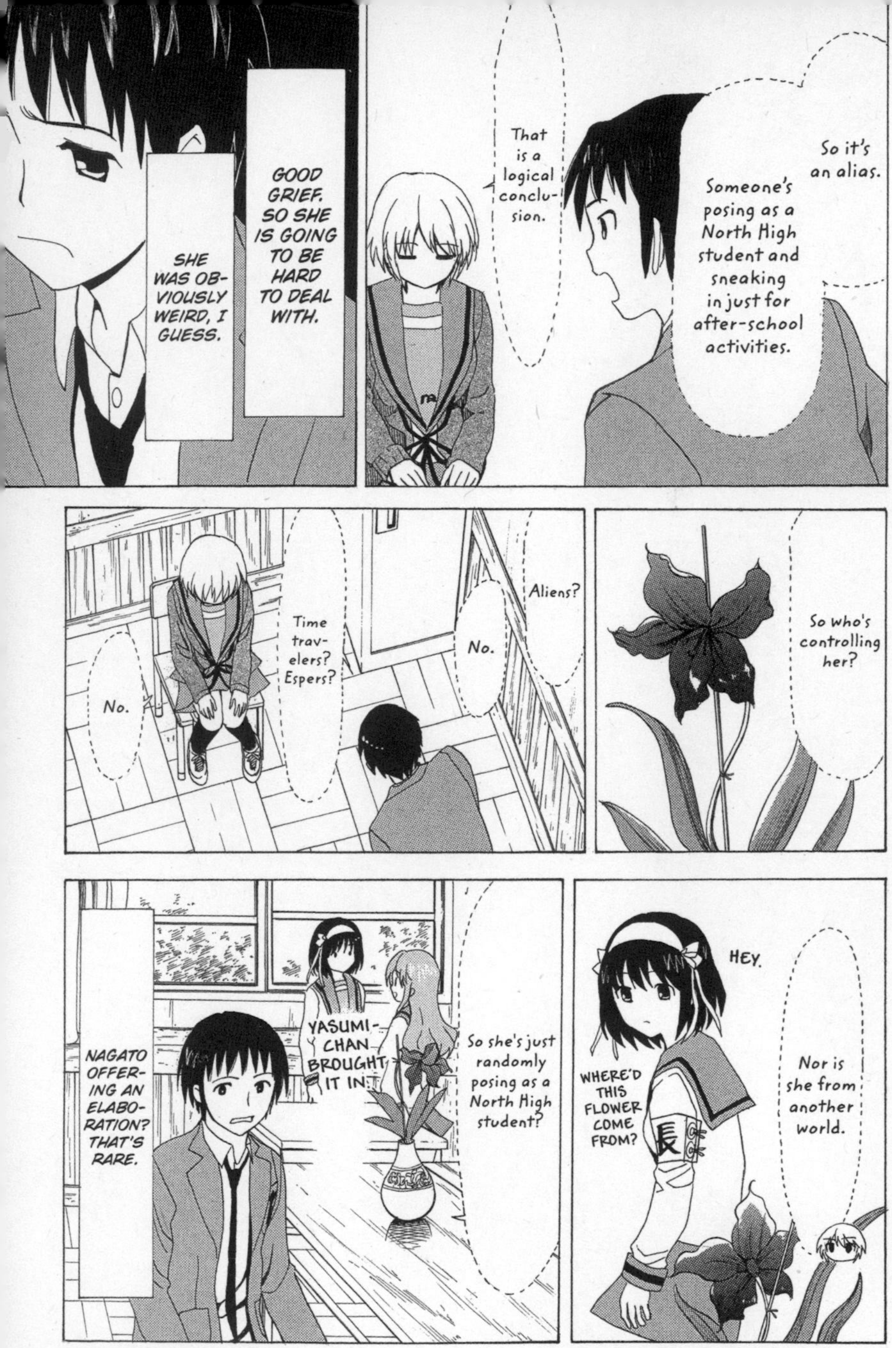
So it's an alias.
Someone's posing as a North High student and sneaking in just for after-school activities.
That is a logical conclusion.
GOOD GRIEF. SO SHE IS GOING TO BE HARD TO DEAL WITH.
SHE WAS OBVIOUSLY WEIRD, I GUESS.
So who's controlling her?
Aliens?
No.
Time travelers? Espers?
No.
Nor is she from another world.
HEY.
WHERE'D THIS FLOWER COME FROM?
So she's just randomly posing as a North High student?
YASUMI-CHAN BROUGHT IT IN.
NAGATO OFFERING AN ELABORATION? THAT'S RARE.

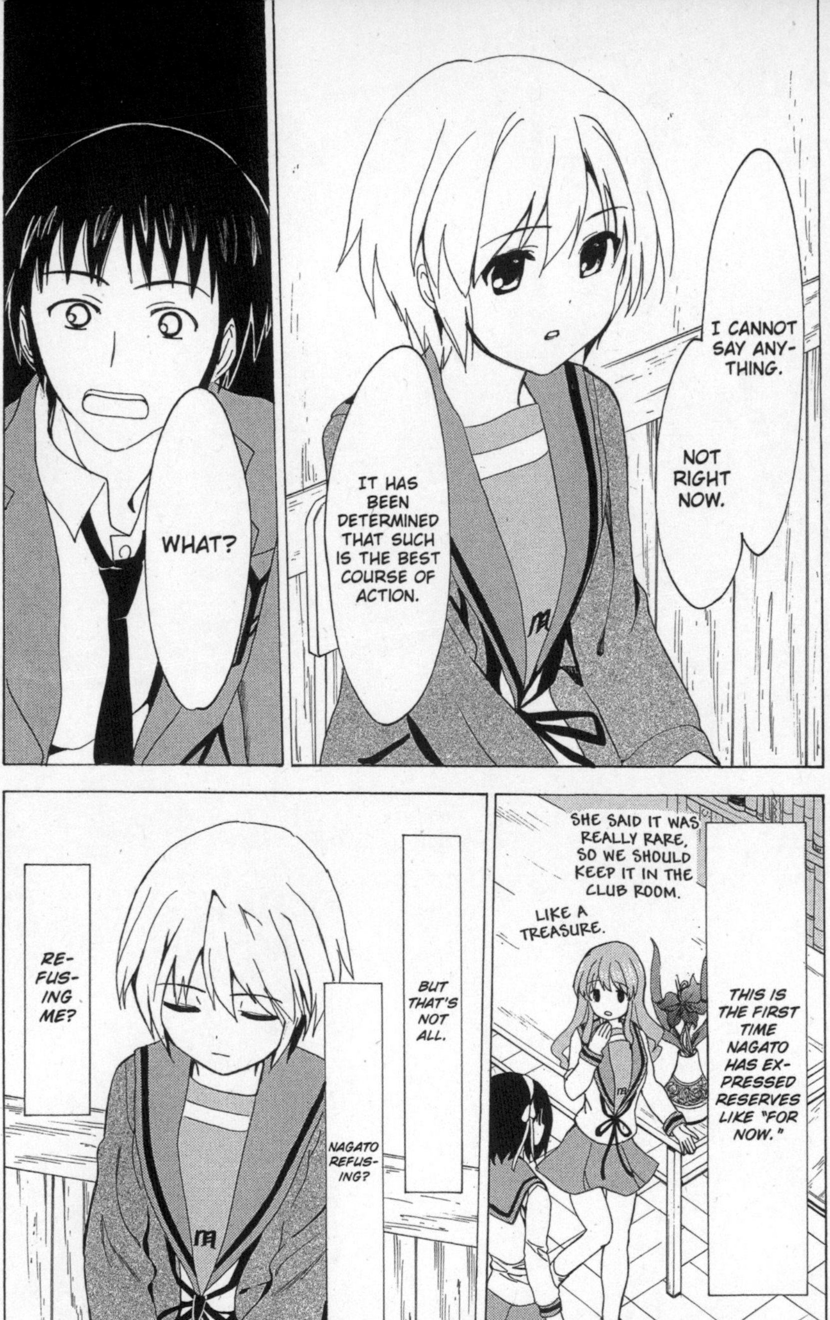
I CANNOT SAY ANY-THING.
NOT RIGHT NOW.
IT HAS BEEN DETERMINED THAT SUCH IS THE BEST COURSE OF ACTION.
WHAT?
THIS IS THE FIRST TIME NAGATO HAS EX-PRESSED RESERVES LIKE "FOR NOW."
SHE SAID IT WAS REALLY RARE, SO WE SHOULD KEEP IT IN THE CLUB ROOM.
LIKE A TREASURE.
BUT THAT'S NOT ALL.
NAGATO REFUS-ING?
RE-FUS-ING ME?

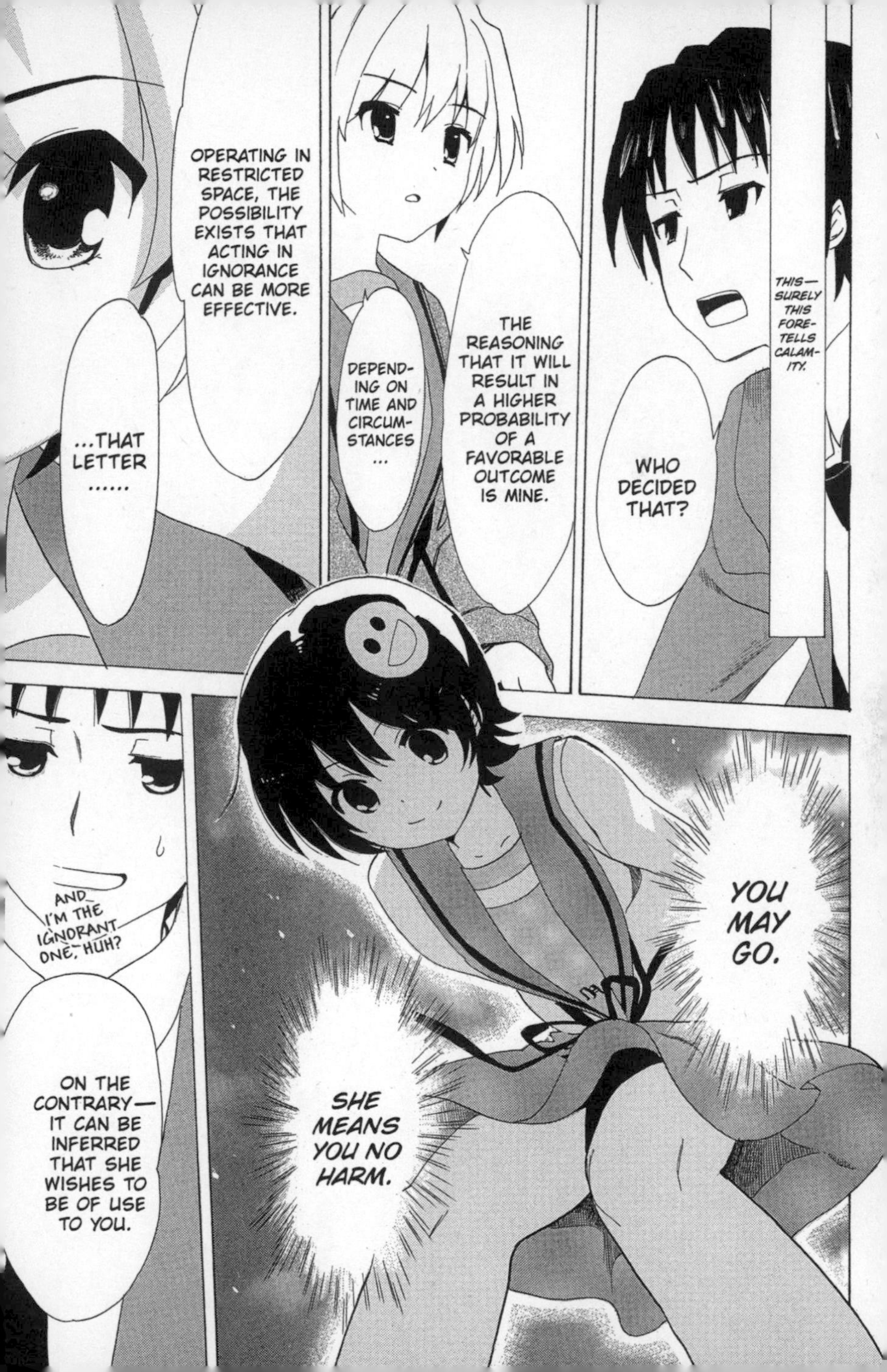
THIS— SURELY THIS FORE-TELLS CALAM-ITY.
WHO DECIDED THAT?
THE REASONING THAT IT WILL RESULT IN A HIGHER PROBABILITY OF A FAVORABLE OUTCOME IS MINE.
DEPEND-ING ON TIME AND CIRCUM-STANCES ...
OPERATING IN RESTRICTED SPACE, THE POSSIBILITY EXISTS THAT ACTING IN IGNORANCE CAN BE MORE EFFECTIVE.
...THAT LETTER ......
YOU MAY GO.
SHE MEANS YOU NO HARM.
AND I'M THE IGNORANT ONE, HUH?
ON THE CONTRARY— IT CAN BE INFERRED THAT SHE WISHES TO BE OF USE TO YOU.

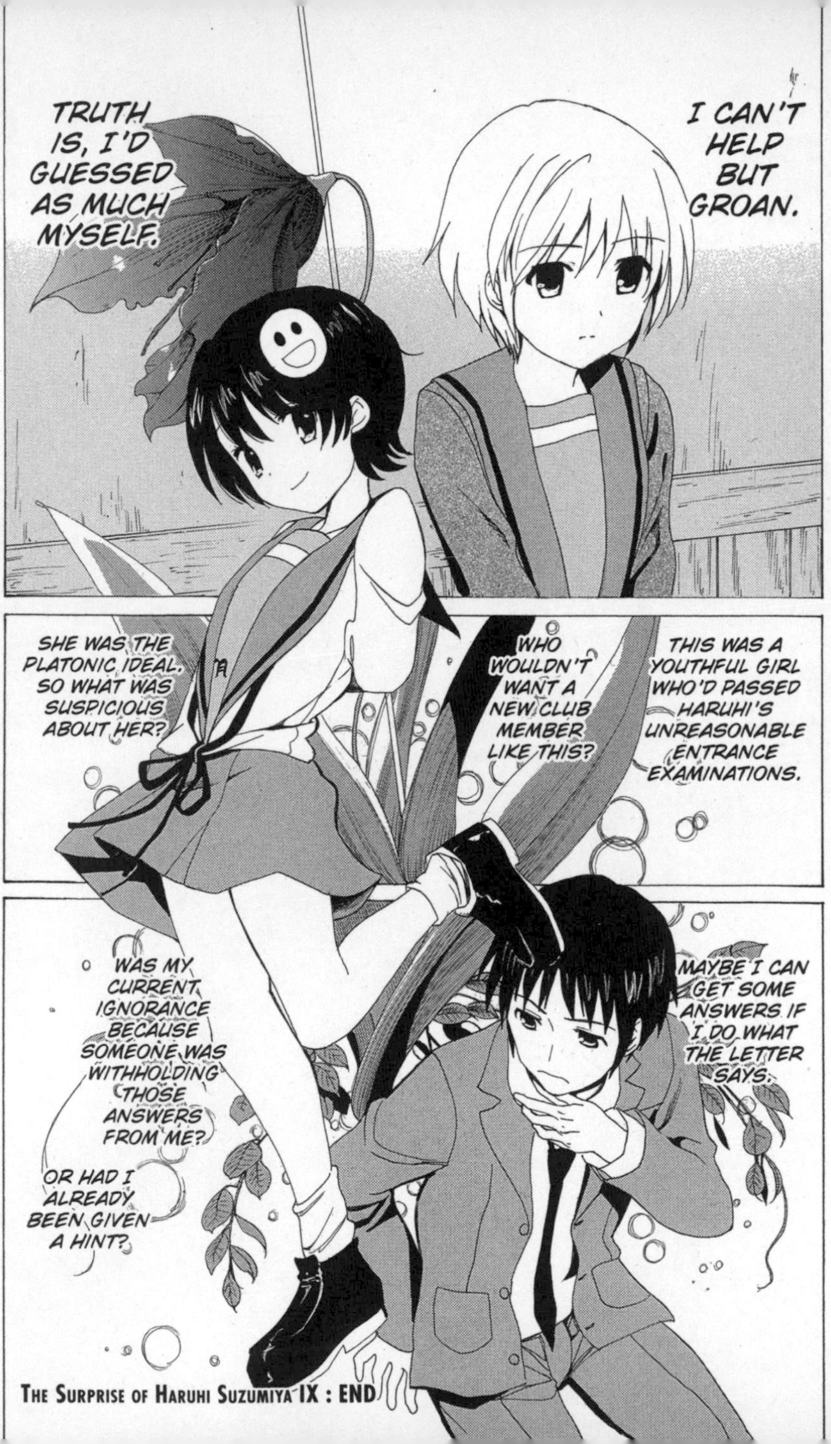
I CAN'T HELP BUT GROAN.
TRUTH IS, I'D GUESSED AS MUCH MYSELF.
THIS WAS A YOUTHFUL GIRL WHO'D PASSED HARUHI'S UNREASONABLE ENTRANCE EXAMINATIONS.
WHO WOULDN'T WANT A NEW CLUB MEMBER LIKE THIS?
SHE WAS THE PLATONIC IDEAL. SO WHAT WAS SUSPICIOUS ABOUT HER?
MAYBE I CAN GET SOME ANSWERS IF I DO WHAT THE LETTER SAYS.
WAS MY CURRENT IGNORANCE BECAUSE SOMEONE WAS WITHHOLDING THOSE ANSWERS FROM ME?
OR HAD I ALREADY BEEN GIVEN A HINT?
THE SURPRISE OF HARUHI SUZUMIYA IX : END

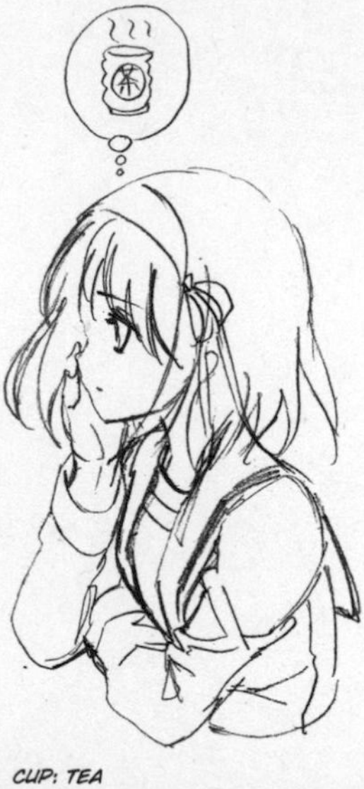
茶

CUP: TEA

THE MELANCHOLY OF HARUHI SUZUMIYA

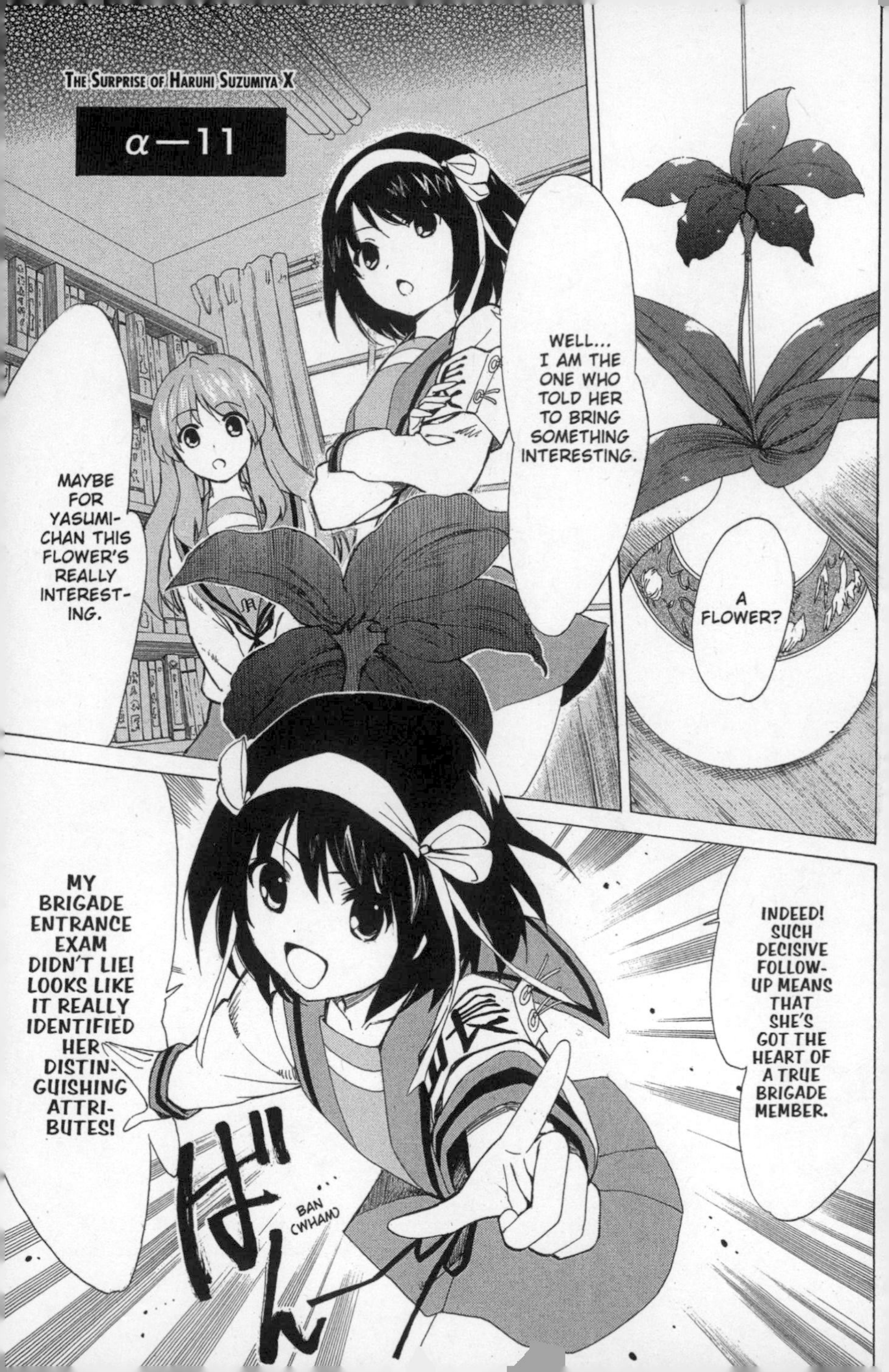
The Surprise of Haruhi Suzumiya X
α—11
A FLOWER?
WELL... I AM THE ONE WHO TOLD HER TO BRING SOMETHING INTERESTING.
MAYBE FOR YASUMI-CHAN THIS FLOWER'S REALLY INTEREST-ING.
INDEED! SUCH DECISIVE FOLLOW-UP MEANS THAT SHE'S GOT THE HEART OF A TRUE BRIGADE MEMBER.
MY BRIGADE ENTRANCE EXAM DIDN'T LIE! LOOKS LIKE IT REALLY IDENTIFIED HER DISTIN-GUISHING ATTRI-BUTES!
ばん
BAN (WHAM)

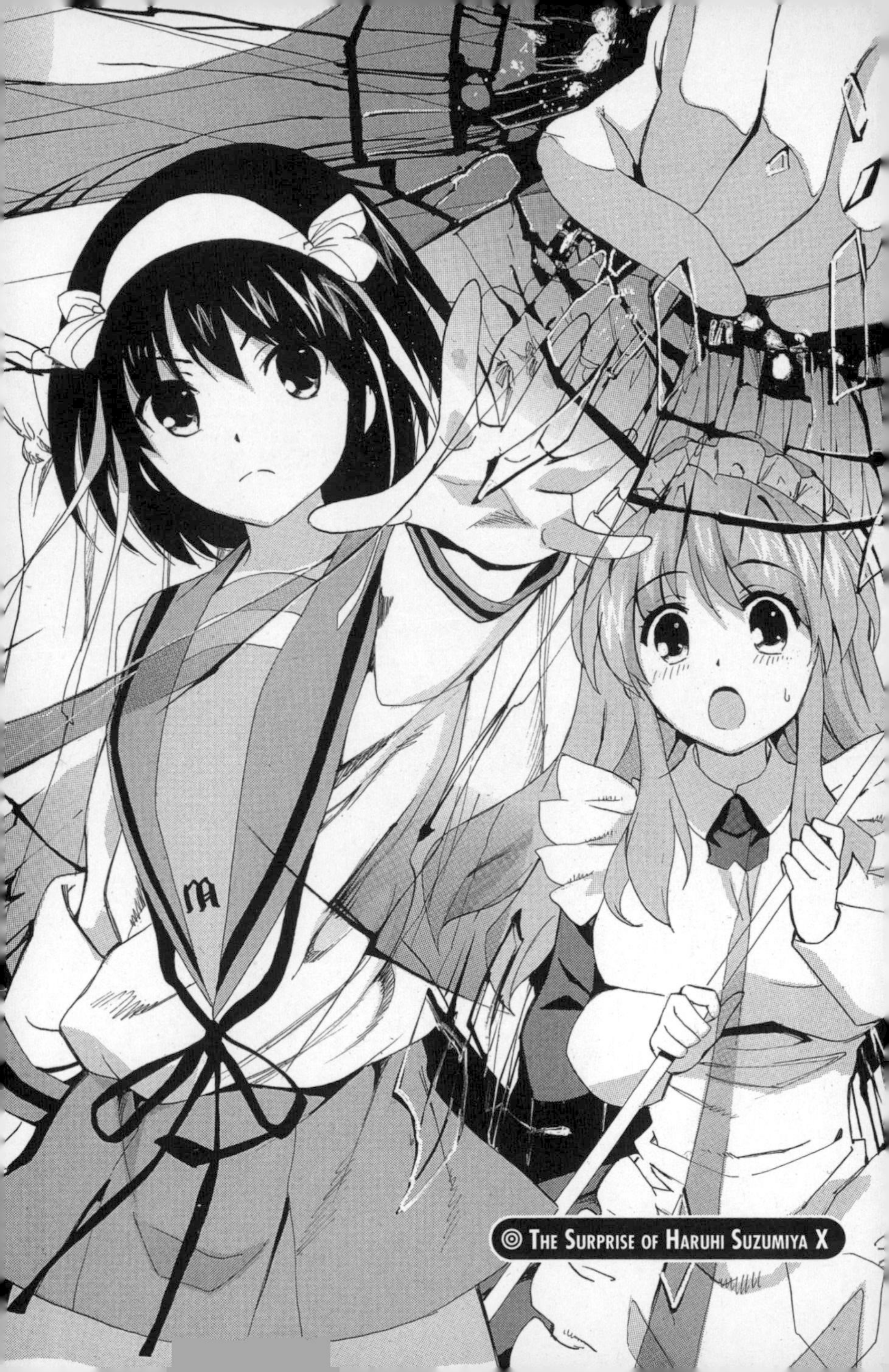
◎ The Surprise of Haruhi Suzumiya X

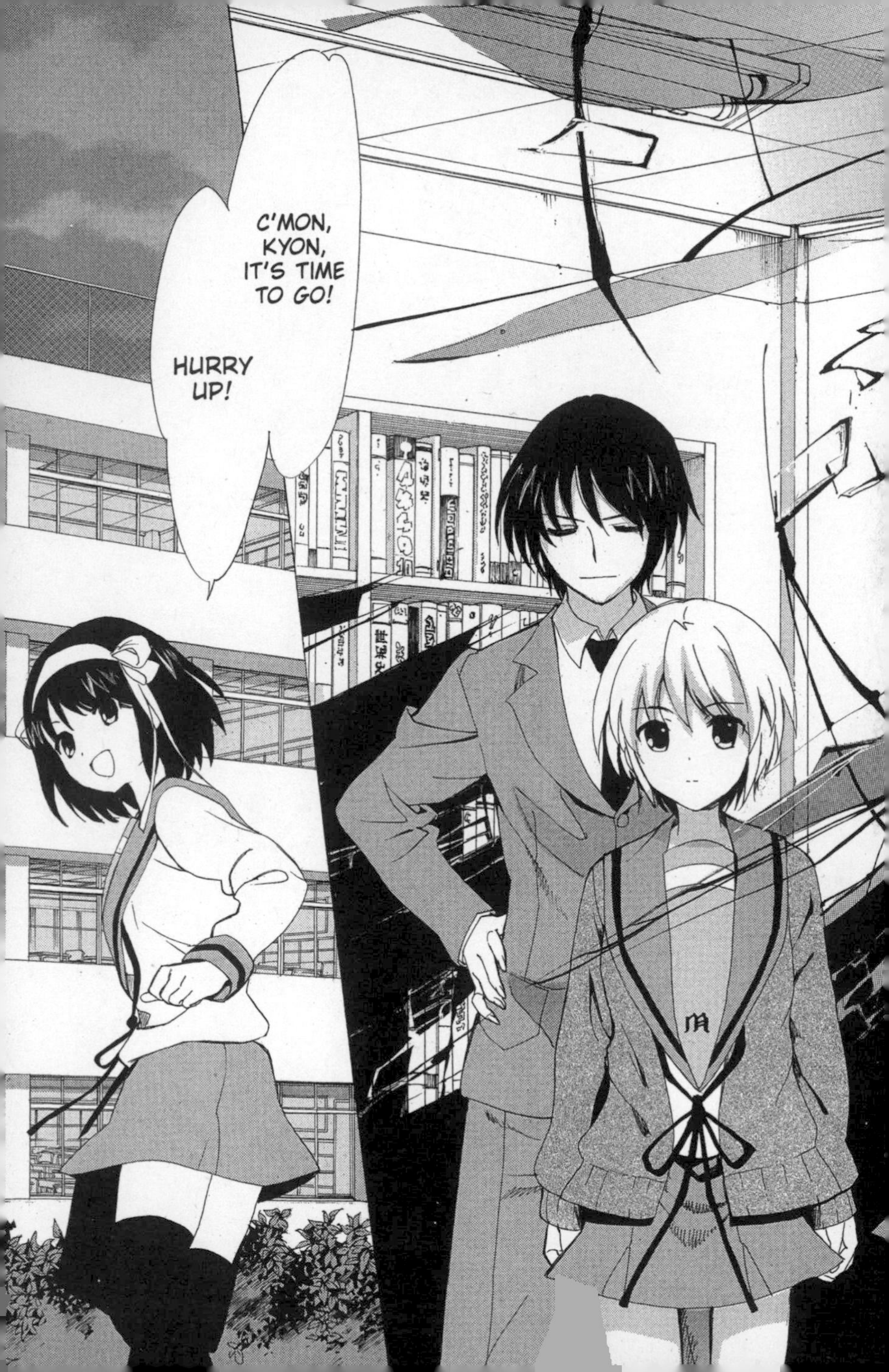
C'MON, KYON, IT'S TIME TO GO!
HURRY UP!

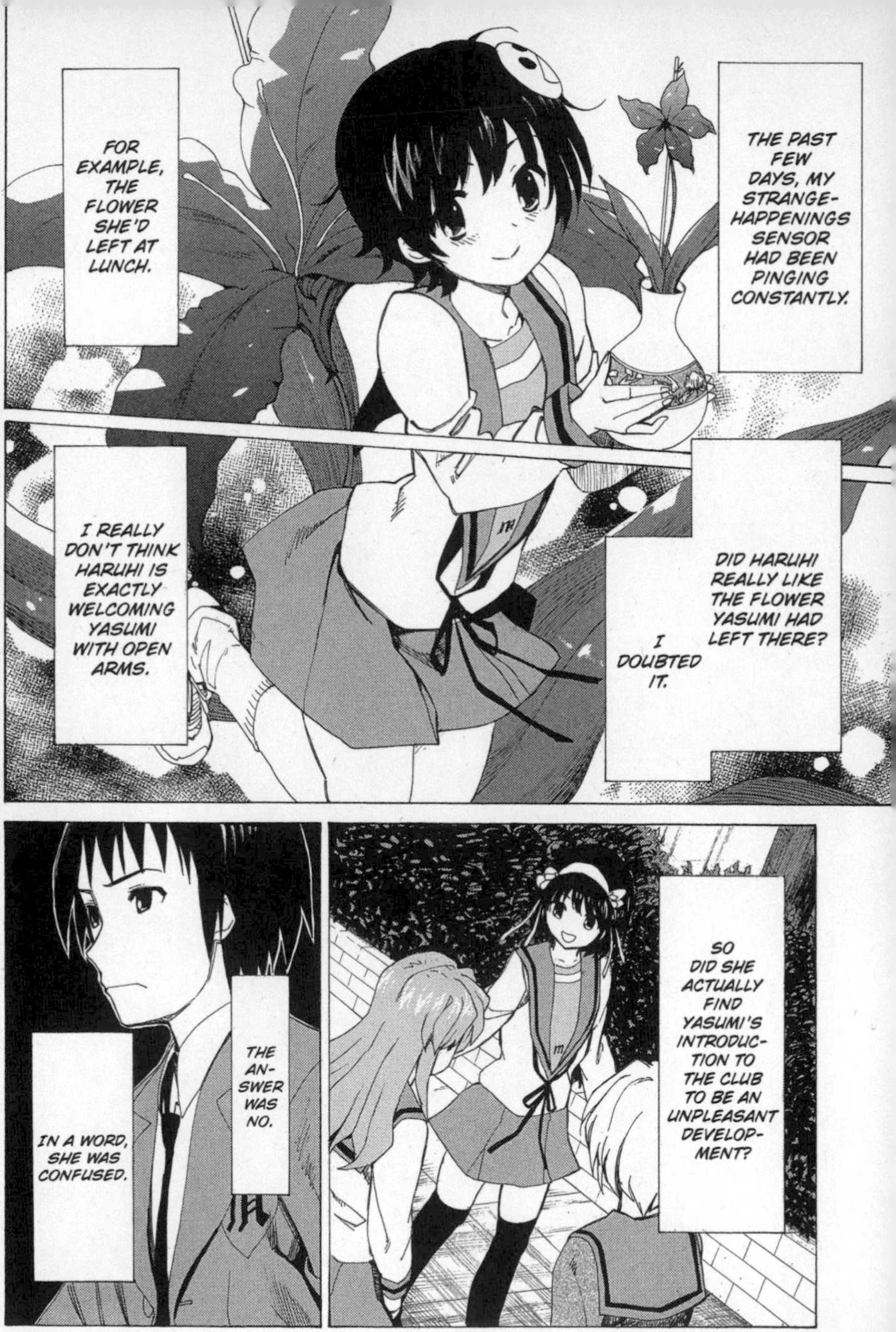
THE PAST FEW DAYS, MY STRANGE-HAPPENINGS SENSOR HAD BEEN PINGING CONSTANTLY.
FOR EXAMPLE, THE FLOWER SHE'D LEFT AT LUNCH.
DID HARUHI REALLY LIKE THE FLOWER YASUMI HAD LEFT THERE?
I DOUBTED IT.
I REALLY DON'T THINK HARUHI IS EXACTLY WELCOMING YASUMI WITH OPEN ARMS.
SO DID SHE ACTUALLY FIND YASUMI'S INTRODUC-TION TO THE CLUB TO BE AN UNPLEASANT DEVELOP-MENT?
THE AN-SWER WAS NO.
IN A WORD, SHE WAS CONFUSED.

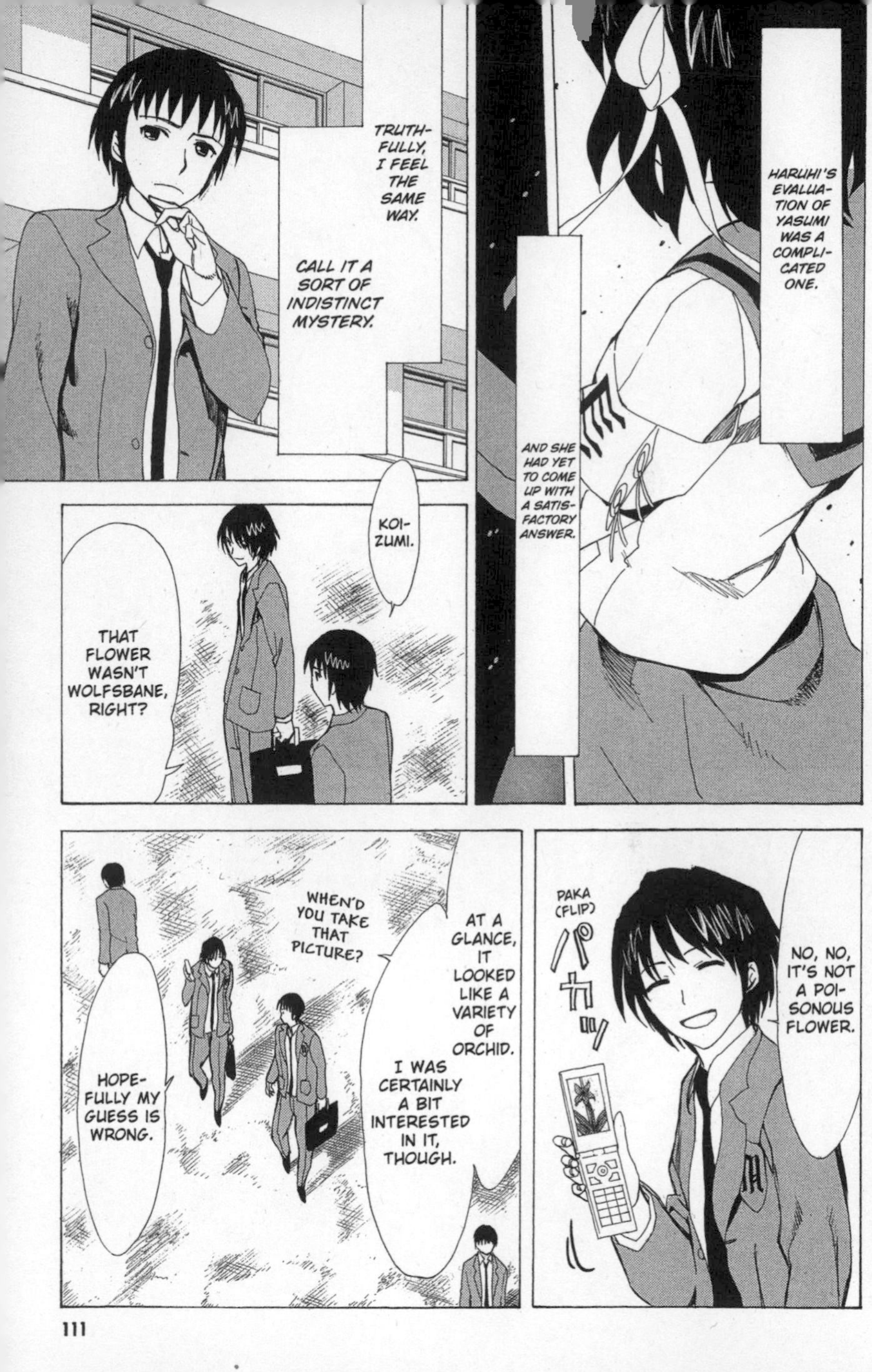
HARUHI'S EVALUATION OF YASUMI WAS A COMPLICATED ONE.
AND SHE HAD YET TO COME UP WITH A SATISFACTORY ANSWER.
TRUTHFULLY, I FEEL THE SAME WAY.
CALL IT A SORT OF INDISTINCT MYSTERY.
KOIZUMI.
THAT FLOWER WASN'T WOLFSBANE, RIGHT?
NO, NO, IT'S NOT A POISONOUS FLOWER.
PAKA (FLIP)
パカッ
AT A GLANCE, IT LOOKED LIKE A VARIETY OF ORCHID.
WHEN'D YOU TAKE THAT PICTURE?
I WAS CERTAINLY A BIT INTERESTED IN IT, THOUGH.
HOPEFULLY MY GUESS IS WRONG.

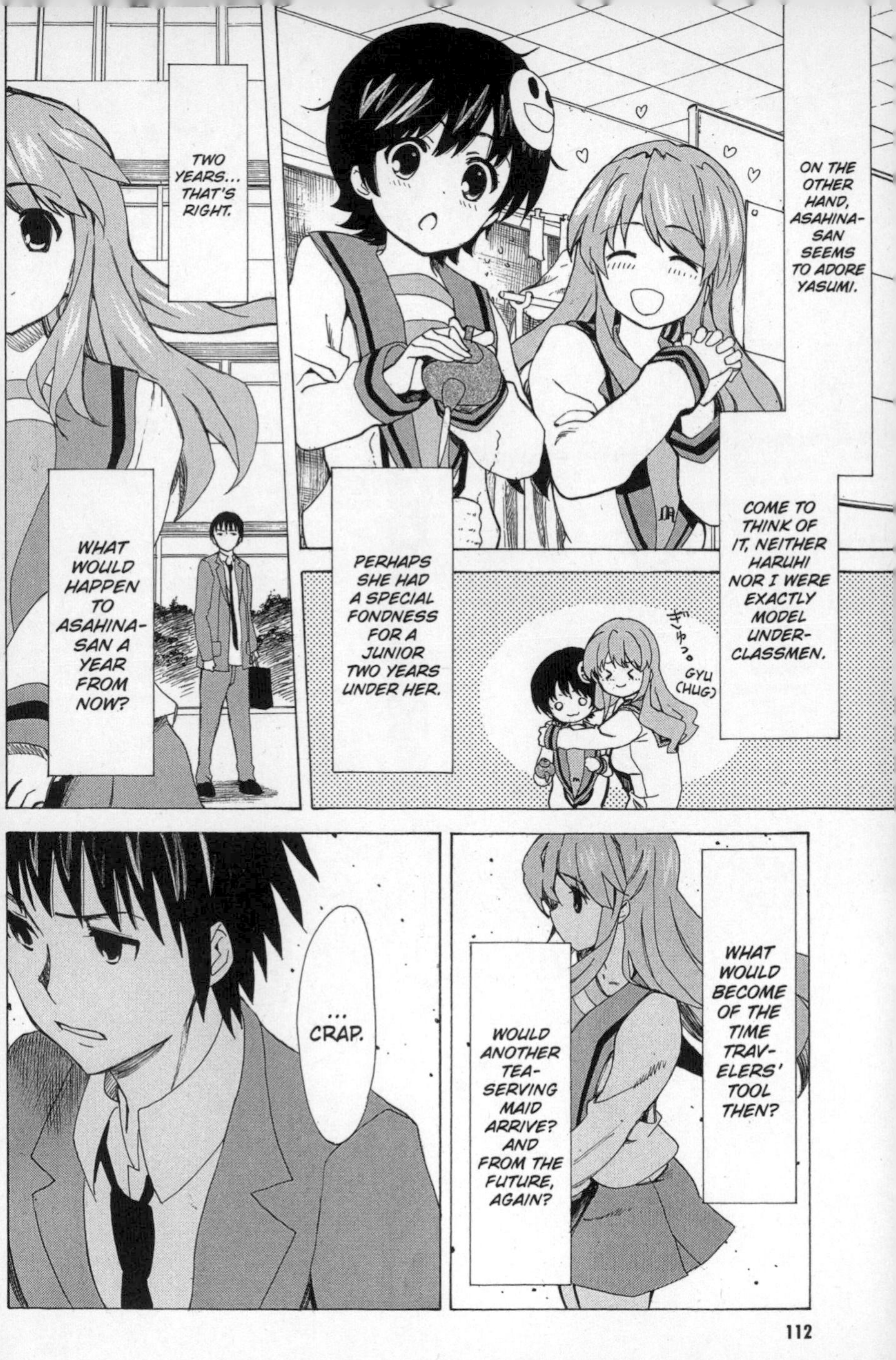
ON THE OTHER HAND, ASAHINA-SAN SEEMS TO ADORE YASUMI.
PERHAPS SHE HAD A SPECIAL FONDNESS FOR A JUNIOR TWO YEARS UNDER HER.
COME TO THINK OF IT, NEITHER HARUHI NOR I WERE EXACTLY MODEL UNDER-CLASSMEN.
ぎゅっ
GYU (HUG)
TWO YEARS... THAT'S RIGHT.
WHAT WOULD HAPPEN TO ASAHINA-SAN A YEAR FROM NOW?
WHAT WOULD BECOME OF THE TIME TRAV-ELERS' TOOL THEN?
WOULD ANOTHER TEA-SERVING MAID ARRIVE? AND FROM THE FUTURE, AGAIN?
... CRAP.

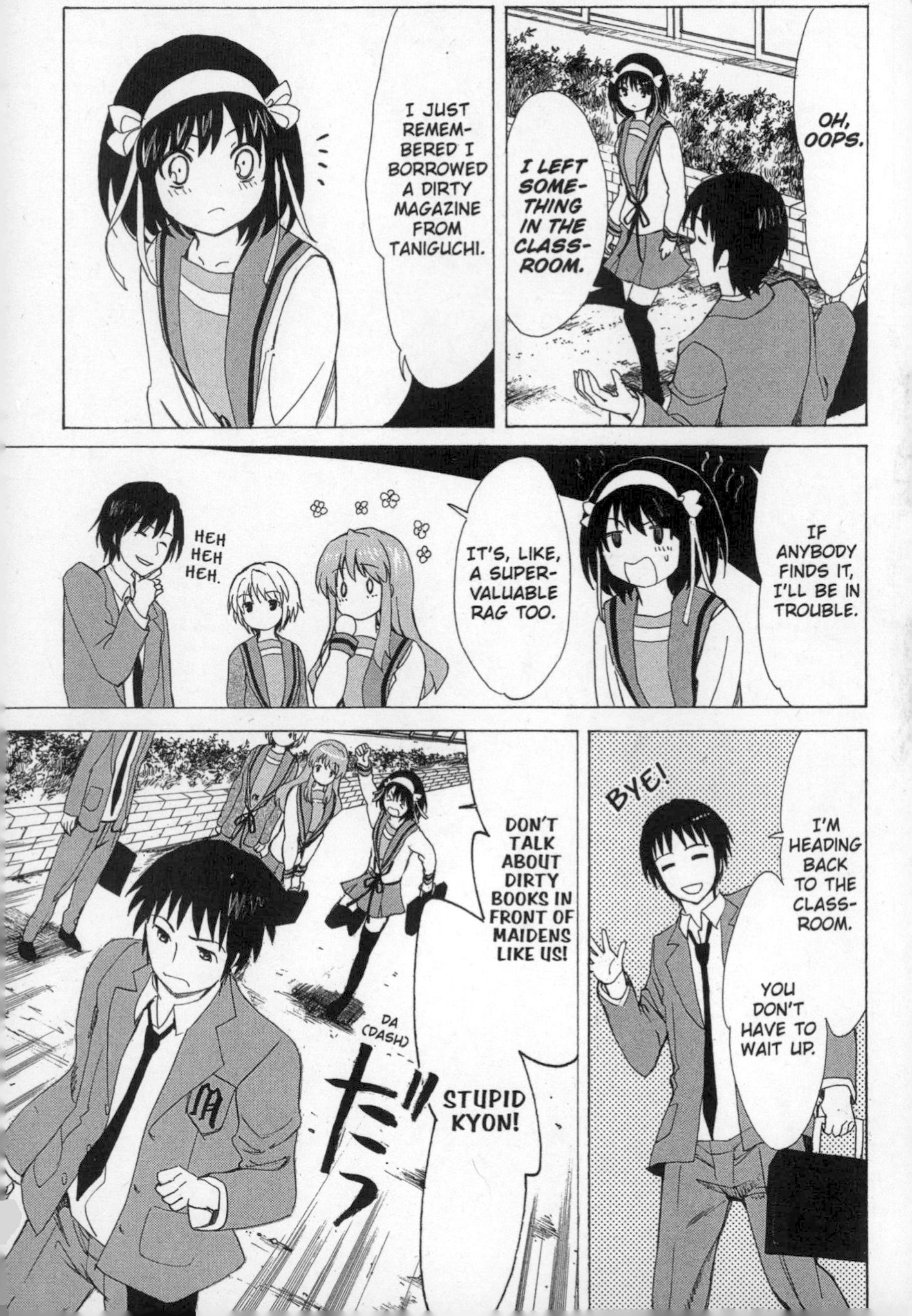
OH, OOPS.
I LEFT SOMETHING IN THE CLASSROOM.
I JUST REMEMBERED I BORROWED A DIRTY MAGAZINE FROM TANIGUCHI.
IF ANYBODY FINDS IT, I'LL BE IN TROUBLE.
IT'S, LIKE, A SUPER-VALUABLE RAG TOO.
HEH HEH HEH.
I'M HEADING BACK TO THE CLASSROOM.
YOU DON'T HAVE TO WAIT UP.
BYE!
DON'T TALK ABOUT DIRTY BOOKS IN FRONT OF MAIDENS LIKE US!
STUPID KYON!
DA (DASH)

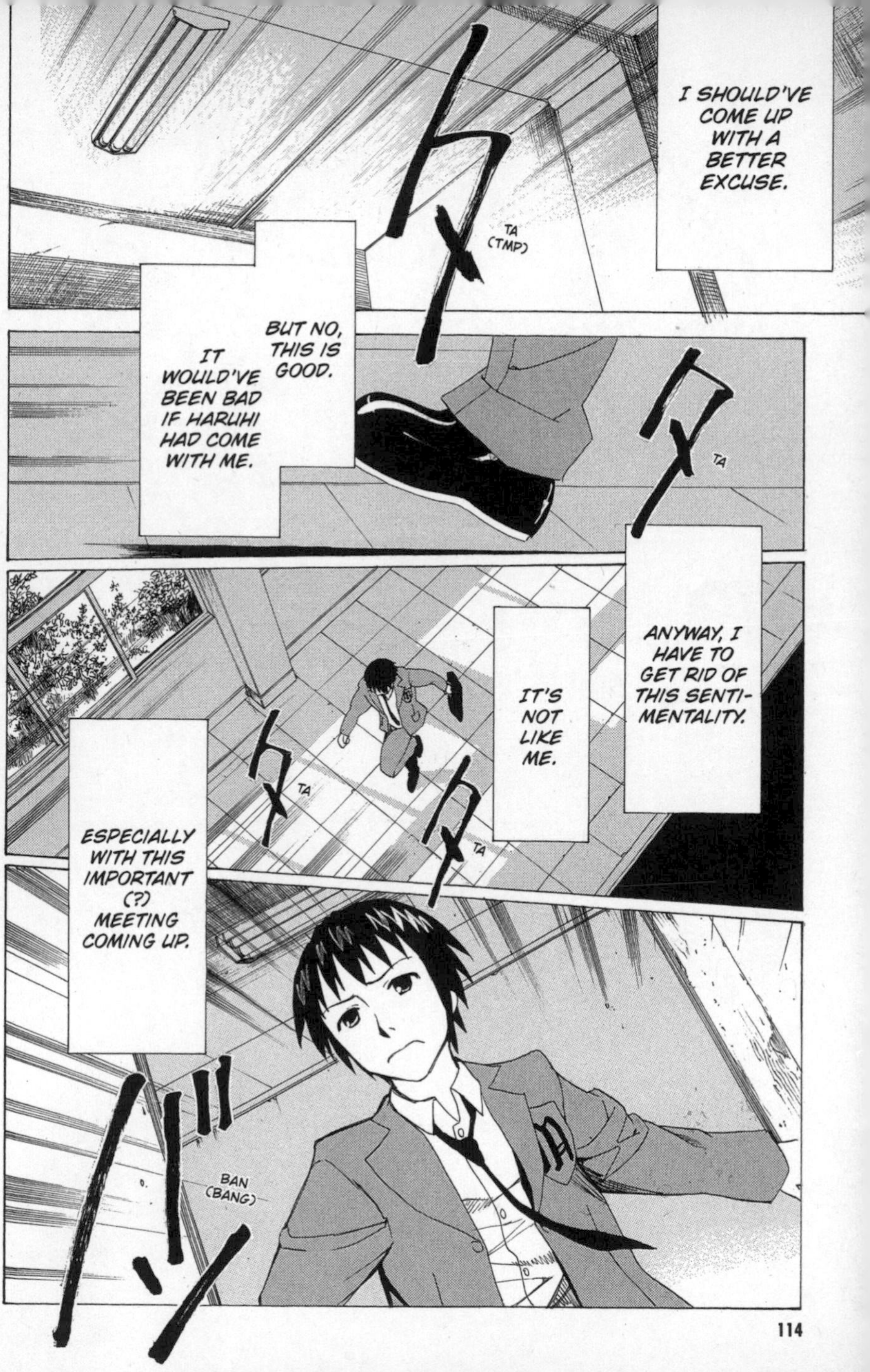

I SHOULD'VE COME UP WITH A BETTER EXCUSE.
TA (TMP)
TA
BUT NO, THIS IS GOOD.
IT WOULD'VE BEEN BAD IF HARUHI HAD COME WITH ME.
ANYWAY, I HAVE TO GET RID OF THIS SENTI-MENTALITY.
IT'S NOT LIKE ME.
TA
TA
ESPECIALLY WITH THIS IMPORTANT (?) MEETING COMING UP.
BAN (BANG)

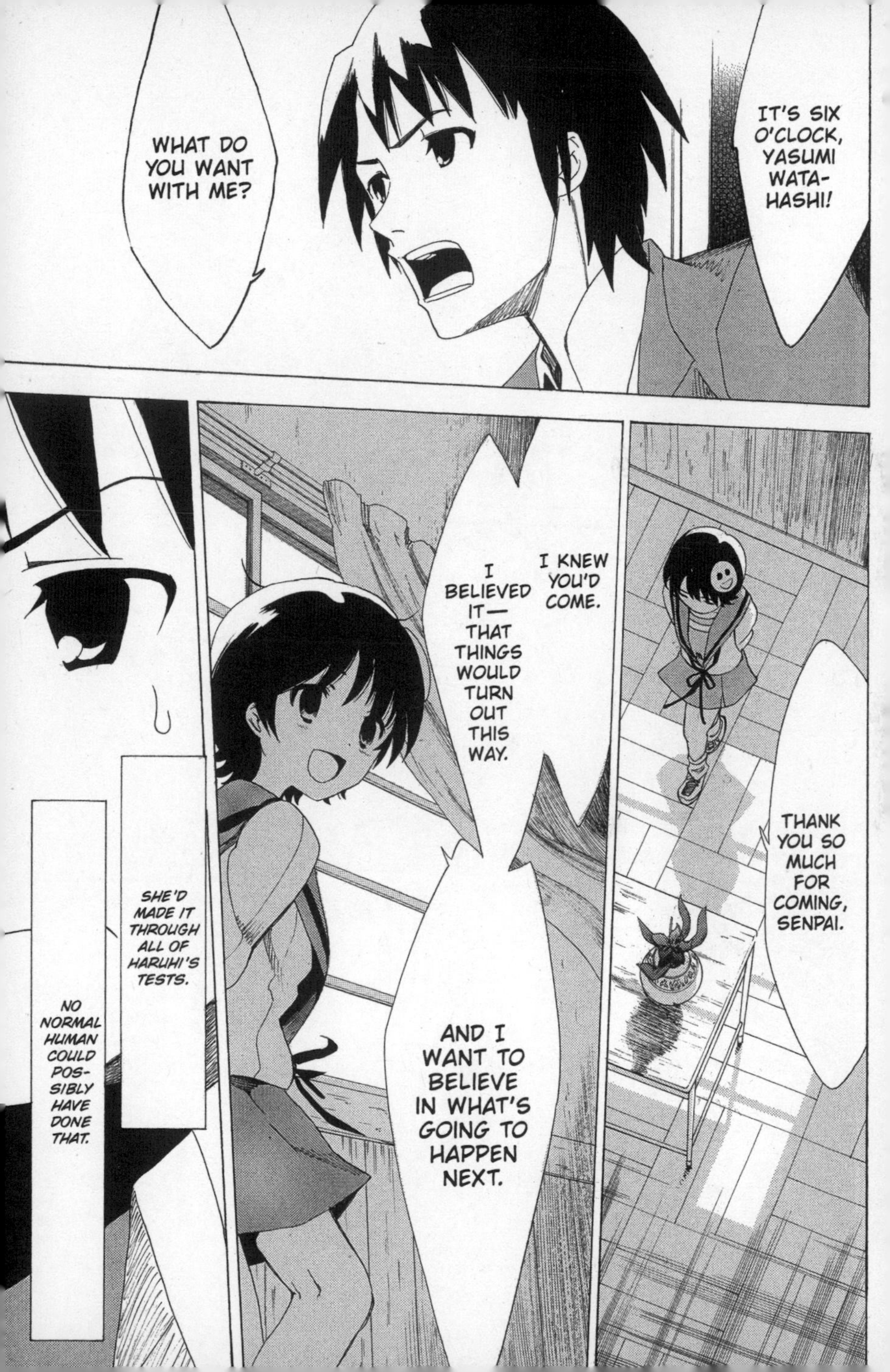
IT'S SIX O'CLOCK, YASUMI WATA-HASHI!
WHAT DO YOU WANT WITH ME?
THANK YOU SO MUCH FOR COMING, SENPAI.
I KNEW YOU'D COME.
I BELIEVED IT— THAT THINGS WOULD TURN OUT THIS WAY.
AND I WANT TO BELIEVE IN WHAT'S GOING TO HAPPEN NEXT.
SHE'D MADE IT THROUGH ALL OF HARUHI'S TESTS.
NO NORMAL HUMAN COULD POS-SIBLY HAVE DONE THAT.

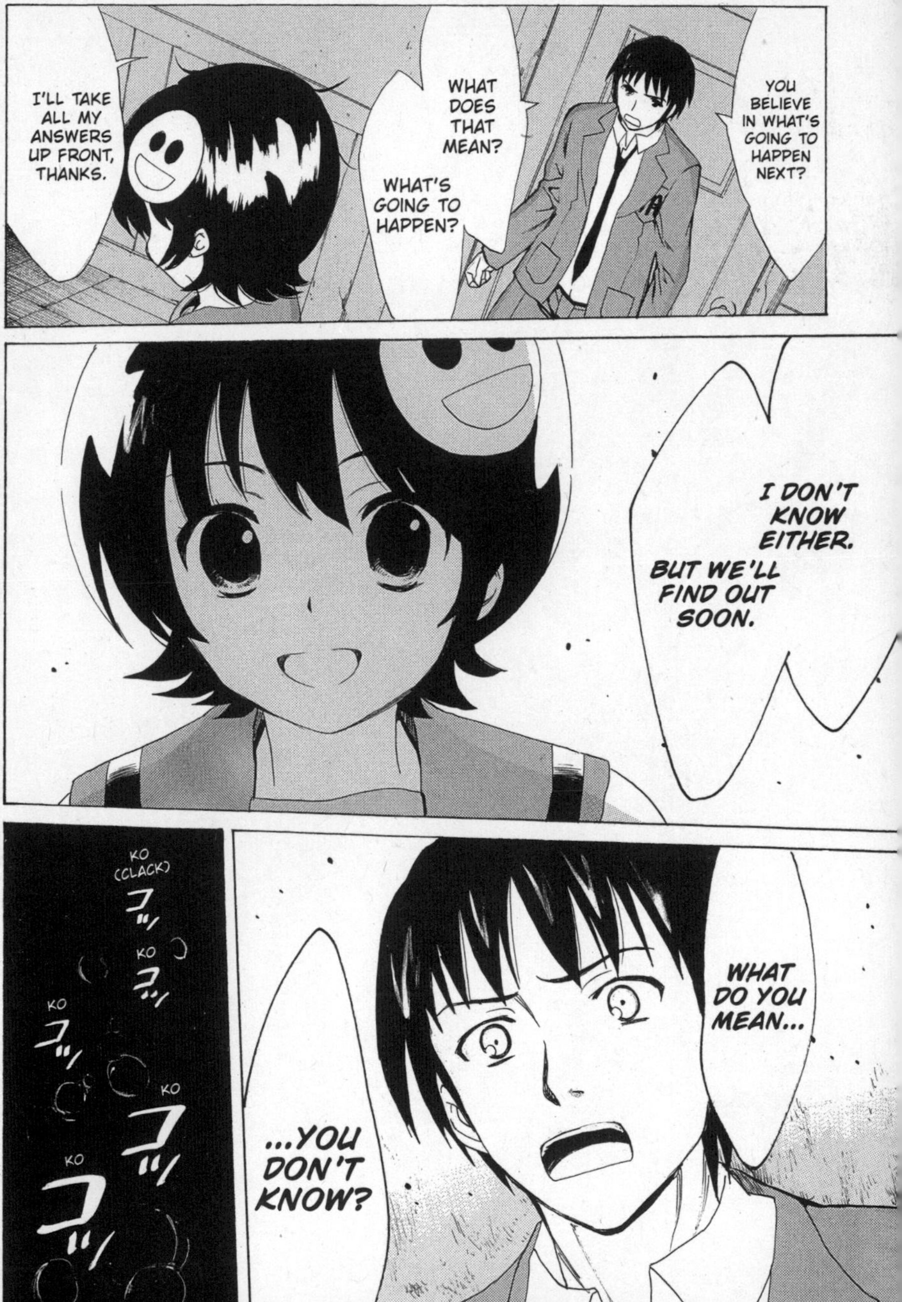
YOU BELIEVE IN WHAT'S GOING TO HAPPEN NEXT?
WHAT DOES THAT MEAN?
WHAT'S GOING TO HAPPEN?
I'LL TAKE ALL MY ANSWERS UP FRONT, THANKS.
I DON'T KNOW EITHER.
BUT WE'LL FIND OUT SOON.
WHAT DO YOU MEAN...
...YOU DON'T KNOW?
KO (CLACK) コッ
KO コッ
KO コッ
KO コッ
KO コッ

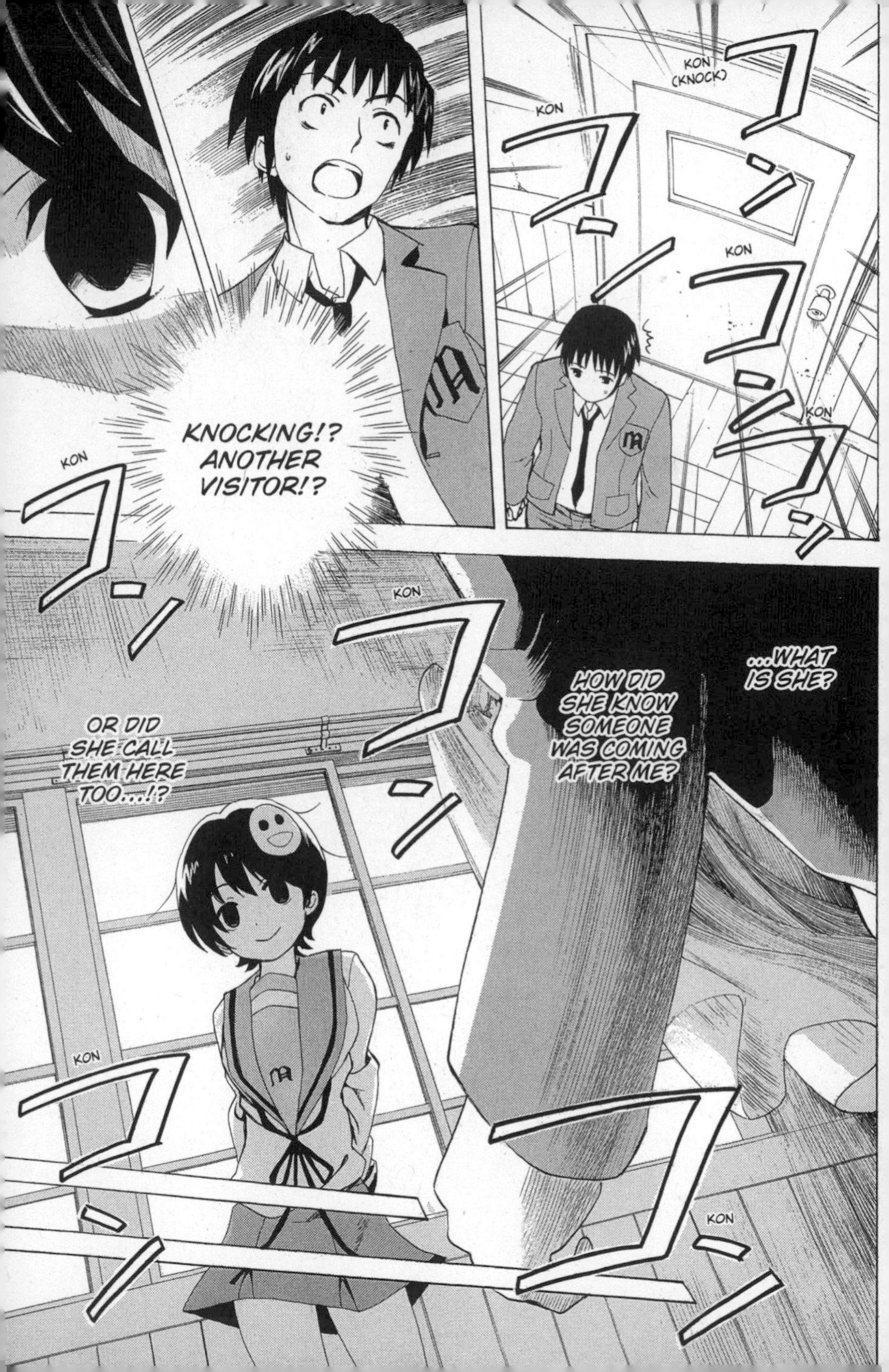
KON (KNOCK)
KON
KON
KON
KNOCKING!? ANOTHER VISITOR!?
KON
KON
...WHAT IS SHE?
HOW DID SHE KNOW SOMEONE WAS COMING AFTER ME?
OR DID SHE CALL THEM HERE TOO...!?
KON
KON

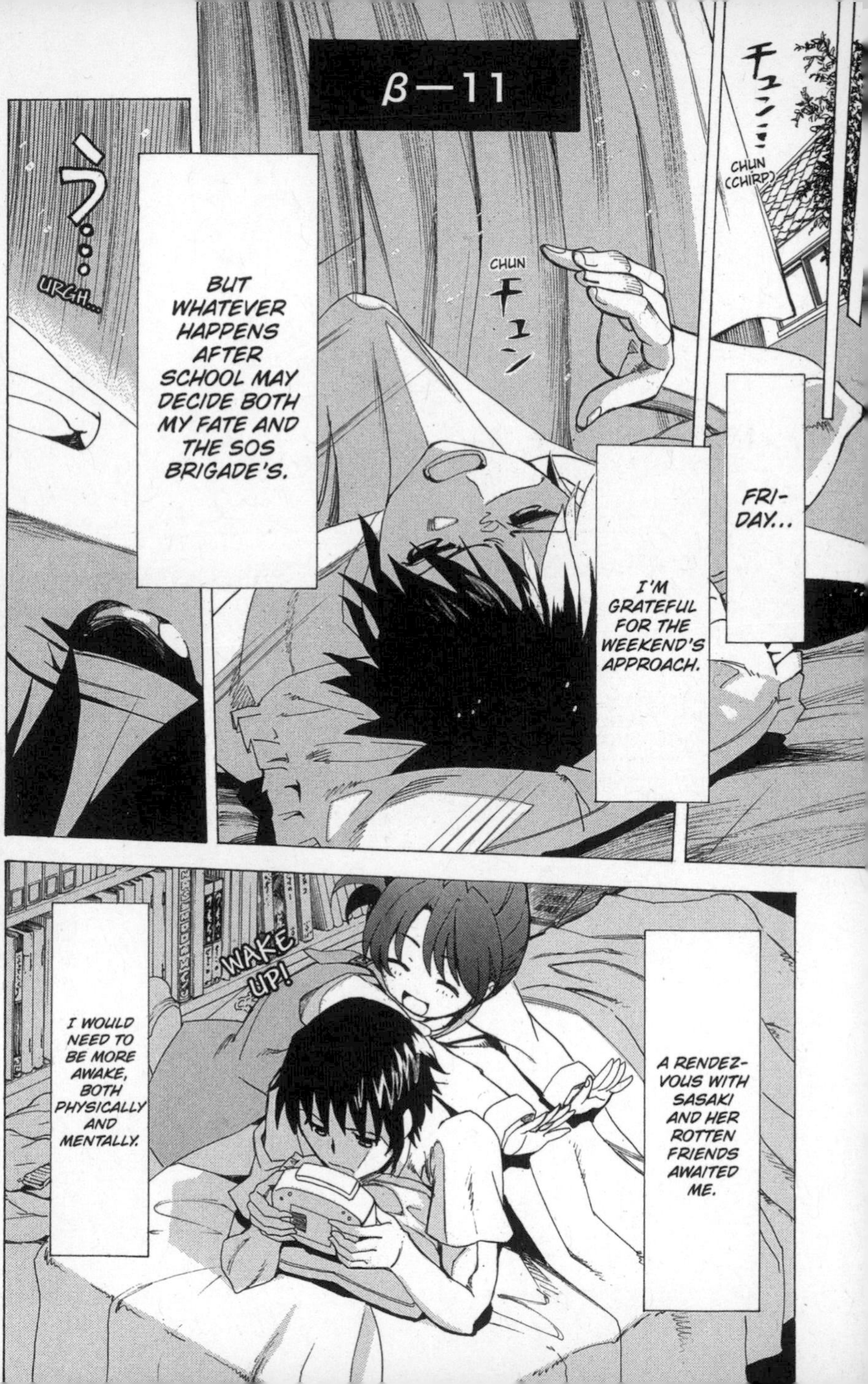
β—11
チュン…
CHUN (CHIRP)
FRI-DAY...
I'M GRATEFUL FOR THE WEEKEND'S APPROACH.
CHUN
チュン
BUT WHATEVER HAPPENS AFTER SCHOOL MAY DECIDE BOTH MY FATE AND THE SOS BRIGADE'S.
う…
URGH...
A RENDEZ-VOUS WITH SASAKI AND HER ROTTEN FRIENDS AWAITED ME.
WAKE UP!
I WOULD NEED TO BE MORE AWAKE, BOTH PHYSICALLY AND MENTALLY.

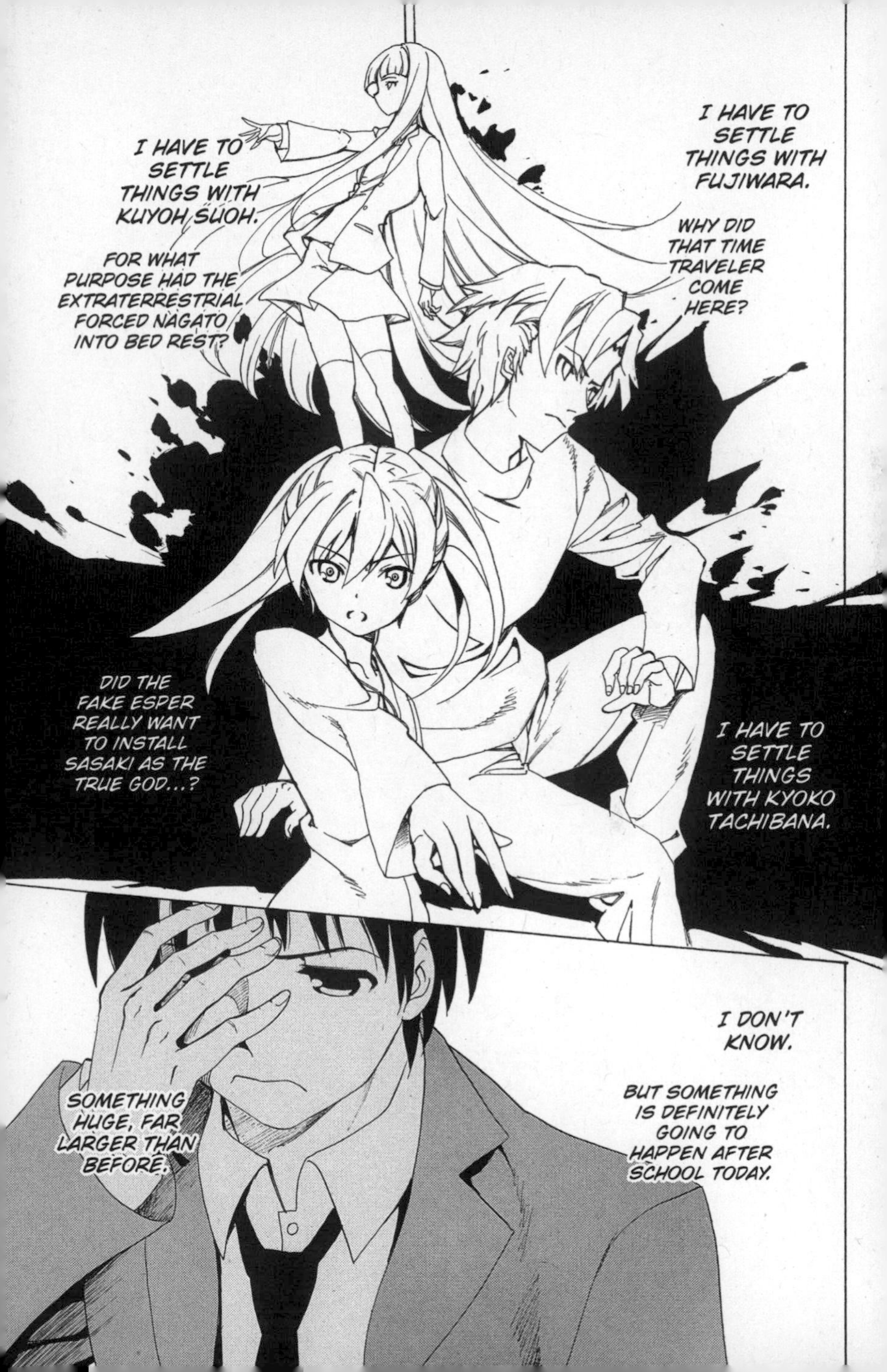
I HAVE TO SETTLE THINGS WITH FUJIWARA.
WHY DID THAT TIME TRAVELER COME HERE?
I HAVE TO SETTLE THINGS WITH KUYOH SUOH.
FOR WHAT PURPOSE HAD THE EXTRATERRESTRIAL FORCED NAGATO INTO BED REST?
I HAVE TO SETTLE THINGS WITH KYOKO TACHIBANA.
DID THE FAKE ESPER REALLY WANT TO INSTALL SASAKI AS THE TRUE GOD...?
I DON'T KNOW.
BUT SOMETHING IS DEFINITELY GOING TO HAPPEN AFTER SCHOOL TODAY.
SOMETHING HUGE, FAR LARGER THAN BEFORE.

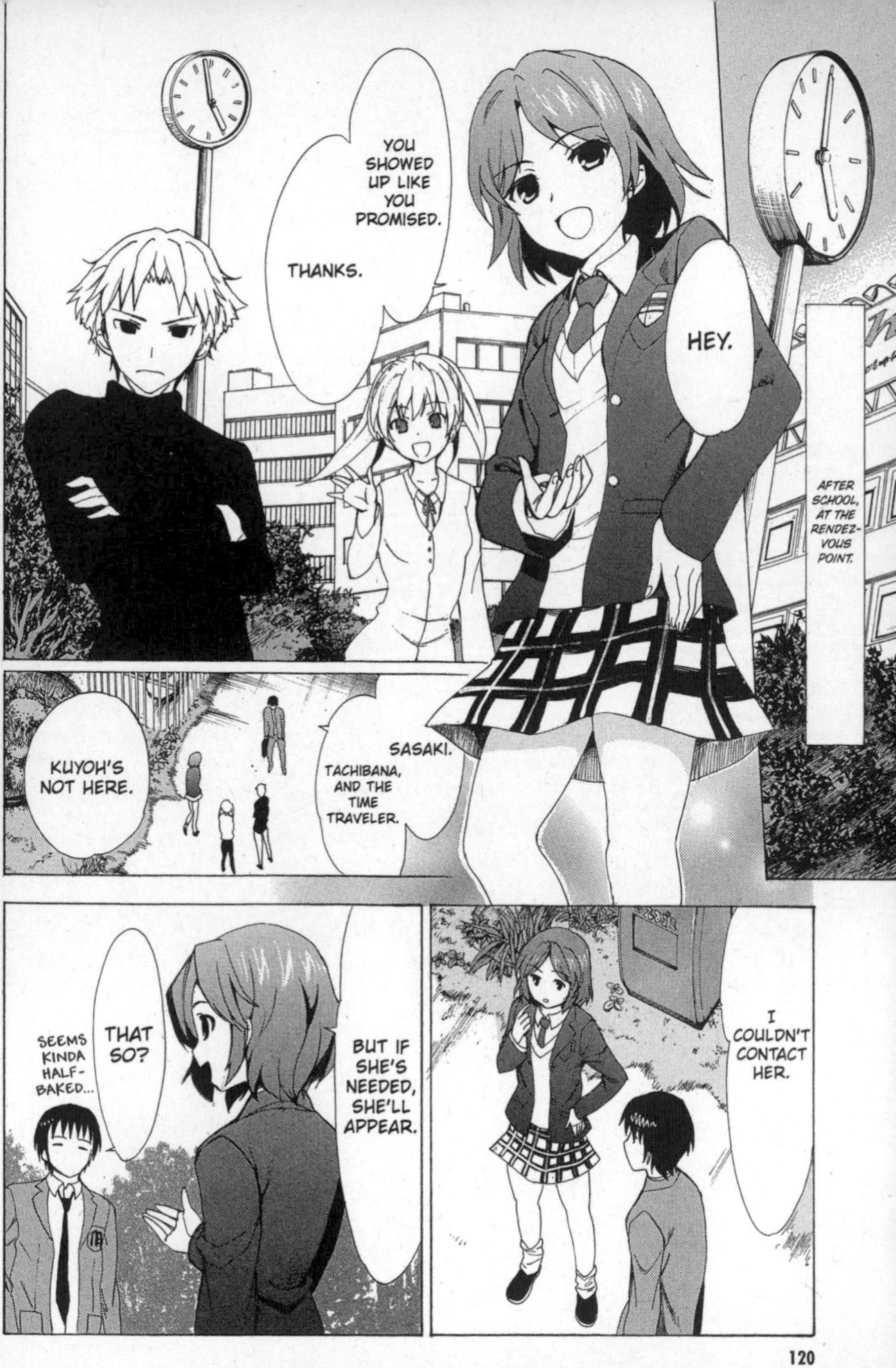
AFTER SCHOOL, AT THE RENDEZVOUS POINT.
HEY.
YOU SHOWED UP LIKE YOU PROMISED.
THANKS.
SASAKI.
TACHIBANA, AND THE TIME TRAVELER.
KUYOH'S NOT HERE.
I COULDN'T CONTACT HER.
BUT IF SHE'S NEEDED, SHE'LL APPEAR.
THAT SO?
SEEMS KINDA HALF-BAKED...

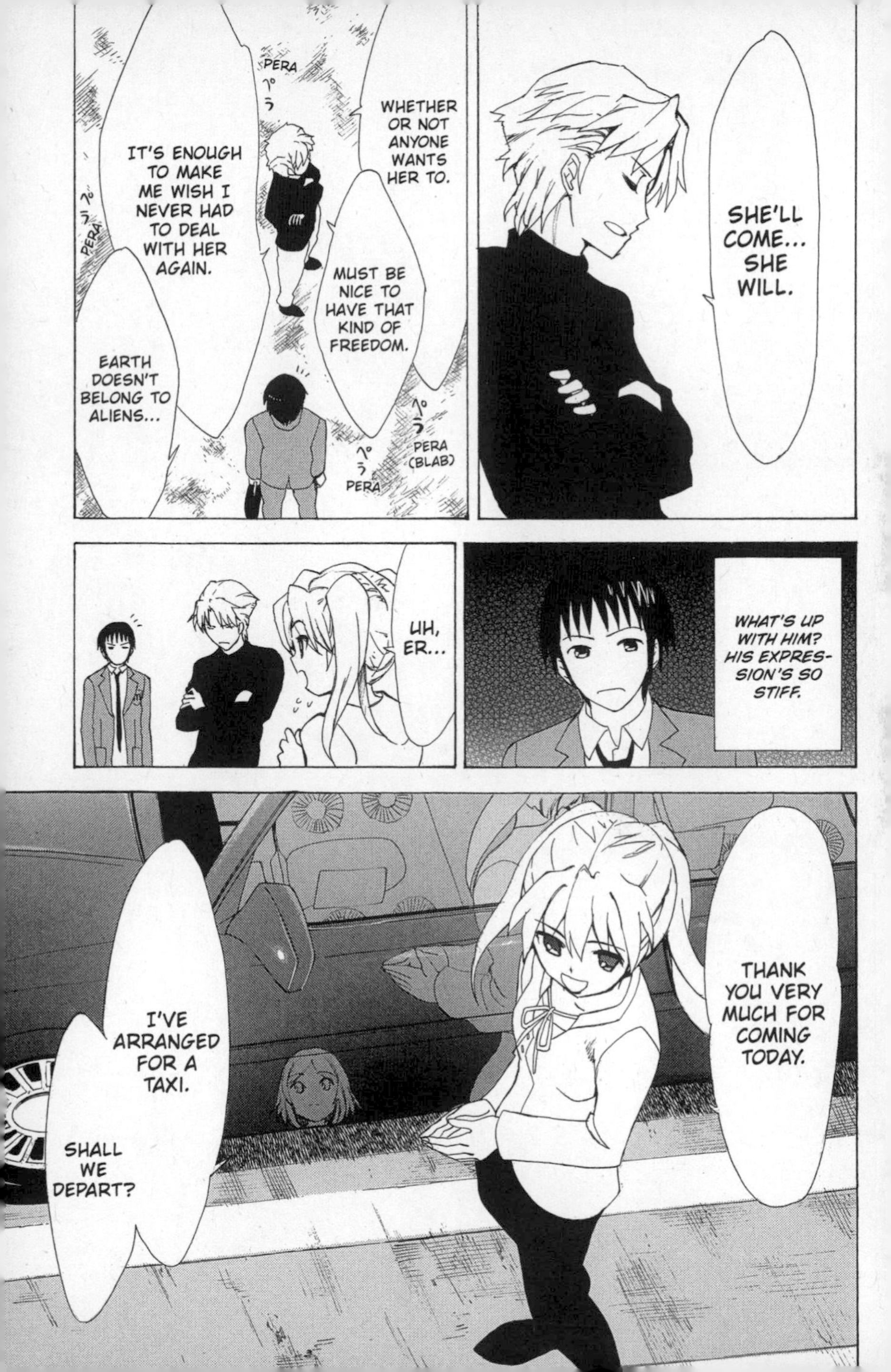
SHE'LL COME... SHE WILL.
WHETHER OR NOT ANYONE WANTS HER TO.
PERA
IT'S ENOUGH TO MAKE ME WISH I NEVER HAD TO DEAL WITH HER AGAIN.
PERA
MUST BE NICE TO HAVE THAT KIND OF FREEDOM.
PERA (BLAB)
PERA
EARTH DOESN'T BELONG TO ALIENS...
WHAT'S UP WITH HIM? HIS EXPRESSION'S SO STIFF.
UH, ER...
THANK YOU VERY MUCH FOR COMING TODAY.
I'VE ARRANGED FOR A TAXI.
SHALL WE DEPART?

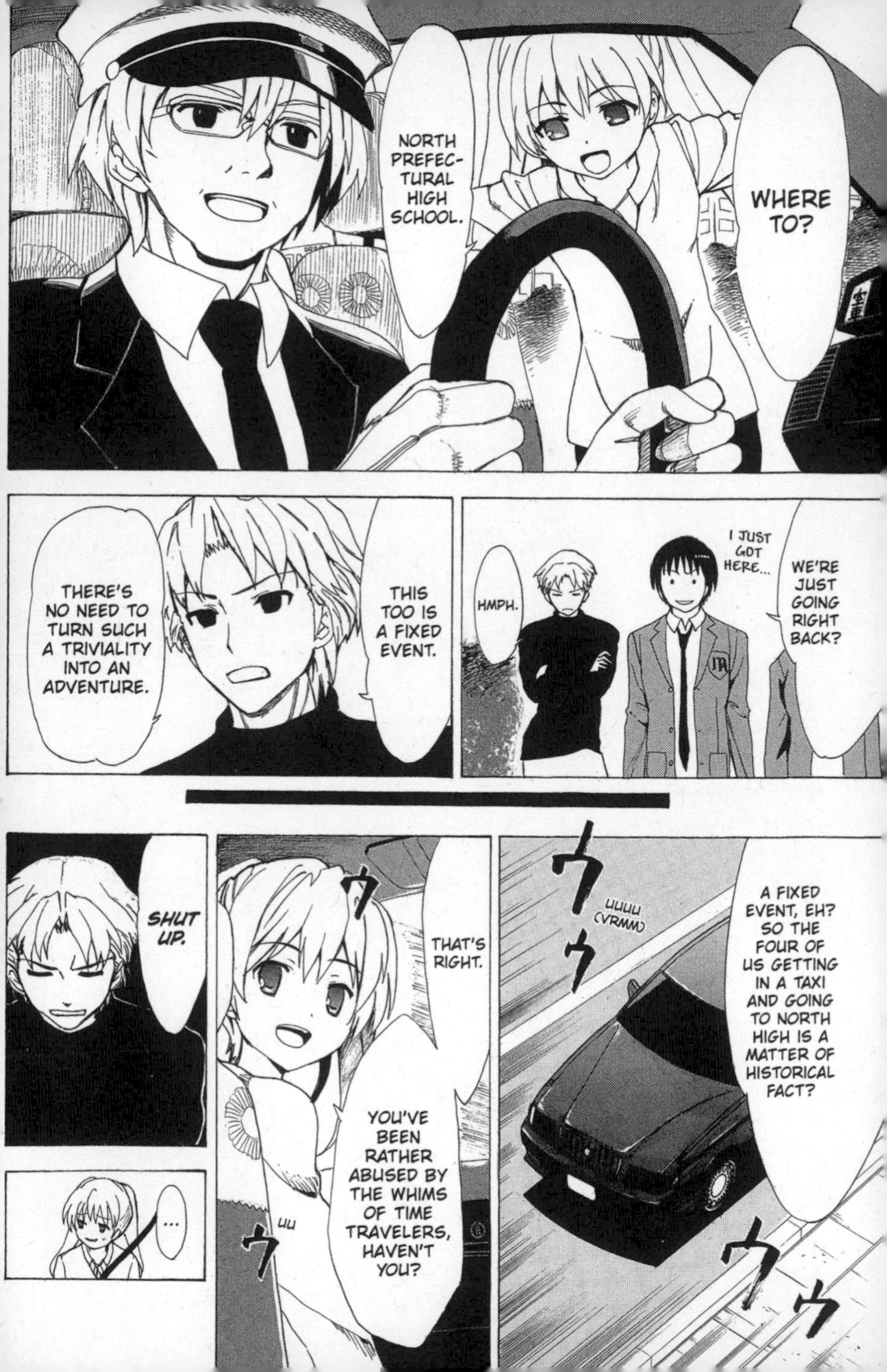
WHERE TO?
NORTH PREFEC-TURAL HIGH SCHOOL.
WE'RE JUST GOING RIGHT BACK?
I JUST GOT HERE...
HMPH.
THIS TOO IS A FIXED EVENT.
THERE'S NO NEED TO TURN SUCH A TRIVIALITY INTO AN ADVENTURE.
A FIXED EVENT, EH? SO THE FOUR OF US GETTING IN A TAXI AND GOING TO NORTH HIGH IS A MATTER OF HISTORICAL FACT?
uuuu (VRMM)
THAT'S RIGHT.
YOU'VE BEEN RATHER ABUSED BY THE WHIMS OF TIME TRAVELERS, HAVEN'T YOU?
uu
SHUT UP.
...

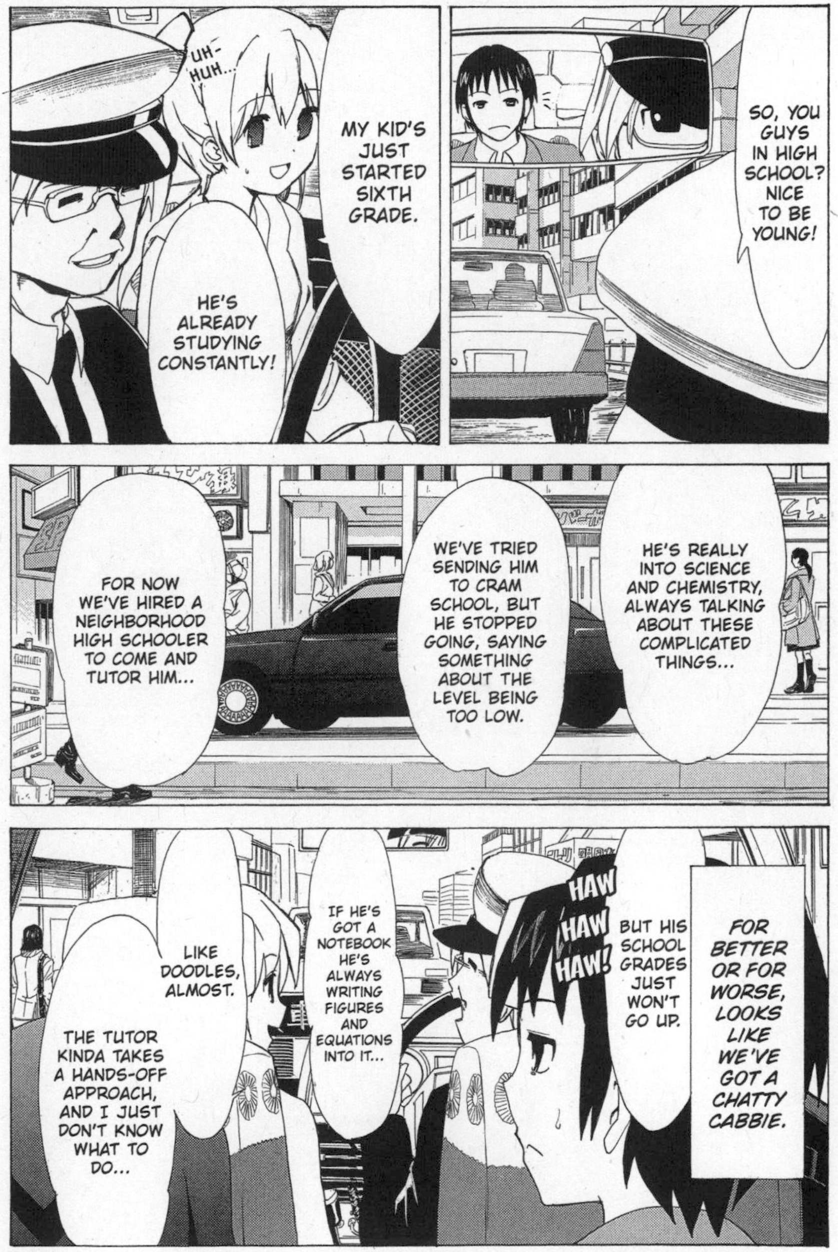
SO, YOU GUYS IN HIGH SCHOOL? NICE TO BE YOUNG!
MY KID'S JUST STARTED SIXTH GRADE.
UH-HUH...
HE'S ALREADY STUDYING CONSTANTLY!
HE'S REALLY INTO SCIENCE AND CHEMISTRY, ALWAYS TALKING ABOUT THESE COMPLICATED THINGS...
WE'VE TRIED SENDING HIM TO CRAM SCHOOL, BUT HE STOPPED GOING, SAYING SOMETHING ABOUT THE LEVEL BEING TOO LOW.
FOR NOW WE'VE HIRED A NEIGHBORHOOD HIGH SCHOOLER TO COME AND TUTOR HIM...
FOR BETTER OR FOR WORSE, LOOKS LIKE WE'VE GOT A CHATTY CABBIE.
BUT HIS SCHOOL GRADES JUST WON'T GO UP.
HAW HAW HAW!
IF HE'S GOT A NOTEBOOK HE'S ALWAYS WRITING FIGURES AND EQUATIONS INTO IT...
LIKE DOODLES, ALMOST.
THE TUTOR KINDA TAKES A HANDS-OFF APPROACH, AND I JUST DON'T KNOW WHAT TO DO...

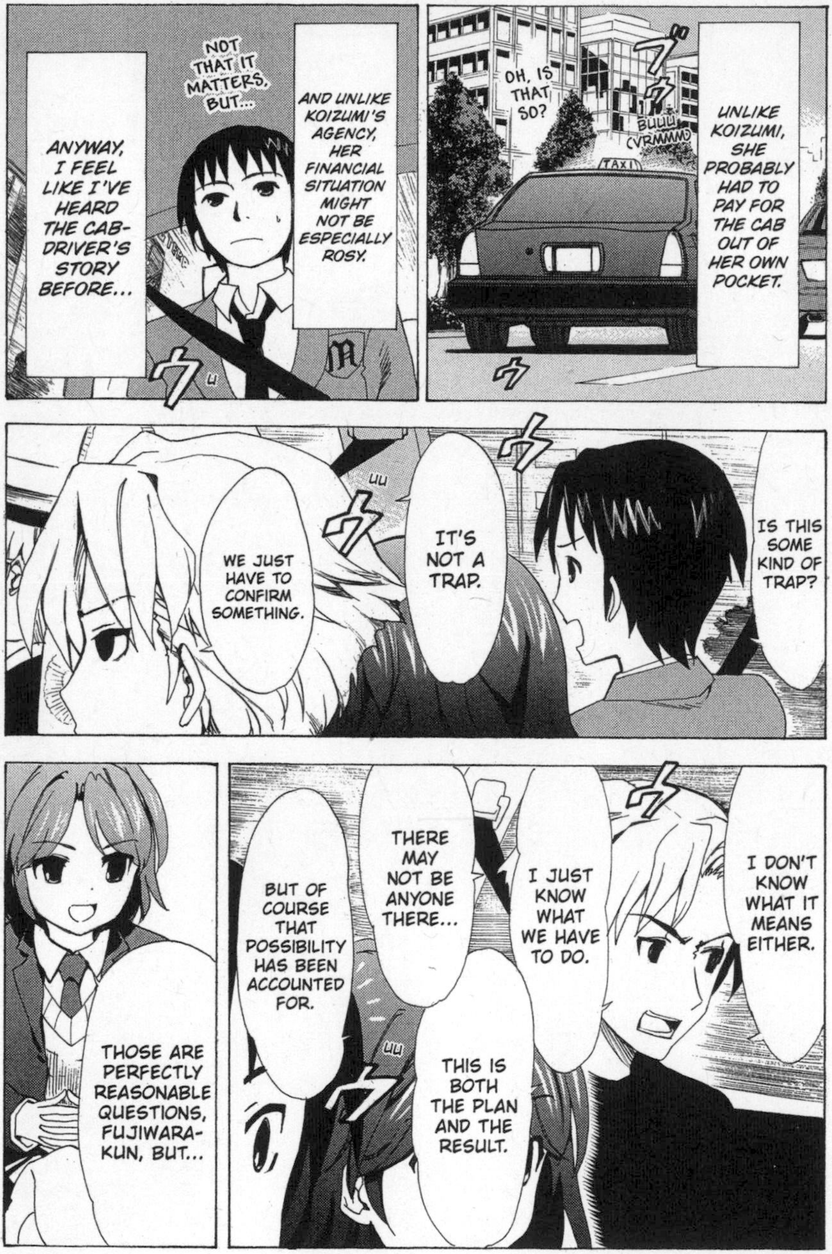
UNLIKE KOIZUMI, SHE PROBABLY HAD TO PAY FOR THE CAB OUT OF HER OWN POCKET.
OH, IS THAT SO?
BUUU (VRMMM)
TAXI
AND UNLIKE KOIZUMI'S AGENCY, HER FINANCIAL SITUATION MIGHT NOT BE ESPECIALLY ROSY.
NOT THAT IT MATTERS, BUT...
ANYWAY, I FEEL LIKE I'VE HEARD THE CAB-DRIVER'S STORY BEFORE...
u
IS THIS SOME KIND OF TRAP?
IT'S NOT A TRAP.
uu
WE JUST HAVE TO CONFIRM SOMETHING.
I DON'T KNOW WHAT IT MEANS EITHER.
I JUST KNOW WHAT WE HAVE TO DO.
THERE MAY NOT BE ANYONE THERE...
BUT OF COURSE THAT POSSIBILITY HAS BEEN ACCOUNTED FOR.
THIS IS BOTH THE PLAN AND THE RESULT.
uu
THOSE ARE PERFECTLY REASONABLE QUESTIONS, FUJIWARA-KUN, BUT...

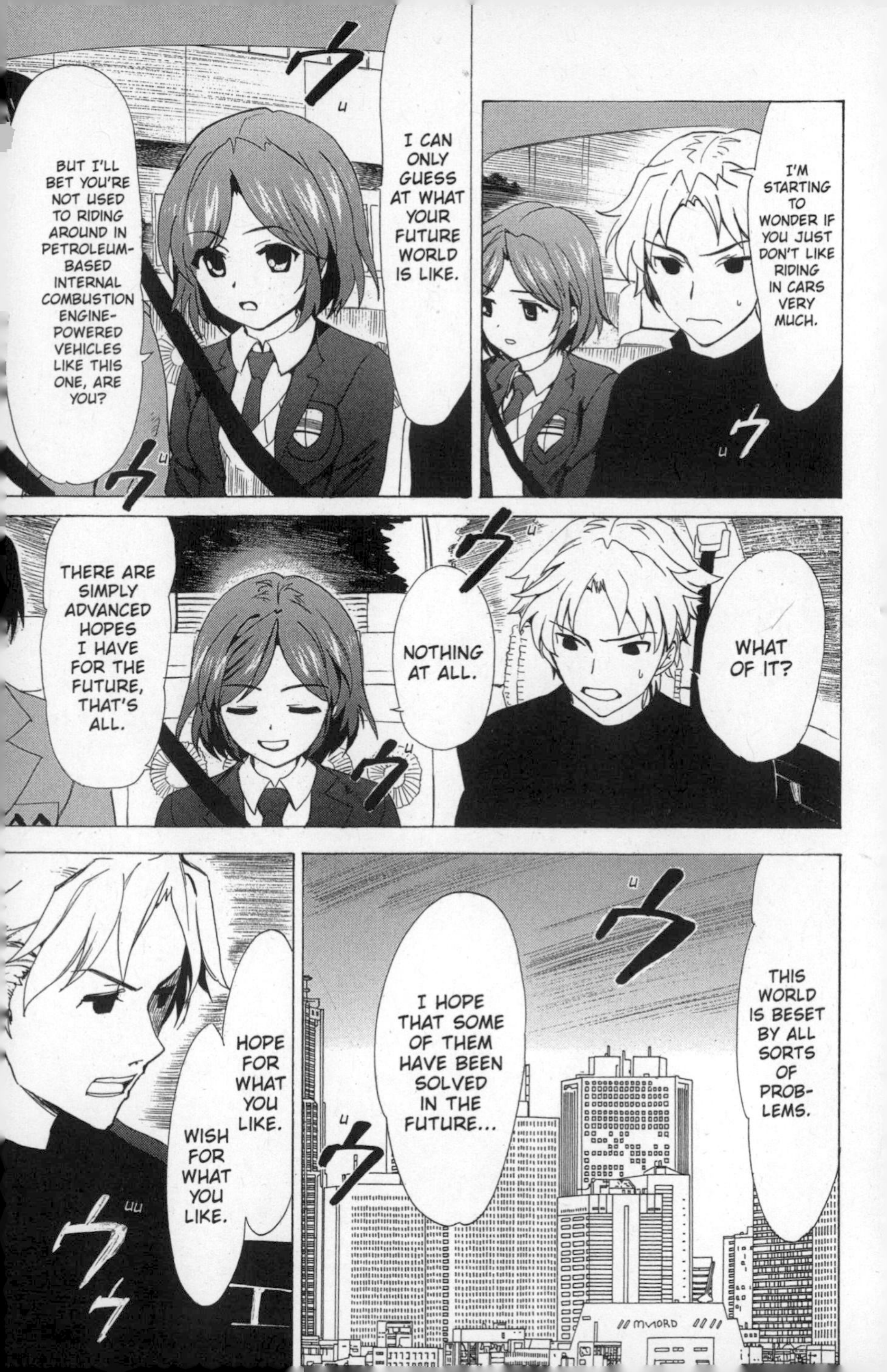
I'M STARTING TO WONDER IF YOU JUST DON'T LIKE RIDING IN CARS VERY MUCH.
I CAN ONLY GUESS AT WHAT YOUR FUTURE WORLD IS LIKE.
BUT I'LL BET YOU'RE NOT USED TO RIDING AROUND IN PETROLEUM-BASED INTERNAL COMBUSTION ENGINE-POWERED VEHICLES LIKE THIS ONE, ARE YOU?
WHAT OF IT?
NOTHING AT ALL.
THERE ARE SIMPLY ADVANCED HOPES I HAVE FOR THE FUTURE, THAT'S ALL.
THIS WORLD IS BESET BY ALL SORTS OF PROBLEMS.
I HOPE THAT SOME OF THEM HAVE BEEN SOLVED IN THE FUTURE...
HOPE FOR WHAT YOU LIKE.
WISH FOR WHAT YOU LIKE.

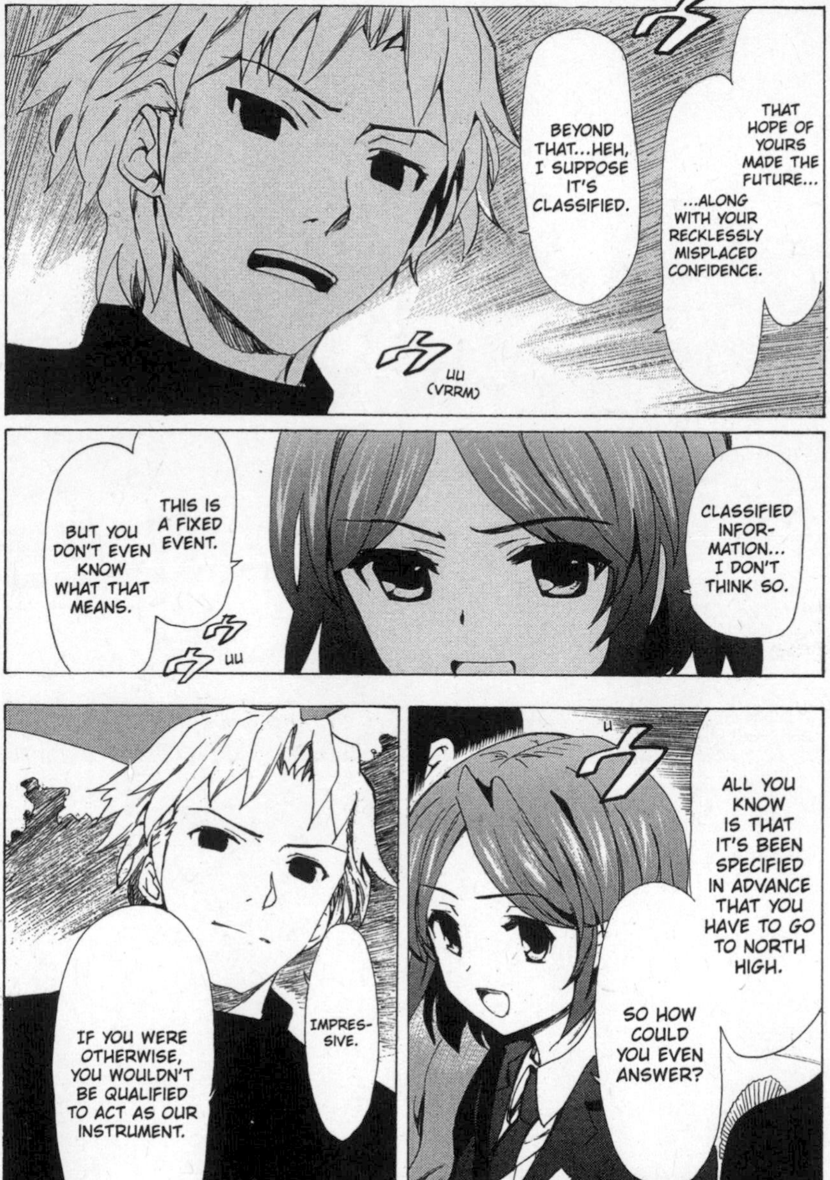
THAT HOPE OF YOURS MADE THE FUTURE... ...ALONG WITH YOUR RECKLESSLY MISPLACED CONFIDENCE.
BEYOND THAT...HEH, I SUPPOSE IT'S CLASSIFIED.
UU (VRRM)
CLASSIFIED INFORMATION... I DON'T THINK SO.
THIS IS A FIXED EVENT.
BUT YOU DON'T EVEN KNOW WHAT THAT MEANS.
UU
U
ALL YOU KNOW IS THAT IT'S BEEN SPECIFIED IN ADVANCE THAT YOU HAVE TO GO TO NORTH HIGH.
SO HOW COULD YOU EVEN ANSWER?
IMPRESSIVE.
IF YOU WERE OTHERWISE, YOU WOULDN'T BE QUALIFIED TO ACT AS OUR INSTRUMENT.

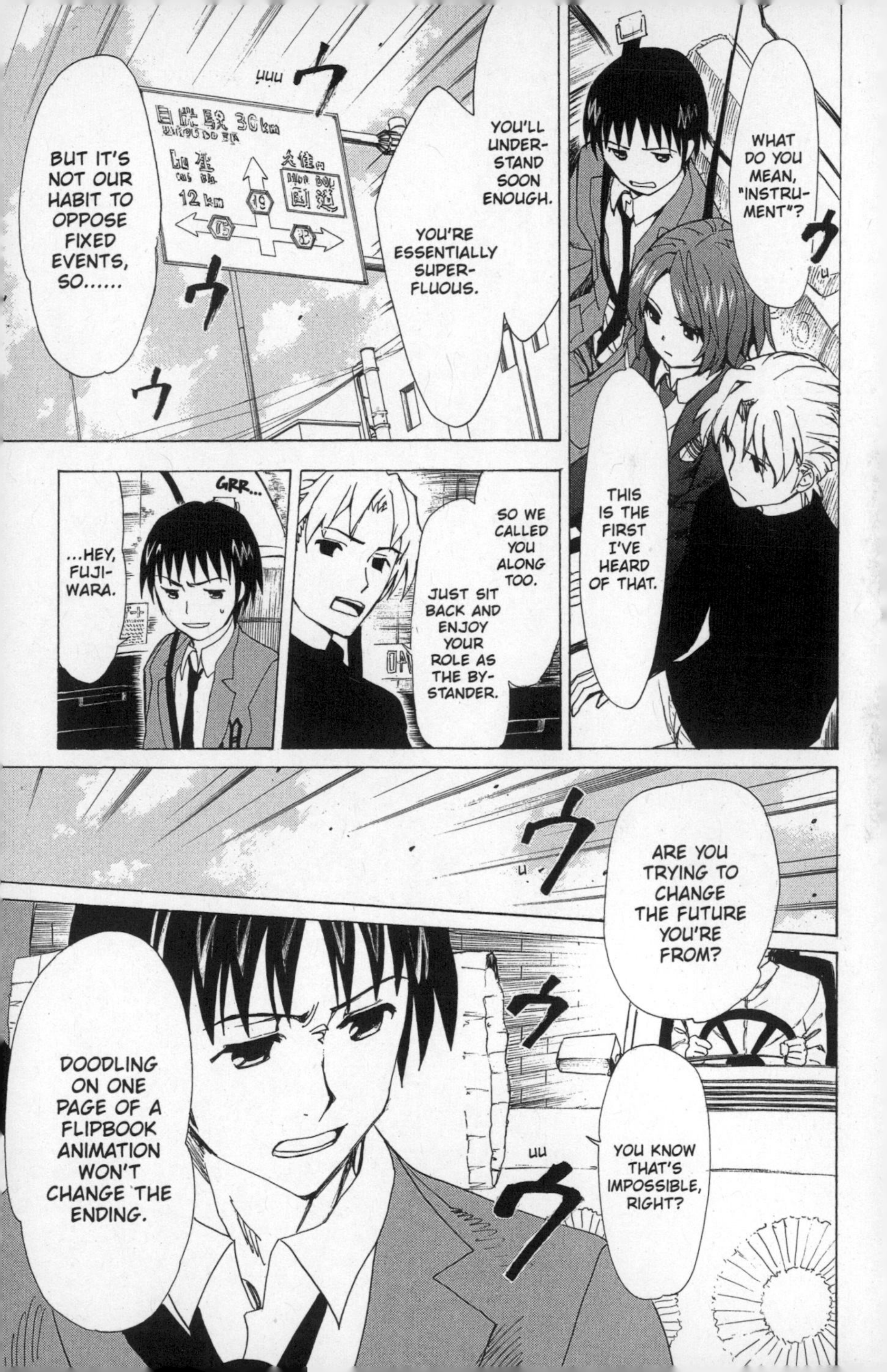

WHAT DO YOU MEAN, "INSTRUMENT"?
u
THIS IS THE FIRST I'VE HEARD OF THAT.
YOU'LL UNDER-STAND SOON ENOUGH.
YOU'RE ESSENTIALLY SUPER-FLUOUS.
uuu
BUT IT'S NOT OUR HABIT TO OPPOSE FIXED EVENTS, SO......
SO WE CALLED YOU ALONG TOO.
JUST SIT BACK AND ENJOY YOUR ROLE AS THE BY-STANDER.
GRR...
...HEY, FUJI-WARA.
ARE YOU TRYING TO CHANGE THE FUTURE YOU'RE FROM?
u
YOU KNOW THAT'S IMPOSSIBLE, RIGHT?
uu
DOODLING ON ONE PAGE OF A FLIPBOOK ANIMATION WON'T CHANGE THE ENDING.

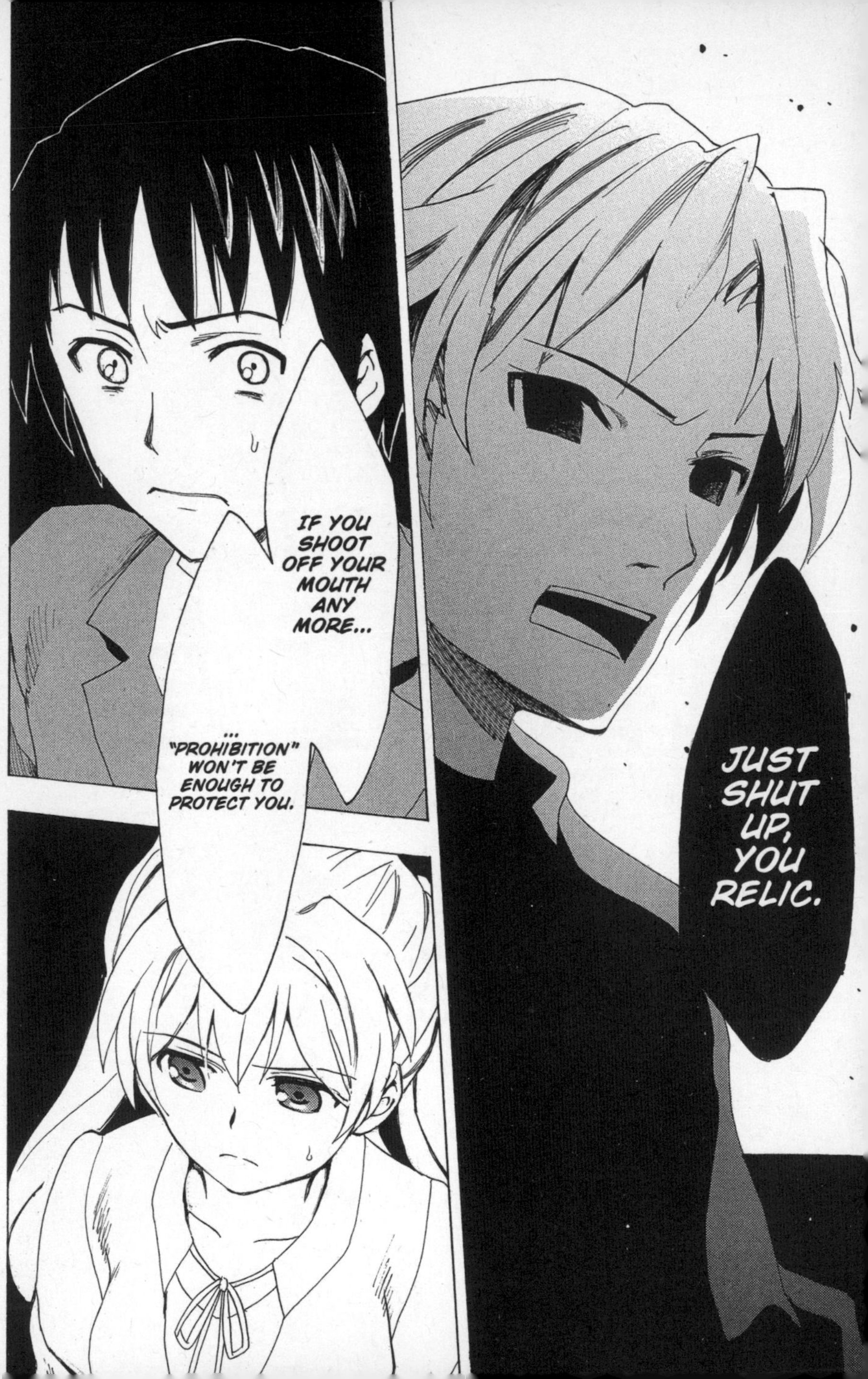
JUST SHUT UP, YOU RELIC.
IF YOU SHOOT OFF YOUR MOUTH ANY MORE...
..."PROHIBITION" WON'T BE ENOUGH TO PROTECT YOU.

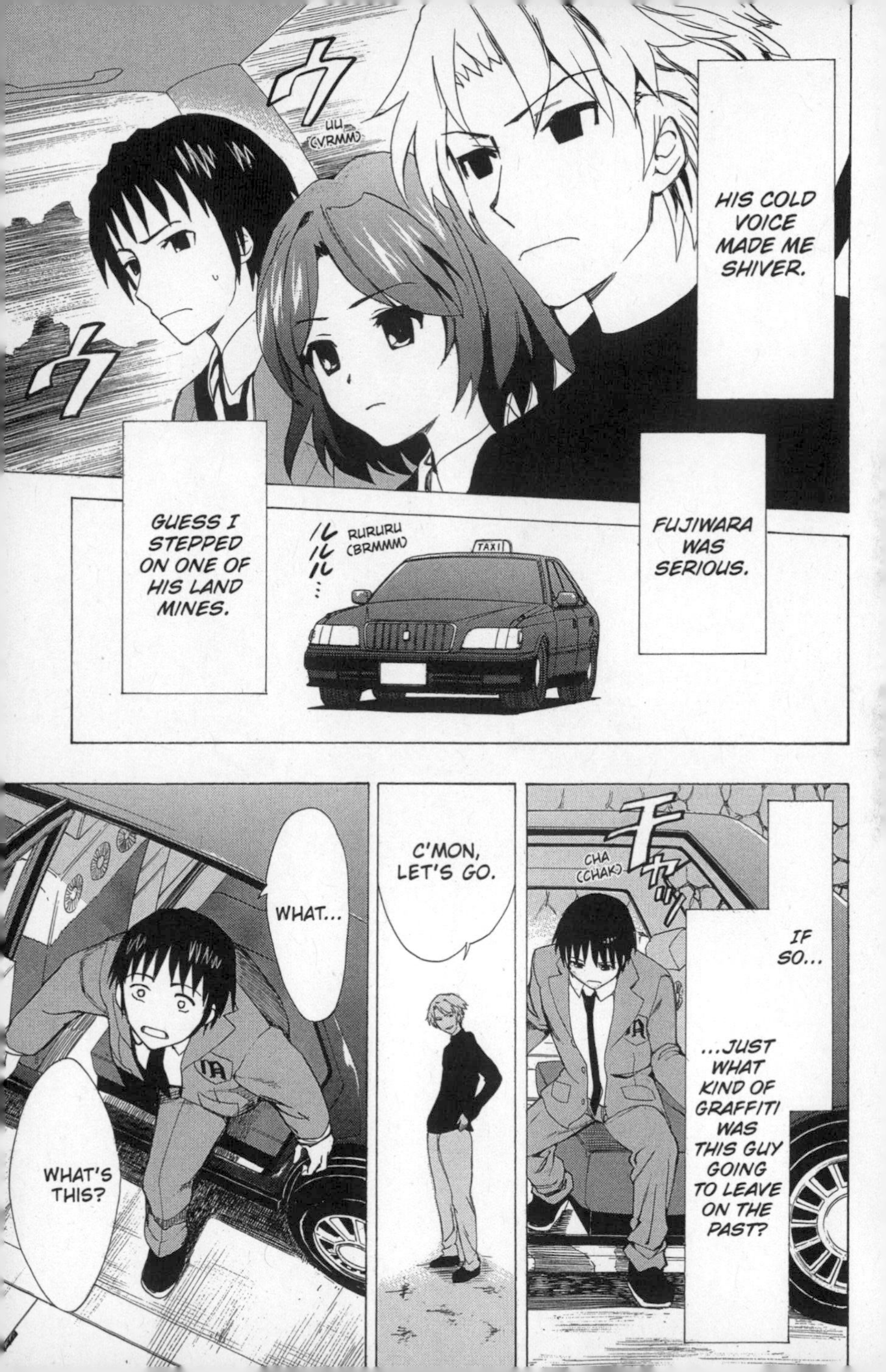
HIS COLD VOICE MADE ME SHIVER.
ウ
UU (VRMM)
ウ
FUJIWARA WAS SERIOUS.
ルルル…
RURURU (BRMMM)
TAXI
GUESS I STEPPED ON ONE OF HIS LAND MINES.
チャッ
CHA (CHAK)
IF SO...
...JUST WHAT KIND OF GRAFFITI WAS THIS GUY GOING TO LEAVE ON THE PAST?
C'MON, LET'S GO.
WHAT...
WHAT'S THIS?

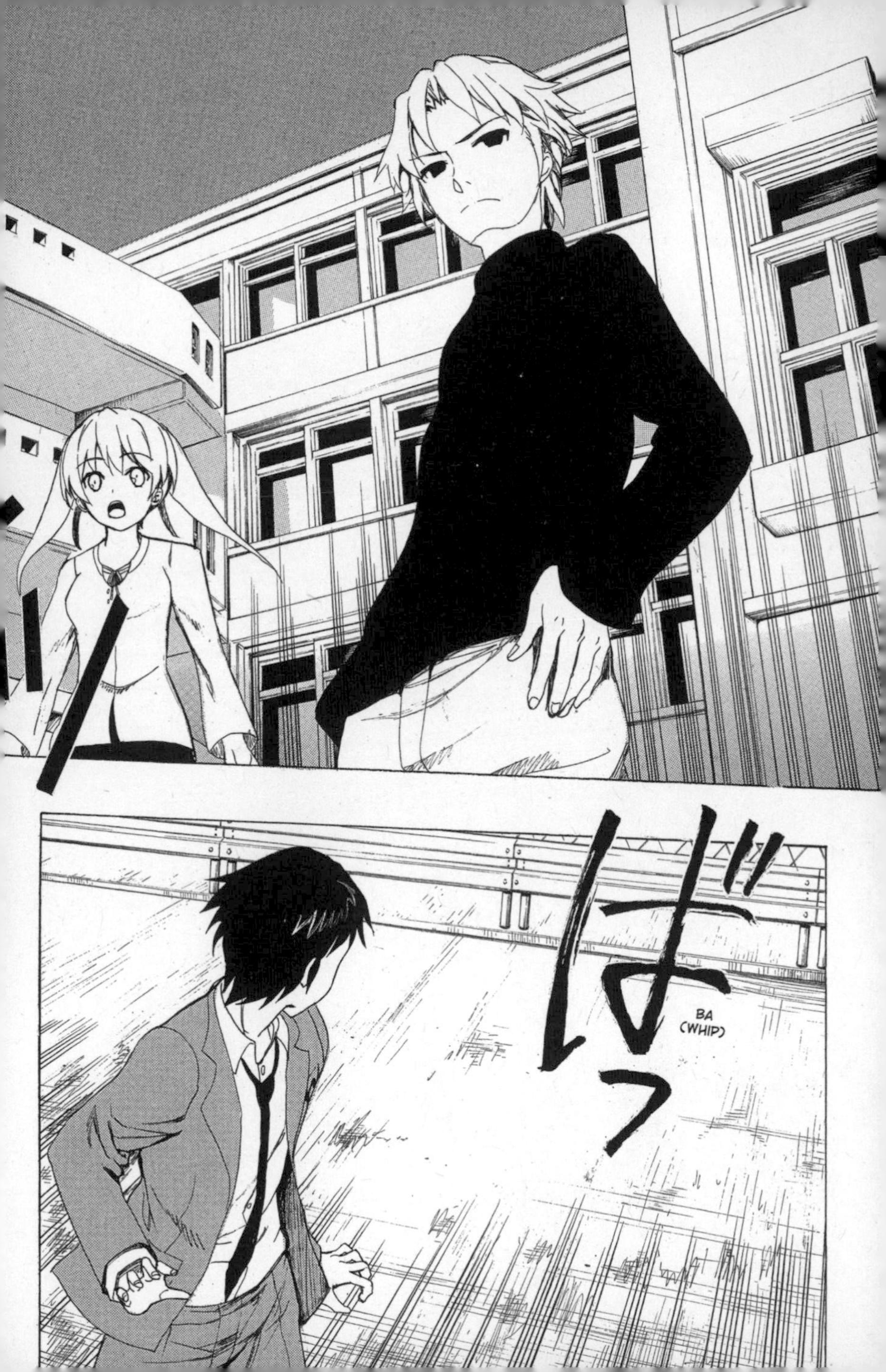
ばっ
BA
(WHIP)

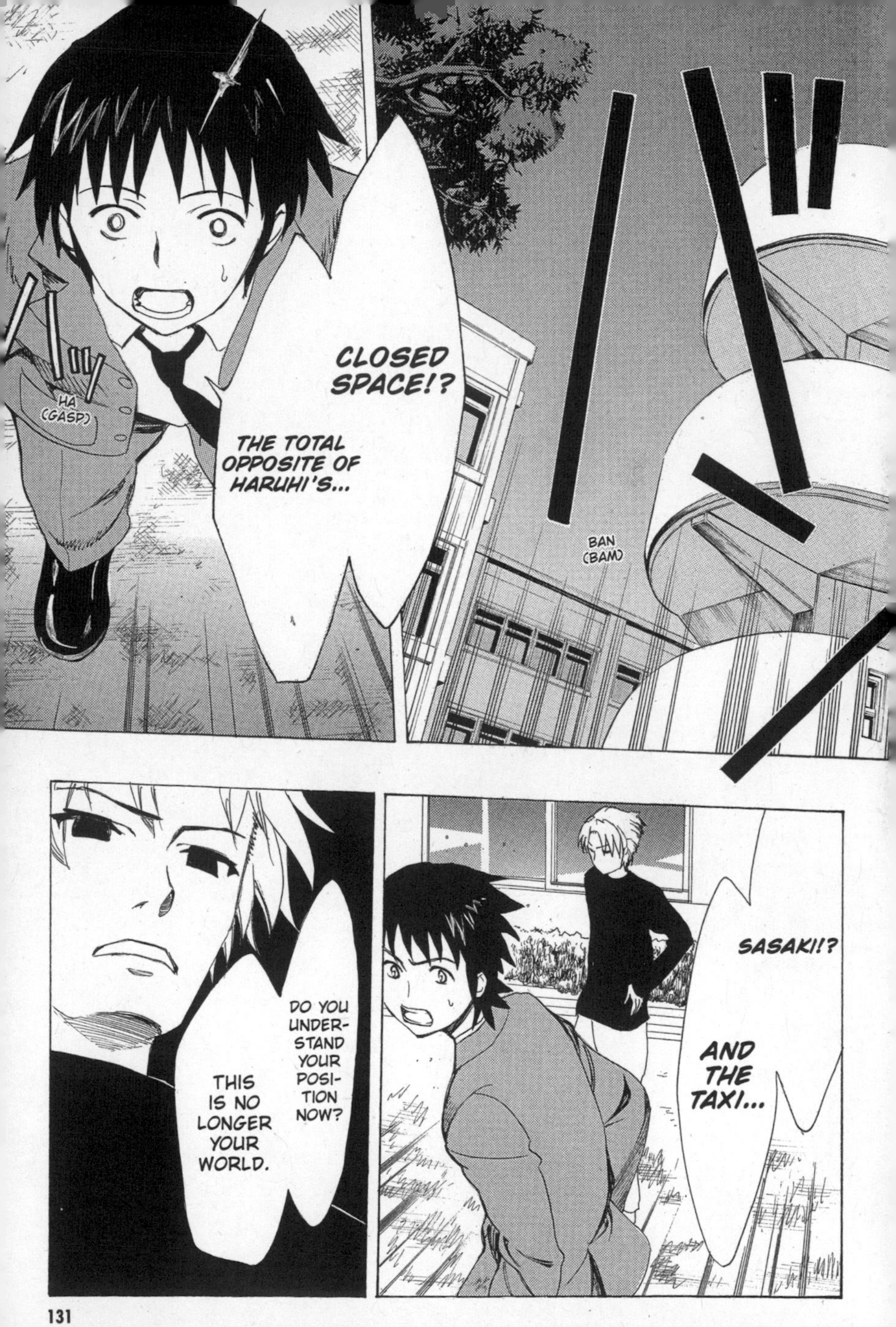
CLOSED SPACE!?
THE TOTAL OPPOSITE OF HARUHI'S...
HA (GASP)
BAN (BAM)
SASAKI!?
AND THE TAXI...
DO YOU UNDERSTAND YOUR POSITION NOW?
THIS IS NO LONGER YOUR WORLD.

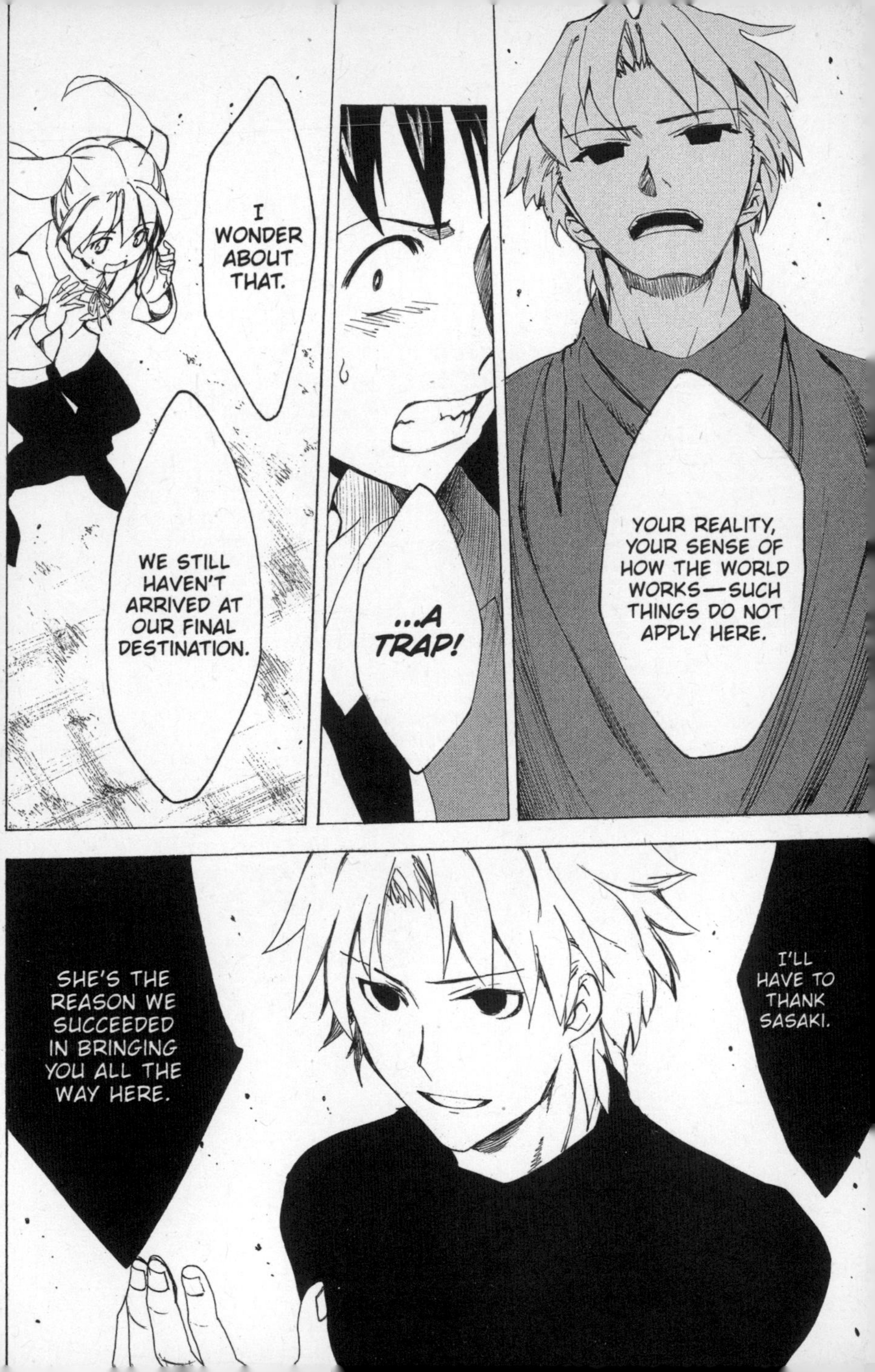
YOUR REALITY, YOUR SENSE OF HOW THE WORLD WORKS—SUCH THINGS DO NOT APPLY HERE.
...A TRAP!
I WONDER ABOUT THAT.
WE STILL HAVEN'T ARRIVED AT OUR FINAL DESTINATION.
I'LL HAVE TO THANK SASAKI.
SHE'S THE REASON WE SUCCEEDED IN BRINGING YOU ALL THE WAY HERE.

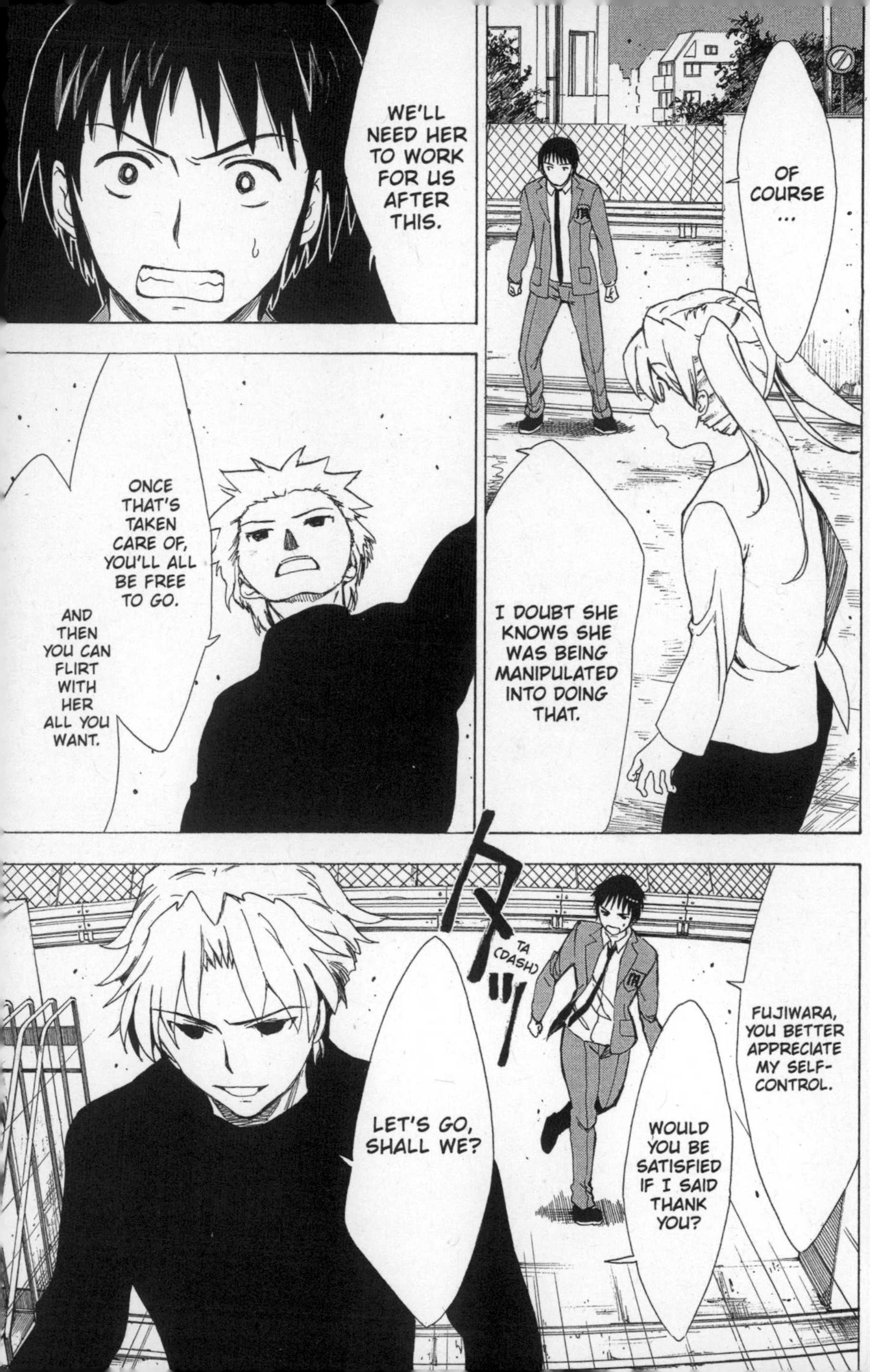
OF COURSE...
I DOUBT SHE KNOWS SHE WAS BEING MANIPULATED INTO DOING THAT.
WE'LL NEED HER TO WORK FOR US AFTER THIS.
ONCE THAT'S TAKEN CARE OF, YOU'LL ALL BE FREE TO GO.
AND THEN YOU CAN FLIRT WITH HER ALL YOU WANT.
FUJIWARA, YOU BETTER APPRECIATE MY SELF-CONTROL.
WOULD YOU BE SATISFIED IF I SAID THANK YOU?
TA (DASH)
LET'S GO, SHALL WE?

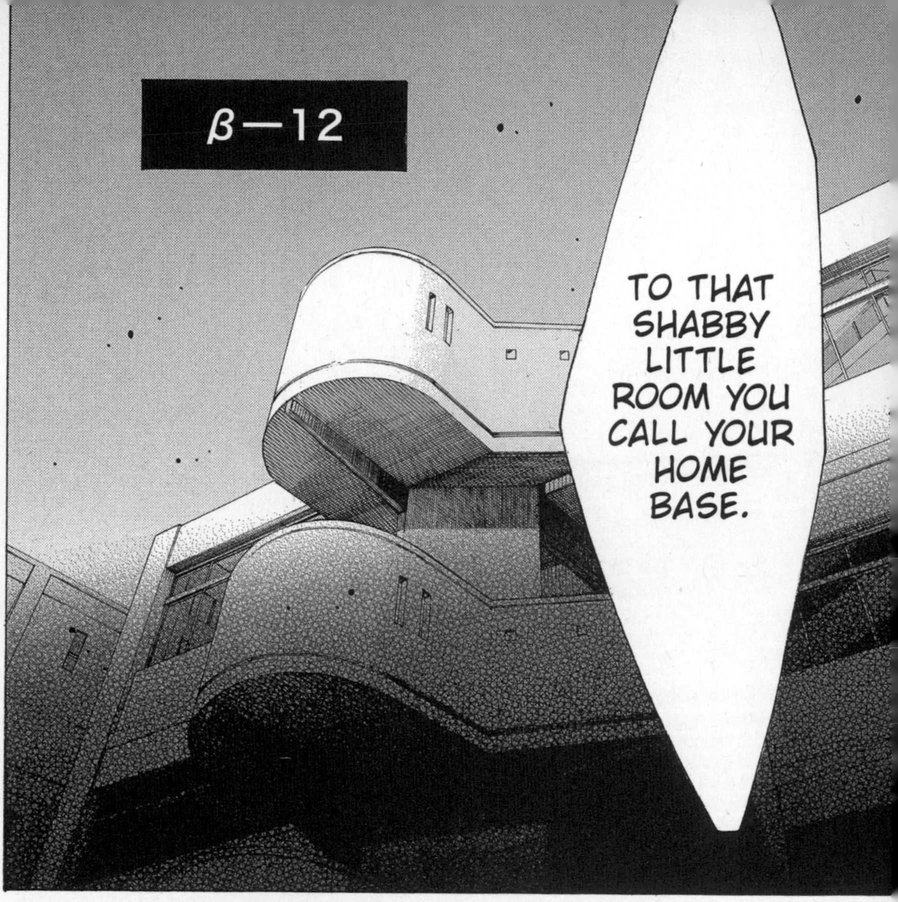
β—12
TO THAT SHABBY LITTLE ROOM YOU CALL YOUR HOME BASE.

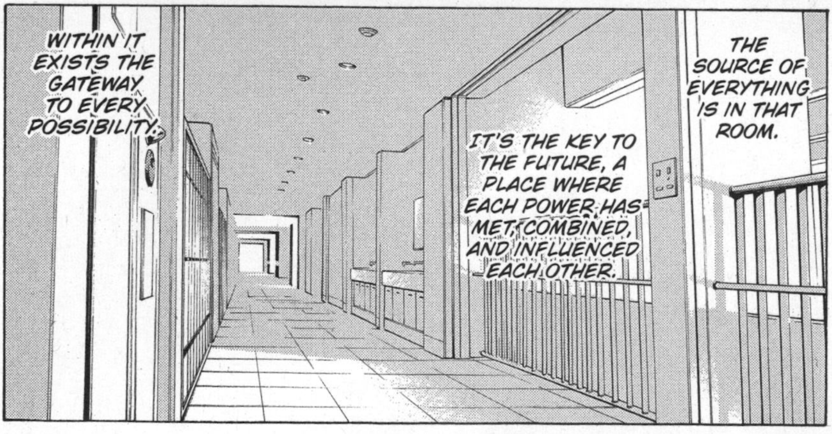
THE SOURCE OF EVERYTHING IS IN THAT ROOM.
IT'S THE KEY TO THE FUTURE, A PLACE WHERE EACH POWER HAS MET, COMBINED, AND INFLUENCED EACH OTHER.
WITHIN IT EXISTS THE GATEWAY TO EVERY POSSIBILITY.

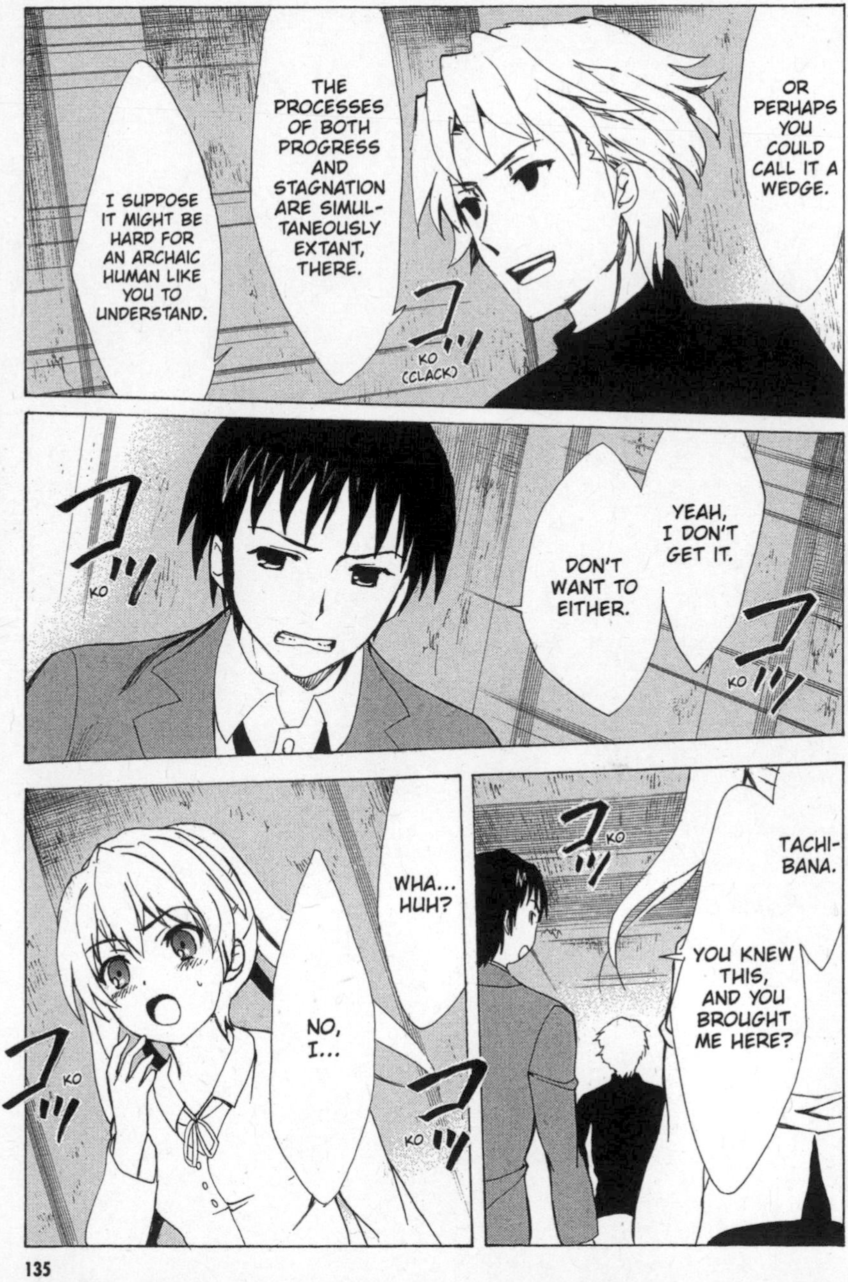
OR PERHAPS YOU COULD CALL IT A WEDGE.
THE PROCESSES OF BOTH PROGRESS AND STAGNATION ARE SIMUL-TANEOUSLY EXTANT, THERE.
I SUPPOSE IT MIGHT BE HARD FOR AN ARCHAIC HUMAN LIKE YOU TO UNDERSTAND.
KO (CLACK)
YEAH, I DON'T GET IT.
DON'T WANT TO EITHER.
KO
KO
TACHI-BANA.
KO
YOU KNEW THIS, AND YOU BROUGHT ME HERE?
WHA... HUH?
NO, I...
KO
KO

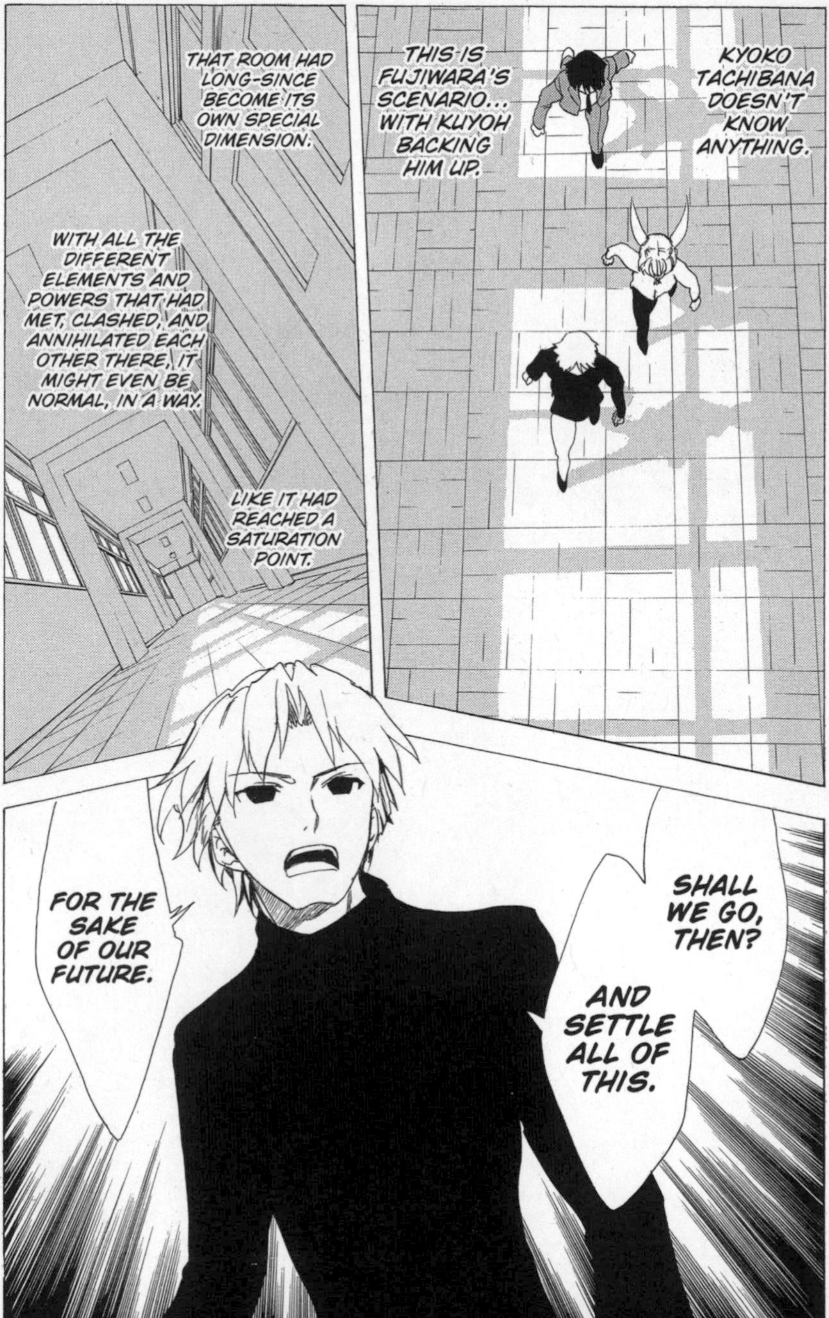
KYOKO TACHIBANA DOESN'T KNOW ANYTHING.
THIS IS FUJIWARA'S SCENARIO... WITH KUYOH BACKING HIM UP.
THAT ROOM HAD LONG-SINCE BECOME ITS OWN SPECIAL DIMENSION.
WITH ALL THE DIFFERENT ELEMENTS AND POWERS THAT HAD MET, CLASHED, AND ANNIHILATED EACH OTHER THERE, IT MIGHT EVEN BE NORMAL, IN A WAY.
LIKE IT HAD REACHED A SATURATION POINT.
SHALL WE GO, THEN?
AND SETTLE ALL OF THIS.
FOR THE SAKE OF OUR FUTURE.

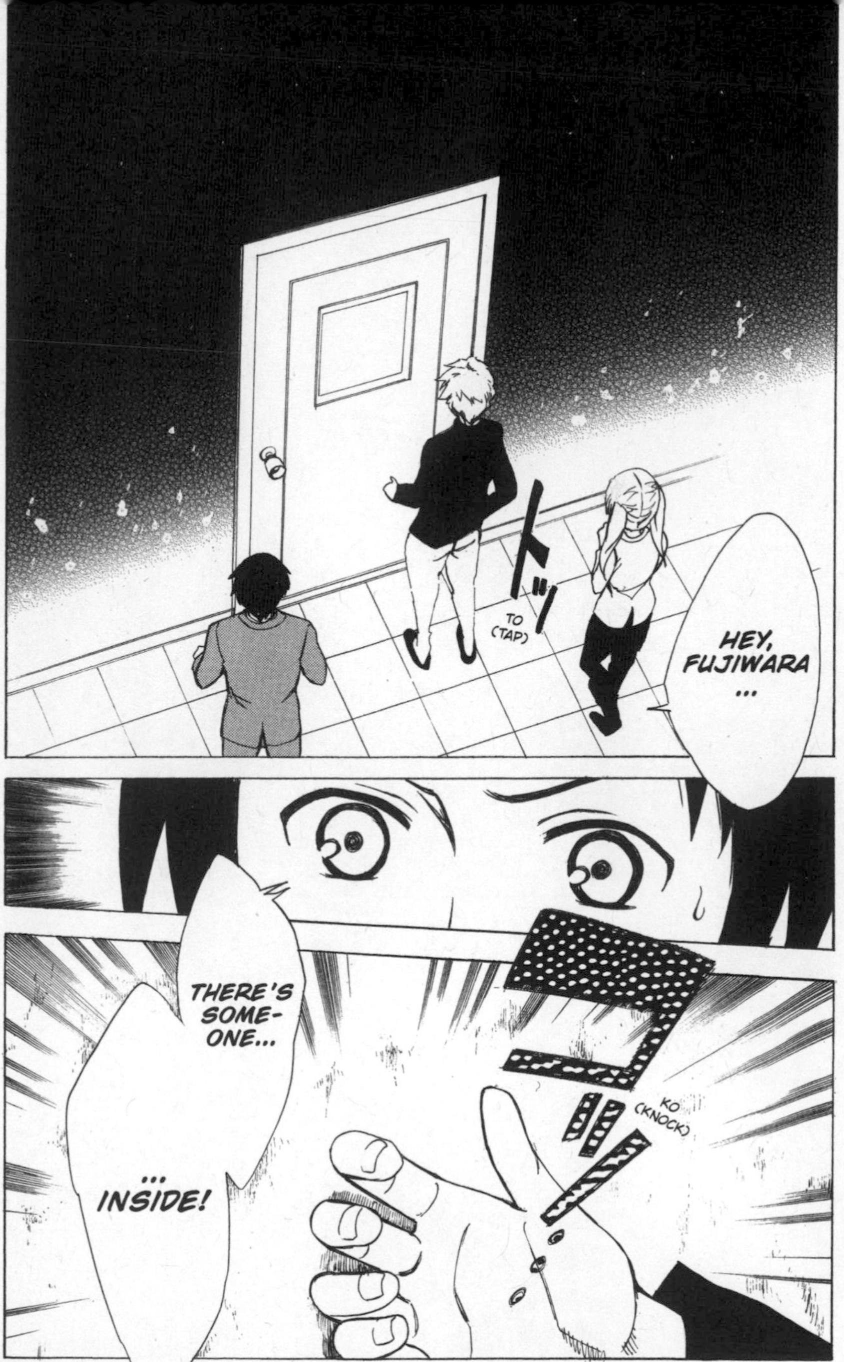

HEY, FUJIWARA ...
TO (TAP)
KO (KNOCK)
THERE'S SOME-ONE... ... INSIDE!

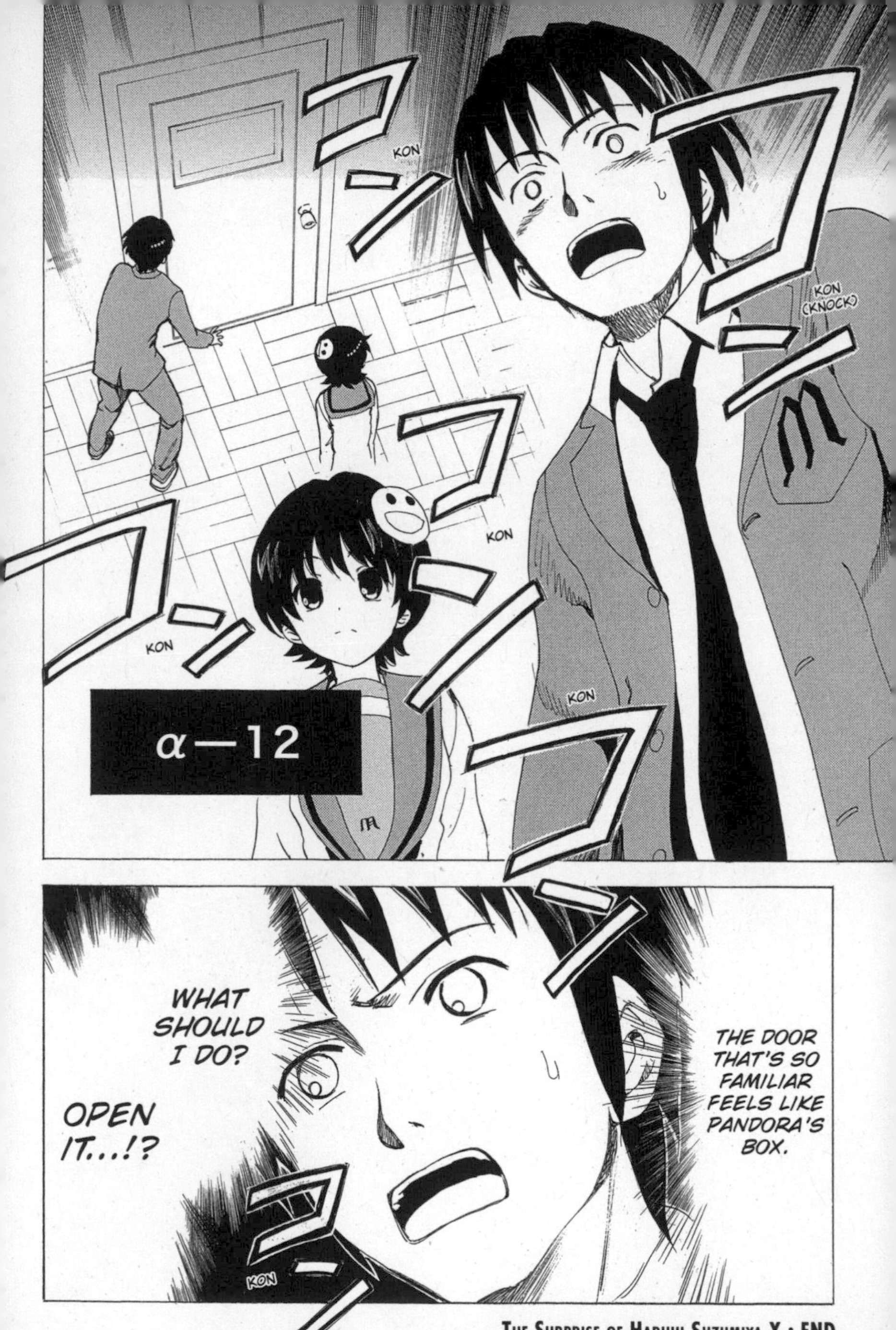
KON (KNOCK)
KON
KON
KON
KON
α—12
THE DOOR THAT'S SO FAMILIAR FEELS LIKE PANDORA'S BOX.
WHAT SHOULD I DO?
OPEN IT...!?
KON

THE SURPRISE OF HARUHI SUZUMIYA X : END

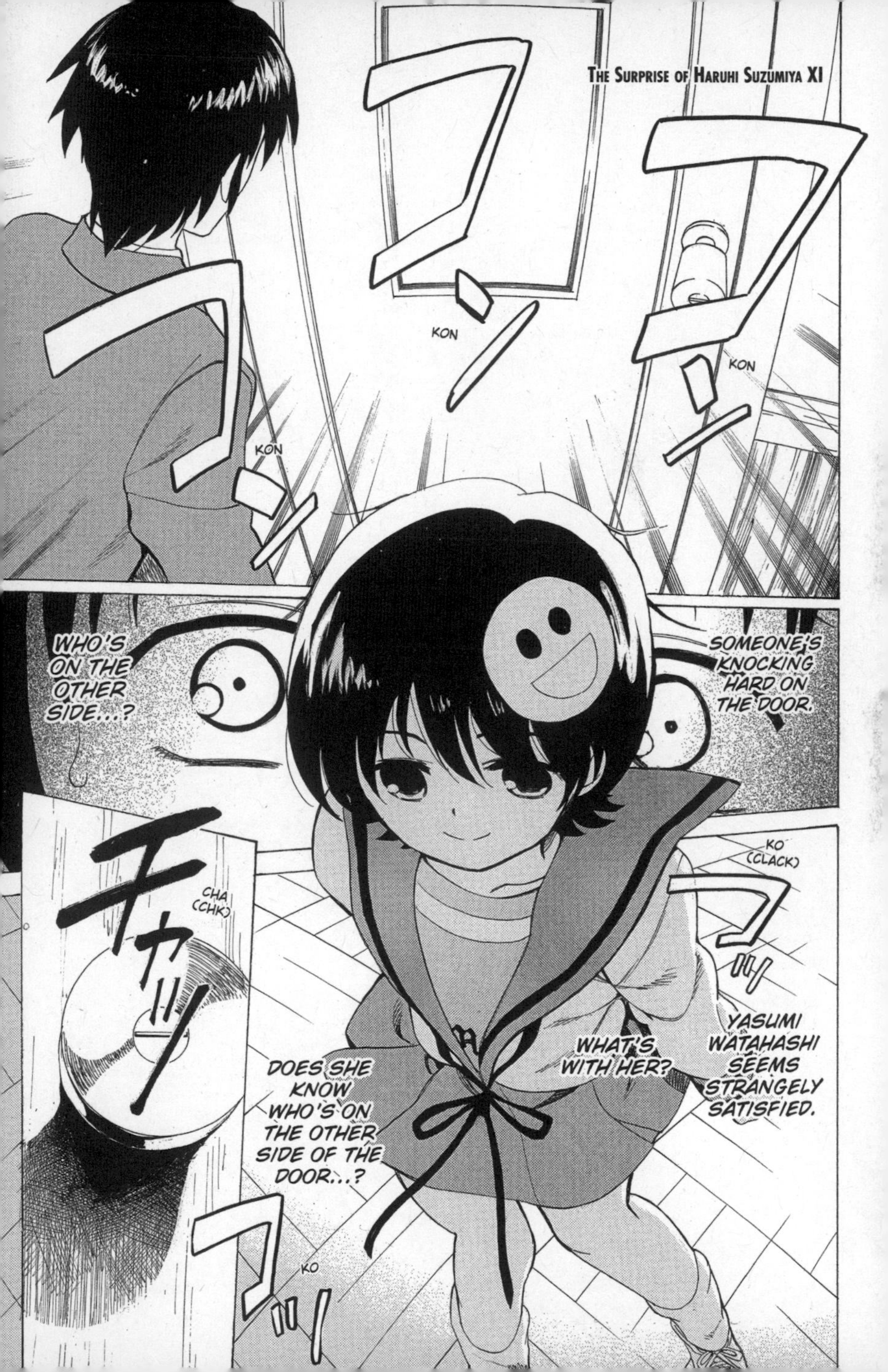
KON
KON
KON
SOMEONE'S KNOCKING HARD ON THE DOOR.
WHO'S ON THE OTHER SIDE...?
KO (CLACK)
YASUMI WATAHASHI SEEMS STRANGELY SATISFIED.
WHAT'S WITH HER?
DOES SHE KNOW WHO'S ON THE OTHER SIDE OF THE DOOR...?
CHA (CHK)
KO

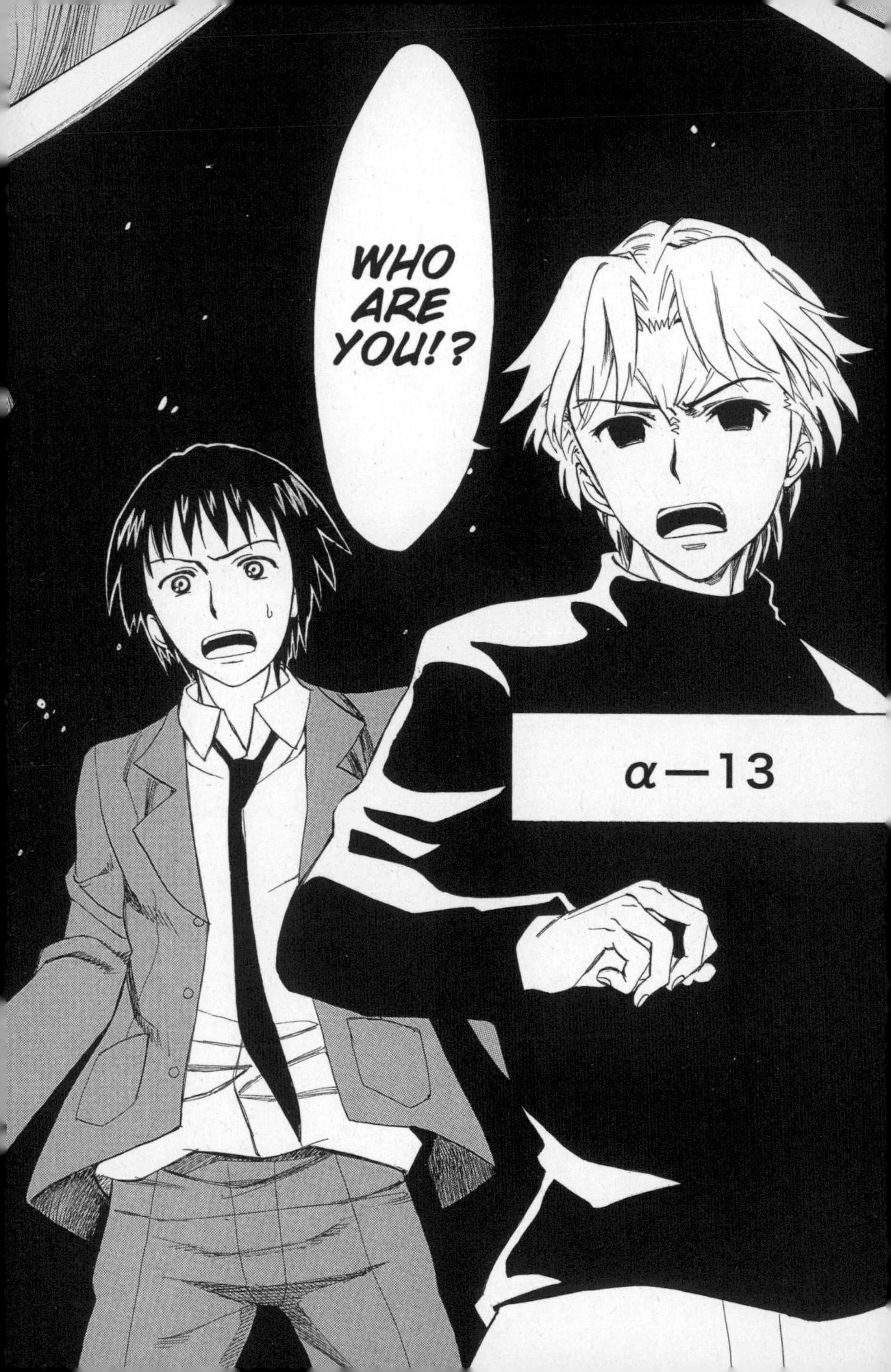
WHO ARE YOU!?
α—13

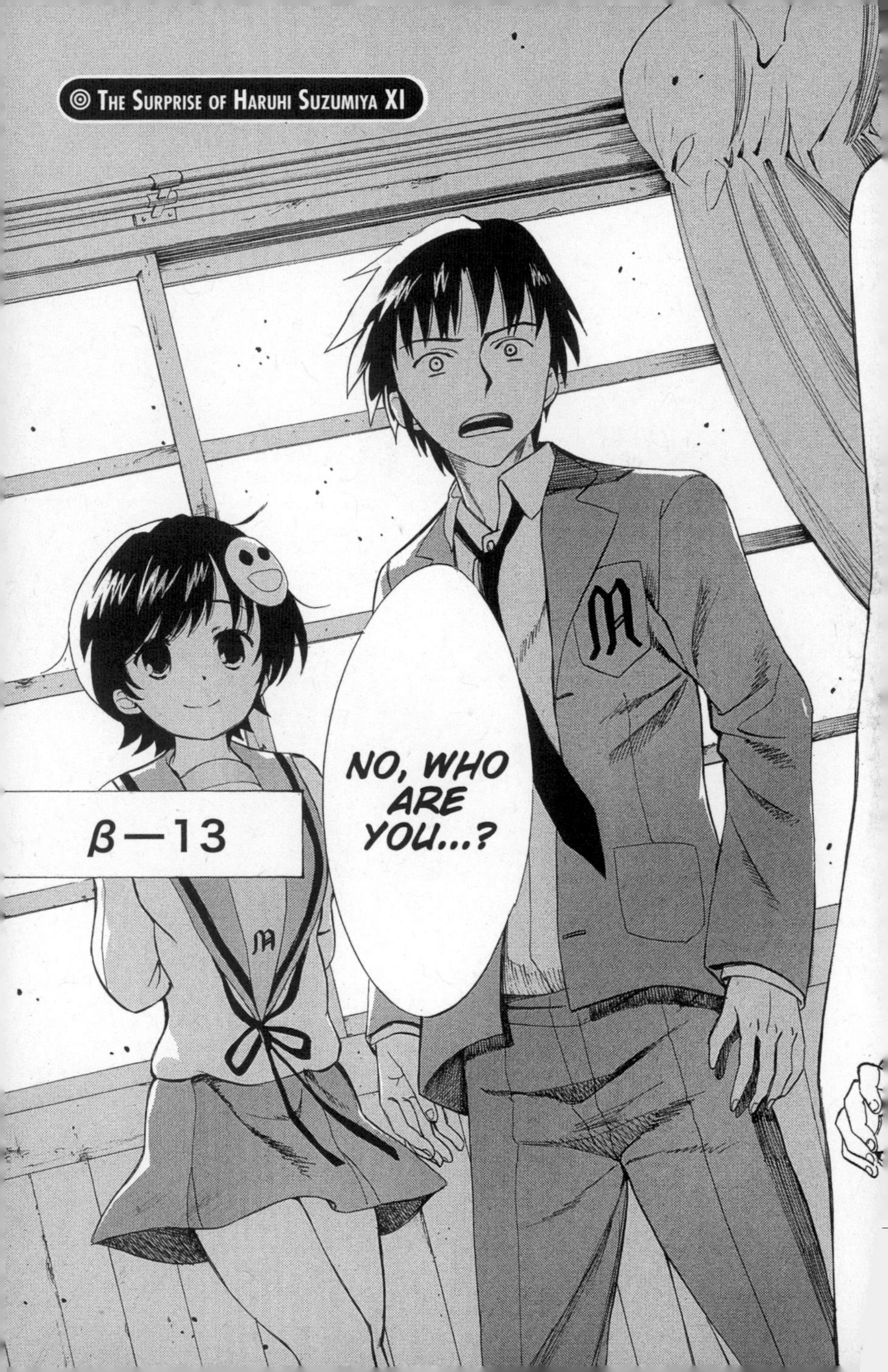

The Surprise of Haruhi Suzumiya XI
β—13
No, who are you...?

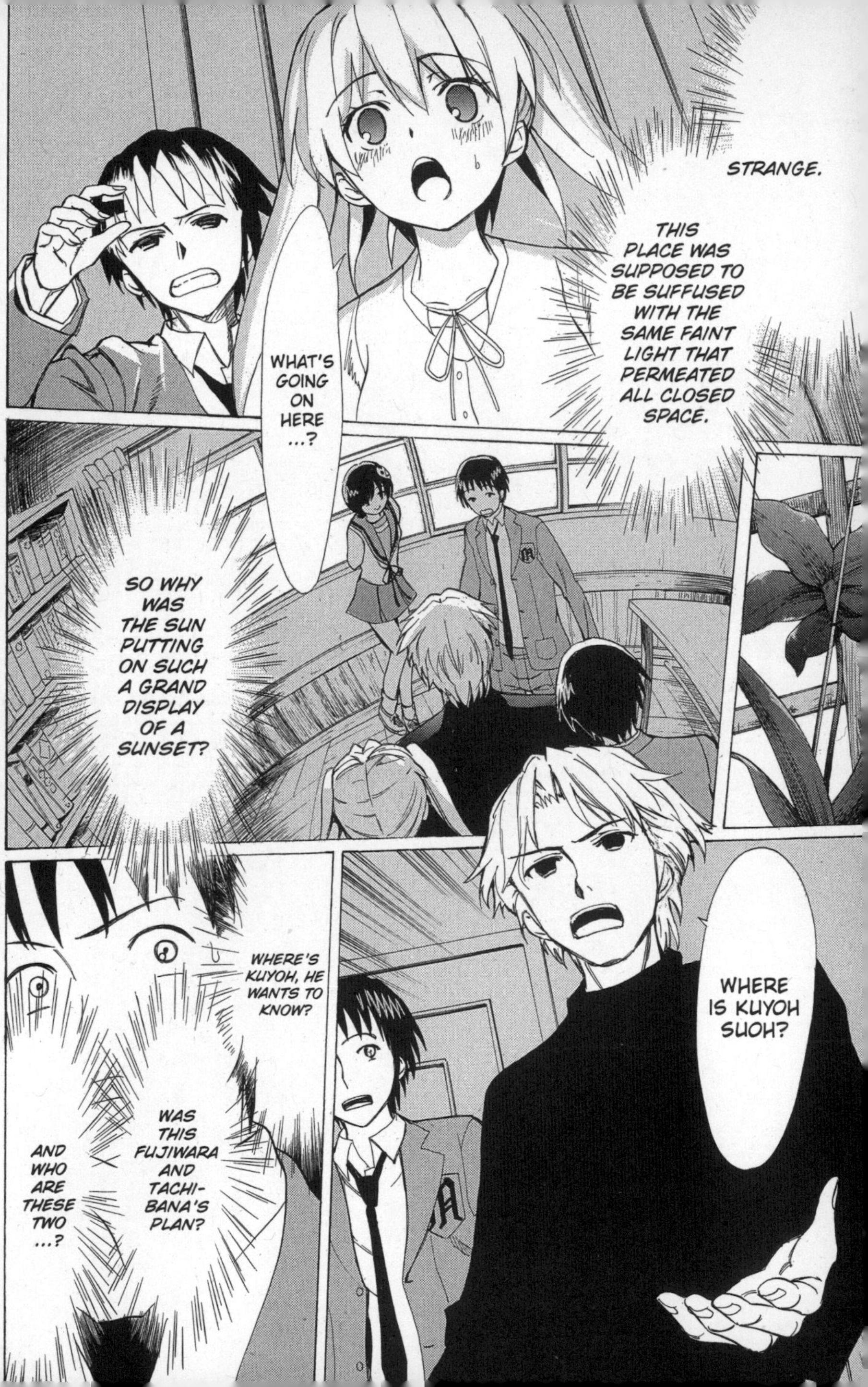
STRANGE.
THIS PLACE WAS SUPPOSED TO BE SUFFUSED WITH THE SAME FAINT LIGHT THAT PERMEATED ALL CLOSED SPACE.
WHAT'S GOING ON HERE ...?
SO WHY WAS THE SUN PUTTING ON SUCH A GRAND DISPLAY OF A SUNSET?
WHERE IS KUYOH SUOH?
WHERE'S KUYOH, HE WANTS TO KNOW?
WAS THIS FUJIWARA AND TACHIBANA'S PLAN?
AND WHO ARE THESE TWO ...?

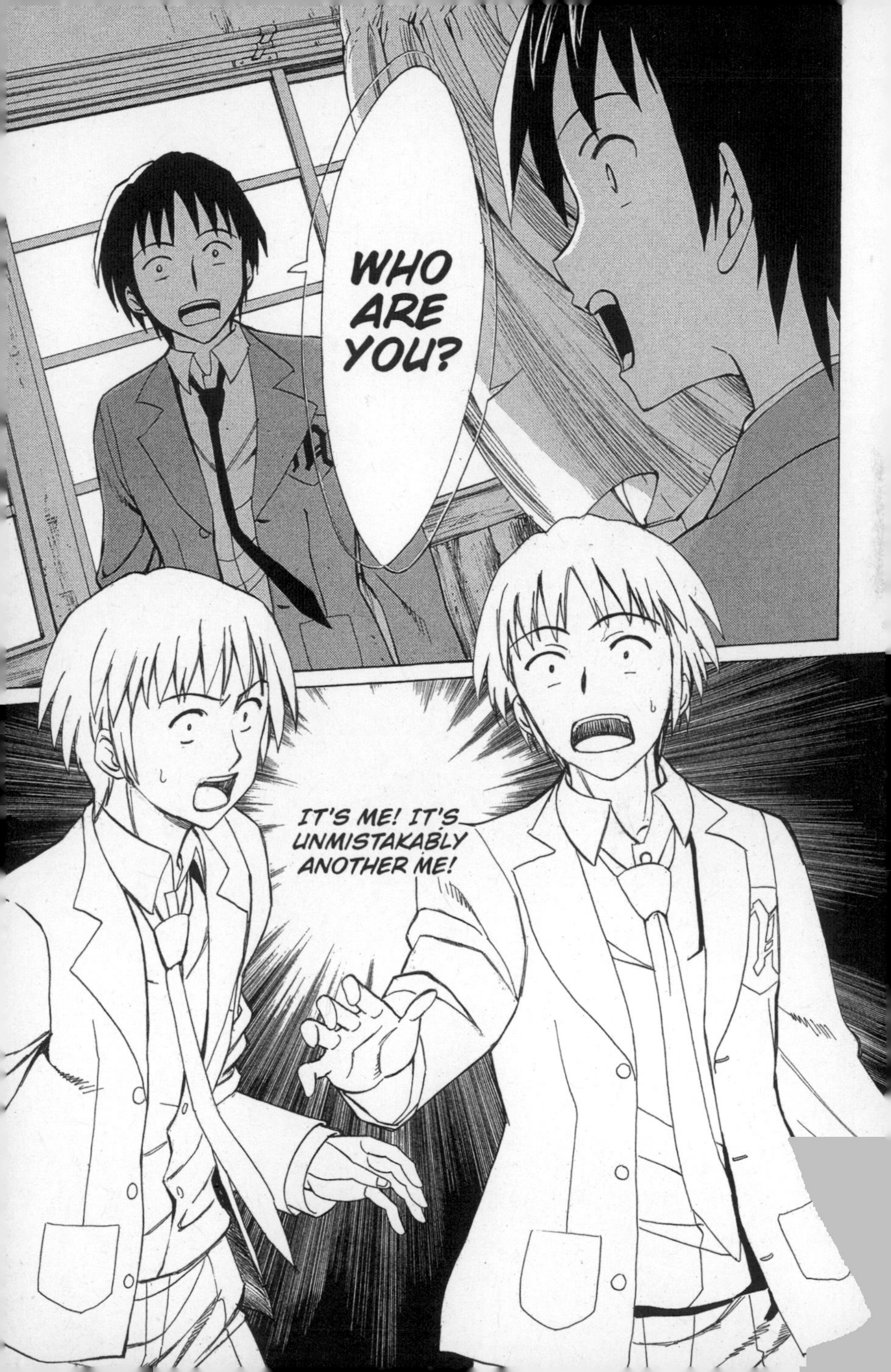
WHO ARE YOU?
IT'S ME! IT'S UNMISTAKABLY ANOTHER ME!

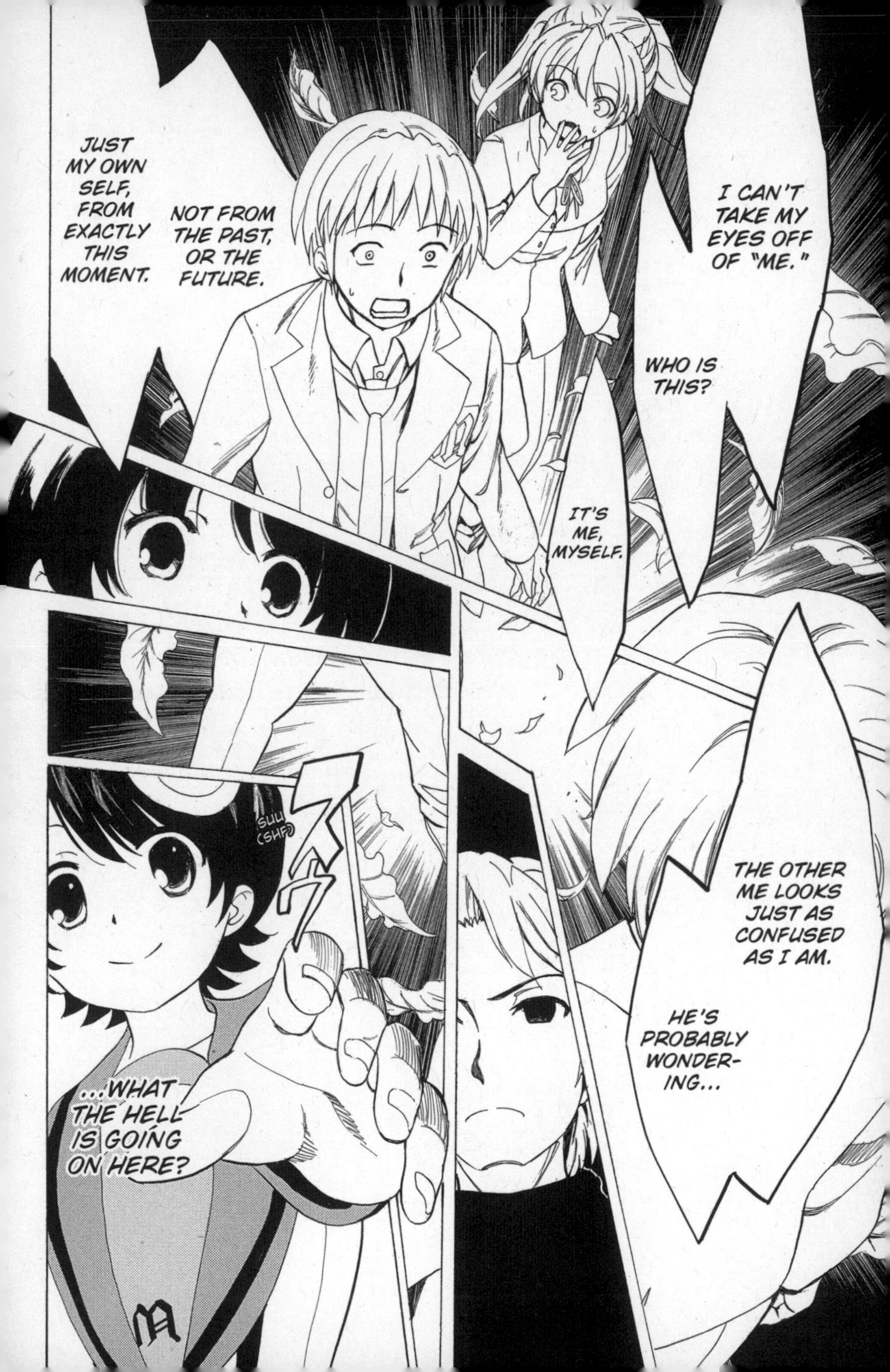
I CAN'T TAKE MY EYES OFF OF "ME."
WHO IS THIS?
IT'S ME, MYSELF.
NOT FROM THE PAST, OR THE FUTURE.
JUST MY OWN SELF, FROM EXACTLY THIS MOMENT.
THE OTHER ME LOOKS JUST AS CONFUSED AS I AM.
HE'S PROBABLY WONDER-ING...
SUU (SHF)
...WHAT THE HELL IS GOING ON HERE?

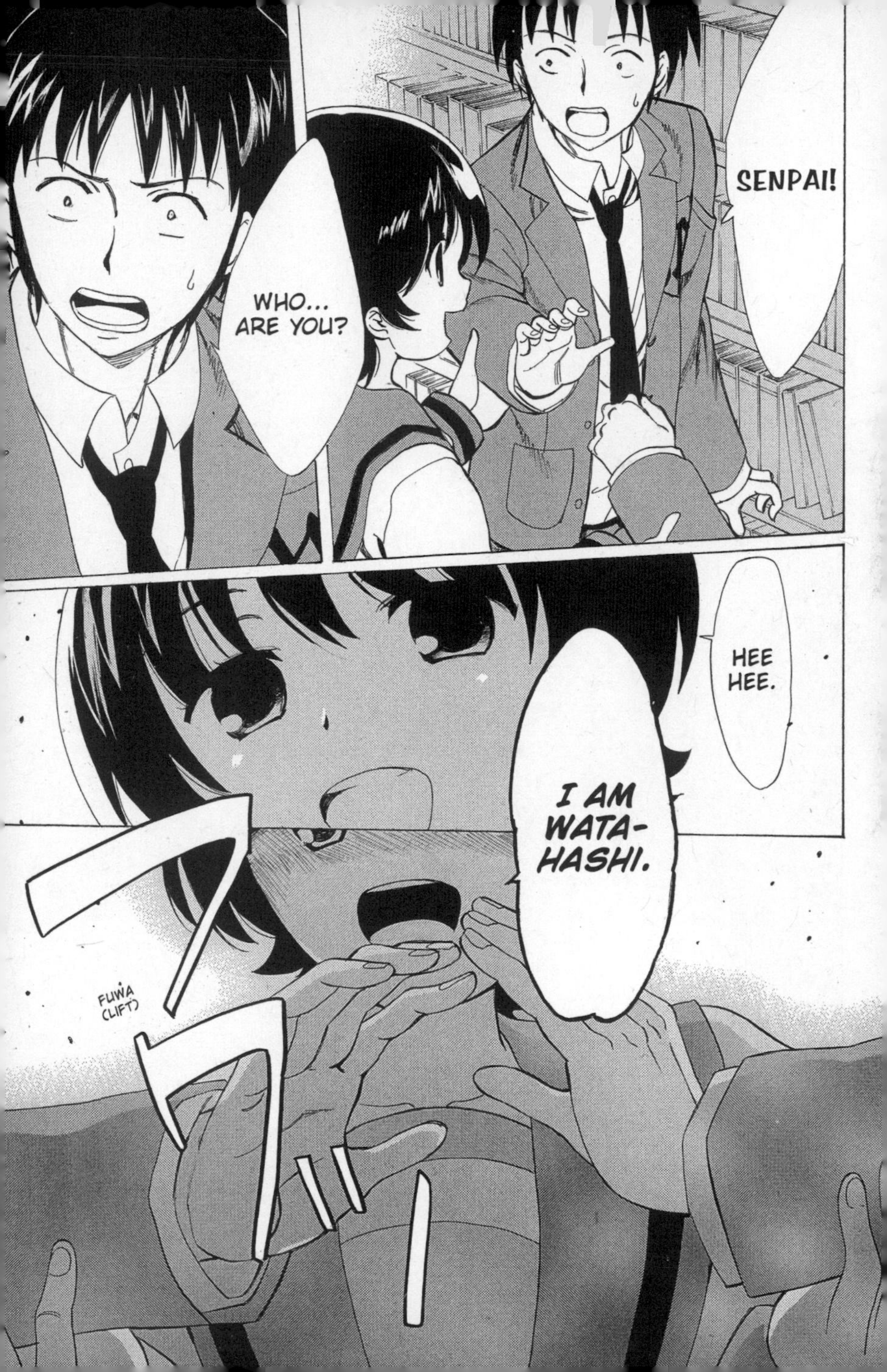
SENPAI!
WHO... ARE YOU?
HEE HEE.
I AM WATA-HASHI.
FUWA (LIFT)

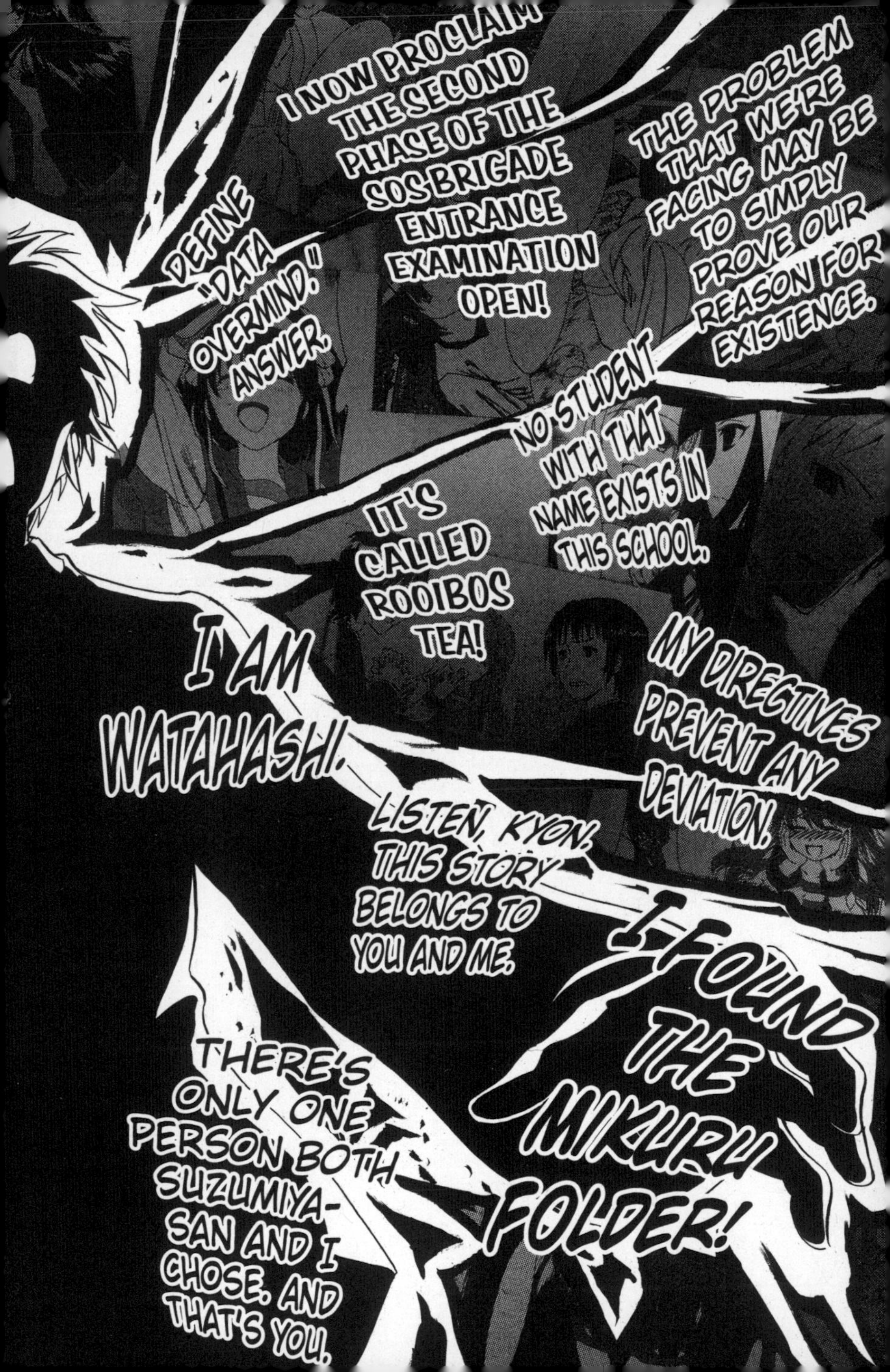
THE PROBLEM THAT WE'RE FACING MAY BE TO SIMPLY PROVE OUR REASON FOR EXISTENCE.
I NOW PROCLAIM THE SECOND PHASE OF THE SOS BRIGADE ENTRANCE EXAMINATION OPEN!
DEFINE "DATA OVERMIND." ANSWER.
NO STUDENT WITH THAT NAME EXISTS IN THIS SCHOOL.
IT'S CALLED ROOIBOS TEA!
MY DIRECTIVES PREVENT ANY DEVIATION.
I AM WATAHASHI.
LISTEN, KYON. THIS STORY BELONGS TO YOU AND ME.
I FOUND THE MIKURU FOLDER!
THERE'S ONLY ONE PERSON BOTH SUZUMIYA-SAN AND I CHOSE. AND THAT'S YOU.

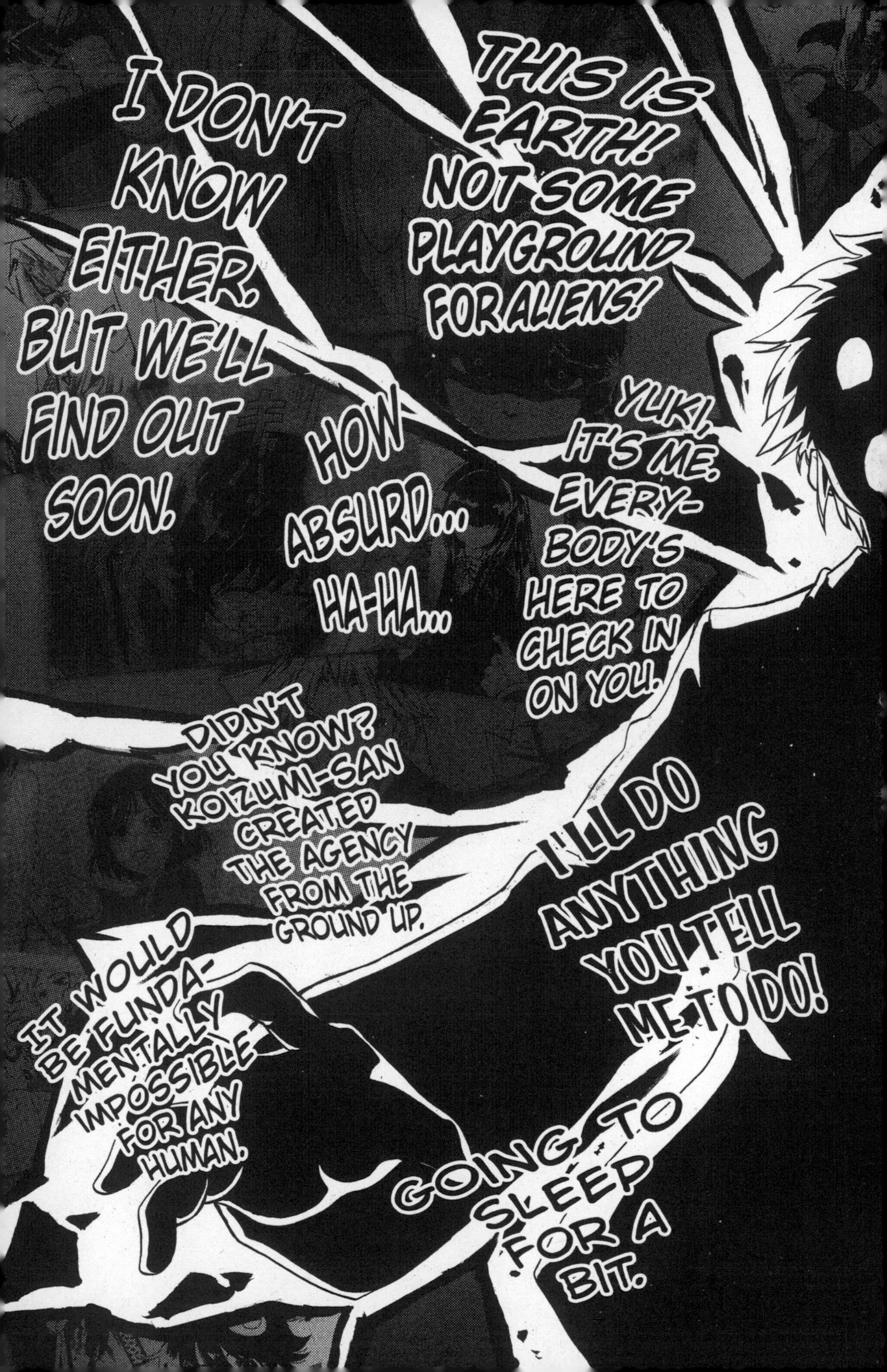
THIS IS EARTH! NOT SOME PLAYGROUND FOR ALIENS!
I DON'T KNOW EITHER. BUT WE'LL FIND OUT SOON.
YUKI, IT'S ME. EVERY-BODY'S HERE TO CHECK IN ON YOU.
HOW ABSURD... HA-HA...
DIDN'T YOU KNOW? KOIZUMI-SAN CREATED THE AGENCY FROM THE GROUND UP.
I'LL DO ANYTHING YOU TELL ME TO DO!
IT WOULD BE FUNDA-MENTALLY IMPOSSIBLE FOR ANY HUMAN.
GOING TO SLEEP FOR A BIT.

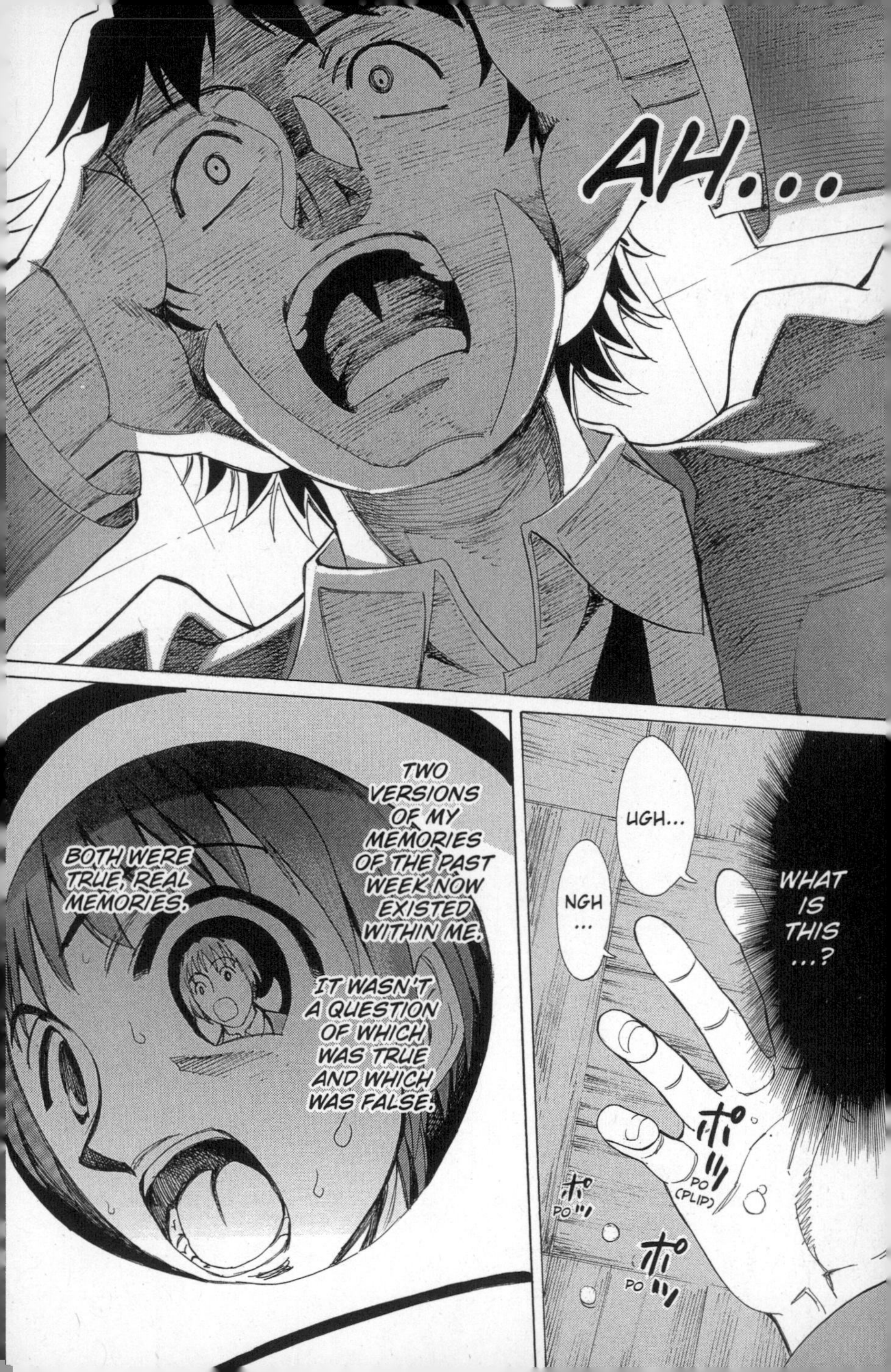
AH...
UGH...
NGH...
WHAT IS THIS...?
ポッ PO (PLIP)
ポッ PO
ポッ PO
TWO VERSIONS OF MY MEMORIES OF THE PAST WEEK NOW EXISTED WITHIN ME.
BOTH WERE TRUE, REAL MEMORIES.
IT WASN'T A QUESTION OF WHICH WAS TRUE AND WHICH WAS FALSE.

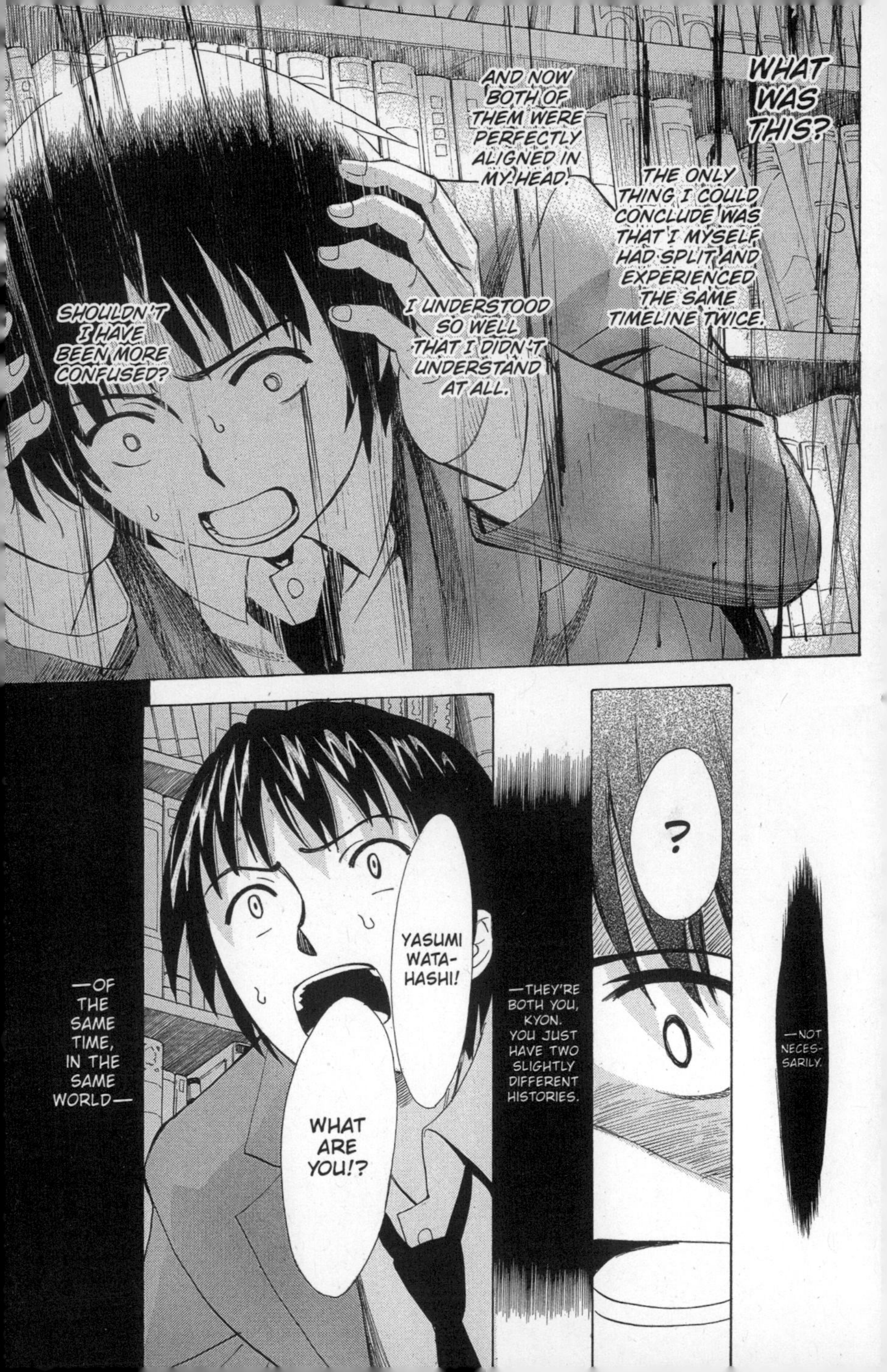
WHAT WAS THIS?
THE ONLY THING I COULD CONCLUDE WAS THAT I MYSELF HAD SPLIT AND EXPERIENCED THE SAME TIMELINE TWICE.
AND NOW BOTH OF THEM WERE PERFECTLY ALIGNED IN MY HEAD.
I UNDERSTOOD SO WELL THAT I DIDN'T UNDERSTAND AT ALL.
SHOULDN'T I HAVE BEEN MORE CONFUSED?
—NOT NECES-SARILY.
?
—THEY'RE BOTH YOU, KYON. YOU JUST HAVE TWO SLIGHTLY DIFFERENT HISTORIES.
YASUMI WATA-HASHI!
WHAT ARE YOU!?
—OF THE SAME TIME, IN THE SAME WORLD—

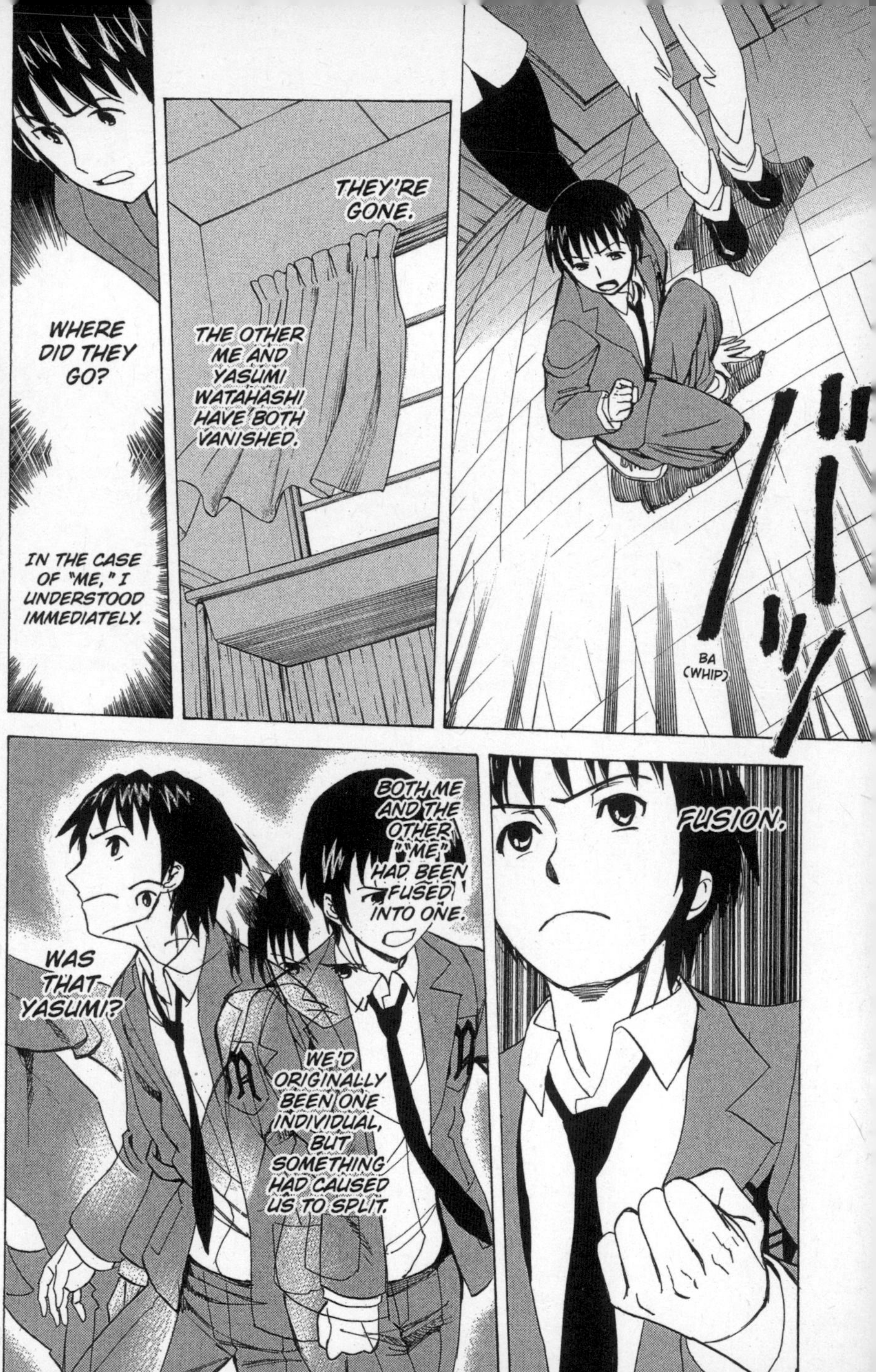
BA (WHIP)
THEY'RE GONE.
THE OTHER ME AND YASUMI WATAHASHI HAVE BOTH VANISHED.
WHERE DID THEY GO?
IN THE CASE OF "ME," I UNDERSTOOD IMMEDIATELY.
FUSION.
BOTH ME AND THE OTHER "ME" HAD BEEN FUSED INTO ONE.
WAS THAT YASUMI?
WE'D ORIGINALLY BEEN ONE INDIVIDUAL, BUT SOMETHING HAD CAUSED US TO SPLIT.

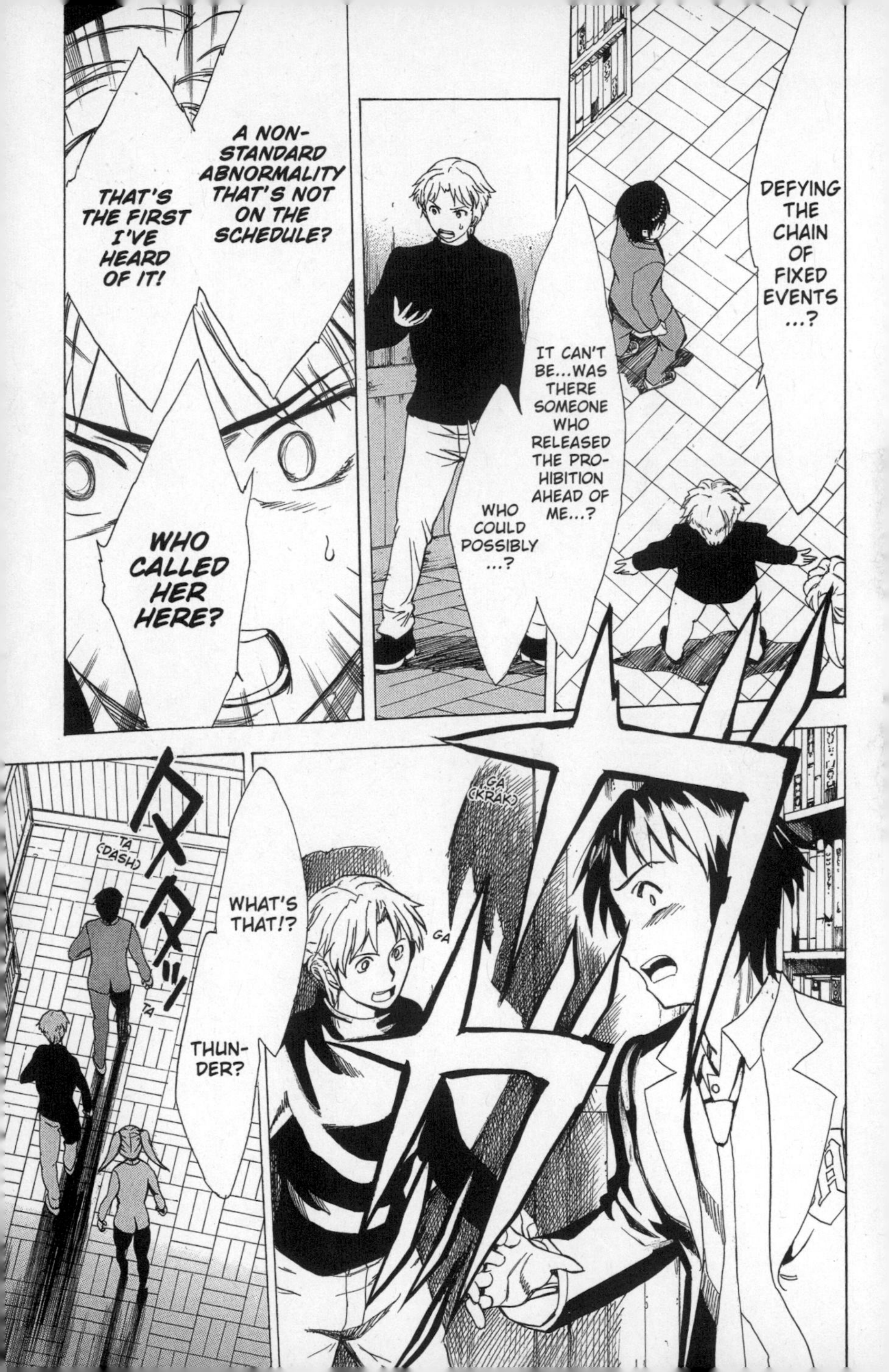
DEFYING THE CHAIN OF FIXED EVENTS ...?
IT CAN'T BE...WAS THERE SOMEONE WHO RELEASED THE PRO-HIBITION AHEAD OF ME...?
WHO COULD POSSIBLY ...?
A NON-STANDARD ABNORMALITY THAT'S NOT ON THE SCHEDULE?
THAT'S THE FIRST I'VE HEARD OF IT!
WHO CALLED HER HERE?
GA (KRAK)
GA
WHAT'S THAT!?
THUN-DER?
TA (DASH)
TA

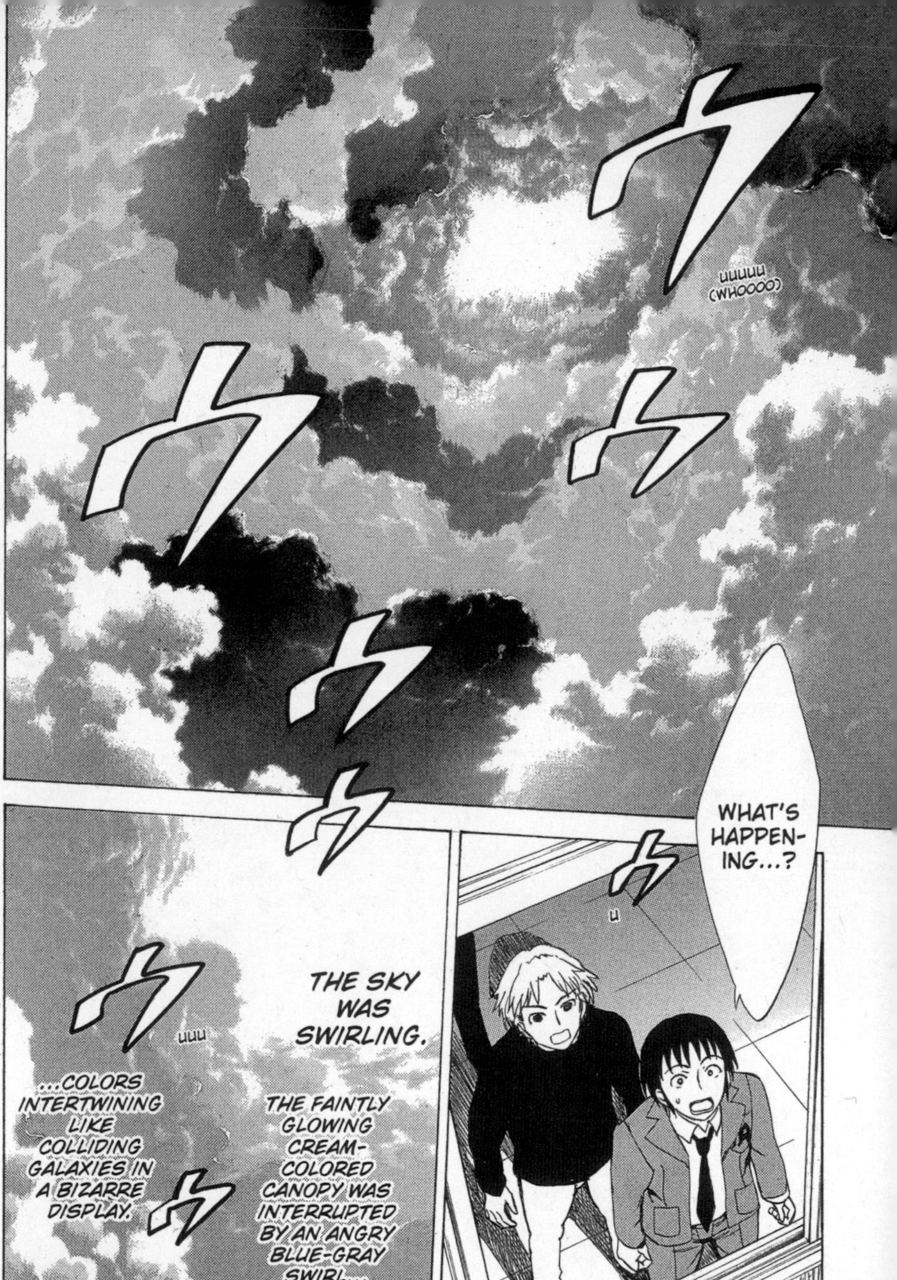
uuuuu (WHOOOO)
WHAT'S HAPPEN-ING...?
u
THE SKY WAS SWIRLING.
THE FAINTLY GLOWING CREAM-COLORED CANOPY WAS INTERRUPTED BY AN ANGRY BLUE-GRAY SWIRL...
...COLORS INTERTWINING LIKE COLLIDING GALAXIES IN A BIZARRE DISPLAY.
uuu

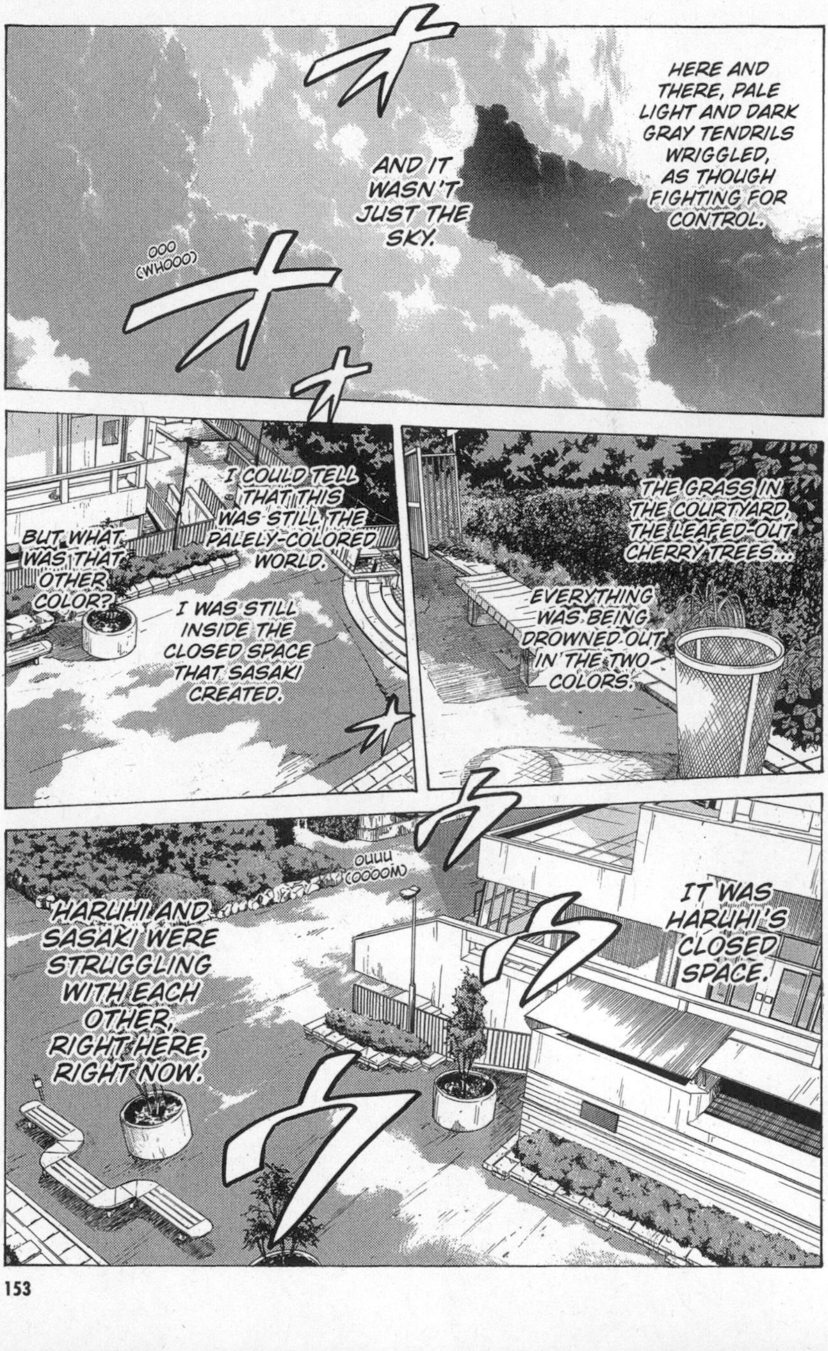
HERE AND THERE, PALE LIGHT AND DARK GRAY TENDRILS WRIGGLED, AS THOUGH FIGHTING FOR CONTROL.
AND IT WASN'T JUST THE SKY.
OOO (WHOOO)
THE GRASS IN THE COURTYARD, THE LEAFED-OUT CHERRY TREES...
EVERYTHING WAS BEING DROWNED OUT IN THE TWO COLORS.
I COULD TELL THAT THIS WAS STILL THE PALELY-COLORED WORLD.
I WAS STILL INSIDE THE CLOSED SPACE THAT SASAKI CREATED.
BUT WHAT WAS THAT OTHER COLOR?
IT WAS HARUHI'S CLOSED SPACE.
OUUU (OOOOM)
HARUHI AND SASAKI WERE STRUGGLING WITH EACH OTHER, RIGHT HERE, RIGHT NOW.

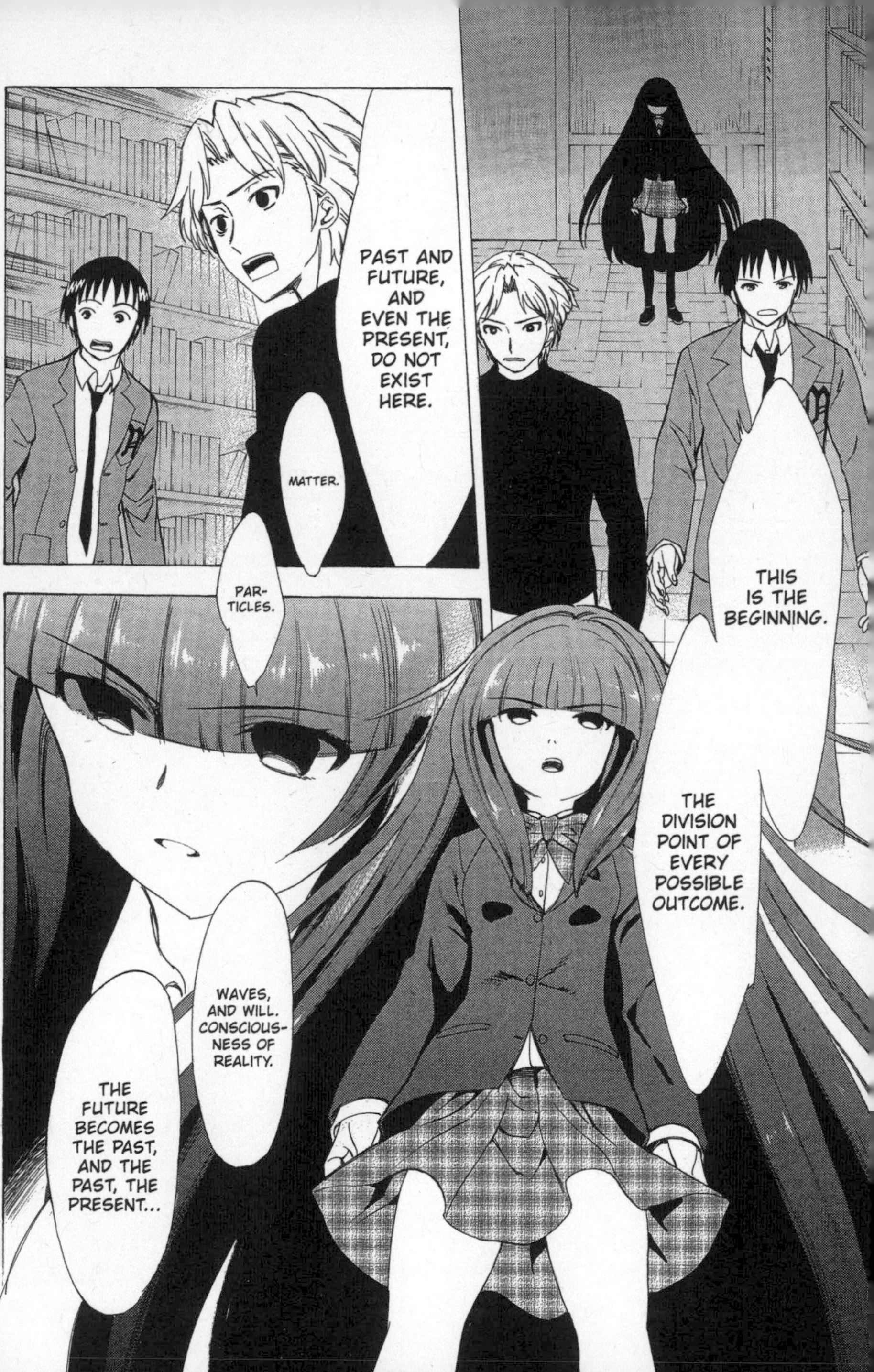
THIS IS THE BEGINNING.
THE DIVISION POINT OF EVERY POSSIBLE OUTCOME.
PAST AND FUTURE, AND EVEN THE PRESENT, DO NOT EXIST HERE.
MATTER.
PAR-TICLES.
WAVES, AND WILL. CONSCIOUS-NESS OF REALITY.
THE FUTURE BECOMES THE PAST, AND THE PAST, THE PRESENT...

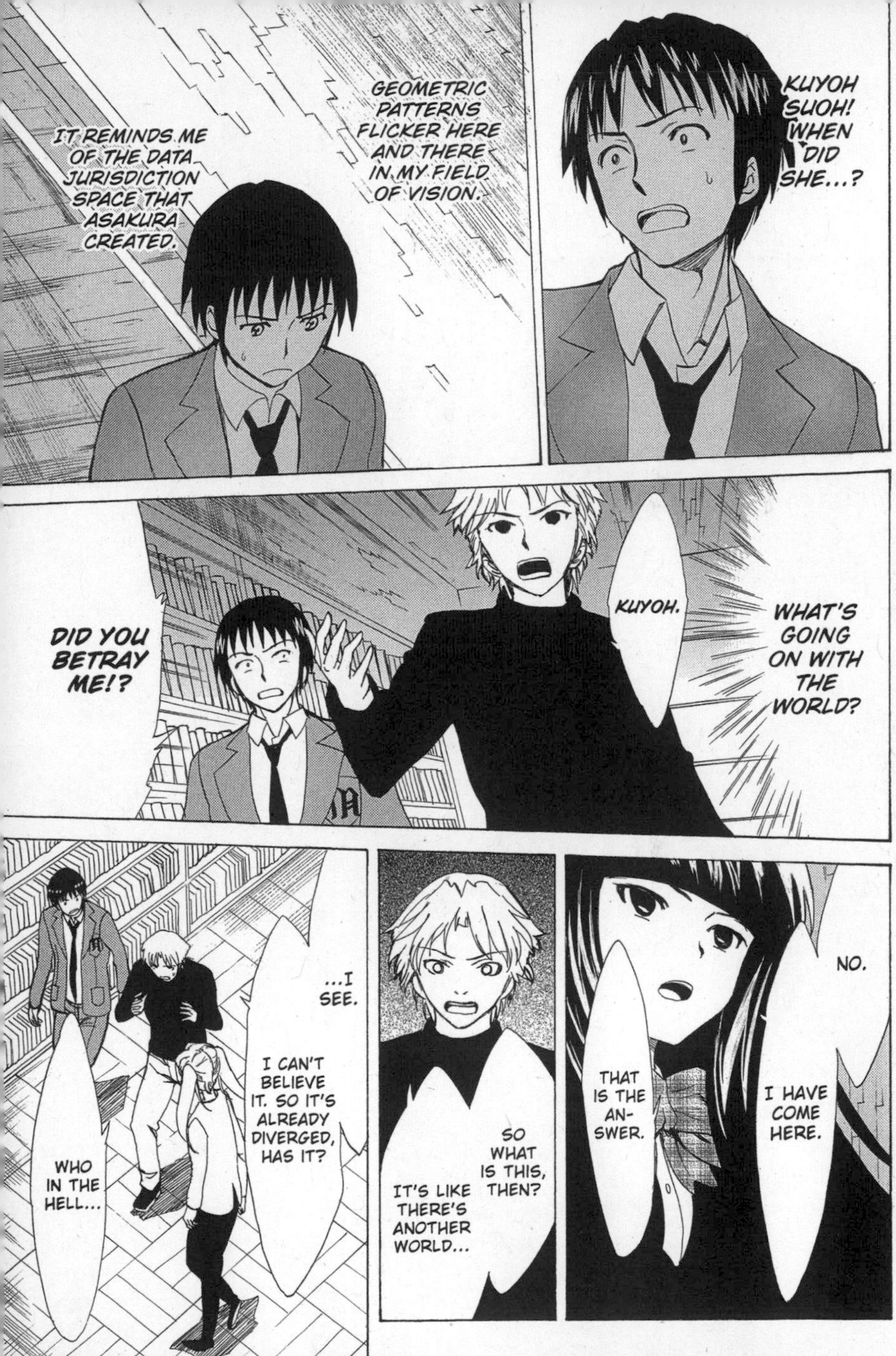
KUYOH SUOH! WHEN DID SHE...?
GEOMETRIC PATTERNS FLICKER HERE AND THERE IN MY FIELD OF VISION.
IT REMINDS ME OF THE DATA JURISDICTION SPACE THAT ASAKURA CREATED.
WHAT'S GOING ON WITH THE WORLD?
KUYOH.
DID YOU BETRAY ME!?
NO.
I HAVE COME HERE.
THAT IS THE AN-SWER.
SO WHAT IS THIS, THEN?
IT'S LIKE THERE'S ANOTHER WORLD...
...I SEE.
I CAN'T BELIEVE IT. SO IT'S ALREADY DIVERGED, HAS IT?
WHO IN THE HELL...

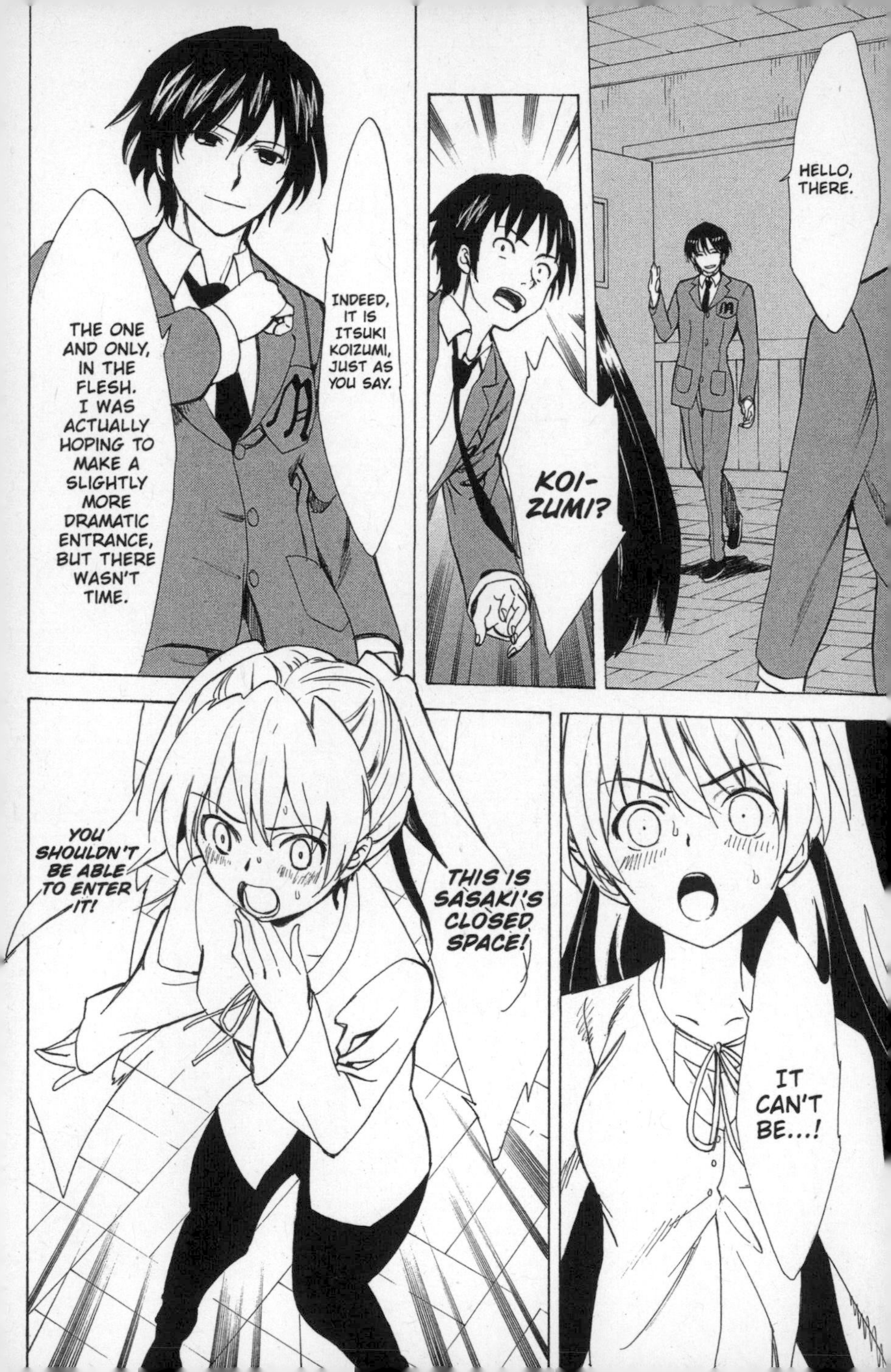

HELLO, THERE.
KOI-ZUMI?
INDEED, IT IS ITSUKI KOIZUMI, JUST AS YOU SAY.
THE ONE AND ONLY, IN THE FLESH. I WAS ACTUALLY HOPING TO MAKE A SLIGHTLY MORE DRAMATIC ENTRANCE, BUT THERE WASN'T TIME.
IT CAN'T BE...!
THIS IS SASAKI'S CLOSED SPACE!
YOU SHOULDN'T BE ABLE TO ENTER IT!

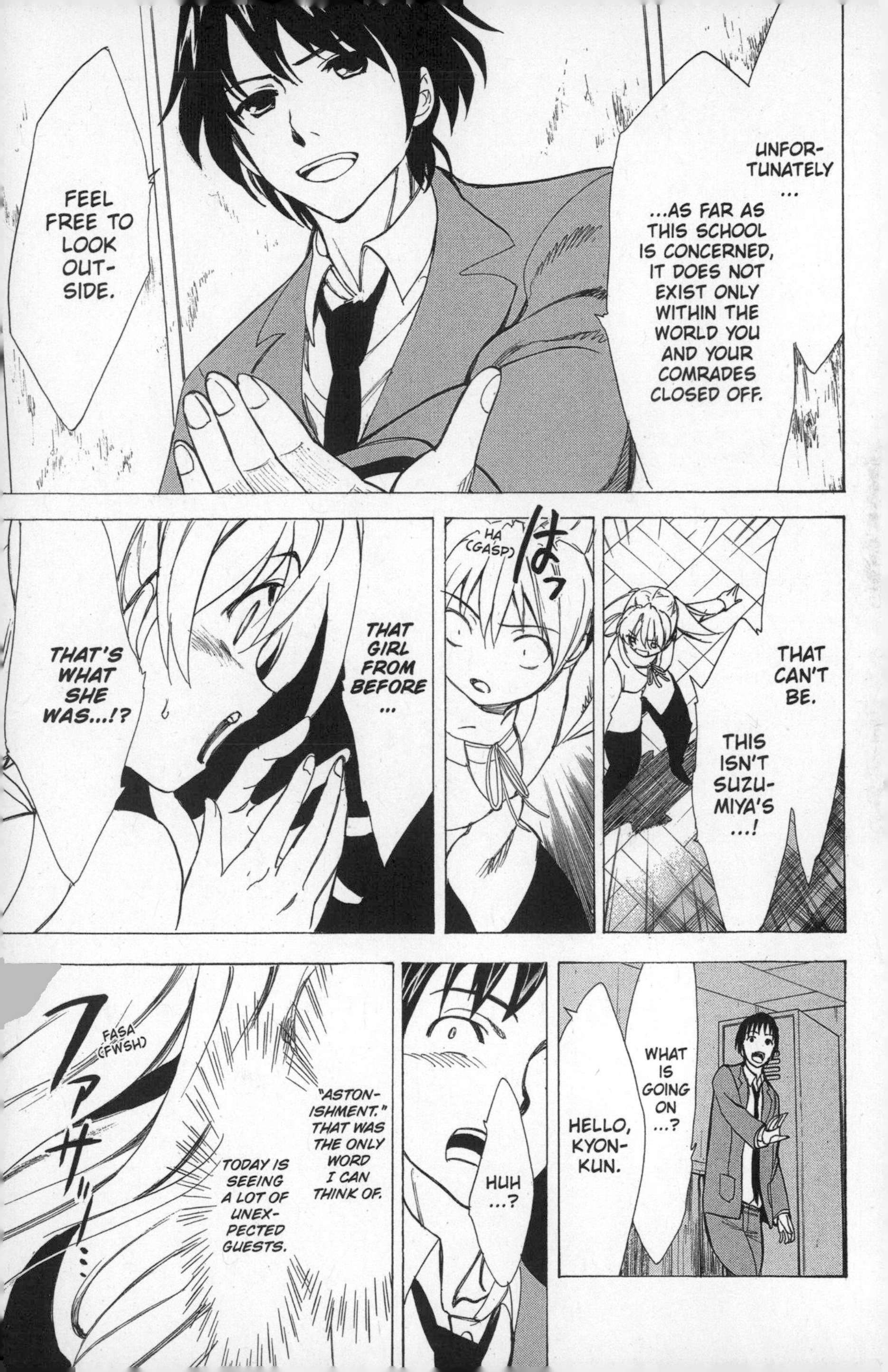
UNFOR-TUNATELY...
...AS FAR AS THIS SCHOOL IS CONCERNED, IT DOES NOT EXIST ONLY WITHIN THE WORLD YOU AND YOUR COMRADES CLOSED OFF.
FEEL FREE TO LOOK OUT-SIDE.
THAT CAN'T BE.
THIS ISN'T SUZU-MIYA'S ...!
HA (GASP)
はっ
THAT GIRL FROM BEFORE ...
THAT'S WHAT SHE WAS...!?
WHAT IS GOING ON ...?
HELLO, KYON-KUN.
HUH ...?
"ASTON-ISHMENT." THAT WAS THE ONLY WORD I CAN THINK OF.
TODAY IS SEEING A LOT OF UNEX-PECTED GUESTS.
FASA (FWSH)
ファサッ…

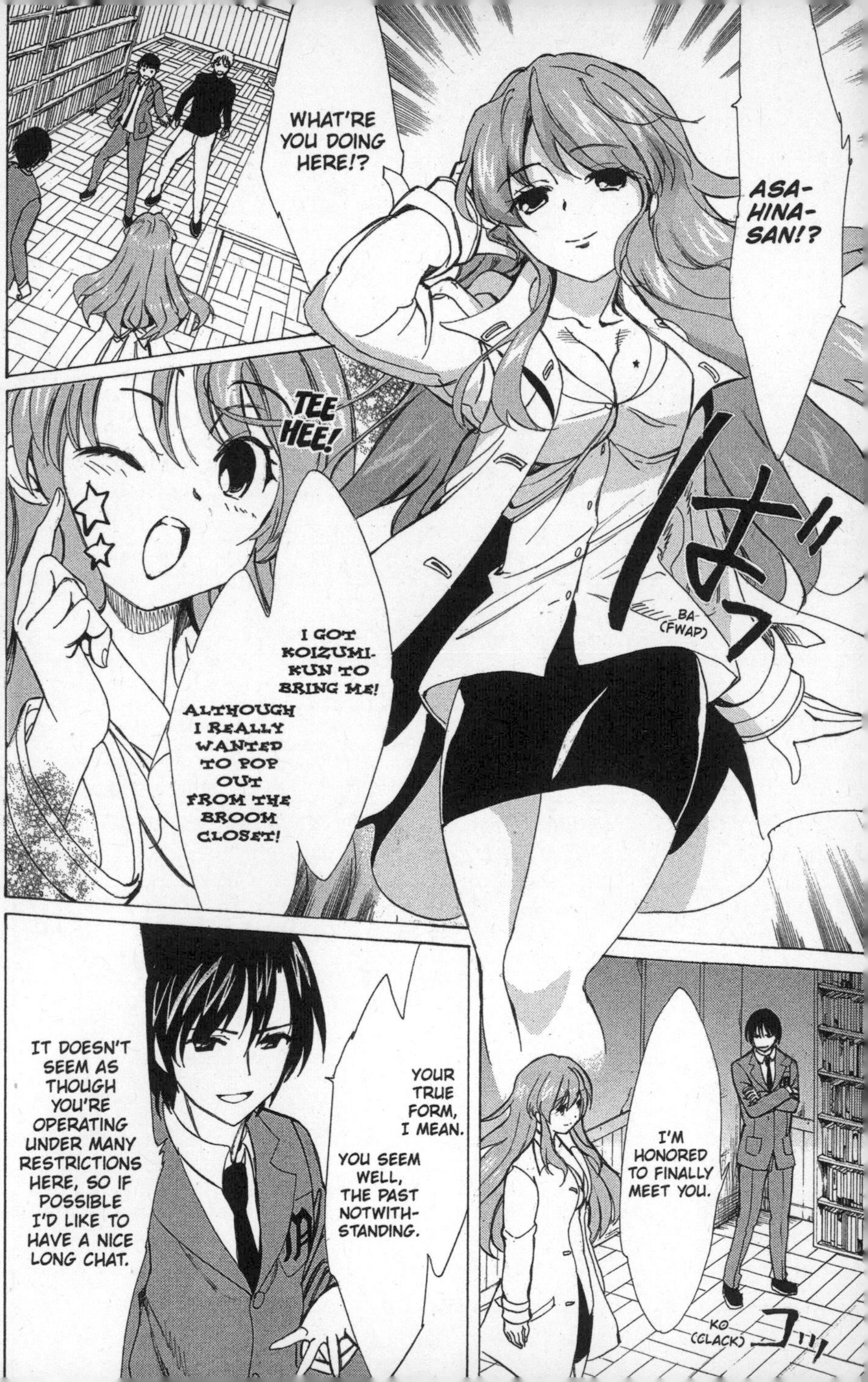
ASA-HINA-SAN!?
BA (FWAP)
WHAT'RE YOU DOING HERE!?
TEE HEE!
I GOT KOIZUMI-KUN TO BRING ME!
ALTHOUGH I REALLY WANTED TO POP OUT FROM THE BROOM CLOSET!
I'M HONORED TO FINALLY MEET YOU.
KO (CLACK)
YOUR TRUE FORM, I MEAN.
YOU SEEM WELL, THE PAST NOTWITH-STANDING.
IT DOESN'T SEEM AS THOUGH YOU'RE OPERATING UNDER MANY RESTRICTIONS HERE, SO IF POSSIBLE I'D LIKE TO HAVE A NICE LONG CHAT.

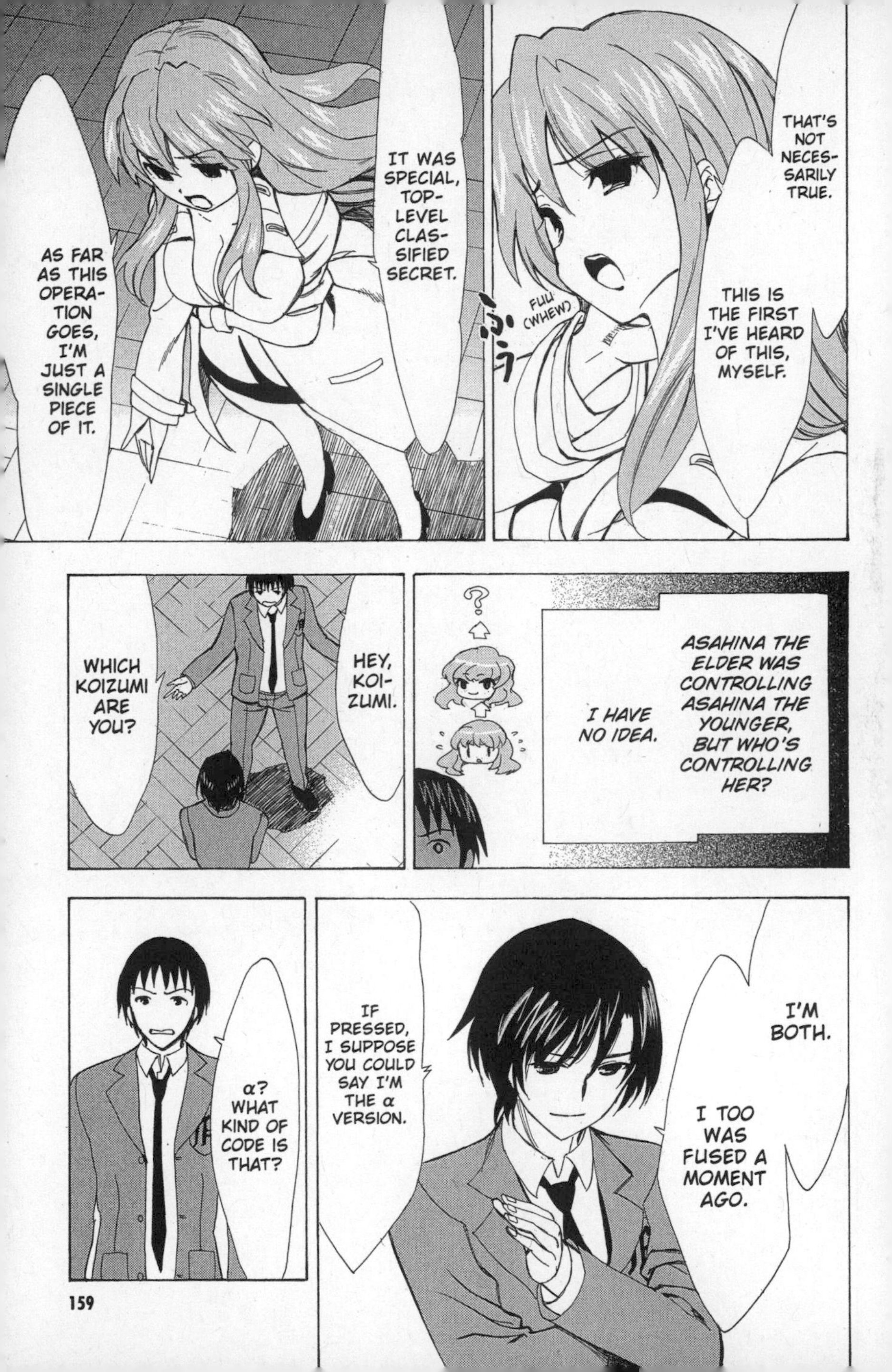
THAT'S NOT NECES-SARILY TRUE.
FUU (WHEW)
THIS IS THE FIRST I'VE HEARD OF THIS, MYSELF.
IT WAS SPECIAL, TOP-LEVEL CLAS-SIFIED SECRET.
AS FAR AS THIS OPERA-TION GOES, I'M JUST A SINGLE PIECE OF IT.
ASAHINA THE ELDER WAS CONTROLLING ASAHINA THE YOUNGER, BUT WHO'S CONTROLLING HER?
I HAVE NO IDEA.
?
HEY, KOI-ZUMI.
WHICH KOIZUMI ARE YOU?
I'M BOTH.
I TOO WAS FUSED A MOMENT AGO.
IF PRESSED, I SUPPOSE YOU COULD SAY I'M THE α VERSION.
α? WHAT KIND OF CODE IS THAT?

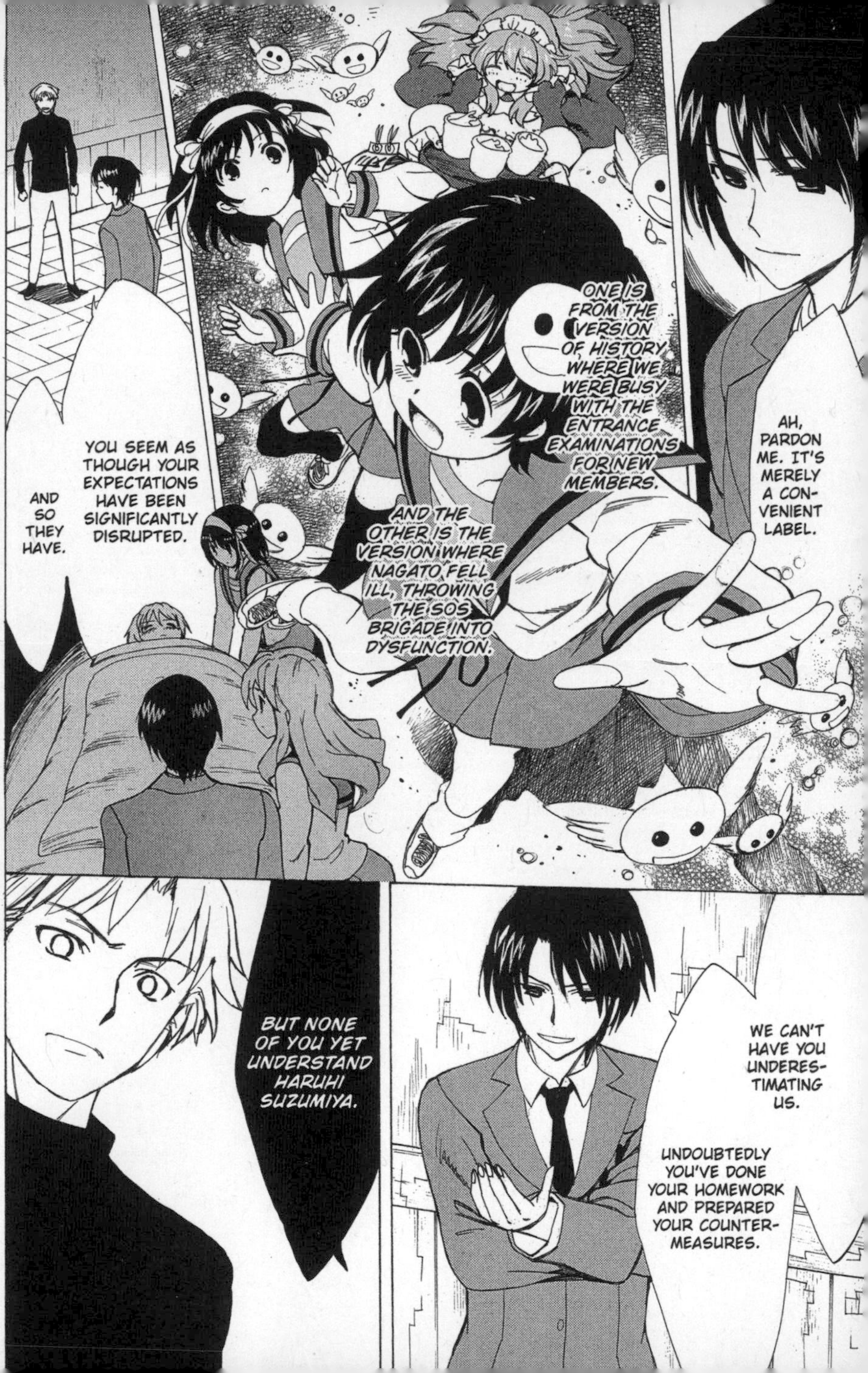
AH, PARDON ME. IT'S MERELY A CON-VENIENT LABEL.
ONE IS FROM THE VERSION OF HISTORY WHERE WE WERE BUSY WITH THE ENTRANCE EXAMINATIONS FOR NEW MEMBERS.
AND THE OTHER IS THE VERSION WHERE NAGATO FELL ILL, THROWING THE SOS BRIGADE INTO DYSFUNCTION.
YOU SEEM AS THOUGH YOUR EXPECTATIONS HAVE BEEN SIGNIFICANTLY DISRUPTED.
AND SO THEY HAVE.
WE CAN'T HAVE YOU UNDERES-TIMATING US.
UNDOUBTEDLY YOU'VE DONE YOUR HOMEWORK AND PREPARED YOUR COUNTER-MEASURES.
BUT NONE OF YOU YET UNDERSTAND HARUHI SUZUMIYA.

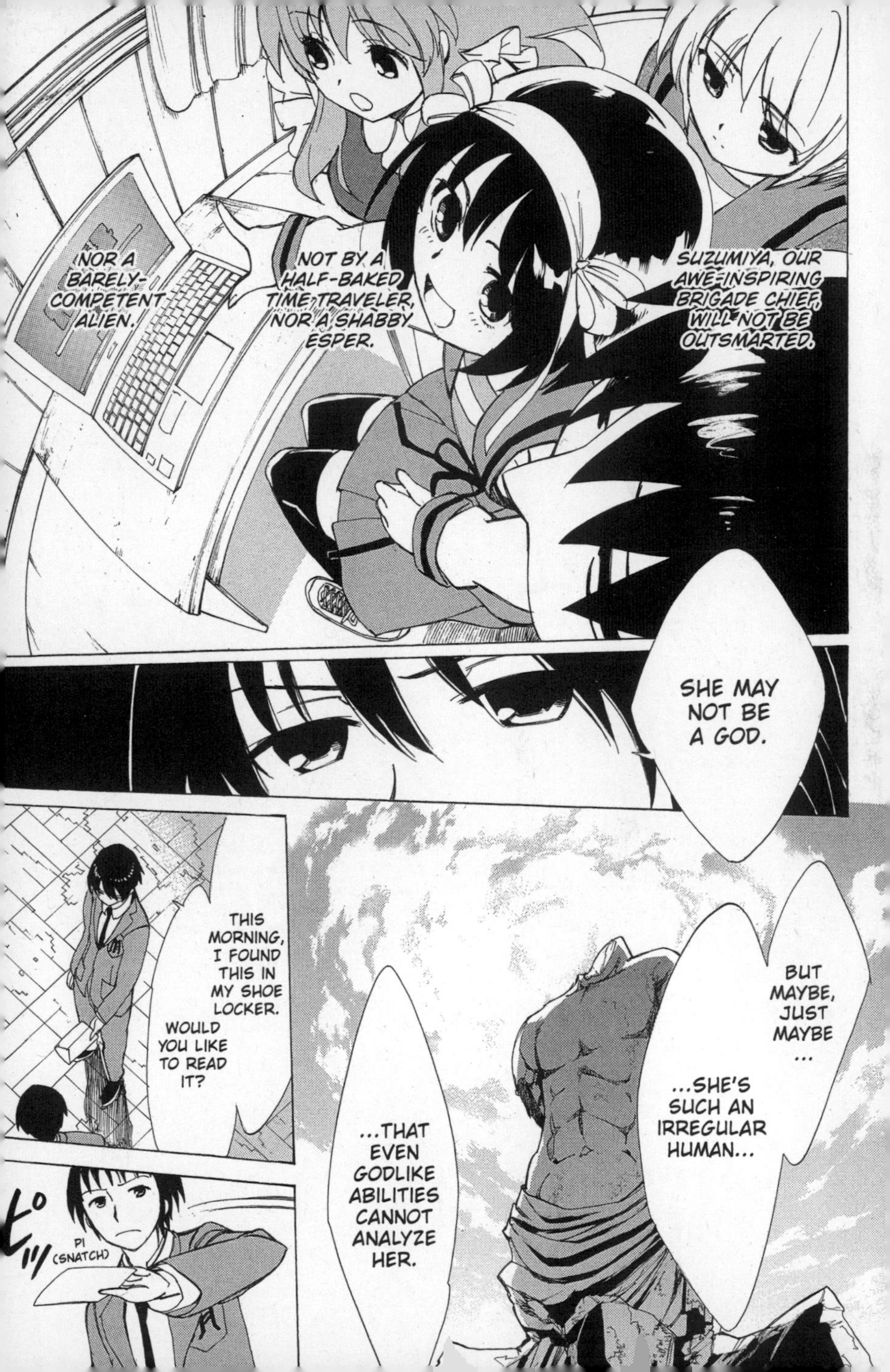
SUZUMIYA, OUR AWE-INSPIRING BRIGADE CHIEF, WILL NOT BE OUTSMARTED.
NOT BY A HALF-BAKED TIME TRAVELER, NOR A SHABBY ESPER.
NOR A BARELY-COMPETENT ALIEN.
SHE MAY NOT BE A GOD.
BUT MAYBE, JUST MAYBE ...
...SHE'S SUCH AN IRREGULAR HUMAN...
...THAT EVEN GODLIKE ABILITIES CANNOT ANALYZE HER.
THIS MORNING, I FOUND THIS IN MY SHOE LOCKER.
WOULD YOU LIKE TO READ IT?
PI (SNATCH)

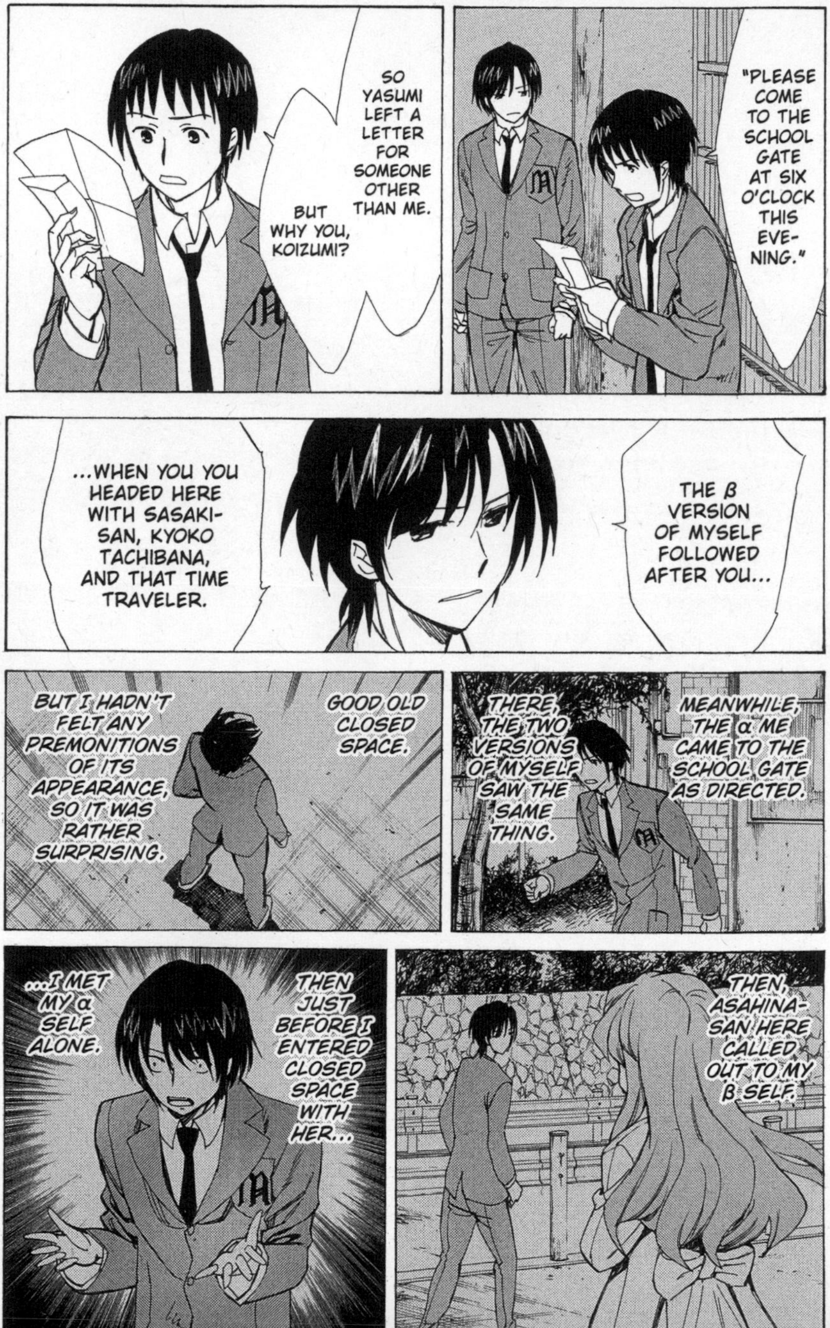
"PLEASE COME TO THE SCHOOL GATE AT SIX O'CLOCK THIS EVENING."
SO YASUMI LEFT A LETTER FOR SOMEONE OTHER THAN ME.
BUT WHY YOU, KOIZUMI?
THE β VERSION OF MYSELF FOLLOWED AFTER YOU...
...WHEN YOU YOU HEADED HERE WITH SASAKI-SAN, KYOKO TACHIBANA, AND THAT TIME TRAVELER.
MEANWHILE, THE α ME CAME TO THE SCHOOL GATE AS DIRECTED.
THERE, THE TWO VERSIONS OF MYSELF SAW THE SAME THING.
GOOD OLD CLOSED SPACE.
BUT I HADN'T FELT ANY PREMONITIONS OF ITS APPEARANCE, SO IT WAS RATHER SURPRISING.
THEN, ASAHINA-SAN HERE CALLED OUT TO MY β SELF.
THEN JUST BEFORE I ENTERED CLOSED SPACE WITH HER...
...I MET MY α SELF ALONE.

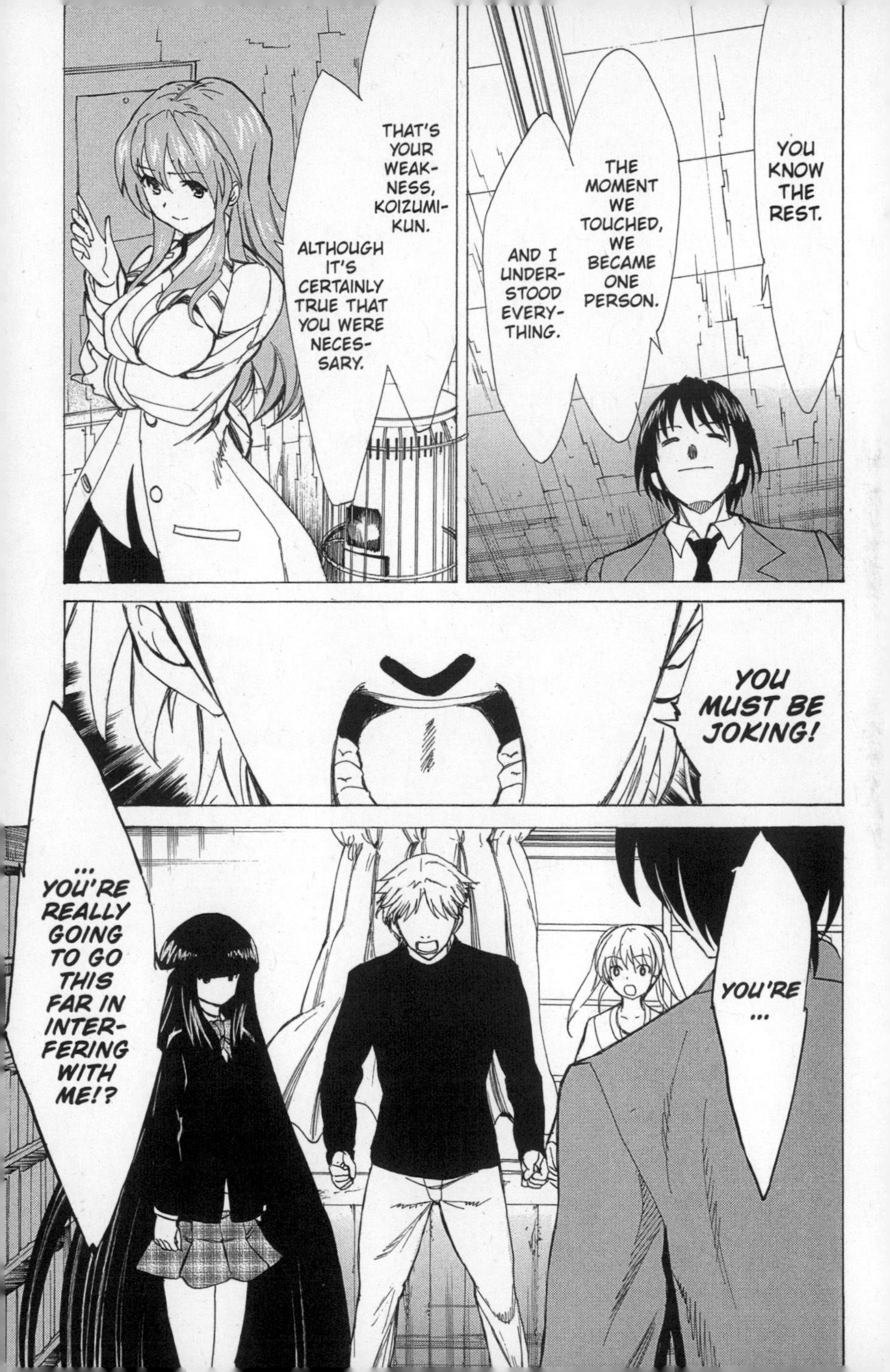
YOU KNOW THE REST.
THE MOMENT WE TOUCHED, WE BECAME ONE PERSON.
AND I UNDERSTOOD EVERYTHING.
THAT'S YOUR WEAKNESS, KOIZUMI-KUN.
ALTHOUGH IT'S CERTAINLY TRUE THAT YOU WERE NECESSARY.
YOU MUST BE JOKING!
YOU'RE ...
... YOU'RE REALLY GOING TO GO THIS FAR IN INTERFERING WITH ME!?

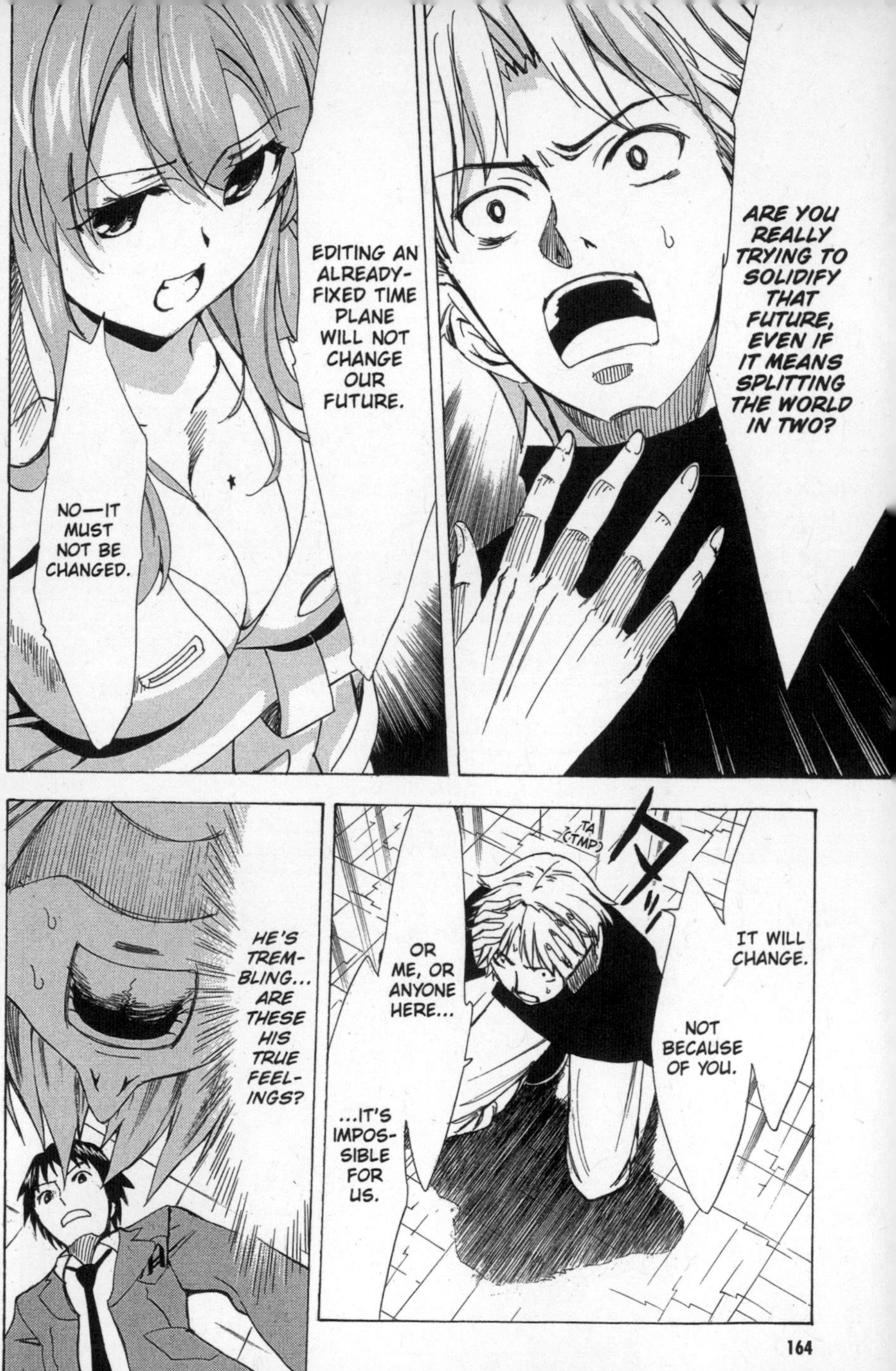
ARE YOU REALLY TRYING TO SOLIDIFY THAT FUTURE, EVEN IF IT MEANS SPLITTING THE WORLD IN TWO?
EDITING AN ALREADY-FIXED TIME PLANE WILL NOT CHANGE OUR FUTURE.
NO—IT MUST NOT BE CHANGED.
TA (TMP)
IT WILL CHANGE.
NOT BECAUSE OF YOU.
OR ME, OR ANYONE HERE...
...IT'S IMPOSSIBLE FOR US.
HE'S TREMBLING... ARE THESE HIS TRUE FEELINGS?

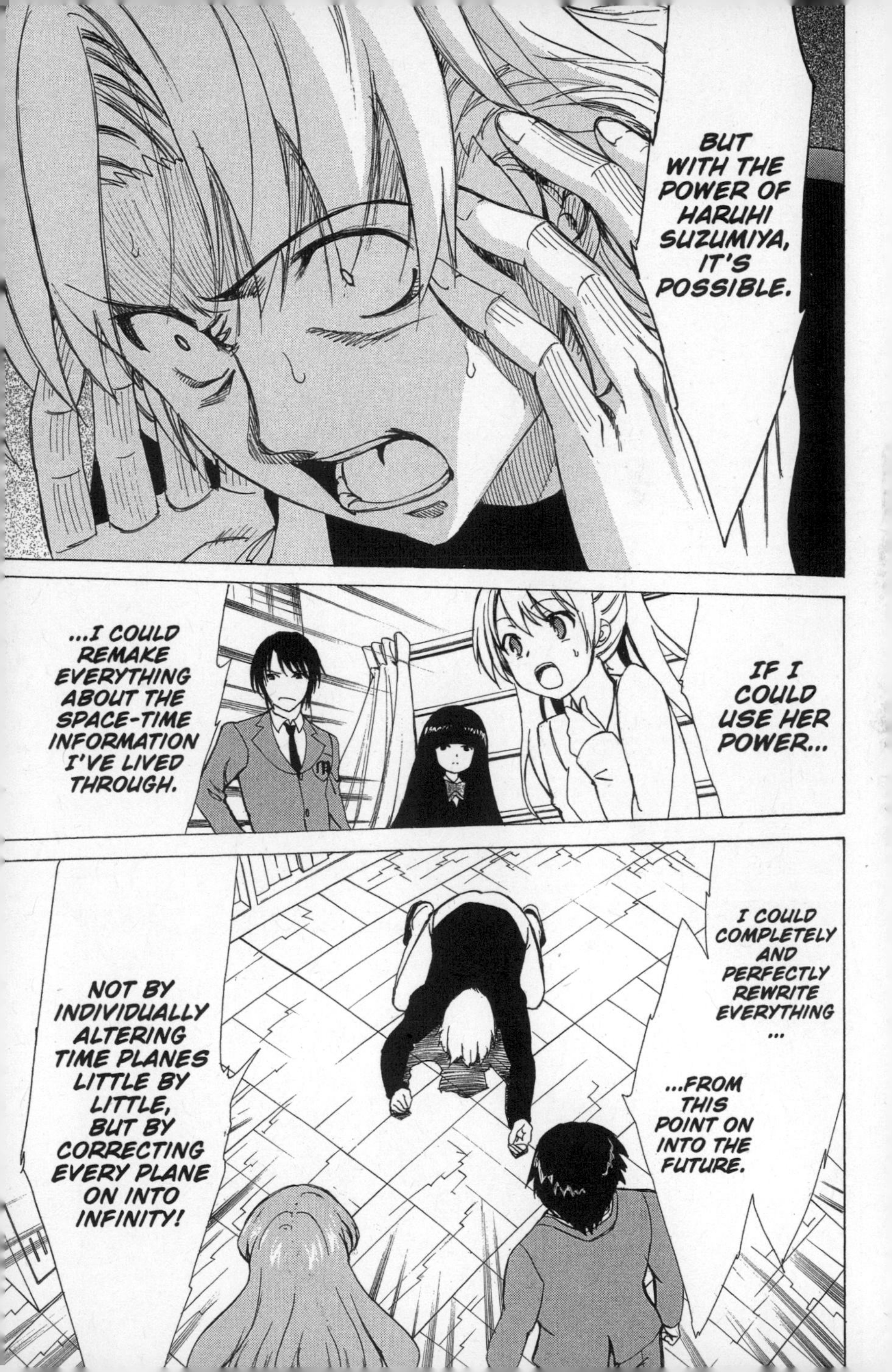
BUT WITH THE POWER OF HARUHI SUZUMIYA, IT'S POSSIBLE.
IF I COULD USE HER POWER...
...I COULD REMAKE EVERYTHING ABOUT THE SPACE-TIME INFORMATION I'VE LIVED THROUGH.
I COULD COMPLETELY AND PERFECTLY REWRITE EVERYTHING...
...FROM THIS POINT ON INTO THE FUTURE.
NOT BY INDIVIDUALLY ALTERING TIME PLANES LITTLE BY LITTLE, BUT BY CORRECTING EVERY PLANE ON INTO INFINITY!

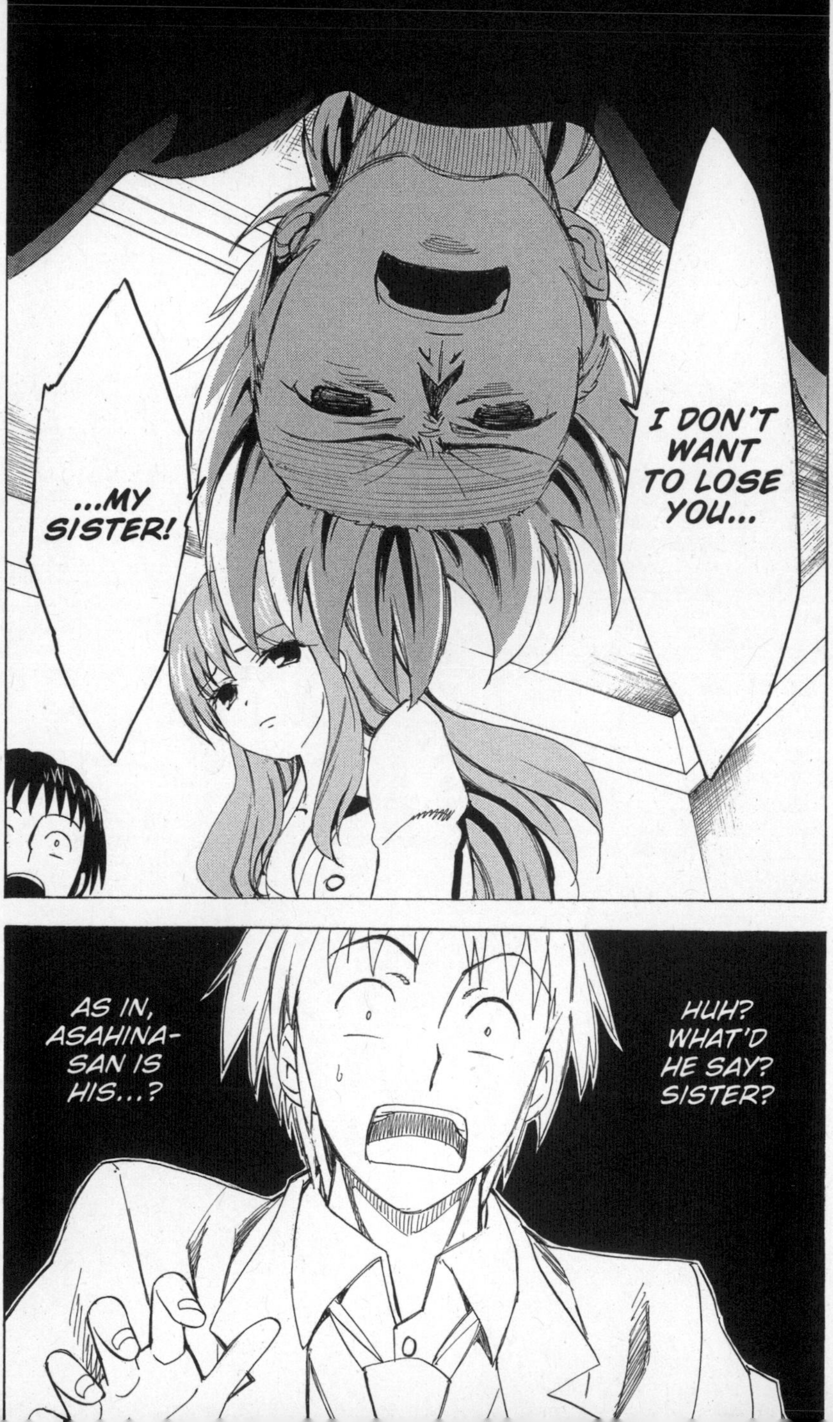
I DON'T WANT TO LOSE YOU...
...MY SISTER!
HUH? WHAT'D HE SAY? SISTER?
AS IN, ASAHINA-SAN IS HIS...?

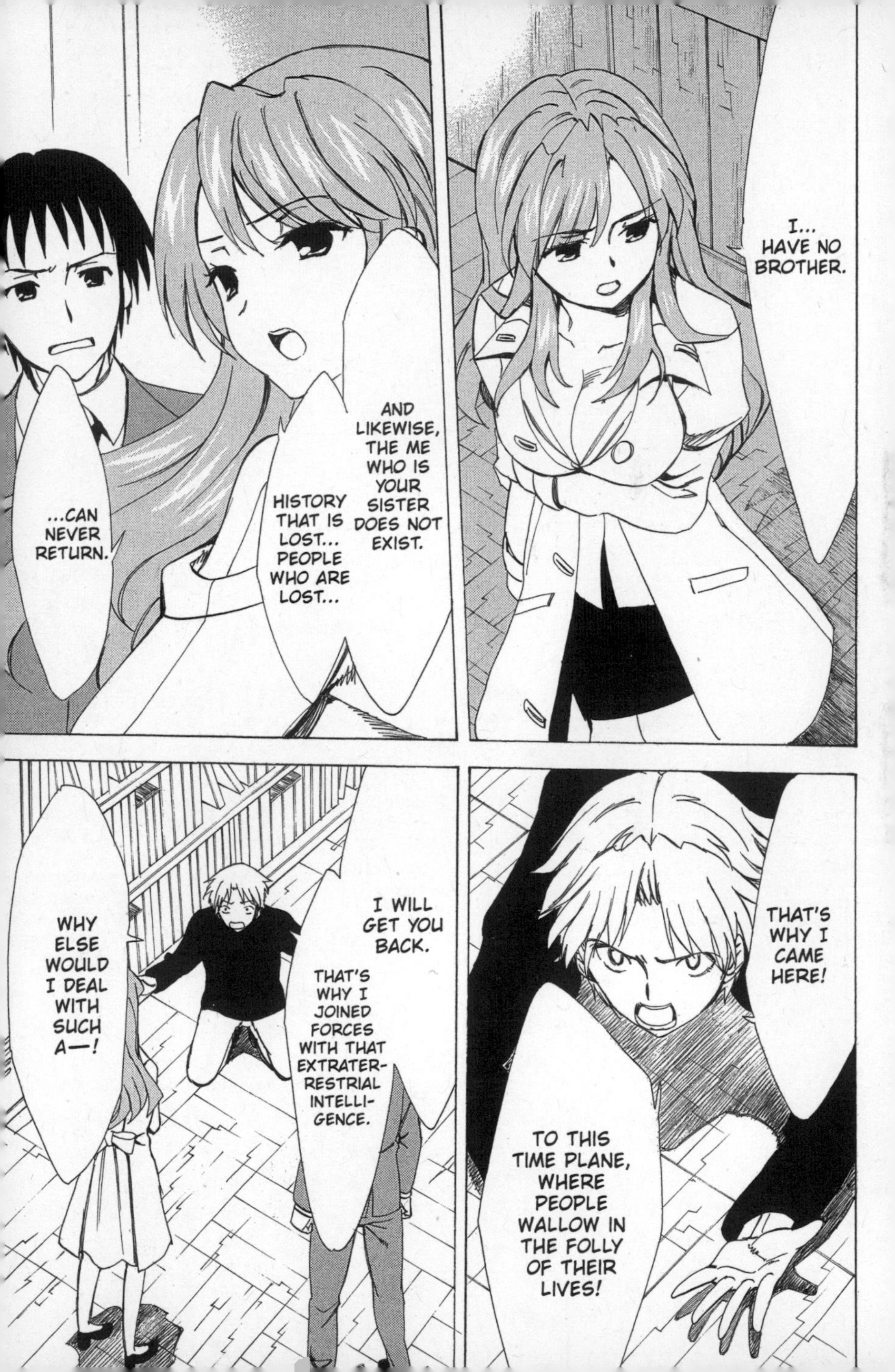
I... HAVE NO BROTHER.
AND LIKEWISE, THE ME WHO IS YOUR SISTER DOES NOT EXIST.
HISTORY THAT IS LOST... PEOPLE WHO ARE LOST...
...CAN NEVER RETURN.
THAT'S WHY I CAME HERE!
TO THIS TIME PLANE, WHERE PEOPLE WALLOW IN THE FOLLY OF THEIR LIVES!
I WILL GET YOU BACK.
THAT'S WHY I JOINED FORCES WITH THAT EXTRATER-RESTRIAL INTELLI-GENCE.
WHY ELSE WOULD I DEAL WITH SUCH A—!

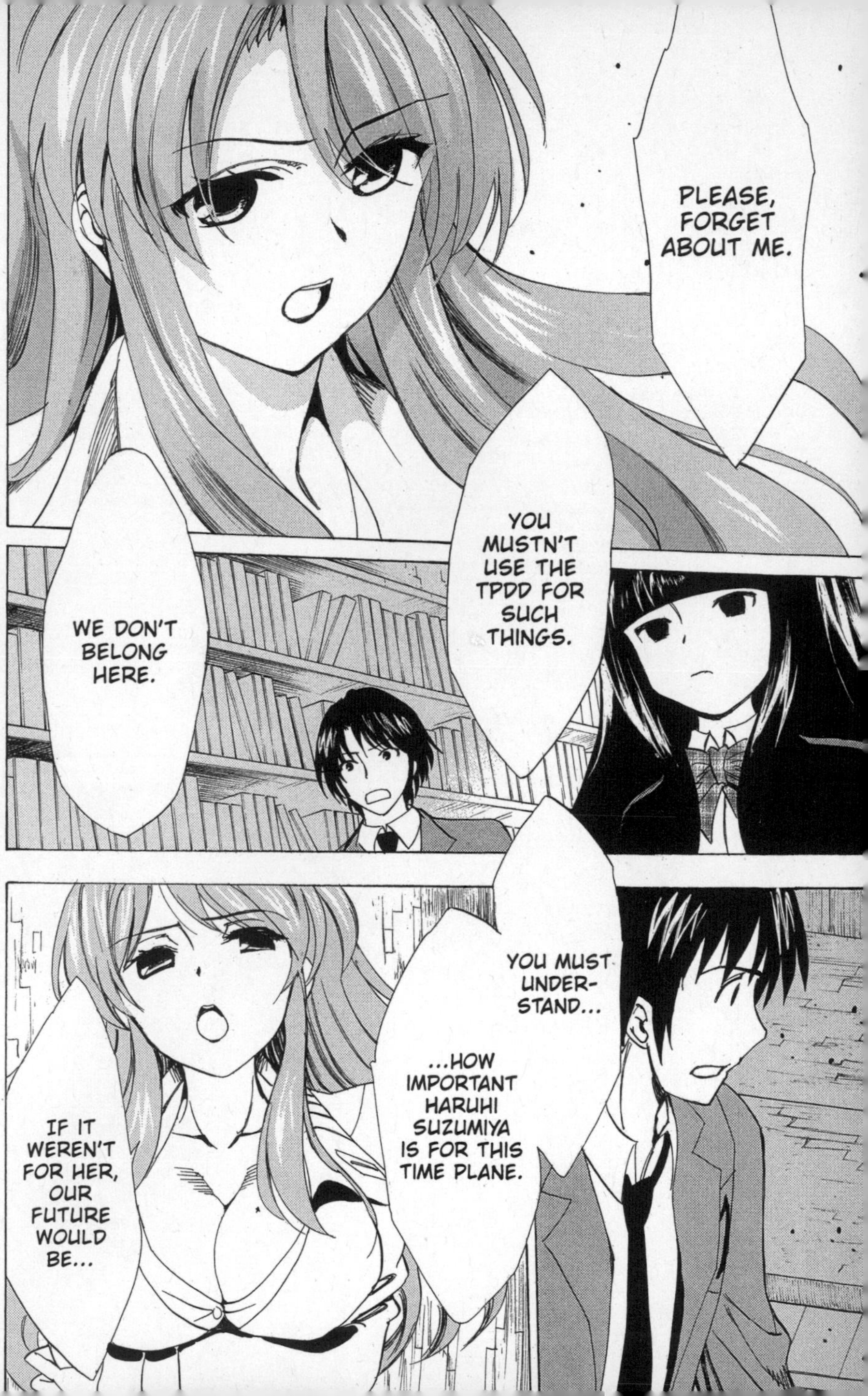
PLEASE, FORGET ABOUT ME.
YOU MUSTN'T USE THE TPDD FOR SUCH THINGS.
WE DON'T BELONG HERE.
YOU MUST UNDER-STAND...
...HOW IMPORTANT HARUHI SUZUMIYA IS FOR THIS TIME PLANE.
IF IT WEREN'T FOR HER, OUR FUTURE WOULD BE...

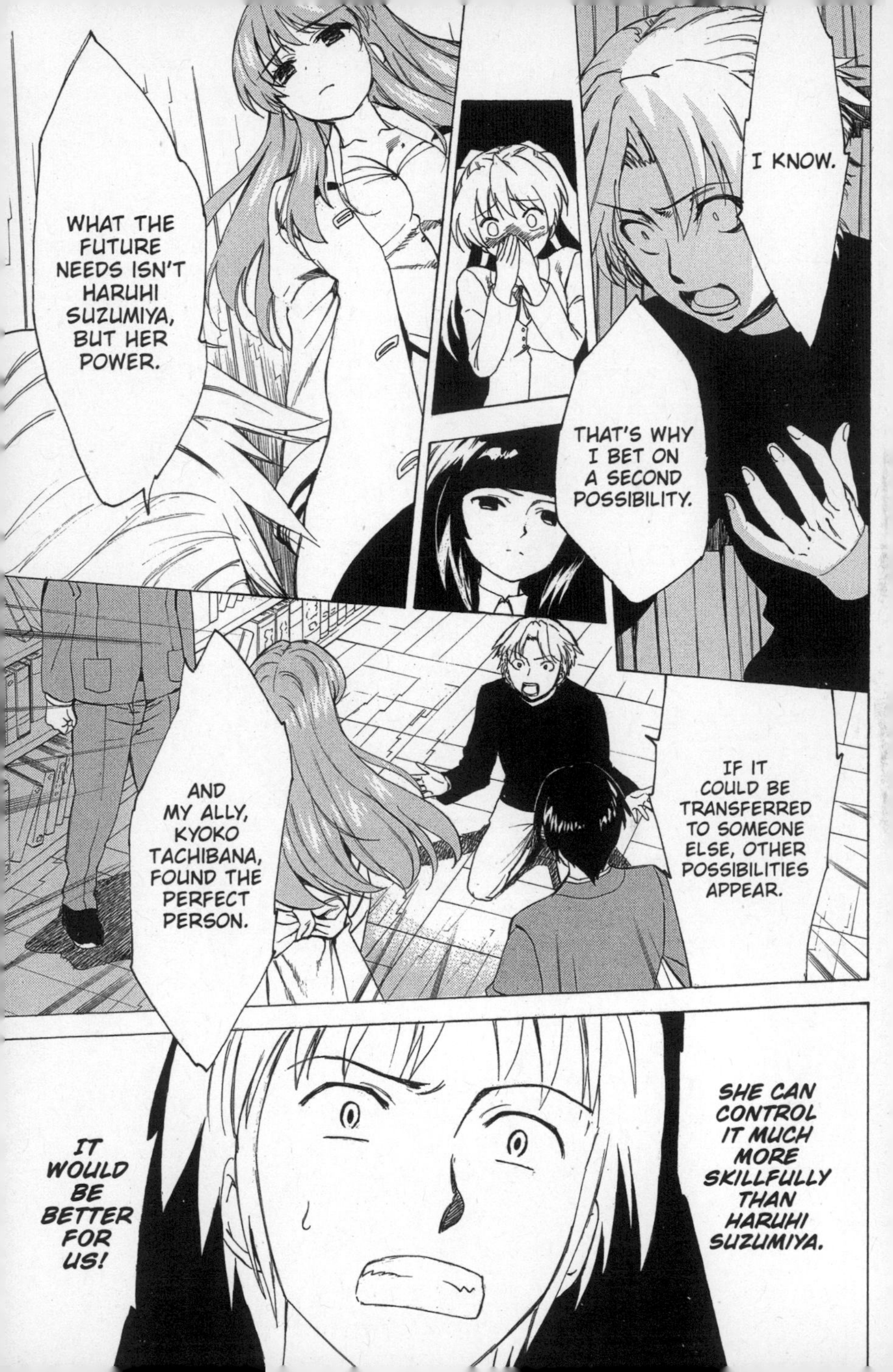
I KNOW.
THAT'S WHY I BET ON A SECOND POSSIBILITY.
WHAT THE FUTURE NEEDS ISN'T HARUHI SUZUMIYA, BUT HER POWER.
IF IT COULD BE TRANSFERRED TO SOMEONE ELSE, OTHER POSSIBILITIES APPEAR.
AND MY ALLY, KYOKO TACHIBANA, FOUND THE PERFECT PERSON.
SHE CAN CONTROL IT MUCH MORE SKILLFULLY THAN HARUHI SUZUMIYA.
IT WOULD BE BETTER FOR US!

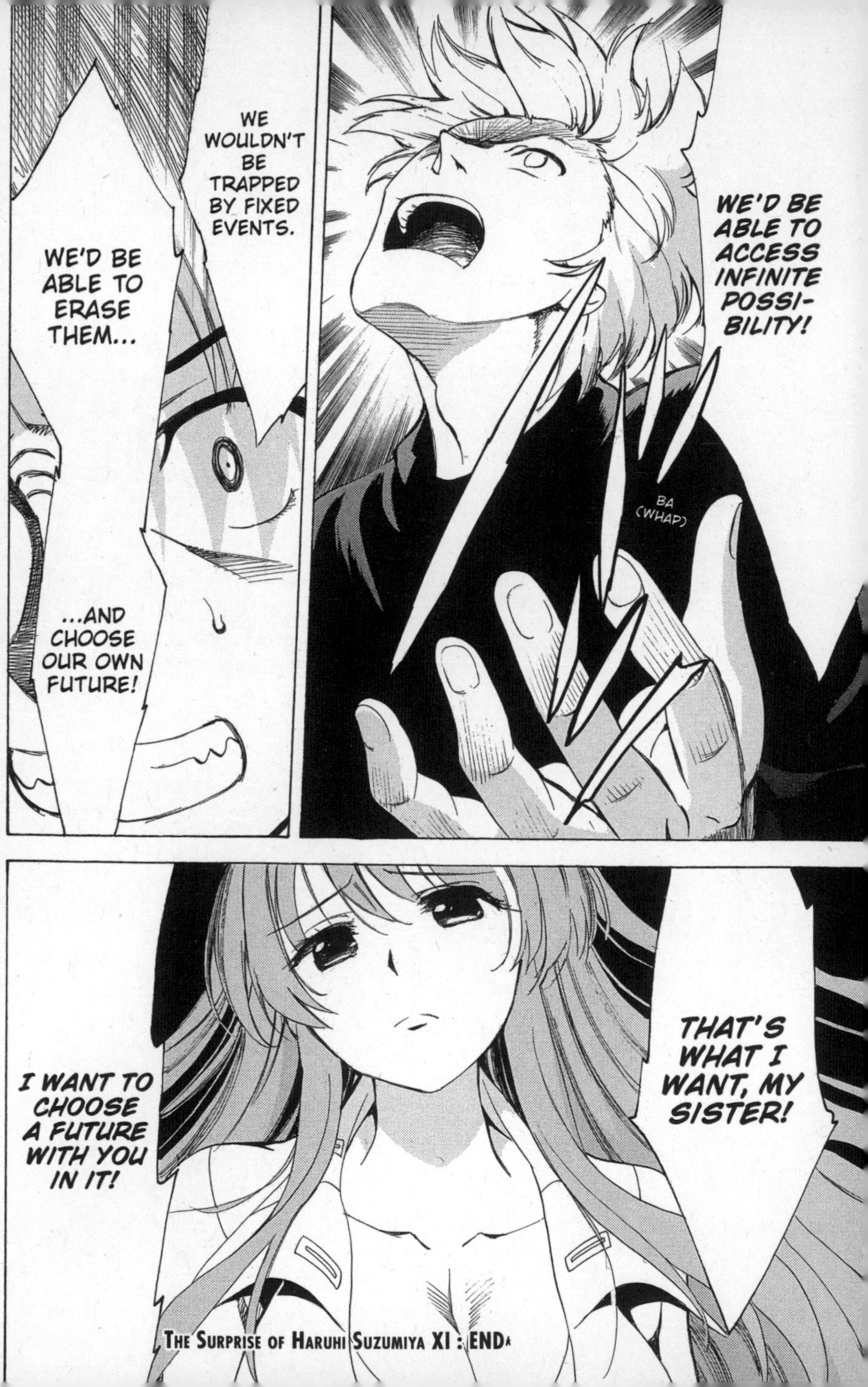
WE'D BE ABLE TO ACCESS INFINITE POSSI-BILITY!
BA (WHAP)
WE WOULDN'T BE TRAPPED BY FIXED EVENTS.
WE'D BE ABLE TO ERASE THEM...
...AND CHOOSE OUR OWN FUTURE!
THAT'S WHAT I WANT, MY SISTER!
I WANT TO CHOOSE A FUTURE WITH YOU IN IT!
THE SURPRISE OF HARUHI SUZUMIYA XI : END

TO BE CONTINUED

THE MELANCHOLY
OF HARUHI SUZUMIYA
PREVIEW

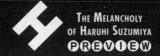

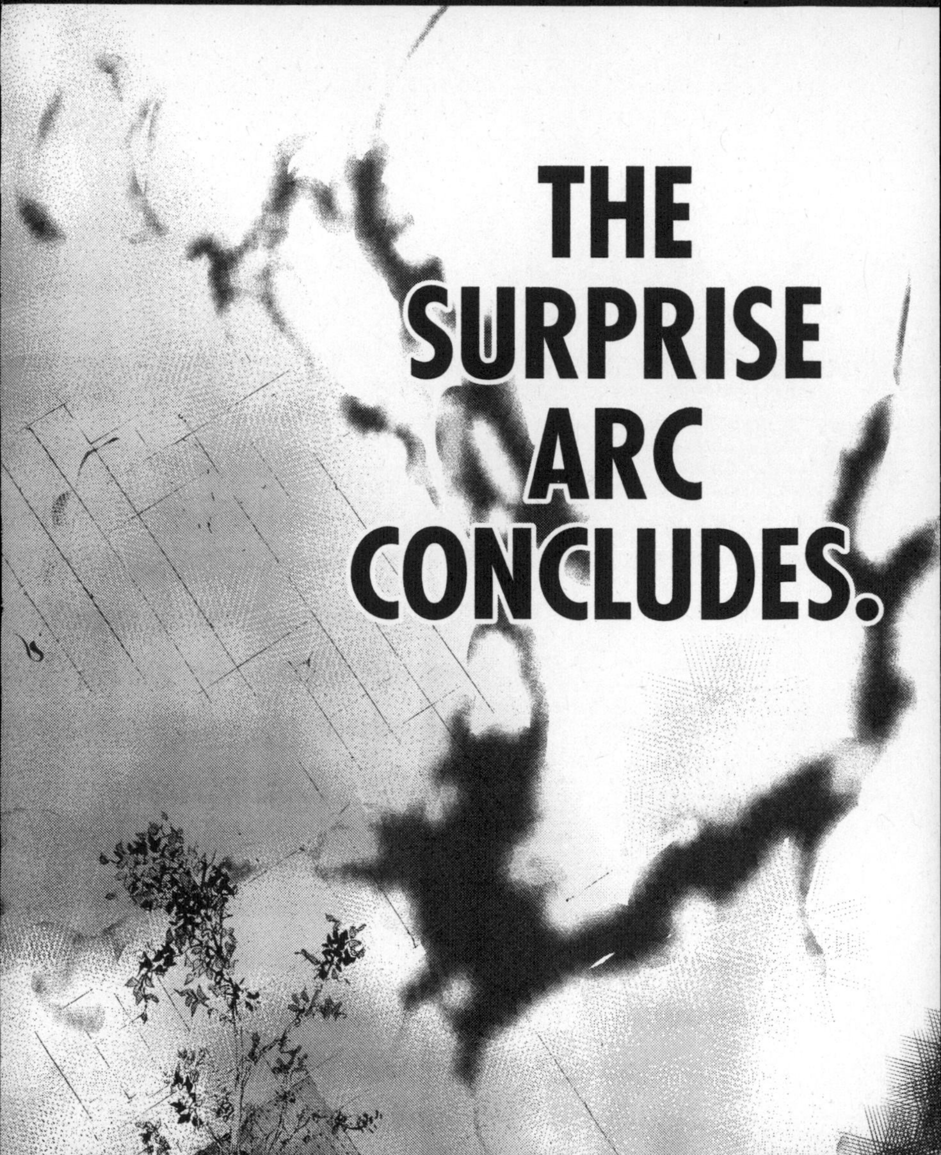
THE
SURPRISE
ARC
CONCLUDES.

THAT AWAIT IN VOLUME 20, AVAILABLE NOVEMBER 2014!

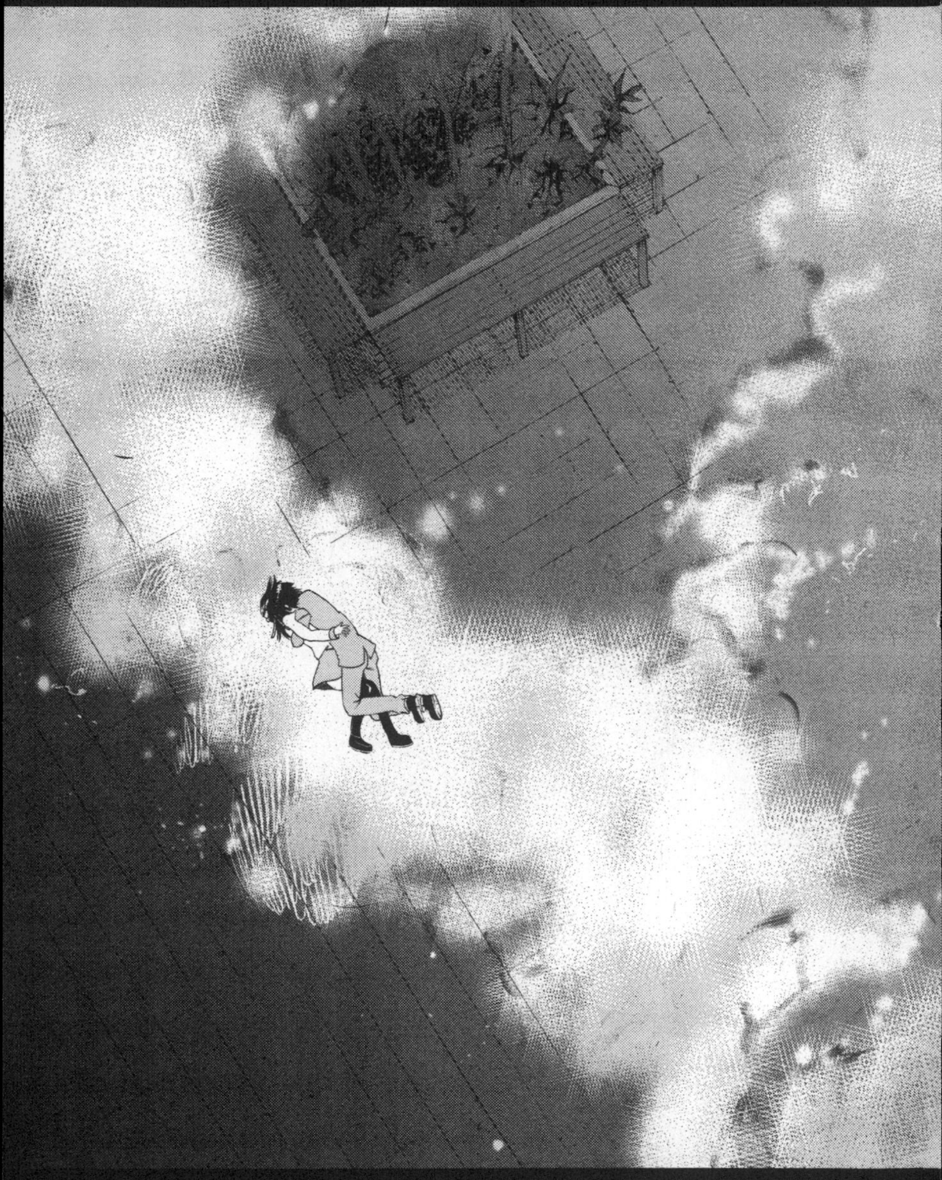

EVENTS ACCELERATE IN THE STAGGERING DEVELOPMENTS

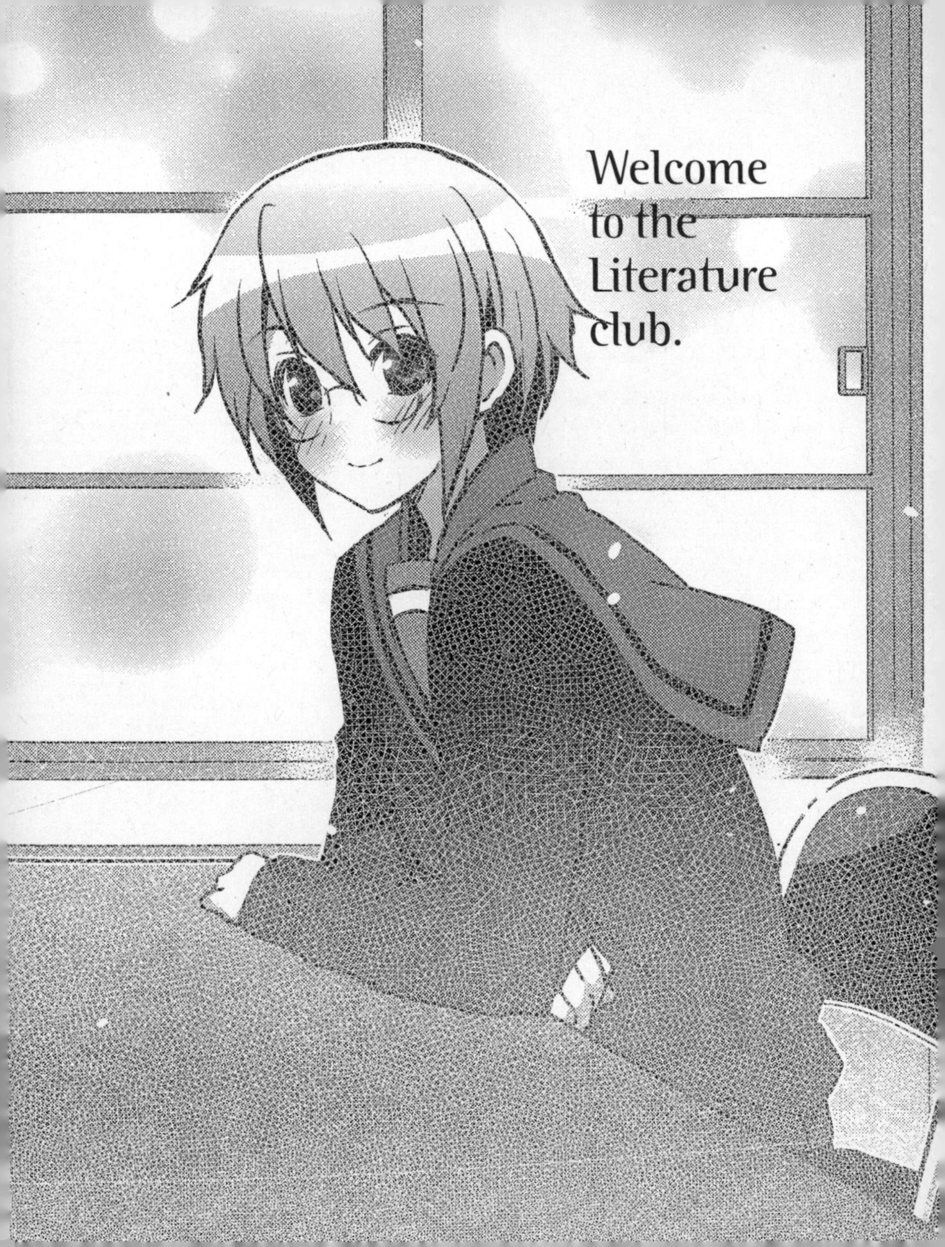
Welcome to the Literature club.

# THE DISAPPEARANCE OF
# NAGATO YUKI-CHAN

## Volume 6 Coming September 2014

STORY: **NAGARU TANIGAWA** ART: **PUYO** CHARACTERS: NOIZI ITO

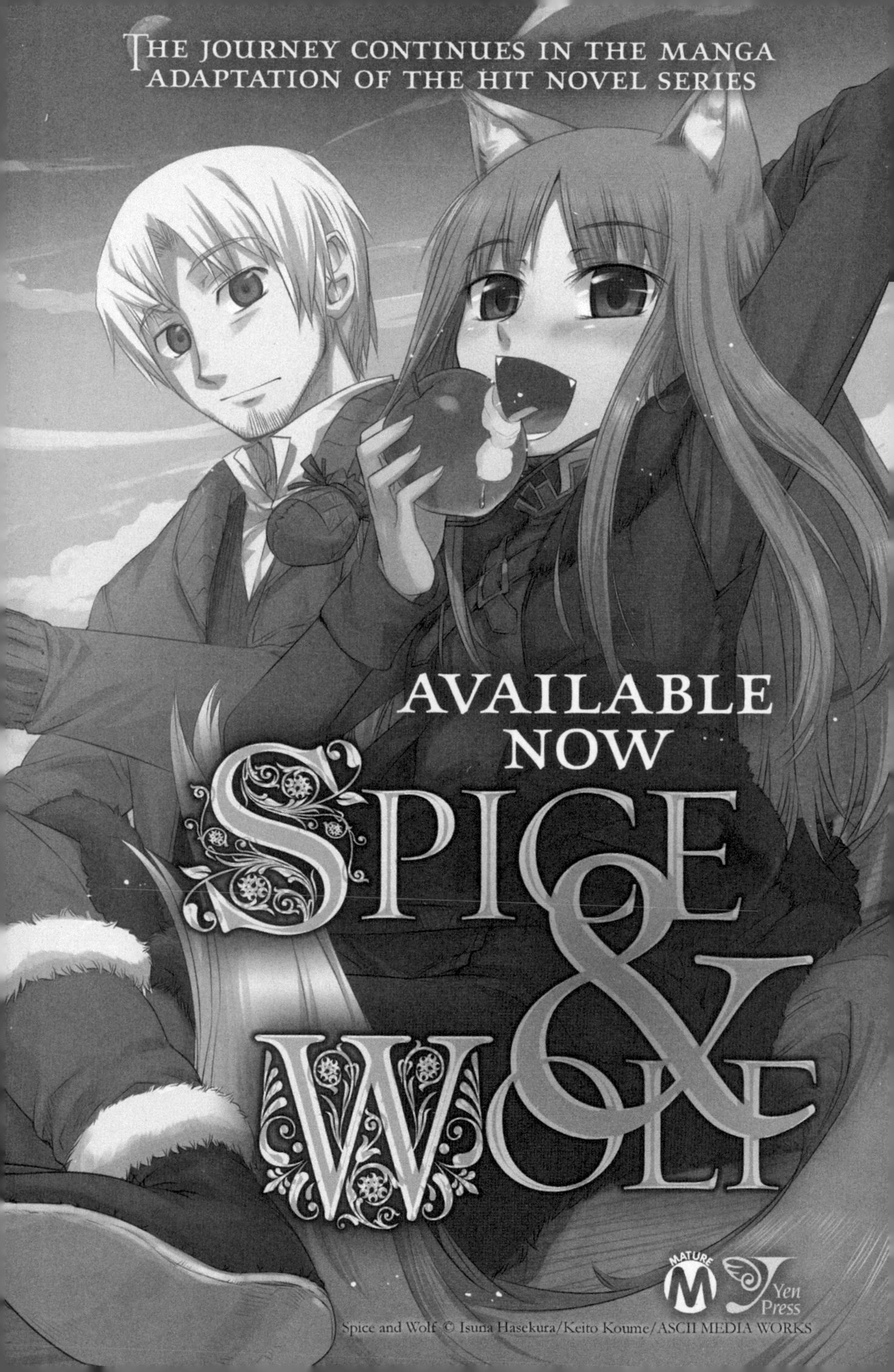
THE JOURNEY CONTINUES IN THE MANGA
ADAPTATION OF THE HIT NOVEL SERIES
AVAILABLE
NOW
SPICE
&
WOLF
MATURE
M
Yen
Press
Spice and Wolf © Isuna Hasekura/Keito Koume/ASCII MEDIA WORKS

# To become the ultimate weapon, one must devour the souls of 99 humans...

## and one witch.

Maka is a scythe meister, working to perfect her demon scythe until it is good enough to become Death's Weapon—the weapon used by Shinigami-sama, the spirit of Death himself. And if that isn't strange enough, her scythe also has the power to change form—into a human-looking boy!

**VOLUMES 1-20 IN STORES NOW!**

The Phantomhive family has a butler who's almost too good to be true...

...or maybe he's just too good to be human.

# Black Butler

## YANA TOBOSO

**VOLUMES 1-16 IN STORES NOW!**

# THE MELANCHOLY OF HARUHI SUZUMIYA

Original Story: Nagaru Tanigawa
Manga: Gaku Tsugano
Character Design: Noizi Ito

Translation: Paul Starr
Lettering: Alexis Eckerman

SUZUMIYA HARUHI NO YUUTSU Volume 19 © Nagaru TANIGAWA • Noizi ITO 2013 © Gaku TSUGANO 2013. Edited by KADOKAWA SHOTEN. First published in Japan in 2013 by KADOKAWA CORPORATION, Tokyo. English translation rights arranged with KADOKAWA CORPORATION, Tokyo, through Tuttle-Mori Agency, Inc., Tokyo.

English translation © 2014 by Hachette Book Group, Inc.

Yen Press
Hachette Book Group
237 Park Avenue, New York, NY 10017

www.HachetteBookGroup.com
www.YenPress.com

Yen Press is an imprint of Hachette Book Group, Inc. The Yen Press name and logo are trademarks of Hachette Book Group, Inc.

First Yen Press Edition: August 2014

ISBN: 978-0-316-37680-8

10 9 8 7 6 5 4 3 2 1

BVG

Printed in the United States of America